Ireland's Own Soil

Ireland's Own Soil

Government and agriculture in Ireland, 1945-65

Paul Rouse

ISBN 0-9534902-1-1

Cover by Liz Hammick
Photo John Caffrey
Printed and bound in Ireland by Johnswood Press Ltd.

Table of contents

List of Abbreviations

A/I	Agricultural Institute
ACC	Agricultural Credit Corporation
AH	*Agricultural History*
AHR	*Agricultural History Review*
ASA	Agricultural Science Association
B/T	Board of Trade
CAP	Common Agricultural Policy
CEEC	Committee of European Economic Cooperation
CIPEAP	Commission of inquiry on post-Emergency agricultural policy
CRO	Commonwealth Relations Office
cwt.	hundredweight
D/A	Department of Agriculture
D/E	Department of Education
D/EA	Department of External Affairs
D/F	Department of Finance
D/FA	Department of Foreign Affairs
D/IC	Department of Industry and Commerce
D/LG	Department of Local Government
D/T	Department of the Taoiseach
DO	Dominions Office
ECA	Economic Co-operation Administration
ECSC	European Coal and Steel Community
EEC	European Economic Community
EFTA	European Free Trade Association
ERP	European Recovery Programme
FAO	Food and Agriculture Organisation
GATT	General Agreement on Tariffs and Trade
GNP	Gross National Product
IAOS	Irish Agricultural Organisation Society
ICA	Irish Countrywomen's Association
ICMSA	Irish Creamery Milk Suppliers' Association
IESH	*Irish Economic and Social History*
IFJ	*Irish Farmers' Journal*
IRA	Irish Republican Army
JSSISI	*Journal of the Statistical and Social Inquiry Society of Ireland*
M/A	Minister for Agriculture
NAI	National Archives of Ireland
NFA	National Farmers' Association
OECD	Organisation for Economic Cooperation and Development
OEEC	Organisation for European Economic Cooperation

OPW	Office of Public Works
PRO	Public Record Office (London)
TCD	Trinity College, Dublin
TD	Teachta Dála
UCC	University College, Cork
UCD	University College, Dublin
UCDA	University College, Dublin Archives
UK	United Kingdom
US	United States of America
USSR	Union of Soviet Socialist Republics
VEC	Vocational Education Committee

Pre-decimal currency is given in the following format:
£   s [shillings] d [pence].

Acknowledgements

This is book is dedicated to my parents, Patsy and Dolores Rouse, without whose support I would never have finished first year of university or, indeed, much else. It is also dedicated to my brothers, David, John and Brian. I cannot begin to explain the depths of gratitude I owe to my family for their toleration.

Professor Mary Daly is also owed a huge debt of gratitude. To state the obvious: this project would never have been completed without her advice and friendship. I would like to thank various other members of the history department in University College, Dublin, most notably, Maeve Bradley, Professor Hugh Gough, Dr Michael Laffan and Dr Tadhg Ó hAnnracháin. Particular thanks to Dr Tim O'Neill for his open door and invaluable wisdom. Also to Dr Brian Cowler, who generously loaned me his excellent doctoral thesis. The staffs of the various archives and libraries visited were unfailingly helpful. Thanks especially to Seamus Helferty in UCD Archives, Paddy and Pauline at the National Archives, Fran at the National Library and Kathy Chance at the Public Records Office.

At the IUE in Firenze, Professor Alan Milward and Professor Jaime Reis offered valuable suggestions, but, most of all, I would like to express my gratitude to the researchers who made my stay such a memorable one. Thanks, in particular, to Nicola Dunleavy, lawyer, author and Irish dancer; Maurice Fitzgerald; Ann-Christina Knudsen; Derry O'Brien, footballer, and the other members of the International Heroes; and the legendary Viale Righi sisters, Dorte Martinsen and Claudia Attucci. Of course, most of all, to the wonderful Elia Marzal: Quan de tu s'allunya, d'enyorança es mor.

In London, Kathleen and David Blackeby, were once again more generous and hospitable than could be imagined. Thanks also to my other aunt and uncle, Helen and Jimmy Lee, and my cousins, Brian, Kevin, Katie and James whose blind optimism as Crystal Palace fans was a source of huge inspiration for this project. Cultural tours of the city, especially Camden, were provided by Mal MacCarthy and Nigel Brennan, from the Ministry of Fun.

Thank you to the Irish Farmers' Journal for the financial support which made this project possible. I would like to pay particular tribute to Matt Dempsey who offered constant support in a thoroughly unobtrusive manner, and to Joe Rea and Paddy O'Keeffe. Further thanks to John Grogan for his clinical efficiency and much-appreciated assistance, and to John Bergin for bringing the entire effort to a conclusion.

Huge thanks to the following people for their friendship over the last four years and beyond: Mark Duncan, for reading these pages and for many slivers of hospitality; Deirdre McMahon; Marie Clarke; James McGuire and Jim Quinn from the Dictionary of Irish Biography; Pauline McKenna; Niall O'Dea and John Dowling; Joe Hughes and Samantha Touhey - my chauffeur and chef - who had to spend many days driving and feeding their very own Miss Daisy; Declan Walsh; Geoffrey; Jude McCarthy; Greg and Cian; Sean, Dick and Figs; Lindsey Earner; Orla Mulligan, Rhode; Diarmaid Ferriter; Dermie Ryan, pool king and catman extraordinaire; Catalina Feeney; Joe Clarke; Ronan MacKay; Gareth Ivory; Ita Kennelly; Susan Conlon; Breege Murphy; Rónán O'Brien, who once again read the first pages; Pat Leahy, hurler, wit and as proud a Gael as ever stood in shoe leather; Peter MacDonagh, the red lad who's doing a fine job above in Dublin as the Minister for Greyhounds; Che, Fidel and the dolphins; Billy B. and Bob D.; the many heroes of Tullamore G.A.A. Club, around which the world orbits; Bennie O'Brien; Margaret Ó hÓgartaigh; the Offaly Express; Anne-Maree Farrell, whose support was vital to the completion of this research; Liam Cullen, the yank from Wexford, for post, print and stories of Ireland, and Sarah Fenton, Westmeath; Duckie, Hopper, Collie, Lemon and Siobhan.

I would most like to thank two people for support which went beyond the call of friendship. Willie Murphy ensured that the many months of archival research were never less than entertaining. Always generous with his time, he provided detailed, insightful comments on this work and, further, offered invaluable encouragement when it was badly needed. More than anyone else, Donal Cahill looked after me when I was hobbling. Never one to shirk danger ('I've been shot') in Hartigan's or beyond, he even risked sharing his apartment with an undomesticated civilian. I remain forever grateful for his friendship and hope someday to repay him.

Introduction

For most of history, the prosperity of agriculture was central to Irish economic development. Following the foundation of the Free State in 1922, agriculture effectively defined the newly independent state's material well-being. Agricultural policy was invested with a significance which travels far beyond economics, however. It was perceived also as the conduit for a social and cultural renaissance which would justify the Irish political revolution. Images of a united Ireland, Gaelic speaking and thriving in populous rural communities had sustained the separatist movement and, later, enjoyed repeated exposure in the political and economic debates of independent Ireland. Fidelity to visions of bountiful farmsteads transcended party and personality. Accordingly, the evolution of Irish agricultural policy involves the convergence of prevailing political, social, cultural and economic forces where past inheritance joined uneasily with present realities and projected future demands.

The constitutional relationship with Britain has formed the prism through which Irish history has been most often viewed. It would be a substantial folly to deny the relevance of this approach, yet it has been accompanied by comparative neglect of the social and economic realities which coloured the nature of Irish independence. The politics of partition and neutrality may inspire as more emotive issues but it was agricultural policy – its successes and failures – which truly shaped the lives of most Irish people. The formulation of agricultural policy is the principal theme of this work which begins with a survey of Irish agriculture in 1945. An understanding of post-1945 policy cannot be contemplated without prior analysis of the traditions which had come to define Irish agricultural structure, policies and politics before the conclusion of World War II. Accordingly, the first chapter traces the development of Irish agriculture, initially, in the years before independence, and then in the years immediately after the founding of the Free State. Although long embalmed in a culture of torpor, in terms of performance, Irish agriculture underwent extraordinary structural change in the century after the famine. It is in this era that the enduring pattern of the agricultural economy was cemented and that the political vision which governed that economy was forged. Similarly, in the first two decades of the post-independence era, there were two readily discernible approaches to agricultural policy by native governments. These divergent policies are outlined, as is the manner in which they rested against the agricultural structure of the country. The chapter concludes with an analysis of the problems facing Irish agriculture as outlined in the *Reports of the commission of inquiry on post-emergency agricultural policy*, and of the debates in government on how best to resolve these problems.

The second chapter opens with an assessment of the attempts in the immediate post-war years to devise policy initiatives to combat the acknowledged flaws in the agricultural economy. Attempts by the Fianna Fáil government to restructure the pigs and bacon sector and the dairying sector are analysed, as is the endeavour to devise a price policy appropriate to Irish circumstances. This is succeeded by an account of the tentative moves by Fianna Fáil to re-establish the Irish position in the British market, moves which were given greater impetus by the first inter-party government on its accession to power in February 1948. In accordance with its fundamental importance to export policy over the following two decades, there is a substantial assessment of the 1948 Anglo-Irish agreement and, in particular, of the relevance of agriculture to the negotiations and the eventual provisions of the accord. Irish involvement in Marshall Aid confirmed the state's desire to reintegrate with the international economy following the relative isolation of the 1930s and of World War II. Attempts to use Marshall Aid money to revitalise agriculture and, crucially, the efforts to establish a progressive grasslands policy are assessed. The chapter closes with a consideration of the attempts of the inter-party government to stamp its imprint on domestic agricultural policy – notably on the dairying sector – before it was removed from office in 1951.

The opening sections of chapter three revolve around the attempts by the Fianna Fáil administration which held office from 1951 to 1954, and of the inter-party government which succeeded it until 1957, to devise effective policies to promote tillage and dairy farming. The strains and similarities in the policies pursued by the respective governments are assessed, with particular focus on wheat acreage and on livestock breeding policy. The impact of the 1948 Anglo-Irish agreement on the development of Irish agricultural policy through the 1950s is also scrutinised, along with the subsequent subsidiary agreements which refined its operation. The effects of the reliance on the export of cattle to Britain as ordained by these agreements is detailed, notably the relationship between export-driven extensive farming and policy governing other elements of the agricultural economy. Critically, the social, economic, political and cultural demands encompassed by land policy are documented. The chapter concludes with a study of attempts to redress the drift from the land so characteristic of that decade and of the sense of stagnation which pervaded agricultural circles through those years.

Chapter four opens with an account of the initiative to revitalise the Irish economy – and, especially, to revitalise agriculture – through the 1958 *Programme for economic expansion*. This chapter outlines the agricultural policy highlighted in that document, the attempts to realise a policy capable of achieving specified targets, and the relative failure of agriculture to meet the demands made of it. The continued failure to develop policies to address the fundamental structural weaknesses of the agricultural economy is traced. Meanwhile, the failure of Irish farmers, themselves, to respond as imagined to the *Programme* is rooted in the flawed research, educational and advisory systems which serviced the industry, and in the inability to develop export markets capable of absorbing the expanded agricultural produce which the *Programme for economic expansion* envisaged. Unconvinced of a market for their produce, farmers retained outdated modes of production and declined to invest in a system of farming which offered a secure, albeit impoverished, existence into the early 1960s. The chapter concludes with an account of how the *Programme*, even if it failed to foster the desired levels of expansion, did assist in ensuring the survival of the livestock export trade through its support for the tuberculosis eradication scheme.

The fifth chapter records the failure to devise a coherent policy framework to address the problems of small farmers, especially those living in the west of Ireland. There is an assessment of the diminution of the role envisaged for agriculture in the *Second programme for economic expansion*, published in two parts in the years 1963 and 1964. The chapter continues with an analysis of the attempts to improve the export market for Irish agricultural produce, firstly in overtures to the British government and then in the drive to secure membership of the European Economic Community (EEC). The effect on agricultural policy of the failure to gain entrance to that community and the subsequent signing of the 1965 Anglo-Irish Free Trade Agreement is explored in depth. This final chapter concludes with an overview of the relative merits of the agricultural policy pursued by successive Irish governments between 1946 and 1965; the factors, both foreign and domestic, which influenced that policy; its impact on the agricultural economy; and its legacy.

It is not suggested how the constraints which limited policy might have been overcome nor is it sought to persuade that options sponsored by others might have produced better results – or worse ones. Although counterfactual history has been something of an intellectual heresy, it can be a worthwhile addition in assessing the past and is far too easily dismissed as more properly the preserve of fiction writers than historians.[1] It does require that the actual history of an era be well recorded, however, and this is not a description which can be accorded to Irish agricultural history. For a similar reason, there is only the most fleeting of attempts to place Irish agricultural policy in a comparative context. A whole range of countries – most notably Denmark, New Zealand and Portugal – hold the potential for comparative analysis which should prove singularly instructive when juxtaposed with the Irish experience. Yet to provide such a comparison on any worthwhile scale would have necessitated substantial shift of focus away from the subject of this study. The existing levels of historical investigation into Irish agricultural policy did not suggest that such a shift would be either justified or wholly profitable. Nonetheless, occasional reference is made to the contrasting fortunes of other agricultures where it is thought that such reference will further illuminate the Irish condition.

It is a commonplace almost beyond parody for historians to justify their endeavours by railing at the previous (and always inexplicable) omission from the canon of Irish history of their latest project. Singing a lament for the neglect of any particular historical theme or topic reeks of self-indulgence, however. Pleas from the bewitched for recognition are generally devoid of perspective and too often descend into cliché. Nonetheless, it is incontestable that the existing

---

[1] Niall Ferguson (ed.), *Virtual history: alternatives and counterfactuals* (1997).

historical literature on modern Irish agriculture does not give adequate expression to the fundamental role played by that industry in the history of the state. That is not to assert that the subject has been ignored, rather it has not enjoyed exploration commensurate with its importance. The principal existing material dealing specifically with the subject includes Raymond Crotty, *Irish agricultural production: its volume and structure* (1966), I.F. Bailie and S.J. Sheehy (eds.), *Irish agriculture in a changing world* (1971), Daniel Hoctor, *The department's story: a history of the Department of Agriculture* (1971), P.J. Drudy (ed.), *Studies 2: Ireland: land, politics and people* (1982) and Brian Cowler's doctoral thesis, *A history of Irish agriculture and European integration, 1956-72* (1998). Innumerable other works treat the fortunes of Irish agriculture in the post-war era *en passant* with varied levels of acumen, but no serious, full-length analysis of Irish agriculture in the two decades after World War II has been offered. Given the extent of the secondary material which alludes to, without ever properly addressing, the subject, it would be possible to circle indefinitely without even contemplating landing. Fear of flying has rooted this work firmly in primary sources, most particularly in the files of the Irish government held in the National Archives in Dublin. Substantial use is also made of other archives, notably the Public Record Office in London, while official publications are also drawn upon frequently.

Ultimately, this book seeks to offer an overall assessment of the relationship between government and agriculture between 1945 and 1965. This assessment seeks to determine the nature of that relationship, yet it does so in the conviction that the presentation of history as neatly-structured argument is often unconvincing. Assailing the work of others – not to mention the desire to stake out a new territory with a forbidding scent – has encouraged a school of history which places confrontation high on the academic agenda and rewards the attitude of those who deal in dogma. Above all, it is seen as important to be certain. There is a cynical comfort in assessing the past with a knowing shrug of incredulity. The passage of time can facilitate a lamentable disdain of failure and a tendency to replace critical analysis of process with patronising foresight of outcome. This is emphatically the case in any assessment of policy, particularly one borne of a seemingly anachronistic political vision, armed with the knowledge of whether that policy has succeeded or failed. Often the factors which determined the fate of policy are more readily apparent and this, again, can induce complacency.

While acknowledging the potential to misrepresent the past amidst a headlong rush to formulate a sustainable interpretation and to suffuse that interpretation with invincible exasperation, it is impossible to ignore the essential truth that Irish agricultural policy from 1945 to 1965 failed by most criteria of assessment. Undoubtedly, elements of that policy were successful and there were many mitigating factors for those elements which failed, but, as a whole, agricultural policy did not bring prosperity to the industry in Ireland and only rarely achieved the targets set by policy makers. It is instructive that, through certain periods, it is difficult to discern any coherent policy. Moreover, elements of policy effectively worked in opposition to each other as government departments engaged in mutually destructive attrition. At best, this produced stagnation – at worst, it resulted in tail-spin. Lack of resources, inherent structural problems in Irish agriculture, a recidivist farming community, an inadequate political culture, an increasingly inhospitable international climate and myriad other problems placed agricultural policy in a hostile context. Even allowing for context, however, agricultural policy in Ireland was ill-conceived and ineffective. Inevitably, it could not possibly have met the expectations of all – that it met those of so few stands as its most dispiriting aspect.

Chapter
1

Longing on a large scale ... 1945 and before [1]

By 1945 Irish agriculture required radical overhaul. Neutrality in World War II had ensured avoidance of the horrors of war but the prosperity which Irish farmers had enjoyed through the Great War was not repeated. Indeed, the Irish experience of war, locally known as 'the Emergency', placed in stark perspective the inadequacies of Irish agriculture and the policy failings which had attended the industry since independence. Legislation enforcing a mandatory minimum area of tillage production per farm had forced Irish farmers to respond to the changed circumstances of the Emergency by altering their traditional pattern of farming and they duly accomplished the task of feeding the populace. The nature of this response, however, vividly exposed inherent structural flaws in the Irish agricultural economy. That farmers had to be compelled by law to till their lands lent eloquent testimony to the dominance of pastoral farming. That dominance had been founded on decades of lucrative livestock exports to Britain in a trade which had survived political independence and all attempts by native governments to foster a more mixed agricultural economy.

Bound into low-intensity pastoral farming, Irish farmers had been ill-equipped to deal with the requirements of World War II. Farmers were reliant on a low-input strategy, which emphasised the need to keep costs at a minimum, rather than on a high standard of technical efficiency. Compulsory tillage, requiring firstly one-eighth, and later three-eighths, of all farmland to be tilled, demonstrated just how dominant pastoral farming was across the country. In many areas, tillage had been neglected to the point of abandonment leaving farmers deprived of basic required techniques. This not only lessened output but exacerbated the problem of the dearth of fertilisers. Had Irish farmers been able to retain undiluted their traditional pattern of farming through the Emergency, the effects on output of war-time shortages of fertilisers would have been relatively minor. Grassland could survive, even prosper, in Ireland with minimal fertiliser usage but, on a long-term basis, tillage could not. The farmers ensured the people of Ireland did not go hungry through the Emergency – but they did so at the cost of starving the land.

Beyond the perspectives of war, farming structure and policy were widely condemned. All observers stressed the importance of the industry and its potential, but none were in any doubt it was failing to achieve levels of production or profit which satisfied even minimal expectations. Projected as the driving force

---

[1] Don de Lillo, *Underworld* (1998), p. 11. De Lillo wrote: "Longing on a large scale is what makes history."

of the economy, Irish agriculture wavered between stagnation and decline. This cacophony of condemnation stressed the low level of technical competence and derided the policies which successive governments pursued. "Our farmers have failed to develop methods of production and organisations for processing and marketing suitable for the realisation of the possibilities of our soil, climate and geographical position," stated one report.[2] Another commentator noted: "No solution is offered except to continue to feed the dog with his own tail."[3]

Nonetheless, economic isolation during World War II facilitated an unprecedented combination of economic analysis and contemplation of planning. The relationship between the state and the economy was fundamentally altered through the contingency planning of the war years.[4] The problems of agriculture were minutely scrutinised in an attempt to postulate a policy to bring prosperity to the industry. The central conduit for this was the 'Commission of inquiry on post-Emergency agricultural policy' established in 1942. Exhaustive debate produced a series of interim reports before the publication, in 1945, of a majority and two minority reports. Although diverging widely on prospective solutions, these reports offered a penetrating insight into the problems of Irish agriculture. In tandem with the production of these reports, various government ministers called for a substantial re-evaluation of policy and stressed the inadequacies of past policies. The conclusion was inescapable: Irish agriculture had achieved only a meagre increase in output in the century since the famine and was treading water in a stagnant pool.

There was a clear acceptance that a critical juncture had been reached. The technical advances made by other countries during the war, as well as the evidence of widespread planning, left it indisputable that change was essential if Irish agriculture was to progress. It is somewhat ironic that it was in this historical poverty of performance that greatest solace was found. The potential for expansion was perceived as immense and it was assumed that there would be an unlimited market for food in the years immediately after the war, placing Ireland, theoretically at least, in a unique position to prosper. Moreover, in the absence of any likelihood of the miraculous visitation of a sustainable industrial sector, agriculture would continue to serve as the mainstay of the economy. If Ireland was to prosper in the post-war world, agriculture would have to thrive – and for agriculture to thrive a radical transformation was imperative.

---

[2] *Commission of inquiry on post-emergency agricultural policy* (CIPEAP) (1945), majority report, p. 47.

[3] Henry Kennedy, *The future of agriculture in Ireland* (1938), in University College Dublin Archives (UCDA), Patrick McGilligan papers, P35c\181.

[4] Raymond J. Raymond, 'Thesis abstract. The economics of neutrality: the United States, Great Britain and Ireland's war economy, 1937–45', in *Irish Economic and Social History* (IESH), vol. x (1983), pp 98–9.

I

Agriculture and Ireland before 1921

Irish agriculture, according to Raymond Crotty, is influenced by climate, system of land tenure and demand for its products.[5] Seemingly oblivious to patterns of land tenure, though, the cattle trade dominated through the comparative advantage arising from climatic conditions and the proximity of the British market. Although tillage production was central to continental Europe's agricultural system, in Ireland it was "practised in a desultory, haphazard way and provided only a very small part of the food requirements of men and beasts."[6] By 1600 the trade in live cattle across the Irish sea was underway and was so attractive it was suggested that Ireland seemed destined for conversion into vast cattle walks while its population might be transferred to provide a helot class in England.[7] The obvious exaggerations of such sentiments should not disguise the essential truth of the enduring romance between cattle and Irish land.

By 1780 trade with Britain accounted for 74 per cent of Irish imports and 79 per cent of Irish exports – this marked a four fold increase in absolute quantity since the beginning of the century. Similarly, the importance of Ireland to Britain's economy also climbed to account for 15 per cent of total trade. Agricultural exports accounted for the vast bulk of this export trade.[8] In the first half of the nineteenth century both pastoral and tillage farming struggled under falling prices, but tillage, with its higher inputs, proved less profitable than grass, thriving, as ever, with little encouragement under Irish conditions. Most critically, cattle prices held more firmly than tillage ones as demand on the British market ebbed from cereals towards livestock. [9] The cold historical analysis of the physical impact of the famine of the 1840s on Irish agriculture is that it stimulated a process of consolidation which would ensure, in time, the virtual elimination of entire classes. In terms of agricultural economy, the famine confirmed the slide from tillage to pasture. Britain's policy of free trade encompassed unlimited food importation on a comparative cost basis and on the lines best suited to the British economy. Imported North American grain on an improved transport network worsened the corn market, while Irish agriculture bowed to the imperatives of climate and allowed natural conditions provide enough grass at negligible cost to feed livestock. Increasingly, it was beef rather than dairying, hampered by the shortage of winter feed and traditionally inefficient seasonality, which held sway in the new order. Between 1847 and 1876, the cattle population rose by almost 60 per

---

[5] Crotty, *Agricultural production*, p. 1. This section draws heavily on Crotty's work, as well as on Cormac Ó Gráda, *Ireland: a new economic history*, 1780–1939 (1994), and on Roy Foster, *Modern Ireland*, 1600–1972 (1988).

[6] Crotty, *Agricultural production*, p. 3.

[7] Foster, *Modern Ireland*, p. 35.

[8] Ó Gráda, *New economic history*, p. 43.

[9] Crotty, *Agricultural production*, pp 36–42.

cent and the sheep population by more than 80 per cent.

The human population suffered a converse experience as between 1845 and 1910 the number of rural labourers fell from at least 700,000 to 300,000. [10] The continued decline in numbers owed much to emigration. [11] The steady demise of the agricultural labouring class was almost mirrored by the decline of the agrarian classes just above it. [12] It would appear that this demographic rupture originated before the famine, but it was that cataclysm which defined its nature. Between 1845 and 1910, the number of cottiers with less than five acres fell from 300,000 to 62,000; while, in that same period, the number of farmers holding between five and fifteen acres fell from 310,000 to 154,000. The farmer with less than fifteen acres to his name did not vanish as conveniently as the labourer. The toehold of land was protected with unrelieved zeal until the family line was ended through emigration or failure to marry. Yet, as surely if not as spectacularly as the labourers, this class too had lurched into a steady, unrelenting decline.

In tandem with recast demographics and the assertion of the primacy of livestock, the drive towards peasant proprietorship gathered pace. This "dynamic element of structural change" dominated the political landscape in the closing decades of the nineteenth century as the agrarian movement joined constitutional and revolutionary nationalism in the unprecedented unity of the Land League. [13] Tenant farmers became the largest social group in rural society and their interests grew increasingly important. In the thirty years after 1847, livestock and butter prices rose and with the rise in prosperity came determined agitation which forced a series of land acts culminating in 1903 with the Wyndham Act. Long-term government loans effectively allowed most tenants buy up the land they farmed and the tenure system became one of peasant proprietorship. By 1916, 64 per cent of agricultural holdings in Ireland were owner-occupied as compared with a mere 3 per cent in 1870.

Peasant proprietorship failed to inspire an improvement in productivity. There was no dramatic or even significant effect on efficiency, investment or land use. [14] J.J. Lee caustically notes that land activist, Michael Davitt, had initially promoted land nationalisation with tenancy secured by a reasonable standard of efficiency but "the farmers were not impressed. There would be no nonsense

---

[10] Samuel Clark, 'The importance of the agrarian classes: agrarian class structure and collective action in nineteenth century Ireland', in P.J. Drudy (ed.), *Land, politics and people*, pp 11–36, 21.

[11] For example, in the 1871–2 annual report of the Massachusetts bureau of statistics of labour, it was noted that half of the farm labourers in the state were Irish born. See Lawanda F. Cox, 'The agricultural wage earner, 1865–1900: the emergence of a modern labour problem', in *Agricultural History* (AH), vol. 22, no. 1 (1948), pp 95–114. That same report noted comments by a local farmer who called for the replacement of the Irish labourers by Asian ones as the Irish were "getting too much Americanized to be very efficient help – the best working for themselves and buying farms and the others earning their wages as easily as they can."

[12] See David Fitzpatrick, 'The disappearance of the Irish agricultural labourer, 1841–1912', in *IESH*, vol. vii (1980), pp 66–92, *passim*.

[13] *Ibid.*, p. 84.

[14] M.A.G. Ó Tuathaigh, 'The land question, politics and Irish society, 1922–60', in P.J. Drudy (ed.), *Land, politics and people*, pp 167–90.

about efficiency as far as they were concerned ... They had not fought the land war to be crucified on the cross of their efficiency."[15] Overall, however, peasant proprietorship brought a stability of output which shaded into stagnation and it was not necessarily the panacea promised by its advocates (see appendix). As James Connolly argued in 1897:

> The agriculture of Ireland can no longer compete with the scientifically equipped farmers of America ... Have our advocates of peasant proprietary really considered the economic tendencies of the time and the development of the mechanical arts in the agricultural world? ... The day of small farmers, as of small capitalists, is gone and wherever they are still found, they find it impossible to compete with the mammoth farmers of America and Australia.[16]

Despite Connolly's dismal prognosis, the potential to develop Irish agriculture was not lost on other observers and the era brought institutional innovation, both realised and imagined.

The principal reformer in Irish agriculture at the time was Horace Plunkett who worked in, and wrote on, the co-operative movement and the establishment of a Department of Agriculture and Technical Instruction in Dublin in 1899. In the course of his 1904 treatise *Ireland in the new century*, Plunkett outlined his interpretation of the problems facing Irish agriculture, the requirements to solve these problems and the means to meet these requirements. Stripped of its self-justification and crass generalisations on the Irish character,[17] the book offers an insightful analysis of Irish agriculture at the beginning of the twentieth century. Like Connolly, Plunkett stressed that peasant proprietorship alone would not bring prosperity to Irish agriculture but that co-operation offered the means to compete against the large-scale farming operations of the New World and the more organised productivity of the old one. He argued that, as foreign competition was not about to disappear, but rather intensify, Irish farming would have to reform itself or perish. To this end, the Irish Agricultural Organisation Society (IAOS) was established to offer a co-operative outlet capable of overcoming the problems facing smallholders. Noting the ready markets now available in the growing industrialised cities, Plunkett wrote of the importance of "the regular consignment of food in large quantities of such uniform quality that the sample can be relied upon to be truly indicative of the quality of the bulk. Thus the rapid distribution of produce in the markets becomes as important a factor in agricultural economy as improved methods of production or cheap and expeditious carriage."

---

[15] J.J. Lee, 'The land war', in Liam de Paor (ed.), *Milestones in Irish history* (1986), p. 114.

[16] In *Shan Van Vocht*; quoted in R.M. Fox, *James Connolly: the forerunner* (1946), p. 39.

[17] Witness such remarks as: "the Irish question is, in its most difficult and most important aspects, the problem of the Irish mind, and that the solution of this problem is to be found in the strengthening of Irish character," and "the conclusion has been forced upon me that the Irish mind is suffering from considerable functional derangement, but not, so far as I can discern, from any organic disease. This is the basis of my optimism," Horace Plunkett, *Ireland in the new century* (1904), p. 59.

Underlying all beneficial change, Plunkett stressed, was the importance of education. Technical improvements in agriculture were rooted in the widespread availability and participation in general and agricultural education. Significantly, he pointed out that agriculture had come to be viewed as intimately associated with "the very existence of the race ... their last resort and sole dependence," but that this was unrealistic and that "not by agriculture alone is Ireland to be saved. The solution of the rural problem embraces many spheres of national activity." While he commented disapprovingly that "the people have an extraordinary belief in political remedies for economic ills," Plunkett made a sharp distinction between political and state remedy. He cast an envious eye on European countries where state intervention "has undoubtedly done much to render possible a prosperous peasant proprietary by, for example, the dissemination of useful information, admirable systems of technical education in agriculture, cheap and expeditious transport, and even state attention to the distribution of agricultural produce in distant markets." Plunkett placed his faith in the new Department of Agriculture's unique position as planned by Irishmen and in its ambitions which included "the aiding, improving and developing of agriculture in all its branches; horticulture, forestry, home and cottage industries; sea and inland fisheries; the aiding and facilitating of the transit of produce; and the organisation of a system of education in science and art, and in technology as applied to those various subjects." [18]

The optimism of these years even gave rise to the suggestion that the department could give free play to "a reawakening life." This was never realised. The co-operative movement showed early prosperity but lost its government funding in a political wrangle and failed to take firm hold. It stumbled onwards yet never attained the vibrancy of continental movements. Similarly, the new department enjoyed little success. On the grounds of output alone, it did not justify the expectations which had attended its inauguration. Nonetheless, the issues raised by Plunkett and what he perceived as the needs of Irish agriculture were repeated at will through the century. Pleas for land redistribution, education, technical efficiency, marketing, transport, co-operation, innovation and a balanced economy – as the century began so would it continue.

Although neither co-operation nor the establishment of a Department of Agriculture succeeded in substantially raising the prosperity of Irish agriculture, the competing powers of Europe had greater success. Despite having "responded lackadaisically," Irish farmers benefited from World War I as exports of farm produce, food and drink rose from £41.6 million in 1914 to £78.3 million in 1918 without ever threatening to fully exploit the lack of competition from Danish and Dutch exports.[19] By then, political unrest in Ireland had brought a new dimension to the agricultural scene. Drawing on the doctrine of James Fintan Lalor who had written that a strong and independent agricultural peasantry was the only base on which a people could be improved or on which a nation could safely rest, the rhetoric surrounding the Easter Rising in 1916 was suffused with the imagery of

[18] *Ibid.*, pp 180, 20–1, 51, 231.

[19] Ó Gráda, *New economic history*, p. 389.

agrarianism. [20] Inevitably, the rhetoric strove to offer all things to all men – the landless man was to be given land; the small farmer was to have his holding increased; and the larger farmer was to have his position safeguarded. Far from merely winning independence, the rebels seemed set fair to extend the landmass of the island. Some were not prepared to await that particular eventuality. Patriotism is rarely more sharply displayed than when founded in acute self-interest and the rural poor sensed their moment had finally arrived. The Great War had curtailed emigration leaving labourers in the countryside who would otherwise have been abroad. The rising prices of the war years and the curtailment of land restructuring fuelled their frustration and it was not long before labourers and small farmers were rallying to the old battle hymn of 'the land for the people'. Whether seeking conacre or the aggrandizement of smallholdings, the motivating force was the seizure of land. From 1917, estate redistribution, cattle driving, ploughing and stripping, and general agrarian unrest were in full swing. Elsewhere, farm labourers organised in trade unions and threatened strike action.

For the strong farmer, equally, freedom was defined in economic not constitutional terms. Some reacted to the groundswell of land agitation by covertly participating to further expand their own property and wealth; others founded the Irish Farmers' Union to defend their position; consideration was even given to setting up an armed Farmers' Freedom Force to defend their property.[21] The republican movement was moved to intervene with a headlong rush to the middle ground in an attempt to preserve unity and earn respect for responsible leadership. A Dáil decree was issued on 29 June 1920 stating: "That the present time when Irish people are locked in a life and death struggle with their traditional enemy, is ill-chosen for the stirring up of strife amongst our fellow countrymen; and all our energies must be directed towards the clearing out [of] – not the occupiers of this or that piece of land – but the foreign invader of our country."[22] Special Land Courts were set up by the Dáil to curtail the activities of the more radical and to enforce, through the Irish Republican Army (IRA), such redistribution as could most easily be effected.[23]

Through all of this the propagandists continued to bang out a familiar beat on the republican drum. In the construction of an alternative vision to the one offered by the traditional enemy, Gaelic revivalists and revolutionary nationalists alike presented the small farming ideal as the genuinely Irish existence.[24] Far from the squalor of industrial cities and their degrading factories, the Irish would create a vibrant rural landscape of small homesteads and thriving cottage industries. Political independence would ensure the agricultural prosperity which would drive this buoyant, self-sufficient economy. Detail was ignored as excessively divisive. Rather, all were assured that economic progress was an essential by-

---

[20] F.S.L. Lyons, *Ireland since the famine* (1971), p. 108.

[21] Fitzpatrick, 'Disappearance', *passim*.

[22] Ó Tuathaigh, 'Land question', pp 170–1.

[23] *Ibid.*, p. 170; Foster, *Modern Ireland*, p. 513.

[24] Mary E. Daly, *Industrial development and Irish national identity 1922–1939* (1992), pp 7–11.

product of independence. Rhetoricians, calmly ignoring market forces, claimed it
was the legislative freedom of Grattan's parliament which had brought the most
sustained era of prosperity in the last decades of the eighteenth century. The
restoration of legislative independence would signify a return to Babylon – and
there basking on the shores of the river would be Irish farmers and farm labourers.

II

Cumann na nGaedheal and agriculture

The Anglo-Irish treaty of 1921, the establishment of the Free State in 1922
and the subsequent descent into civil war carried obvious consequences for Irish
agriculture. The opposing sides did not divide merely on matters constitutional –
economics were of definite importance. Notwithstanding the danger of over-
simplifying the equation given the cross-class allegiances of both factions,
opponents of the treaty enjoyed their greatest support amongst the labourers and
smallholders of the south and west. Agrarian radicals tended to find a more
accommodating home in anti-treaty forces than in the government party which
was dominated by the more conservative elements of society, and, most notably, by
large farmers. It is unnecessary here to document the nature of the conflict except
to reflect that its impact on agriculture was, perhaps, more pronounced for what
did not happen than for what did. A radical restructuring of agriculture may not
have occurred in any event, but the manner in which the republican movement
cleaved in the months after the signing of the treaty was a major determining
factor in the development of agricultural policy in the nascent Free State.

When Cumann na nGaedheal assumed office in January 1923, it "was
without any policy save to ensure the survival of the state."[25] With the civil war still
in progress there was no appetite to experiment with economic policy. The
precarious nature of the state dictated that even had there been a strong
governmental desire for radical redesign of the economy, this would have been an
exercise fraught with unjustifiable risk. The common market, as well as the
currency, banking and transport systems shared with the British were not about to
be discarded at a time of such peril. The leading lights of the government party
and their principal supporters were drawn from the elements of society which had
most to gain from preservation of the social and economic status quo. Moreover,
the continuity offered by civil servants surviving from the departing British
administrative system emphasised a tradition of financial austerity and avoidance
of government intervention. A largely conservative party advised by a thoroughly

---

[25] *Ibid.*, p. 14.

conservative administrative elite resulted in economic orthodoxy – policy would reflect the ethos of the era not of the revolution. Cumann na nGaedheal effectively disregarded the social and economic sloganeering which attended the path to political independence when faced with the realities of government. The abandonment of the doctrines of self-sufficiency and protectionism was born of circumstance and of mentality. Dilution of proclaimed policy when faced with actual implementation is an intractable characteristic of the political process. It was, wrote one commentator, "a classic example of this triumph of pragmatism over dogma."[26]

This 'pragmatism' was further determined by the loss of the industrial corner of north-east Ulster. It may be something of a generalisation to note that partition effectively severed an industrial head from its agricultural body but it still remains that, in 1911, the proportion of the labour force engaged in industry in the counties that came to constitute Northern Ireland was 35 per cent, while in the rest of the country it was a mere 13 per cent. This statistic is exacerbated by the fact that, in the south, manufacturing was tending more and more towards food and drink processing which, by the 1920s, accounted for two-thirds of total manufacturing net output.[27] The manner in which political independence failed to impinge upon existing economic trends is illustrated by the 1924 returns where exports to Great Britain comprised £50.59 million of total export sales of £51.58 million. Of this total, agricultural, food and drink products stood at 86 per cent.[28] "The externalities were changed – the emblem, the flag, the anthem – but not the fundamentals," observed one historian.[29] Another wrote: "The economic policy of Cumann na nGaedheal during this decade shows remarkable fidelity to British practices."[30] The Free State slipped easily into a dependency groove.

The primacy of agriculture was enshrined as the government accepted that the economy depended on it for prosperity, that agricultural prosperity depended on the export market, that that market essentially comprised of Britain, and that the most profitable Irish product in Britain was cattle. Policy revolved around these essential verities and as the new Minister for Agriculture, Patrick Hogan, stated in January 1924: "National development in Ireland for our generation at least is practically synonymous with agricultural development." Industry was to be fostered only if it did not conflict with the primary aim of raising farming income. Hogan argued that farmers would have to be compensated for any cost increases consequent to industrial protection, that local governments should curb spending to reduce taxes on farmers, while "spending on unemployment, housing, or industrial development was ruled out."[31] George O'Brien, professor of national

---

[26] T.K.D. Daniel, 'Griffith on his noble head: the determinants of Cumann na nGaedheal economic policy, 1922–32,' in *IESH*, vol. iii (1976), pp 55–65, p. 55.

[27] Kieran A. Kennedy, Thomas Giblin and Deirdre McHugh., *The economic development of Ireland in the twentieth century* (1988), pp 9–11.

[28] Daly, *Industrial development*, p. 15.

[29] Raymond Crotty, *Farming collapse: national opportunity?* (1973), p. 6.

[30] Daly, *Industrial development*, p. 56.

[31] *Ibid.*, pp 16, 17.

economics at University College, Dublin (UCD), in an oft-quoted article, noted that Hogan's belief was that national economic policy

> should be directed to maximise farmers' income, because the farmers being the most important section of the economy, everything that raised their income raised the national income of the country. Prosperity among farmers would provide the purchasing power necessary to sustain demand for non-agricultural goods and services, and it was useless to encourage secondary industries unless the primary industry was in a position to purchase their products.[32]

In essence, Hogan championed policies which emphasised the expansion and development of methods already being applied.[33]

To accomplish this, he established, in November 1922, a commission to advise on agricultural policy, chaired by J.P. Drew, a professor of agriculture at UCD. The majority report, agreed by eight of the ten commission members, confirmed Hogan's creed. It noted that agriculture must "find its salvation from within, or it must perish" and that salvation was not to be found in the cult of state intervention, rather through "voluntary effort, collective and individual, on the part of the people themselves." To this end, Edmund Burke was approvingly quoted: "To provide for us in our necessities is not in the power of government. It would be a vain presumption in statesmen to think they can do it. The people maintain them, and not they the people. It is in the power of government to prevent much evil, and it can do very little positive good in this or perhaps anything else."[34] The only concession was support for government assistance to the co-operative movement and the expansion of the education system. While not entirely dismissing tillage, the majority report agreed that Ireland was "especially suited to stock raising and dairy farming," and that the recent trend from tillage to cattle farming was rooted in the greater profitability of the latter. Accordingly, the report warned of the dangers of excessive redistribution of land as conducive to subsistence farming where "a bad season may precipitate a famine," and argued that the much-reviled grazier was an integral part of the agricultural economy as an outlet for the small farmer to sell his cattle. The report continued:

> While fully alive to the disadvantages attendant on the use of rich pasture lands merely as pasture, we are inclined to support the view that either greater profit to the occupier or greater advantage to the community at large will not follow from their use in any other way, and we therefore recommend the government to proceed with due caution in the matter of their re-division.

---

[32] George O'Brien, 'Patrick Hogan: Minister for Agriculture 1922–32', *Studies*, 25 (1936), p. 37.

[33] Crotty, *Agricultural production*, p. 113.

[34] *Report of the commission on agriculture* (1924), pp 26–7. The commission held fifty-six public meetings, thirty-eight private ones, heard one hundred and twenty-one witnesses and issued five interim reports, before eventually issuing concluding majority and minority reports.

The minority report contained fundamental differences. Recommending that agricultural policy should be directed towards self-sufficiency and "away from the conception that the Irish farmer exists solely to supply the British consumer all he can produce of beef, pork, butter and eggs at an internationally competitive price," the minority report rejected the notion that prosperity for the individual farmer equalled prosperity for the nation. Pointing out that tillage provided greater national wealth than grazing, even if grazing did offer higher personal profit, it called for the state to make positive efforts to increase the area under tillage. Not only was this tillage produce to be used to feed livestock, but there should be a guaranteed price for wheat, while the government should stipulate a minimum percentage of Irish wheat which must be milled by Irish millers.[35]

The five interim reports, which the commission produced, dealt with tobacco, butter, eggs, agricultural credit and the licensing of bulls. These reports, most particularly the ones on butter and eggs, were highly critical of elements of the agricultural economy. During World War I Irish farmers had focussed more on quantity of produce than on quality and had been unable to resist the option of sending over 'bad eggs and worse butter' in their exports to Britain.[36] Not only was the reputation of this produce "considerably impaired,"[37] but the return of continental competitors meant that the conditions of trade were now a matter of "extreme urgency."[38] In particular, the grading, packaging and marketing of butter, as well as the packaging and cleanliness of eggs, were undermining the position of Irish produce in the British market. The reports recommended regulation and the immediate introduction of legislation to raise standards in the trade. Ignoring the minority report, government policy followed the broad philosophical sweep of the majority report and espoused non-interventionism. There were to be no guaranteed prices, no protective tariffs, no subsidies, although a number of initiatives were designed to expedite the expansion of existing trends. Farmers were to be left free to follow the market, but there were to be a small number of schemes to assist them. Principally, Hogan sponsored a series of acts "considered draconian in their day, [which] established systems of inspection and control that enabled Irish produce to recover from the reputation it had acquired during the war."[39] It was in this policing of quality control that government policy found its greatest success. Other initiatives involved the establishment of the Dairy Disposal Company to acquire co-operative and private creameries in financial trouble and the establishment of the Agricultural Credit Corporation (ACC), designed to offer loans to co-operative societies, as well as to individual farmers.

The perennially durable land question was set high on the agenda. Although

---

35 *Ibid.*, pp 29, 34, 35, 76–8, 80–2, 94–5.

36 Ó Tuathaigh, 'Land question', p. 175.

37 National Archives, Ireland (NAI), Department of Taoiseach (D/T), S 2392, Irish White Cross memo to Minister for Agriculture, 15 Mar. 1922.

38 *Commission on agriculture, second interim report (butter)*, May 1923, p. 14.

39 Daniel, 'Griffith', p. 61.

there was to be no wholesale redistribution of land, it was a political imperative that initiatives in place before independence be sustained, if not intensified. The Land Act, 1923 established the Land Commission and accorded it the task of transferring the ownership of large estates from the remaining landlords to smallholders taking the view that a viable holding constituted a minimum of twenty-two acres. It further assumed the role of the Congested Districts Board which was dissolved and its assets, staff and operations encompassed in a special branch of the Land Commission. In its operations up to 1923 the Congested Districts Board had rearranged 10,000 holdings in the western region – the branch of the Land Commission which assumed its function rearranged 1,000 such holdings between 1923 and 1950.[40] Through the 1923 act, the Land Commission was given only limited powers and limited resources – it was to redistribute land but it was to do so without interfering with property rights and at minimal cost.

Given the opportunities on the British market, and with market forces supplemented by natural and institutional impulses, government policy was, perhaps, the logical way forward. Yet, Ireland's share of the British market did not significantly expand, although in terms of what was to follow, agriculture enjoyed a decade of relative prosperity.[41] Between 1924 and 1928 Free State butter increased its share of the British market from 8.7 per cent to 9.1 per cent, but that of eggs slipped from 23.1 per cent to 19.6 per cent. The cattle trade registered no sustained increase beyond yearly fluctuation.[42] Overall output did increase but not on anything approaching the scale required to raise living standards in the wider community. By 1929/30, gross agricultural output was 4 per cent below its pre-World War I level.[43] Net agricultural output was equally disappointing and in 1929/30 had fallen by 5 per cent since the middle of the decade. Although crop yields improved, between 1922 and 1932 the area of tilled land fell by 17 per cent. In that same period the number of cattle fell by 8 per cent.[44] It has been argued that, judged by the limits imposed on it, Cumann na nGaedheal's economic policy achieved a substantial, if unspectacular, measure of success – the state was solvent and enjoyed fiscal stability, exports rose, industrial employment increased, farm wages improved and emigration fell.[45] Nonetheless, a singular frustration was experienced by those convinced that all that had restrained Ireland was the denial of legislative independence and it is difficult to avoid the conclusion that "the achievements of government in the first decade of independence lay in the political rather than in the economic sphere – in establishing the framework of democratic government and in peacefully handing over the reins to another government with a quite different outlook on economic policy."[46] This different

---

[40] P. Commins., 'Land policies and agricultural development', in P.J. Drudy (ed.), *Land, politics and people*, pp 217–40, esp. p. 218.

[41] Ó Tuathaigh, 'Land question', p. 177. In 1929 the total value of Irish exports reached £47 million – a figure not reached again until 1949.

[42] Ó Gráda, *New economic history*, p. 391.

[43] Kennedy *et al., Economic development*, p. 36.

[44] Ó Gráda, *New economic history*, p. 391.

[45] Daniel, 'Griffith', p. 65; Daly, *Economic development*, p. 57.

[46] Kennedy et al., *Economic development*, p. 40.

outlook ensured a radically altered agricultural policy. Non-interventionism was condemned to a watery grave – the state would now attempt to direct the road that agriculture should travel.

III

Fianna Fáil and agriculture in the 1930s

The return to democratic politics in 1927 of the vast bulk of the alienated republicans who had refused to enter the Dáil in the wake of the civil war dramatically altered the political landscape. There was no return to the consensus politics of the movement's pre-1921 form. From its inception Fianna Fáil embarked on a populist crusade to win power. Understanding that its electoral rehabilitation would not profit from a devotion to constitutional issues alone, it prioritised economic matters.[47] It appealed to the sections of society seemingly ignored by Cumann na nGaedheal's austerity. One of the founding aims of Fianna Fáil was to provide for the greatest possible number of families to live on the land through redistribution. Promises to redefine and intensify the work of the Land Commission were accompanied by similar declarations of fidelity to self-sufficiency in food production, principally through the extension of the tillage acreage. This was to be complemented by a vigorous policy of industrialisation, particularly through the cultivation of small industries in rural Ireland. Both agricultural and industrial development, with the ultimate target of self-sufficiency, were to be aided by widespread protectionism.

In its last years in office, Cumann na nGaedheal had not so much mellowed on protectionism as undergone a "noisy abandonment of its commitment to free trade." A combination of world-wide depression and the pressing need to respond to the aggressive posturing of Fianna Fáil had forced the government into action. With Hogan arguing that their protectionism was "pragmatic rather than dogmatic,"[48] the government weakened its position on tariffs and by December 1931 butter, bacon and oats were all protected.[49] Patrick McGilligan later fondly recalled to Richard Mulcahy that "our derided policy of those days withstood the blizzard."[50] Mulcahy, himself, claimed that Ireland was one of two countries who had safely come through "that world disaster ... because its agricultural policy was

---

[47] William Murphy, 'In pursuit of popularity and legitimacy: the rhetoric of Fianna Fáil's social and economic policy 1926–34' (M.A., UCD, 1998), *passim*.

[48] Ó Gráda, *New economic history*, p. 387.

[49] D. Hoctor, *The department's story: a history of the department of agriculture* (1971), p. 169.

[50] UCDA, Richard Mulcahy papers, P7c/58, McGilligan to Mulcahy, 3 Oct. 1963.

firmly based on the production of livestock and livestock products."[51] The electorate were convinced by neither the agricultural policy nor the deathbed conversion to protectionism. The election of February 1932 saw Fianna Fáil gain office they were not to lose until 1948 – and the impact on agricultural policy was dramatic.

Perversely, the trauma of the Great Depression appeared tailor-made for Fianna Fáil policies. The collapse of the world trade in agriculture and the effective cessation of emigration for the first time in many generations necessitated a radical redrawing of policy. Similarly, the global embrace of subsidisation and protectionism saw the mood of the decade swing sharply from the one which preceded it.[52] The mood of relations between the Irish and British governments swung with equal force. Within months of taking power the new government, fulfilling a major aspect of its electoral promises, withheld the payment of the land annuities due to the British government as part of the post-independence settlement. Britain duly responded in July 1932 by placing a duty of 20 per cent ad valorem on the principal Irish agricultural exports, notably cattle, and this was increased by a further 10 per cent in November 1932. The Irish replied in kind with the imposition of duties on British coal and assorted industrial products in a whirlwind escalation of hostilities. By 1936, of almost 2,000 categories on the official Irish import list, over one-half were subject to tariffs, generally in the range of 50 to 75 per cent.[53] Grandiosely styled as an 'economic war', the dispute was only ended with the signing of the Anglo-Irish trade agreement of 1938.

Although the 'war' was, at least in part, an economic manifestation of political grievance, the perception has emerged that, even without it, trade relations between the two countries through the 1930s would have proved distinctly turbulent.[54] The 'war' rendered the impact of that turbulence more acute, gave it political connotations which might otherwise have been avoided and delayed constructive solution, but it did not define the pattern of trade which emerged. It is clearly unsustainable to deny that the 'war' was a factor in the commerce of the era but, on the Irish side, it was "incidental to and not a condition of the protective policy of those years."[55] While, in Britain, there had already been a swift move from free trade to protectionism through the introduction of import quotas and tariffs. The establishment of marketing boards for milk, bacon, pigs and potatoes under the Agricultural Marketing Act, 1931, as well as the introduction of a guaranteed price for wheat in 1932, altered the free trade landscape which so recently had appeared immune from change.[56]

It was not as a consequence of the 'war', but as part of its overall economic

---

[51] UCDA, Richard Mulcahy papers, P7/C/121, copy of speech in Portumna, Co. Galway, 27 Oct. 1946.

[52] Ó Tuathaigh, 'Land question', p. 183; Crotty, *Agricultural production*, p. 133.

[53] Kennedy *et al.*, *Economic development*, pp 42, 43.

[54] See, for example, *ibid.*, pp 42–3.

[55] Crotty, *Agricultural production*, p. 134.

[56] Hoctor, *The department's story*, p. 168.

policy, that Britain imposed strictures on the import of cattle. These also applied to other suppliers, although, as the main supplier of live cattle, Ireland suffered greatest penury. Pressure at home forced the British government to act to assist its own farmers. The price of fat cattle had been in decline through the 1920s and the sharp fall in the early months of 1932 reduced the price of livestock almost to pre-World War I levels. When British producers complained that they were receiving insufficient protection, the 30 per cent ad valorem duty was strengthened by quantitative restrictions on the import of cattle and the prohibition of the import of Irish beef. The Irish cattle trade fell into steep decline. Between 1929 and 1934 the export of live animals fell in value from £19.7 million to £6.1 million and that of animal-derived foodstuffs from £14.5 million to £5.2 million.[57] In June 1934, the Department of Finance suggested that the living standards of Irish farmers had fallen by 15 per cent between 1929 and 1933, but that even without the 'war' the decline would have been 13 per cent.[58] The traditional market was disappearing and the Taoiseach and leader of Fianna Fáil, Eamon de Valera, declared it "gone forever."[59]

The fate of other nations and their markets was mere background music, however, as Fianna Fáil was intent on pursuing the economic agenda of pre-independence separatism regardless of context. Protectionism was designed to provide employment and reduce emigration. In de Valera's particular denomination of the tariff creed, the industries established were not expected to compete internationally, but were to service the home market. In May 1932, *ad valorem* duties ranging from 15 to 75 per cent were placed on 38 classes of goods – the drive for industrial self-sufficiency was underway. The domestic market was further shielded from external infiltration by the use of such non-tariff methods as quotas, import licences and compulsory milling orders.[60] The new emphasis on industrial expansion was confirmed by the establishment of the Turf Development Board (later Bord na Móna), Ceimicí Teoranta and the Industrial Credit Corporation. Industrial development did not signify a turning away from agriculture. Fianna Fáil promoted industry more vigorously than Cumann na nGaedheal, but the primary element of its social and economic policies was agricultural restructuring. This restructuring brought a new interpretation to the role of government whose spending increased from 24 per cent of Gross National Product (GNP) in 1931 to 30.3 per cent by 1933, before averaging 30 per cent for the remainder of the 1930s. Agricultural spending claimed 46 per cent of this increase, with a further 23.3 per cent allocated to land redistribution.[61] Much of this money went initially in the form of bounties to subsidise exporters who were struggling to maintain a hold in Britain. By 1934 duties on animals imported into Britain could reach two-thirds of the value of the animal and even allowing for its

[57] Kennedy *et al.*, *Economic development*, p. 45.

[58] Ó Gráda, *New economic history*, p. 413.

[59] Quoted in, Louis Smith and Sean Healy, *Farm organisations in Ireland: a century of progress* (1996), p. 18.

[60] Kennedy *et al.*, *Economic development*, p. 43.

[61] Daly, *Industrial development*, p. 62.

antipathy to the dominance of cattle farming, the government could not allow the trade to entirely disintegrate. Diminution of status of the cattle trade and not its disintegration was the avowed aim of policy.

A realignment from cattle farming to tillage farming was fundamental to the success of Fianna Fáil policies. This substitution of intensive for extensive farming was seen as the key to a revitalised social order allowing smallholders improve their incomes and larger farmers to employ more labourers thus stemming emigration and the drift from the land. A concerted campaign was launched to encourage farmers to convert from pastoral to tillage production. A bounty was offered for calf skins, subsidies were introduced for wheat and sugar beet, import controls were imposed on sugar and tobacco, and relief was offered on rates in proportion to the amount of non-family farm labour employed.[62] The measures only partially succeeded. As Hoctor recorded: "At all times ... farmers clung to livestock. There were more cattle, including a higher proportion of dairy cows, in the country at the end of the economic war than there were at the beginning ... Although financial losses had been heavy the country's capacity for livestock expansion was not impaired."[63] If the livestock industry emerged undaunted, though not unscathed, from an unfavourable climate, tillage, as a whole, did not profit from the support it received. Between 1932 and 1938 the wheat acreage was increased from 22,000 acres to more than ten times that figure and, in the same period, the area under sugar beet grew from 13,000 to 51,000 acres. These expansions supplied 30 and 60 per cent of the national requirement, respectively.[64] Despite mid-decade expansion, though, by 1939 tillage acreage was only 2 per cent higher than it had been at the start of the decade. Government initiatives in wheat and sugar production enticed farmers to sow those crops, but at the expense of other crops, not at the expense of cattle (see appendix). On neither a county nor a provincial basis was there evidence that increased tillage had provided more rural employment. Indeed, Leinster, which enjoyed the greatest increase in tillage between 1929 and 1939, suffered the greatest decline in agricultural employment.[65]

With tillage failing to increase rural employment, government policy was dependent on land redistribution to fuel the repopulation of rural areas and to combat emigration. In a pamphlet issued before it assumed power, Fianna Fáil promised to "work resolutely to ... break up the large grazing ranches and distribute them amongst young farmers and agricultural labourers, such as those at present compelled to emigrate."[66] The small farmer was portrayed as the foundation of the nation – those already in existence were to be joined by as many as the land could conceivably hold. In 1933 the Land Commission was given extra powers to acquire and redistribute land and the amount spent on redistribution

---

[62] Cormac Ó Gráda, *A rocky road: the Irish economy since the 1920s* (1997), p. 145.

[63] Hoctor, *The department's story*, p. 197.

[64] NAI, D/T S11445-7, Department of Agriculture (D/A) memo to govt., (n.d.).

[65] Crotty, *Agricultural production*, p. 146.

[66] UCDA, Patrick McGilligan papers, P7/c/140, Fianna Fáil election pamphlet, (n.d.).

rose from £2.7 million in 1931 to £7.6 million in 1936.[67] It was, said the Minister of Lands, Joseph Connolly, "work of supreme national importance," and was to be carried out "equitably and expeditiously."[68]

To ensure the maximum number of people on the land, the Fianna Fáil government, despite dissenting voices, retained 22 acres as the desirable farm size with "the policy of 'tillage and work' stressed as answer to any objections that may be raised – as also the possibility that, taking the long view, there may not, eventually, be enough land to go round in larger allotments."[69] Twenty-two acre farms were not viewed by all as economically feasible. In 1936, the Chief Inspector of the Land Commission, J.J. Waddell, argued that the minimum requirement for "sound and practical farming" was 32.5 acres. He noted that the last migrant colony from the west to Rath Carn in Co. Meath was allocated 20-22 acres per family and now "practically every family is sending members across the water to England to assist the occupiers in living on these holdings and help to pay the annuity and rates, and to exist on them."[70] By 1937 there was general agreement that 22 acres was incapable of supporting "an ordinary family in reasonable comfort," and that 25 acres of good land and up to 35 acres of poor land would be required in future.[71] The government agreed to increase the basic amount of good land required to 25 acres, but made no mention of land in poorer areas.[72]

These poorer western areas continued to offer the greatest problems and by 1939 Fianna Fáil had accepted that additional families could be placed on the land only beyond the congested districts and that migration offered the most likely solution. Originally, the Land Commission proposed a 25 year scheme for the large-scale migration of 40,000 families at the cost of £8 million, but the objections of the Department of Finance ensured that a greatly restricted five-year scheme was approved.[73] Even this more limited scheme ran into trouble when local landless claimants in Meath reacted against the influx of westerners and the Land Commission was forced to distribute a conciliatory 4,000 acres amongst them despite the fact that the migrants only received 600 acres.[74] The passion for land showed no signs of relenting, even if it was obvious that there was not enough of it to satisfy demand. The initial wave of Land Commission enthusiasm had broken in the mid-1930s and the sheer scale of the problem remained overwhelming. The government did not, or could not, commit the resources required to effect any more than a moderate impact. But this was not enough to counteract the forces of nature or to placate the desperate who could see a secure future only in land. By the late 1930s, the support for Fianna Fáil amongst small western farmers was diminishing and a new smallholders' party, Clann na Talmhan, claimed a strong

[67] Patrick Sammon, *In the Land Commission: a memoir 1933–78* (1997), p. 9.

[68] NAI, D/T S6490 A, Department of Lands (D/L) memo to govt., 11 Oct. 1933.

[69] *Ibid.*

[70] NAI, D/T S6490 A, J.J. Waddell memo to govt., Dec. 1936.

[71] NAI, D/T S6490 A, D/L memo to govt., 9 Jan. 1937; D/A memo to govt., Jan. 1937.

[72] NAI, D/T S6490 A, cabinet minutes, 19 Jan. 1937.

[73] NAI, D/T S6490 A, cabinet minutes, 29 Aug. 1939.

[74] NAI, D/T S6490 A, T. Smiddy letter to de Valera, Apr. 1942.

vote in the 1938 elections, particularly along the western seaboard. That it should begin to lose the very voters who had formed its backbone is testimony to the government's failure to achieve, or even make much headway towards, another of its central policy objectives.

In overall terms, government policy did not induce a reordering of the existing agricultural structure and the various strands of policy did not raise output. It was the farmers' dole rather than any agricultural directive on tillage or redistribution that most benefited the western smallholder.[75] Government initiatives in price support were misplaced and inspired a distortion rather than an increase of output.[76] Indeed, government policies may have brought a long-term contraction in certain commodities – such as bacon – where the rise in the cost of inputs was not offset by price support.[77] Further, a substantial portion of the high cost to the consumer of bread and sugar probably did not reach farmers due to economic waste, monopolies and cartels.[78] And for all the tariffs and trade dislocation, Britain was still the market for over 90 per cent of all Irish exports.[79] "Again, following an iron precedent – the basic pattern of Irish agriculture showed little sign of change," wrote one historian.[80]

In the absence of such change, it was imperative to reach an accommodation with Britain. The prospect of securing other markets abroad had all but been abandoned:

> A sustained effort has been made during the past four years to find alternative markets for agricultural products. These attempts have not succeeded except to a limited extent. ... There is no element of permanence in markets for cattle, butter, eggs, etc., in continental countries. ... **It is absolutely certain that there is no prospect of securing within any period of time that can be foreseen any real market for our agricultural exports.**[81]

For all the aspirations of autarky, *realpolitik* required a more integrationist approach. The market could only be denied for so long and Fianna Fáil's radical agrarianism went into full retreat, in practice if not in posture. The fear of a continued decline in living standards pushed the government back into the arms of its erstwhile foe. This rapprochement had begun with the coal cattle pact of 1935. This had gone some way towards drawing the sting from the economic crisis when the Irish were granted an increase of 150,000 in their yearly import quota of

[75] Ó Gráda, *New economic history*, p. 396.

[76] Crotty, *Agricultural production*, p. 144; Ó Gráda, *New economic history*, p. 393.

[77] Alan Matthews, 'The state and Irish agriculture, 1950–80', in P.J. Drudy (ed.), *Land, politics and people*, pp 241–69, *passim.*

[78] Crotty, *Agricultural production*, p. 148.

[79] Ó Gráda, *New economic history*, p. 416.

[80] Foster, *Modern Ireland*, p. 541.

[81] NAI, D/T S9420, Memorandum from departmental secretaries of Finance (D/F), Industry and Commerce (D/IC), External Affairs (D/EA) and Agriculture to cabinet, 4 Dec. 1936 [bold type used by authors of memorandum].

cattle and the penal duties on some classes of livestock were reduced.[82]

The reunion was confirmed with the conclusion of the 1938 Defence, Financial and Trade Agreements, described as "a three-leaved shamrock" by British Prime Minister, Neville Chamberlain, at an inter-governmental conference.[83] In it, both countries sacrificed economic interests for political gain and, although the Irish side of the bargain generally received a favourable press, it was the financial and defence aspects, rather than the trade one, which drew most plaudits.[84] In general terms, the agreement gave Ireland clearer access to the British agricultural market. But, as the British Minister for Agriculture, W.S. Morrison, pointed out in the course of negotiations, the years since 1930 had brought a vast change in the conduct of agricultural trade: "In the interval powers have been secured and an organisation built up to prevent unregulated imports of agricultural products which would threaten the stability of markets … No-one now had a free entry into the agricultural markets of this country."[85]

Indeed, Irish deliberations during the talks had conceded as much with the cabinet agreeing that one of the points on which negotiations should proceed was the understanding that "where there is quantitative restriction on agricultural products, the quantities fixed for Irish exports will be sufficient to enable this country to export the whole of its surplus production to the United Kingdom market."[86] During the negotiations it was industrial matters which concerned de Valera most. He stated he wanted to see Irish agricultural production improved – even doubled – but he did not "envisage a purely agricultural life for Eire. Without embarking on unnecessary developments, he wished to see his country produce as much manufacturing goods as it possibly could. His government could not forgo their right to build up their industries."[87] He reiterated this point in the Dáil when arguing that the "trade agreement section was a bargain, give-and-take … The difficulty in making the Agreement was to make sure that any concessions which we gave in it should not handicap us unduly in pursuance of our policy of building up industries here, industries that we regard as necessary for the national life." In that same debate, William Cosgrave prophesied that farmers would find the agreement "a disadvantage."[88] Despite the *Irish Press* claim that the agreement was an unquestionable triumph for the farmers and "abundant and rich reward" for their sacrifices in recent years, Cosgrave would ultimately be proved correct.[89] The Irish were unable to reverse the deleterious impact on trade of changes in British agricultural policy. Most pointedly, the acceptance of the principle of quantitative restrictions, and the failure to secure or possibly even seek, removal of the price differential between Irish and British cattle which was introduced in 1937 proved

---

[82] Ó Tuathaigh, 'Land question', p. 174.

[83] NAI, D/T S10389, minutes of British–Irish conference, 23 Feb. 1938.

[84] *Irish Times*, 26 Apr. 1938, *Manchester Guardian*, 26 Apr. 1938.

[85] NAI, D/T S10389, minutes of British–Irish conference, 17 Jan. 1938.

[86] NAI, D/T S10389, cabinet minutes, 3 Feb. 1938.

[87] NAI, D/T, S10389, minutes of British–Irish conference, 17 Jan. 1938.

[88] NAI, D/T, S10638 A, copy of extract from Dáil Debates, vol. 71, no 1, cols. 29–54.

[89] *Irish Press*, 26 Apr. 1938.

costly in the following decades. The concept of 'orderly marketing' would plague
Irish exporters. The Irish were now operating in a market where British producers
were receiving guaranteed prices for cattle, and the price the Irish would receive
was pegged rigidly below these. The advantage of comparative costs did not now
appear so wholesome.

The accord signalled the restoration of relative normality to Irish
agriculture, however. That normality entailed an agricultural structure effectively
unchanged despite a decade of upheaval. In the years from 1932 to 1939 forty acts
dealing with agriculture were passed by the Dáil but this "feverish activity" was
often short-term in aspect and in impact: "How to survive the economic blizzard
was the all-important thing; long-term planning for the future appeared to be of
little moment in a disordered world."[90] The world was about to enter a period of
even greater disorder and economic survival would once more be the primary
objective of policy. On this occasion, however, isolation offered an opportunity for
the assessment of long-term planning. It also occasioned an introspective analysis
of Irish agriculture which, in the context of the previous avoidance of reality, was
almost Flaubertian in nature.

IV

Responding to war

The isolation of World War II presented the Fianna Fáil government with
the ultimate climate to test national self-sufficiency. It was bitterly ironic that that
doctrine had been condemned to an ideological gulag barely a year previous to
the outbreak of war, when, the 1938 agreements with Britain, emphasised the true
nature of Irish economic independence. Political demarcations entailed the
regular airing of the ideal but actual attempts at implementation would be
insubstantial. Occasional, tempered gestures would be necessary to pay homage to
the past and the seduction of the inherited vision, but reality meant dependence
on the British market. Shadows of war forced immediate reappraisal and the goal
of self-sufficiency was stunningly resurrected, albeit in a fundamentally altered
manner. No longer the basis of a preferred political, social and cultural dogma, it
was now an imperative of national survival. That survival determined the
implementation of programmes which expanded tillage and required a move away
from cattle. Yet, this was done in manner which tacitly acknowledged that the pre-

---

[90] Hoctor, *The department's story*, p. 170.

war structure of farming would reassert itself in time. The farmers were asked to sacrifice their traditional operations in the national interest, but the question was posed in such a way as to promise permission to return to the old patterns as soon as possible.[91]

Even as the self-sufficiency programme was cranking into action, the Department of External Affairs in Dublin was drafting a letter to the British government in advance of a proposed conference which suggested "it would be advisable, as a matter of long-term policy, to determine the nature of agricultural production in this country in relation to the requirements of the home and British markets," and, in particular, of the relationship between production, export price and imported raw materials.[92] Even though this letter eventually spoke more ambiguously of the desirability of policy being of "mutual advantage," the essential message remained clear: whatever the immediate future would hold, the long-term one revolved around the British market.[93] In the interim, Irish agriculture was faced with the task of feeding the country. The food production campaigns marked incremental government involvement in agriculture. In September 1938 the Department of Agriculture established committees to prepare plans to secure increased production of food and feeding stuffs, the maintenance and regulation of an export trade in agricultural produce, and the regulation of the importation and distribution of agricultural requisites. In a series of reports, these committees recommended the introduction of compulsory tillage, the institution of arrangements to facilitate the importation of essential requisites, and the instigation of a propaganda campaign to encourage food production – it was assumed that all these powers would be centralised in a single authority established by legislation.[94] It further recommended consultations with the British government who had intimated that war would entail the suspension of private imports in favour of central purchase by the British Ministry of Food.[95]

The Department of Supplies was established in September 1939 and compulsory tillage was introduced on 17 October 1939 in an order made under the Emergency Powers Act, 1939. Initially, farmers were compelled to till one-eighth of their land and in 1941 this was increased to one-sixth. [96] There was no concession to farm size, soil type or location. Through 1940, there were no serious shortages, but in 1941 "imports of wheat, sugar, feeding stuffs, artificial fertilisers

---

[91] Although much was made of farmer sacrifice during the war years in altering their pattern of farming and many tributes were paid to their performance by government spokesmen, not everybody was quite so enamoured. For some, the farmers had exploited the situation for their personal gain – an interpretation bolstered by the increase in farmer income through the war years.

[92] NAI, D/T S11846 A, D/EA memo to govt., 27 Mar. 1940.

[93] NAI, D/T S11846 A, D/EA memo to govt., 29 Mar. 1940.

[94] The propaganda consisted of lectures, radio talks, newspaper advertisements and "films, including a special documentary sound film, entitled Tomorrow's Bread, with an Irish version Arán an Lae Amáireach, [which] were shown in cinemas. The film, Tomorrow's Bread, which was produced specially for the Department by Richard Hayward, excited great interest and was seen by over 400,000 people". See Hoctor, *The department's story*, pp 206–7.

[95] NAI, D/T S11445–7, D/A memo to govt. on wartime measures, (n.d.).

[96] *Ibid.*; Crotty, *Agricultural production*, pp 158–9.

and agricultural machinery dwindled to a fraction of the pre-war figures, and this country was thrown back upon its own resources for the production of food for man and beast."[97] Although sugar requirements were largely met, wheat remained the primary concern. Notwithstanding the efforts to increase production including the increase of the guaranteed price, the wheat acreage dropped from 575,000 acres in 1942 to 509,000 acres in 1943, and the compulsory tillage minimum was raised to three-eighths. Acute shortages were avoided from 1944, aided by the ban on the feeding of wheat to animals, but compulsory tillage orders remained in place until 1948. The effective evaporation of imported feeding stuffs adversely affected the dairying industry. The committee established by the Department of Agriculture before the war had declined to make definitive recommendations on the dairying industry on the grounds that the numbers of cows could not be rapidly increased, and that an appreciable increase in the production of dairy produce could not be obtained within four years. The fragility of the sector soon became apparent – milk yields fell, butter production declined and only large state subsidies kept the price of butter within reach of the average consumer. By 1942 exports had been prohibited and butter was being rationed. Dependence on imported feeding stuffs also left the pig and poultry industries immensely vulnerable. From a position where they represented 10 per cent of the export trade in 1938, these sectors went into steep decline. By 1941 exports of eggs had decreased considerably, exports of pigs were negligible, and exports of bacon and other pig products ceased altogether. In line with the growth in its own powers, the Department of Agriculture noted that the Emergency "involved comprehensive measures of governmental control and the dynamic conditions which prevailed during the war years necessitated frequent changes in the nature and extent of the control exercised." With a twofold object, the government was obliged to control prices on the home market. Prices paid to producers were raised in order to stimulate production, while consumer prices had to be controlled in order to keep the cost of living within reasonable limits. The Department of Agriculture observed with understatement that "these two aims were sometimes incompatible" and the government was forced to pay steadily increasing subsidies to maintain some balance in the economy.[98]

Subsidies could not cloak all of the difficulties, however. Increased food production was impeded by the inability to import adequate agricultural machinery or even machinery parts. In a neat cameo commentary on the parameters of the Irish agricultural economy, individual farmers were hindered by the shortage of both diesel and horse-shoeing iron. If the lack of such commodities as diesel, iron and machinery parts slowed the food production drive, the acute shortage of fertiliser provided an enduring legacy. Except for a small quantity provided by Britain, potash was unobtainable; attempts were made to excavate phosphate deposits from west Clare and pyrites from Wicklow but these were limited by the exorbitant subsidy required to put them in reach of the

---

[97] NAI, D/T S11445–7, D/A memo to govt. on wartime measures, (n.d.).
[98] *Ibid.*

farmer. Only 50,000 tons per annum of fertilisers were available in 1943 and 1944, ensuring that tillage crops were very inadequately manured while pastures and meadows were almost entirely neglected.[99] Fortunately, Irish grass was long used to being starved of all but the minimum application of fertiliser and natural conditions enabled it to carry on regardless. Tillage was an altogether different matter, however, and the dearth of artificial fertilisers stripped the soil of its nutrients – the pond was being drained to catch the fish.

Some factors were immune to change. While overall gross agricultural output fell by 10 per cent, the cattle trade, stoic to the last, seemed oblivious to the crisis all around.[100] As the Department of Agriculture stated: "the main character of agricultural production did not alter during the Emergency, although the margin moved in favour of tillage crops to the extent of one million acres." It continued: "the effect of the Emergency on the cattle industry was not so pronounced as on other branches of agriculture. The total number of cattle in the country varied very little, and the cattle export trade was generally maintained during the war years, apart from a dislocation caused by foot and mouth disease."[101] Neither pestilence nor government decree, not even world war, could shake the structure of Irish agriculture.

V

Reassessing agricultural policy for post-war progression

If the immediate demands of World War II centred on the need to expand and alter the pattern of food production, the backdrop was filled by a radical reassessment of agricultural policy. The capacity of the Irish people to take legislative action to shape and direct their own economy and its institutional framework had not brought positive results..[102] Indeed, agricultural policy had more likely been of harm than of benefit: "In the first ten years of the Irish Free State, policy followed the lines of encouragement of exports and distrust of agricultural protection. It was sharply reversed after a change in government in 1932. It goes without saying that the advancement of agriculture has not been helped by such oscillations of policy."[103] The rhetoric of the divergent policies of those decades would not fade for many years – the politics of posture required at

---

99 Hoctor, *The department's story*, pp 208, 209.

100 Crotty, *Agricultural production*, p. 159.

101 NAI, D/T S11445-7, D/A memo to govt. on war-time measures, (n.d.).

102 Crotty, *Agricultural production*, p. 111.

103 James Meenan, 'Irish agricultural policies in the last twenty years', in Bailie and Sheehy (eds.), *Irish agriculture in a changing world*, pp 44–55, esp. p. 48.

least the illusion of difference. Electoral demands and traditional pieties demanded that a façade be maintained. In substance, though, there was no escape from the convergence of policy. Difference of emphasis would emerge on occasion, born from divergent visions and political imperatives, but there was no longer a sharp divide.[104] Fleeting glimpses of the idealism of earlier days appeared – but these proved the exception, not the norm. In terms of actual implementation of policy, the radical agrarianism of Fianna Fáil had diminished as surely as the death of free trade had been accepted by Cumann na nGaedheal.

Equally, there was general acceptance that, beyond the calamity of war-time deprivation, agriculture was in a deplorable state. A Land Commission employee wrote of "appalling poverty and hardship," and of "agricultural slums" in the west of Ireland and other congested areas.[105] The *Irish Press* was moved to comment: "We have a long way to go really to justify the title of an agricultural country as distinct from a cattle country."[106] It was not just the pattern of production which the newspaper deplored, but the failure to increase production for almost a century. Acceptance of the need to raise production had led to the establishment of a commission on agriculture in January 1939 charged with recommending how best to promote and maintain increased agricultural production. Before it had concluded its deliberations the government decided, in June 1940, to suspend its function "until such time as circumstances would permit of their deliberations being carried out under more suitable conditions."[107]

Actual conditions were hardly more conducive, but governmental attitude had evolved sufficiently by 1942 to favour the establishment of a new investigative commission. Evidence of planning being undertaken in other countries, both belligerent and non-belligerent, and war time planning at home had fostered a new consciousness that the economy might be directed into desired channels.[108] In June 1942 the government discussed the need for systematic planning and in September 1942 the Department of Agriculture formally appointed an eight-person 'Commission of inquiry on post-Emergency agricultural policy' under the chairmanship of Professor T.A. Smiddy. The commission produced interim reports on poultry production, veterinary services, and on the cattle and dairying industries, before, in 1945, it issued a majority and two minority reports.[109] The disagreements in the reports effectively rested on what the aim and philosophy of agricultural policy should be but on more technical matters, particularly in

---

[104] Paul Bew and Henry Patterson, *Seán Lemass and the making of modern Ireland* (1982), pp 28–9.

[105] NAI, D/T S11555 A, G. Deegan, Land Commission to Minister of Lands, 7 Dec. 1942.

[106] *Irish Press*, 6 Sept. 1944.

[107] NAI, D/T S12888 A, D/A memo to govt., 26 Oct. 1943.

[108] Raymond, 'Economics of neutrality', p. 98; See also NAI, D/T S13341 where there are copies of the Swiss programme for post-war economic expansion, the American post-war plan, and information on nationalisation, collectivisation and state planning programmes in industry and agriculture in the USSR. NAI, D/T, S13101 A and B also contain copies of planning initiatives in Britain regarding employment policy, and of the Beveridge report.

[109] The majority report was signed by Professors Smiddy, Drew, Boyle and Johnston, and by R.C. Barton; the first minority report was signed by Professor E.J. Sheehy and James Mahony; the second minority report was signed by Henry Kennedy of the IAOS.

comment on the state of the agricultural economy, there was virtual unanimity.

That unanimity constituted a shaming indictment of Irish agriculture. The feelings crystallised in the majority report with the lament:

> The condition of many farms in this country is deplorable. Outlying fields usually show greater deterioration as they recede from proximity to the farmyard. Many of them, because of over-grazing and annual haymaking, have reached a state of impoverishment that renders them of little output value ... There are many thousands of acres of moderate and poor pasture which, over a period of many years, no effort has been made to improve the quality or quantity of herbage and from which the annual output is the minimum which nature provides. For various reasons, some subjective, others fortuitous, the fertility of thousands of farms is now so low that they yield but the barest maintenance to their occupiers and frequently subsistence is obtained by annual lettings or the repeated sale of hay, or by part-time alternative employment; judged by modern standards of agriculture such land is derelict.[110]

The cattle industry, although accepted as the most powerful, was condemned for seasonality of production, inefficient marketing, lack of winter feed, poor quality breeding and sub-standard pastures.[111] The reports noted there was an often justified perception of a pastoral system of "considerable disrepute," where the majority of farmers left grass to grow naturally on "derelict and poor-class pastures," and without the benefit of a modernising scientific approach, whereas "high-grade nutritive grass is as far removed from the natural product as the modern potato is from the primitive tuber of Ecuador and Peru."[112] Much of this was due to a dismissive attitude to the use of fertiliser and "the remedying of this defect must have a high priority in the post-Emergency era," because "if there is to be a greatly increased agricultural production, much greater consumption of fertilisers will be needed."[113] The pigs and bacon industry was described as inefficient in production, processing and marketing whose only solution was "very drastic changes," and "a reorganisation of the industry."[114]

Further general points were made. There was a regret that in the absence of farmers' organisations the producers "exert little influence on government policy."[115] Massively increased co-operation, particularly in view of the number of small farmers was "absolutely essential."[116] Land policy should be reviewed as the farm structure had proved inimical to modernisation, although the size of a

---

110 CIPEAP, *majority report*, p. 78.

111 CIPEAP, *majority report*, pp 48–9; *first minority report*, p. 127.

112 CIPEAP, *majority report*, p. 59; *first minority report*, p. 145; *second minority report*, p. 175.

113 CIPEAP, *majority report*, p. 57 and p. 78; *first minority report*, p. 174.

114 CIPEAP, *majority report*, p. 74; *second minority report*, p. 210; *first minority report*, p. 132.

115 CIPEAP, *majority report*, p. 12; *second minority report*, pp 199–202.

116 CIPEAP, *majority report*, pp 50–1; *second minority report*, p. 209.

holding did not necessarily determine its success. In terms of food processing, there was "considerable opportunity for expansion." Marketing was "not highly organised," and was in need of a "thorough examination."[117] A great expansion of investment was required as "it is no more possible to increase production in agriculture without essential capital than it is in any other industry."[118] Such capital would help mechanise farming and "an obvious example of the need for mechanisation is machine milking."[119] Vastly expanded research and advisory services were seen as crucial.[120] And underpinning the entire exercise, "a vigorous and comprehensive educational programme is an imperious necessity."[121]

The reports offered a range of solutions to the problems. The livestock industry would benefit from the extension of artificial insemination and the import of high-class breeding stock.[122] Grassland could be improved by fertiliser subsidies and the importation of fertilisers, seeds and feeding stuffs without import duties or quantitative restrictions.[123] This would be complemented by a soil survey and the establishment of a soil analysis and advisory branch. In general, the need for more thorough exploration of the demands of agriculture should be met by the establishment of research institutes for grassland, potato, agricultural engineering, farm economics and plant breeding development.[124] This research should be directed by a permanent agricultural inquiry and advisory council which would also advise the Minister for Agriculture on a multitude of issues which might arise.[125] The transmission of ensuing development from the theoretical to the practical would require an extended educational system and a substantial increase in the number of agricultural instructors.[126] These instructors would play a vital role in the move towards greater mechanisation,[127] a move which would be funded by improved credit facilities for farmers and a higher level of investment of state capital.[128] Similarly, the marketing of produce would have to be streamlined – co-operatives should be given a much greater role, the replacement of fairs with marts should be investigated.[129] To determine policy on a scientific rather than a speculative basis, there should be a comprehensive survey of the social and economic conditions of the agricultural community which would ensure that the "formulation of state policy ... would be considerably facilitated and rendered

---

[117] CIPEAP, *majority report*, pp 10, 90, 11, 77.

[118] CIPEAP, *second minority report*, p. 207.

[119] CIPEAP, *majority report*, p. 57; *second minority report*, p. 190.

[120] CIPEAP, *first minority report*, p. 151; *second minority report*, pp 203–4.

[121] CIPEAP, *majority report*, p. 51.

[122] CIPEAP, p. 77; *first minority report*, p. 150; *second minority report*, pp 217–8

[123] CIPEAP, *majority report*, p. 85 and pp 89–90; *first minority report*, pp 147–8; *second minority report*, p. 174.

[124] CIPEAP, *majority report*, p. 62 and p. 85; *second minority report*, p. 217.

[125] CIPEAP, *majority report*, p. 91; *first minority report*, p. 147; *second minority report*, p. 216.

[126] CIPEAP, *majority report*, p. 89; *first minority report*, p. 151; *second minority report*, p. 203.

[127] CIPEAP, *majority report*, p. 57, *first minority report*, p. 151; *second minority report*, p. 190.

[128] CIPEAP, *majority report*, p. 89; *first minority report*, pp 120–2 and p. 150; *second minority report*, p. 207.

[129] CIPEAP, *majority report*, p. 50; *first minority report*, p. 150;

[130] CIPEAP, *majority report*, p. 90.

more authoritative."[130]

This "remarkable measure of agreement between the majority and minority reports on almost all problems of technical policy," conflicted with the "total disagreement on what the aim of production should be."[131] In essence, the conflict rehearsed the arguments which had so divided policy-making in the first two decades of independence. The majority and second minority reports were in broad agreement.[132] The chief aim of post-war agricultural policy should be the increased production of livestock and livestock products for export, in particular to the "complementary" British market. Government expenditure should steer clear of price supports and any non-productive schemes which would increase the burden of taxation on farmers. The only exception to be made, in terms of guaranteed prices, was for wheat and sugar beet which should be maintained at a level not appreciably above the world price, but preferably only until world peace and international stability was assured. Permanently guaranteed and subsidised wheat would lead the indigent and careless farmer to grow crop after crop on a disproportionate area ignoring rotation. On the whole, price subsidies were seen as "enabling farmers to continue the use of out-of-date or expensive methods of production. Price subsidies which seem likely to be permanent, afford neither incentive to economy of production nor encouragement to organisation." Government aid should, instead, be directed towards the reduction of the costs of farm inputs. Compulsory tillage was not favoured and regarded as suitable only to extreme national emergency. Protectionism was similarly dismissed and "as far as our policy for the future is concerned it would be most unwise to base it on restrictionist ideas borrowed from the economic policies of the inter-bellum years."[133]

By contrast, protectionist policies stood at the core of the philosophy which governed the first minority report.[134] It recommended that improved production should be stimulated by concentration on the home market which should be maintained by the absolute prohibition on the import of certain commodities and by restrictions on the import of others. It was argued that the farming community could be encouraged to expand production only by the presence of a guaranteed market, governed by the certainty of guaranteed prices: "Experience has shown that guaranteed prices fixed at a level calculated to give a reasonable margin of profit stimulate farmers to increased efficiency." The expansion of exports was obviously desirable and should be pursued, particularly by bargained trade agreements, but it would be a fundamental mistake to concentrate on producing for the speculative export market: "We cannot contemplate with equanimity our re-entry into an international suicidal competition in the production of cheaper and still cheaper foods for industrial markets."[135]

---

131 Meenan, 'Agricultural policies', p. 48.

132 CIPEAP, *majority report, passim.; second minority report, passim.*

133 CIPEAP, *majority report*, pp 24, 65, 64, 33–4.

134 CIPEAP, *first minority report, passim.*

135 CIPEAP, *first minority report*, pp 139, 160–1.

This fundamental divergence of philosophy needed resolution in terms of government policy and the majority report recognised it would be necessary to await the end of the war to finalise matters of long-term agricultural policy. It stressed, however, the transcendent importance of immediate moves to make the technical improvements which would improve efficiency and expand production, regardless of overall direction.[136] In a letter to the Taoiseach, Eamon de Valera, T.A. Smiddy wrote:

> Emphasis cannot be laid too strongly on the real necessity of nothing being left undone to increase agricultural efficiency and adopt drastic measures if necessary to achieve this object. The methods of the past have failed to increase efficiency even a little. Hence the necessity for attempting more radical methods. Those which the committee suggest are moderate and the minimum required to increase our output.[137]

Wary of past failures of policy and of performance, the commission expressed itself as "moderately optimistic about the feasibility of agricultural advance."[138]

VI

Political perceptions of the way forward

The feasibility and favoured form of advance, meanwhile, had already served as the battleground for a strong exchange of views in cabinet. Growing tension within the ruling Fianna Fáil party, and the stark realisation that the need for change was critical, was laid bare as land and agricultural policy came under scrutiny. Even as the 'Commission of inquiry on post-Emergency agricultural policy' was embarking on its deliberations, a Land Commission official articulated dismay that two decades of independence had done little to improve the lot of the smallholder. Connemara, he wrote, was home to "an immense population crowded on to the worst land in Ireland (if land is indeed the word to use)," and "it is clear that we have been able to do very little indeed so far for these poor, over-crowded localities." In a passionate plea for an immediate change of policy, he claimed that schemes seeking solutions through such ventures as bog reclamation were "the rankest folly." He expounded that a substantial migration scheme was the only manner in which to give effective relief and further stressed that the halfway house of the partial schemes then in operation was only perpetuating the

---

[136] CIPEAP, *majority report*, pp 67–8.

[137] NAI, D/T S12888 B, T.A. Smiddy to de Valera, 4 Dec. 1944.

[138] CIPEAP, *majority report*, p. 58.

problem:

> If we cannot move a reasonable number of these smallholders out of
> each village or estate we must make up our minds to leave them where
> they are and let the state improve their conditions in the over-crowded
> 'agricultural slums' in which they live by the operation of the various
> social services and in particular by such methods as better housing,
> establishment of industries, public works and so on. But that is an
> attitude which the Land Commission should not adopt until they have
> tried the only alternative which is the migration of as many as possible
> to under-populated localities and the distribution amongst the
> remainder of the land so acquired.[139]

The memorandum brought no change in policy, but the issue could not be
easily ignored and formed the subject of a memorandum from Seán Moylan,
Minister for Lands, in September 1943. Moylan argued that the Land Commission
had now fulfilled its original task of the transfer of land from landlord to tenant
and its role now should revolve around the provision of farms for "trained, capable
and experienced agriculturalists."[140] In essence, this would involve the rejection of
all claims from labourers and from the landless, except those who had through
thrift and energy built up capital and stock. He deplored the existing policy of
giving three, five or ten acres to cottiers and agricultural labourers because "these
smallholdings are incapable of affording him a livelihood. The practice of such
allotment should cease. It has no economic recommendation and if the economic
condition of the agricultural labourer is to be improved this is not by any means
the method to be adopted." Moylan contended that the practice of distributing
such allotments was very often "because of local agitation and a complete
misconception as to what the uses of land should mean ... This can be regarded
only as a subsidy to incapacity and idleness and an unjustifiable surrender to a
prejudiced local clamour." All uses of land which fell beyond the task of giving
land to farmers to create viable farms were "quite unimportant in comparison,"
and the only time any class other than a farmer should be considered was when
they could be provided with "sufficient land to permit them to successfully
establish themselves as farmers and should not be utilised as material for the
recreation of serfdom." Moylan agreed that the policy of migration from the
congested districts should be "continued and intensified ... The work of dealing
with congestion is practically at a standstill. Without further acquisition there are
in Land Commission hands a large number of vacated holdings which should now
be rearranged and allotted. The longer this commitment is untouched the greater
becomes the difficulty of dealing with the problem." To this end, he called for a
reviewed statement of policy, the designation of set yearly targets for the Land
Commission to meet and the immediate return to the Department of Lands of
staff seconded to other departments during the war – a return agreed to by all

---

[139] NAI, D/T S11555 A, G. Deegan, Land Commission, to Minister for Lands, 7 Dec. 1942.

[140] NAI, D/T S12890 A, Seán Moylan memo to Department of the Taoiseach (D/T), 1 Sept. 1943.

other departments save the Department of Finance. The memorandum
concluded: "If the government is in earnest about the policy of a speed-up then
the Department of Finance should be instructed to place no obstacles in the
way."[141]

Criticism of existing policy intensified in a joint memorandum from Seán
Lemass and Seán Moylan on the economic and social aspects of land policy.[142] It
noted that land acts had hitherto viewed the matter in social rather than economic
terms and, as such, were "a palliative rather than a remedy." Arguing that the state
would have to recognise the right of property but could not allow land to be held
out of production or uneconomically farmed, the ministers stated:

> A holding of 250 acres need not be regarded as undesirably large,
> assuming that it is capably run and adequately capitalised ... The
> economic objection to holdings of this size is that their owners are
> frequently incapable or lack sufficient capital to run them properly ...
> A policy tending to the breaking up of these farms is therefore
> recommended. Owners who do not adequately comply with some
> suitable standard of productive efficiency should be listed for action by
> the Land Commission.

They also argued for the retention of some measure of compulsory tillage,
because incapable farmers "regard the present system of control as undesirable
and will revert to their pre-war system at the earliest opportunity, because,
although such a system may give lesser grass returns, it may be operated with much
less expenditure of energy."

The ministers wrote that the actual size of the holding did not matter, but
that the ideal of 25 acres was based erroneously on ill-judged European
comparisons as only the market gardeners around Dublin had similar
circumstances to their continental counterparts. Ultimately, though: "There is no
justification for the creation of uneconomic holdings." Similar doubts were also
cast on the worth of migration as a solution as "a general translation of the small
rundale holders to the really economic holdings will not increase agricultural
prosperity. The condition of such people should be dealt with as a special problem

[141] *Ibid.* In a memorandum, the Department of Lands noted the laborious nature of the work in which it
was involved, as well as the 20,000 letters a year received by the purchase division of the commission, and
complained that "unfortunately, the Land Commission is regarded in the rural mind as a sort of Universal
Benefactor." Eventually, in July 1944, the government decided that the desirability of resuming Land
Commission work on a normal scale required that seconded staff, which comprised one half of its normal
staffing level, be returned to the department. Nonetheless, the requirements of the compulsory tillage
programme were such that the government later decided to allow the Department of Agriculture to retain
15 of the 35 officials it had received. See NAI, D/T S12890 A, D/L memo to govt., 7 Mar. 1944.

[142] NAI, D/T, S11980 B, committee minutes, 22 Nov. 1944, Seán Lemass and Seán Moylan, joint memo
to govt., 7 Feb. 1945. A meeting of the cabinet committee on economic planning on 22 November 1944
had agreed that Moylan and Lemass should outline the "*various social and economic* aspects of the problem
on which a definition of policy was desirable." In a neat reversal of priority, the ensuing memo was
entitled: "*Economic and social* aspects of land policy."

and without reference to general policy." This special problem of

> the destruction of rural slumdum [sic] is urgent and essential. It
> cannot be tackled solely by way of land distribution and arrangement.
> There is not enough land; there is not enough land in the right places;
> local demand, prejudice, and influence will tend to create an
> opposition to the most desirable activity and measures. This, the
> resuscitation of the congested districts, may, in relation to an ideal
> land policy, be regarded as a burden but it is a burden that must be
> carried. The hard fact, however, imposes itself that the problem of the
> congested districts is only in part soluble by operations in land. A
> general increase in agricultural prosperity would make it possible to
> evolve alternative methods of tackling the evil.

The ministers went on to claim that land policy had contributed to the standard of living in the farming community being "in general very low," to farmers being without modern comforts or services, to the failure of farmers to purchase many industrial goods, and to the fact that "the farming system is poor and the farming equipment primitive." Moylan and Lemass concluded:

> Land administration must in future take a more specific cognisance of
> the contribution to national income which economic policy demands
> of agriculture, and must on the one hand forcibly combat the misuse
> or inadequate use of land and on the other must endeavour to make
> provision and create such conditions as will enable farmers to make an
> adequate contribution.[143]

The Department of Finance responded saying that the government must not take any further actions to break up large farms without "exhaustive examination," as "with mechanisation it is probable that a minimum of 200 statute acres is necessary for the development of full efficiency." The break-up of such farms would deprive the farming community of "all hope of obtaining the leadership which they need," and, in any event, the small farmers needed the big farmers to buy the cattle they reared.[144] It claimed it was difficult to imagine any justification for the resumption of Land Commission activity on a pre-war scale. Effectively, however, Finance did not adequately deal with the substantive points of policy raised by Moylan and Lemass. There was further evasiveness when policy was considered by the cabinet committee on economic planning which agreed that the Taoiseach, in consultation with the Minister for Lands, would prepare for consideration at an early date a series of propositions embodying suggested heads of policy in relation to land division.[145] No record of further action has emerged.

Moylan and Lemass had argued in their aborted attempt to redesign policy

---

143 NAI, D/T, S11980 B, committee minutes, 22 Nov. 1944, Seán Lemass and Seán Moylan, joint memo to govt., 7 Feb. 1945.

144 NAI, D/T S11980 B, D/F memo to govt., 29 Mar. 1945.

145 NAI, D/T S11980 B, minutes of cabinet committee on economic planning, 27 Apr. 1945.

that it was utterly invidious to consider land policy and agricultural policy as other than so closely interrelated as to be whole.[146] Inevitably, the issues manifest in the debate on land policy resurfaced in agricultural policy, primarily when the Department of Finance circulated its impressions on the British white paper on post-war employment policy in November 1944. Finance echoed the belief that approaches to policy should become more economically determined:

> a high or rising standard of living is sometimes regarded in Ireland and elsewhere as implying something hedonistic ... The maintenance of a reasonably high standard of living is one of the most important objects of state-craft. It is sought not merely or mainly for the sake of physical enjoyment and comfort, though they are not altogether despicable aims, but because it is a condition of culture and health, and of social peace and contentment. In a free society, if the general standard of living is low, the standard among the poorer classes will be miserable. A low standard of living can be a danger to the survival of a nation.[147]

Most pressingly, this survival was endangered by emigration: "Every improvement in the national standards of the countries with which our people have intimate contact will impose upon us the choice of raising our own standard or losing population."

Finance argued that continued national survival and population maintenance was best achieved through agricultural development as the history of the booms and depressions of the previous thirty years showed that an agricultural country could maintain greater stability over a long period than an industrial country and that an agricultural country could expect a relatively more stable demand for its produce. Industrialisation was not envisaged: "Irish prosperity on which the level of employment depends can best be increased by developing the prosperity of agriculture, by maximising its efficiency and thereby increasing its productivity." The absorption into the labour force of returning emigrants and demobilised personnel from the defence forces would only be achieved through an expanding agriculture. To this end, it was crucial to review land division policy and to undertake a study of "all existing controls, tariffs, quotas, etc., with the object of removing unnecessary restrictions on trade and whatever makes for higher costs of agricultural production."[148]

In immediate response, Seán Lemass agreed that Irish prosperity could best be developed by improved efficiency and improved production in agriculture, but "even under the stimulus of increased demand and rising prices, agricultural production responds very slowly and in our circumstances a very substantial increase in agricultural output would not result in full employment for all born on

---

[146] NAI, D/T S11980 B, Moylan and Lemass memo to govt., 7 Feb. 1945.
[147] UCDA, Seán MacEntee papers, P67 264 (2); NAI, D/T S13101 A, D/F memo to govt., 1 Nov. 1944.
[148] *Ibid.*

the land." Lemass pointed out that Irish plans for agricultural expansion would be of no benefit in dealing with the immediate post-war unemployment problem, and that an industrialised country was far more capable of responding to improved conditions through the application of sound plans and better international trade. As an aside, Lemass wondered whether, in future, the location of industries should be limited to the cities as "the establishment of industries in smaller towns has had an unsettling effect on agricultural labour and on local general labourer wage rates, which is not conducive to the increased efficiency of the agricultural industry."[149]

In a comprehensive second salvo, Lemass argued that price policy as a weapon for expanding agricultural production had been ineffective, as for all the fluctuations in price over the previous fifteen years, there had been no expansion in the volume of agricultural production.[150] He reiterated his belief that inefficient farmers should be removed from farms and "policy must be directed to ensuring that ownership will be confined to persons willing and capable of working them adequately." Improved co-operation, mechanisation, education, availability of credit and marketing should be complemented by reduction of costs through a more efficient transport system, cheaper and more effective veterinary care, and the removal of local rates. Further, Lemass recommended the intervention of the state as a wholesaler in various commodities to ensure certainty of sale and stability of price. The producers' margin of profit would be guaranteed by low costs, not by high prices to the consumer. The application of state trading or market regulation was not contemplated for the livestock trade, except if the market abroad was not proving remunerative, as "any interference with it would create immense difficulties … The prosperity of agriculture is however so intimately linked with the profitableness of the livestock trade that some method of maintaining it in all circumstances is desirable as part of a comprehensive plan."

As a long-term goal, it was crucial to replace live exports with the dressed meat trade as "the development of agricultural exports in the form of processed goods – meat, bacon, butter, cheese, condensed milk, etc – should be the main aim of policy." In the meantime, the export trade should be refined and expanded as "the enforcement by a responsible authority of efficiency in equipment and management, and the elimination of uneconomic units, is essential to the expansion of exports." This expansion could best be accomplished by state organisations as, when the market fell, private enterprise would protect itself by reducing the prices given to producers. Similarly, the state would have to involve itself more in agriculture than in other industries to ensure that the reorganisation of agriculture and the stimulation of greater demand for products would not be frustrated by the small farmers' inability to organise themselves: "only the state has the power and the resources to do the job properly."[151]

---

149 UCDA, Seán MacEntee papers, P67 264 (3); NAI, D/T S13101 A, D/IC memo to govt., 21 Nov. 1944
150 UCDA, Seán MacEntee papers, P67 264 (4); NAI, D/T S13101 A, D/IC memo to govt., 24 Jan. 1945.
151 *Ibid.*

The Minister for Agriculture, James Ryan, entered the fray with the acknowledgement that "the broad problem is to devise and put into operation effective measures of an economically sound and practicable kind which would result in greater output in the farming industry as a whole, and at the same time contribute to the solution of the employment problem." He propounded a system of mixed farming as the one most likely to provide full employment in agriculture. Tillage concentration was inadvisable due to seasonality of employment, while grazing provided little employment at any time. In terms of specific action, the livestock industry could be improved by better breeding, improved veterinary services and refined marketing and "that is all that reasonable men would expect in respect of livestock." Ryan disagreed with the proposal to displace inefficient farmers as "a most delicate and difficult matter," which would provoke the "danger of serious agitation and public disturbance." He agreed that there were many farmers in the country who made a poor contribution to general output but the state should only consider inserting new owners for extreme reasons such as complete lack of capital, senility or mental trouble. He accepted there were a number of holdings

> in every parish falling below a reasonable productive capacity due to some failing on the part of the present owner but who probably has a young family growing up, one member of which would in time pull the place together and become in due course a first-class farmer. In the meantime the family somehow or other are reared and set out in life as useful citizens. Indeed the lessons which the poverty of the home teach them very often make them good workers wherever they go. It would be unthinkable to disturb the family in such cases no matter how much below the desired standard the farm might presently be.

The right to be poor was both guaranteed and educational. The lesson of poverty was a syllabus in itself, however, as "at present, it cannot be said that we are doing much more than pilot or pioneer work in education." Winter classes, lectures and farm visits were needed, as well as a big increase in agricultural courses and schools. Agricultural research, demonstration and advisory work also required great expansion, while it was intended to implement in full the recommendations on breeding of the 'Commission of inquiry on post-Emergency agricultural policy'. Ryan recited again the liturgy of agricultural flaws awaiting correction. He pronounced himself "in entire agreement that stability of price and certainty of sale are the most important incentives to high production," agreed that it was "preferable to lower the cost of production than to raise prices of farm products," and asserted that farm production, in terms of the pattern favoured, if not in actual volume of output, had always responded to a remunerative price. Nor was there acceptance that "the farmer looks for a certain income and when he reaches it he slacks off his work and goes for more leisure rather than a bigger income." He disagreed that there should be any limitation on production but could only suggest stall-feeding of cattle at the tax-payers' expense or "trivial forms of production such as culture under glass or mushroom growing" as means to diminish the seasonal nature of labour. Arguing that an increase in the number of cattle in the country was neither advisable nor feasible, Ryan agreed with Lemass that the expansion of exports should largely be in pig products, butter, poultry and eggs. Nonetheless, there was but a limited conception of the nature of export marketing:

> I am not so sure that better marketing intelligence will have much effect. The exporters are competent men: they know the conditions of the market in Great Britain and, I am quite sure, get the last penny that can be got for any animals they send over. There is a very large number of exporters and they pay the best possible prices through competition to producers.[152]

Ryan's memorandum was essentially an unimpressive response to what Lemass had earlier written. Again, there was general acceptance of the need for change, but no agreement on the means to bring it about. The debates on land policy, and those fomented by the circulation of British plans for full employment, confirmed that all sections of the government understood the importance of the radical restructuring of agriculture contemplated contemporaneously in the *Reports of the commission of inquiry on post-Emergency agricultural policy*. There was acceptance also that it was the government which would have to drive any restructuring programme. The capacity to resolve the dilemma of conflicting interpretations on how to make that great leap forward would determine its success or failure. A positive solution required foresight, bravery and the willingness to abandon old shibboleths in favour of dynamic integrated policies. An *Irish Times* editorial remarked that, in choosing its agricultural policy, the government would have to "make a bet on the history of the world to come."[153] Noting that the divergent reports of the commission had offered the government two separate avenues to progress along, the paper emphasised the overriding need to choose: "To adopt either course will take courage: but one must be taken". Ominously in light of the stalemate in cabinet on the way forward, the editorial concluded: "Our one fear is that the reports, as a whole, will be 'marked read', and that the government, confronted with so much apparent divergence of opinion, will do nothing at all."

---

152 UCDA, Seán MacEntee papers, P67 264 (5); NAI, D/T, S13101 A, D/A memo to govt., 14 Mar. 1945.

153 *Irish Times*, 29 Nov. 1945.

Chapter
2

Making a bet on history ... 1945–51

In the dying days of World War II, *The Economist* issued an impassioned plea for the development of a more innovative, efficient culture of business in Britain:

> There is far too much talk of protecting rights and defending established positions rather than of creating opportunities for advancing into fresh ground. In economics, as a nation, we are thinking in terms of Maginot lines. But in economics, more even than in strategy, a defence that does not permit any forward movement is doomed to failure ... There has never been a greater opportunity for economic statesmanship. Where is the Pitt or Peel to seize it?

Devoid of such leadership, political parties had nothing to offer "save a doctrine that is almost wholly irrelevant," leading them to seek "refuge in an impolicy of purely temporary expedients, judging every case on its demerits."[1] It was a call to arms which applied equally to Ireland, as the *Irish Times* noted: "All preconceived ideas regarding economics and finance ... have been blown sky-high ... The whole problem is in the melting pot, and may remain there for some time ... Meanwhile, it may not be impertinent to wonder what policy is being followed by the Irish government."[2]

In assessing the failures of Free State government policy in the pre-war era, one commentator remarked with a certain understatement that "the translation of dreams into realities is no easy task."[3] Indeed, for many separatist visionaries, reveries had turned to rust. The economic platitudes so valuable in the pre-independence construction of the image of Ireland free, prosperous and secure, while the rest of humanity was cast adrift on a "filthy modern tide," had fallen through the trapdoor of implementation.[4] Prosperity, and more particularly agricultural prosperity, remained as elusive as language revival and the ending of partition. The passing of the years, however, did nothing to diminish allusion to a vision increasingly defiled by political cant. Escapist rhetoric is not a talent peculiar to the Irish condition yet the middle decades of this century saw its elevation to spectacular heights. And the more the old separatist vision was sundered from reality, the more tightly politicians clung to its rhetoric.

---

[1] *The Economist*, 14 Oct. 1944.

[2] *Irish Times*, 15 Nov. 1944.

[3] Liam Skinner, *Politicians by accident* (1946), p. 34.

[4] W.B. Yeats, *Collected poems* (1973), p. 365.

It was in this gulf between rhetoric and reality that the cabinet debate on the nature of agricultural policy was fought. The impossibility of denying the demands of the present invariably forced consideration of the more prosaic task of furthering national development. Neither, though, could the demands of the past be denied – the political realities of electoral expectation always loomed large. The unstable international scenario required openness to new ideas, yet that, in itself, implied acceptance that the canons of republican thought be repudiated. But too many had invested too much for there to be a wholesale acquiescence in that. The past continued to impinge on policy-making even if it did not define it. Now, however, what had once been radical was, in turn, restraining the formulation of the radical agricultural policies which all available evidence demanded. As the ruminations of the war years demonstrated, there was definite understanding of the need for policy renewal and a slowly growing acceptance that Irish prosperity was dependent upon reintegration with the outside world.[5] Employing 38 per cent of the labour force, producing 32 per cent of GNP and accounting for 75 per cent of foreign exchange earnings, agriculture would have to provide the launchpad if Ireland was to prosper in any post-war scenario.[6] Expansion of output through technical improvements was the first prerequisite of post-war agricultural prosperity. The basic measures to secure this expansion had been clearly outlined and their implementation stressed as the minimum needed to revitalise the industry.

Revitalisation was reliant on a policy which would purge existing agricultural inefficiency and structural weaknesses. The extent of that purge would be determined by the uneasy balance between past and present in shaping government policy. A meeting of the cabinet committee on economic planning reviewing attempts by the Minister for Agriculture to prepare post-war policy proved that the debate had been far from conclusive. Dreams of old collided with the demands of a new era but perceptions of agriculture as the panacea for social, economic and cultural ills remained dominant as the meeting stressed

> the need to promote economic agricultural production, (b) the importance of the export market from the point of view of the maintenance and improvement of the standard of living, and (c) the importance, from the national and social point of view, of the maintenance on the land in economic security of as many families as might be practicable.[7]

Britain was not alone in requiring a Pitt or a Peel to carve a path to a glorious future.

---

[5] Kennedy *et al.*, *Economic development*, p. 52.

[6] Matthews, 'The state and Irish agriculture', p. 241.

[7] NAI, D/T S12888 B, minutes of the cabinet committee on economic planning, 5 Sept. 1944.

I

Immediate post-war attempts to revitalise agriculture

Ongoing difficulties in constructing agricultural policy were outlined in the Department of Agriculture estimate debates in 1945. The minister, James Ryan, told the Dáil he hoped the main recommendations of the interim reports of the 'Commission of inquiry on post-Emergency agricultural policy' would be adopted, but he first had to secure the agreement of other departments.[8] He looked forward to using the main report

> to advise the government on some of the big problems in front of us and on some of the big decisions we have to make. For instance, there is the whole problem of feeding stuffs – whether it is advisable that we should, for all time, produce our own feeding stuffs or go back to complete freedom of trade, throwing the gates open and letting them come in from other countries, or whether there should be some compromise between the two extremes.[9]

This indecision proved to be the single consistent feature in the policy process which emerged from the war years. Accepting an inability to investigate many aspects of agriculture in sufficient depth, one of the central recommendations in the commission's majority and minority reports, alike, was the establishment of a permanent council drawn from all sections of the industry to advise the Minister for Agriculture. Ryan duly accepted the principle of a permanent advisory council, but entirely amended its substance. In October 1945 he established an agricultural advisory committee drawn solely from members of his own department, defending the exclusion of non-civil service personnel as "the most expeditious way ... of getting advice." Ryan's "modified" advisory committee was duly charged with investigating a number of pressing issues, principal among which was the reorganisation of the pigs and bacon industry.[10]

Legislation in 1935 had established a 'Pigs and bacon commission' to assist the industry combat the upheavals then afflicting it. Deprived of adequate powers and of the co-operation from the interests concerned, it proved ineffective. This

---

[8] *Dáil Debates*, vol. 97, no. 3, col. 643, 17 May 1945. Ryan was the longest serving Minister for Agriculture in the history of the state. According to Hoctor, "only a strong man, with a well-balanced mind, could have borne the stresses and strains of those difficult years, but Dr Ryan, with a rare philosophy, stood four-square to every wind that blew." A doctor, Ryan spent the rising on Easter Week, 1916 in the General Post Office as officer in charge of the medical unit where he displayed qualities of courage and devotion which Hoctor argued prepared him well for his ministerial assignment. See Hoctor, *The department's story*, p. 171.

[9] *Dáil Debates*, vol. 97, no. 3, col. 643, 17 May 1945.

[10] *Dáil Debates*, vol. 99, no. 1, col. 24, 30 Jan. 1946.

was in marked contrast to the success of the 'Northern Ireland pigs marketing board' which was led by producers, and which had extensive powers and resources. Continued malaise in the industry provided fertile ground for the first interim report of the 'Commission of inquiry on post-Emergency agricultural policy' which recommended "complete re-organisation of the bacon industry with a view to its rationalisation." Similarly, in 1943 the 'Commission on vocational education' had claimed the pigs and bacon sector would continue to prove uneconomic unless it was replanned and reorganised with a thoroughly co-ordinated policy encompassing all sectors.[11] The minister's advisory committee echoed these sentiments. It furnished a report in December 1945 which argued that

> the failure of pig production to increase during the past hundred years seems at first sight all the more remarkable in view of the great expansion in the British market during most of the period ... The explanation is probably to be found mainly in the fact that the secular trend in agricultural prices favoured increased production of cattle and poultry, so far as this country was concerned, rather than pigs.

Arguing that the inefficient, fragmented structure of the industry was responsible for its stagnation by reducing the profit margin, it recommended the establishment of one unified organisation:

> Unless pig production, bacon curing, the home trade in pigs and pig products, and the export trade in pigs and pig products, are controlled by a single unified authority with a coherent policy, the difficulties of the pigs and bacon industry which have persisted for so many years cannot be overcome. Further renovation of the present machinery cannot be expected to provide a remedy ...

Such an organisation would facilitate the rationalisation and standardisation of product, and the negotiation of export contracts with the British Ministry of Food. All pigs would be purchased on a weight basis with grading to encourage better breeding and marketing. Again, Britain was expected to provide the principal market for exports and should offer greater scope than previously, but it was stressed that these exports should be unsubsidised. If export proved unsustainable without subsidy then the aim should be to limit production to satisfy the home market. Noting that in the past large-scale maize importation had not increased production nor made exports more competitive, the committee members did not "visualise the unrestricted importation of maize, and indeed do not consider it desirable in the interests of agriculture as a whole."[12] Instead, home-grown foods – potatoes, oats and barley – would be far more desirable.

---

[11] UCDA, Patrick McGilligan papers, P35/228, *Report on re-organisation of the pig and bacon industry* (1946), p. 8.

[12] NAI, D/T S12846 B, Agricultural advisory departmental committee: report on the pigs and bacon industry, Dec. 1946.

Further, existing accommodation could be improved but was not retarding production, while a scheme of pig recording should be introduced immediately. Having considered the report and accepted its recommendations, the Minister for Agriculture impressed on the government the need to set up a board to regulate the pigs and bacon industry. The proposed new board was to include curer and producer representatives under an independent chairman. Ryan argued that the existing 'Pigs and bacon commission' should be dissolved and the new board should have the power to compulsorily acquire all bacon-curing firms; require existing firms to improve their layout, efficiency, equipment and management; close down redundant factories; erect, equip and operate factories as it saw fit; direct the fresh pork export business; arrange the importation, purchase, processing and distribution of feed; fix prices for pigs and pig products on the home market subject to a set formula relating prices to feeding costs; and retain the sole right of purchase of pigs offered for slaughter, for production of bacon and for export.[13]

The Department of Finance, and the Department of Industry and Commerce accepted the scheme in principle, but the Department of Local Government strongly opposed the moves. The minister, Seán MacEntee, clearly hankering for his days as Minister for Finance, argued that previous commissions and boards had been counter-productive and "if control hitherto has been so inefficient it is highly unlikely that the strait-jacket of nationalisation will suddenly make it so efficient that the anticipated economies will be realised."[14] Claiming that monopolies however well meaning, when formed by the state "may be an even greater public menace than a rapacious private one," he noted that "dissatisfaction with the handling of the industry by the pigs and bacon commission might have led to the defeat of the government in 1943 were it not for the bigger issues that occupied the minds of the people. There may not be present in the times ahead a corresponding distraction." As other countries could not always be relied upon to be so considerate as to time their wars to coincide with the Irish electoral process, the minister circulated an article outlining the failures of state planning in the USSR to reinforce his opposition.[15]

Ryan and the cabinet agreed only that the proposal to compulsorily acquire premises be removed, but beyond that the minister was instructed to proceed with the preparation of a white paper.[16] The report was duly published in May 1946 with the comment that its objectives had been "accepted by the government and will be implemented as soon as possible by legislation."[17] The announcement was met with some hostility. It was, claimed the *Irish Independent*, "another board of dictators ... putting it on the pig," following in a long line of boards and

---

[13] NAI, D/T, S12846 B, D/A memo to govt., 9 Mar. 1946.

[14] NAI, D/T S12846 B, Department of Local Government and Public Health (D/LG) memo to govt., 21 Mar. 1946.

[15] NAI, D/T S12846 B, D/LG memo to govt., 15 Apr. 1946.

[16] NAI, D/T, S12846 B, cabinet minutes, 18 Apr. 1946.

[17] UCDA, Patrick McGilligan papers, P35/228, Report on reorganisation of pig and bacon industries (1946), p. 10

commissions which had "helped to make the chaos more chaotic." Recalling the days when the country made millions of pounds by selling surplus pig products to Britain, the paper contrasted this with present scarcity where "bacon and ham are today rare luxuries, harder to get than cigarettes or champagne."[18] The paper later issued a cry for the abolition of all pig boards and commissions which had proved so "utterly worthless," and "an insurmountable obstacle" to the provision of bacon and ham.[19]

By June 1946, the Department of Agriculture itself had had second thoughts on the matter. It claimed that the climate was not opportune to proceed with its earlier proposals in respect of the regulation, closure, erection and amalgamation of factories, but it was still proceeding with proposals on price fixing, marketing and licensing in a modified white paper. Little appreciable progress was made on the modified proposals until events in the summer of 1947 brought a complete reversal of direction. By then Paddy Smith had been installed as Minister for Agriculture while Ryan had been moved to Social Welfare.[20] Smith considered that his new department's proposals were more properly designed to fit into a long term plan to be proceeded with only when indigenous and imported feeding stuffs became available to rehabilitate pig stocks. In the short term, the minister determined that the industry's trauma required a radically altered approach. Acute pig shortages had provoked intense competition in the industry and the distribution of bacon in an orderly manner by the 'Pigs and bacon commission' was "utterly impossible." Similarly, the importation of sufficient maize had proved exceptionally difficult so an early improvement in pig stocks could not be expected for some time – the provision of home-grown feed was not considered an option due to continued bread shortages.

Given that a substantial increase in pig production seemed unlikely, even in the medium term, the minister argued that "the chaotic conditions which obtain in the manufacture and distribution of bacon are bound to grow worse. The measures of control now in operation, for which the Minister for Agriculture has to take responsibility as long as they are in operation, are not effective in present conditions and cannot be made effective. Consequently, Smith proposed the removal of all controls on bacon distribution, the removal of the minimum price for pigs and the fixed price for bacon, and the abolition of the 'Pigs and bacon commission'. Of the alternatives available, the removal of all controls, he claimed, was the least objectionable.[21] The cabinet remained unconvinced, however, and

---

18 *Irish Independent*, 31 May 1946.

19 *Ibid.*, 21 Oct. 1946.

20 Ryan moved from the Department of Agriculture in December 1946 and was replaced by Paddy Smith. Not unlike his party leader, Smith was credited with the ability to know instinctively what his people needed: "Few knew so well as he did how countrymen were thinking or what their problems were." He brought to the Department of Agriculture "a rare blend of natural intelligence and other human qualities, amongst which patience and tolerance were prominent." He was also "frank to the point of bluntness in expressing his convictions and intentions." Hoctor, *The department's story*, p. 202.

21 NAI, D/T S12846 B, D/A memo to govt., 8 Aug. 1947.

decided not to adopt the proposals.[22] Then, in September 1947, the reorganisation of the sector was withdrawn from the agenda and the minister was instructed to announce publicly that it had been decided not to proceed with any restructuring.[23] That subsequent announcement stressed that the key to the revival of the pig industry lay in the availability of an adequate supply of feeding stuffs which were not expected to be available for at least four or five years, thus forcing the government to abort its initiative.[24] The cabinet's attempts to restructure had oscillated wildly from rigid control to absolute freedom of trade in a period of eighteen months. In the end, though, it chose to do nothing. More perversely, the very dependence on imported feeding stuffs which the original departmental agricultural advisory committee report had so heavily criticised was now perceived as the *sine qua non* of successful restructuring.

If the world shortage in grain had limited the import of feeding stuffs, home producers never threatened to fill the void. Nonetheless, the importance of maintaining a significant area under tillage in the aftermath of the war was viewed as critical to the development of a balanced, progressive agriculture, and not just vital to national security. The Minister for Agriculture had outlined the importance of mixed farming as the most viable way forward for Irish agriculture, yet all indications suggested that farmers would abandon tillage as soon as the orders compelling them to till were ended. Even with compulsion there were many who did not till their lands. In Meath and Westmeath in 1940, 706 farmers were found to have failed to comply with the tillage orders, constituting almost 40 per cent of all farmers actually inspected. In 1941, the number of defaulters fell to 421 in those counties, an average of 14 per cent of all inspections.[25] Yet, this still represented a considerable rump who remained unfazed by the prosecutions and confiscations suffered by their colleagues. As the area required for compulsory tillage had grown to three-eighths of all land by 1944, the number of prosecutions continued to grow. Compulsion did ensure, however, that the acreage under tillage grew significantly, even if yields remained particularly low.

By September 1944, the Department of Agriculture had accepted it was unlikely to increase the acreage of tillage crops, especially wheat. The focus now was to maintain production and this, it was argued, was dependent upon continued compulsion.[26] By September 1945, circumstances had changed little and the department noted "it is almost certain that large numbers of farmers would give up wheat growing if they were no longer obliged to grow it under the Tillage Order."[27] The anti-wheat sensibilities of Irish farmers crossed all divides. The monetary return from the marginal lands was poor, particularly without fertiliser application, while in potentially the best wheat-growing areas the belief

---

[22] NAI, D/T S12846 B, cabinet minutes, 13 Aug. 1947.

[23] NAI, D/T S12846 B, cabinet minutes, 12 Sept. 1947.

[24] NAI, D/T S12846 B, D/A memo to govt., 9 Oct. 1947.

[25] NAI, D/A AGI G 1944/1941, D/A note, 17 Sept. 1941.

[26] NAI, D/T S11402 D, D/A memo to govt., 25 Sept. 1944.

[27] NAI, D/T S11402 D, D/A memo to govt., 4 Sept. 1945.

persisted that wheat was harder on the land than other crops. Compulsion was seen as the only alternative in time of war, but its post-war operation had provoked contrasting opinions in the *Reports of the commission of inquiry on post-emergency agricultural policy*. All reports emphasised the importance of tillage, particularly for use as animal feed, whose widespread adoption "would amount to a revolutionary change in our agricultural economy and outlook."[28] Despite this the majority and second minority reports viewed compulsion as abhorrent except in extreme circumstances, regardless of the benefits tillage production might secure, while the first minority report viewed it as a necessary evil.

Faced with the short-term requirements of feeding the country and cognisant of the long-term need to ensure a high level of tillage production, the department employed a holding operation. It continued to renew the compulsory tillage orders annually, maintained a high price for wheat and charged the departmental agricultural advisory council with the task of preparing a report on future tillage policy. On receiving that report, the Minister of Agriculture presented his policy to the government which subsequently published it as a white paper.[29] The white paper agreed that ideally farmers should be free to develop their holdings as they saw fit, but it was undesirable in the public interest to allow tillage cultivation to be lost for the second time in a generation. It claimed that many previously antagonistic farmers had come to realise the benefits of tillage, yet there were others who would not be made to till either by propaganda or inducement. Compulsion was the only remaining alternative. To that end, the minister felt

> the balance of advantage is in favour of some measure of compulsory tillage as a permanent feature of the country's agricultural policy. He, accordingly, proposes to introduce legislation at an early date providing for such a measure ... The intention is to reduce the tillage quota as soon as world conditions warrant it, to a level which, while not imposing an unreasonable burden on any class of occupier, would ensure the widespread maintenance of tillage technique and the generous adoption of proper rotations.

The Department of Agriculture had suggested that a minimum of 20 per cent of arable land on holdings of 10 acres or over be tilled, but the government decided that neither this figure nor the suggested wheat acreage of 250,000 acres should be made public.

Acknowledging that some farmers had complied with compulsory tillage by subletting or contracting, the department believed that such defaulters would rectify their misbehaviour in light of the permanency of the programme. As greater encouragement, legislation would include penalties for prosecuted defaulters and the power for inspectors to enter defaulting holdings and cultivate

---

[28] CIPEAP, *majority report*, pp 55–6.

[29] NAI, D/T, S11402 D, D/A memo to govt., 18 Apr. 1946; NAI, D/T S13528, *Policy in regard to crops, pastures, fertilisers and feeding stuffs*, W.P. no. 7597 (May 1946) and cabinet minutes, 3 May 1946.

the land on behalf of the Minister for Agriculture. There would be freedom of choice on which crops to grow, but steps would be taken to administer the act to ensure that soil fertility would be safeguarded through sound crop rotation and not in "a spirit of mere perfunctory compliance."[30] Although there would be no compulsion to grow wheat, guaranteed prices notified two years in advance would encourage sufficient production and permit rotation. Sugar beet would be encouraged in order to maintain all factories in production. A soils advisory service would assist in improving fertility through the application of lime and phosphates and would operate in conjunction with the farm improvements scheme which should be continued as a permanent measure, although without expanded funding.[31] Despite all this there should be no restriction on the import of protein feeding grains as "the experience of the last 6 years has shown that home production alone could not supply sufficient feeding stuffs to maintain livestock in proper condition, and to provide any substantial export trade in certain classes of livestock and livestock products."[32]

The Minister for Finance objected to the proposal to introduce compulsory tillage as a permanent measure of policy. He pointed out that the compulsory tillage orders required an extensive array of inspectors and advisors who had to be paid. He was concerned that the continued growing of wheat on poor land would force subsidy payments when the land could be used more profitably for other crops, for dairying or for livestock. On liming and the farm improvements scheme, the minister noted that that scheme incurred high administrative costs. For 1946/7, such costs would ensure that over 25 per cent of the total grant was not reaching the farmer. Moreover, Finance believed that interest in the scheme had been so high – there were 35,000 grantees in 1944/5 – due to "the unnecessarily attractive terms." It was further requested that the prior sanction of the department be sought if there was contemplation of a ground limestone scheme and, in respect of phosphate fertilisers, there should be "no question of introducing a new subsidy scheme until all payments under the costly fertiliser credit scheme have been completed."[33] This rearguard action from Finance brought the government to publish its white paper on policy without committing to figures outlining the percentage of land to be compulsorily tilled, the extent of the wheat acreage and the financial resources to back the overall policy.

Publication of the white paper brought sanguine comment from the *Irish Times* on compulsory tillage:

[30] NAI, D/T, S11402 D, D/A memo to govt., 18 Apr. 1946; NAI, D/T S13528, *Policy in regard to crops, pastures, fertilisers and feeding stuffs*, W.P. no. 7597 (May 1946) and cabinet minutes, 3 May 1946.
[31] The Farm Improvements Scheme had originated in 1940 as a replacement for the Land Reclamation Scheme which had operated in the congested districts. The new scheme was open to applicants in all areas of the country and provided for the payment of grants amounting to half the estimated cost of a wide variety of farm improvements, including land reclamation and drainage work.
[32] NAI, D/T, S11402 D, D/A memo to govt., 18 Apr. 1946; NAI, D/T S13528, *Policy in regard to crops, pastures, fertilisers and feeding stuffs*, W.P. no. 7597 (May 1946) and cabinet minutes, 3 May 1946.
[33] NAI, D/T S12888 C, D/F memo to govt., 18 Apr. 1946.

The necessity is regrettable; any form of rigid control over the farmer's way of life is a bad thing … It is a sorry commentary on the outlook of many Irish farmers. Every expert during the past 50 years has recognised that the salvation and prosperity of this country lies in a policy of mixed farming, and that an undue concentration on grazing to the exclusion of crops, can result only in the decline and death of the fertility of the soil. Can the farmers not be brought to understand that a short-sighted reluctance to till, while it may produce early and rapid returns in another direction, deprives them of the chance of long and steady profits? We are sorry that the government seem to have abandoned hope of their conversion.

The paper commented that compulsion would place exceptional demands outside of wartime:

A different rotation suits different farms: it may be that the farmer himself often is unaware of what is best for his land; he will be entitled to accurate information, without expense … A difficulty which must be overcome, somehow or other, lies in the farmer's natural reluctance to accept advice from a central department, however well qualified its personnel may be. His instinct is to believe that he, with generations of farming 'in his blood', is bound to know better than the man in the laboratory.[34]

As the legislation for long-term compulsory tillage was being prepared, the short-term renewal of the existing orders was continued in 1946 and 1947.[35] In those years harvesting had been greatly hampered by appalling weather, further fuelling farmers' antipathy to tillage. In 1947 the government, with its purse strings loosened by looming elections, increased the guaranteed price of wheat from 55s per barrel to 62s 6d per barrel of top quality wheat and increased the maximum price for barley to 45s from 40s per barrel. The increase in price was less than the minimum which the Department of Agriculture had recommended as necessary to maintain farmers' incomes and to placate the "general antagonism to wheat growing … Farmers have been expecting some relaxation of the tillage obligations especially in regard to the compulsory wheat growing provision, and there will be a good deal of disappointment when it is announced that there will be no easing in 1948 of what they regard as an onerous burden."[36] That 'onerous burden' was resting on fewer shoulders as the area under tillage – although still at a higher level than in the 1930s – declined, regardless of compulsory orders (see appendix). Although it had decided on compulsory tillage legislation, the government made no attempt to introduce it. Just as with the pigs and bacon industry, the policy initiative which had been born of wartime review, ground to a halt. Electoral concerns were again to the fore. Weary of sacrifice 'in the national

---

[34] *Irish Times*, 5 Jun. 1946.

[35] NAI, D/T S12888 C/D, cabinet minutes, 4 Sept. 1945, 9 Nov. 1946 and 10 Oct. 1947.

[36] NAI, D/T S11402 D, D/A memo to govt., 4 Oct. 1947.

interest', the Irish farmer wished to return to his traditional farming pattern. With an election due in 1948 at the latest, Fianna Fáil understood just how odious farmers found compulsory tillage. As it slid into the last months of its term in office, there was no question of the government pursuing a policy which would condemn it to certain defeat.

As it was, the government was defeated in the January 1948 election and the establishment of the new inter-party government sealed the fate of the mooted compulsory tillage legislation. The new government did not revoke the existing compulsory tillage orders but rather failed to renew them. Neatly appraising the new government's policy, its Minister for Agriculture, James Dillon, stated: "The greatly increased acreage of barley, oats, root crops, and grass crops, which our economy requires will be better produced by the farmers acting on their own initiative rather than under my or anybody else's orders."[37] Prosecutions for contravention of previous tillage orders were abandoned.[38] The great compulsory tillage crusade ended without fuss. It was never to be revived.

II

The Decline of Dairying

Neither centralisation nor compulsion stood at the heart of the government's attempts to rehabilitate the dairy industry. Although butter had been one of Ireland's principal exports in the eighteenth and nineteenth centuries, the industry had suffered a steady decline.[39] Ireland, with its highly salted farm-produced butter, lost its prominent position in the British market to the Danes whose centralised creamery system, powered by the invention of the mechanical cream separator, produced fresh, lightly flavoured fare which proved more palatable and, crucially, more efficient. Attempts to establish a creamery system in Ireland encountered considerable difficulties. The co-operative creameries established at the turn of the century by the IAOS proved too numerous and inefficient, and were unable to defy the enduring seasonality of production. The pre-war trend of export through the summer and import during the winter proved exceptionally difficult to alter.[40]

---

[37] NAI, D/T S11402 E, *Dáil Debates*, vol. 111, no. 1, 1 Jun. 1948. Dillon also revisited Paddy Hogan's old slogan: "The government policy may be summarised in the phrase 'one more cow, one more sow, and one more acre under the plough'". See NAI, D/T S12888 D, Dillon note, (n.d.).

[38] NAI, D/T S11402 E, D/A memo to govt., 17 Jan. 1949.

[39] Peter M. Solar, 'The Irish butter trade in the nineteenth century: new estimates and their implications', in *Studia Hibernica*, no. 25 (1990), pp 134–161; Liam Kennedy, 'The decline of the Cork butter market: a comment', in *Studia Hibernica*, no. 16 (1976), pp 175–8.

[40] *Report of the survey team on the dairy product industry* (1962), pp 14–5.

The establishment by the government of the Dairy Disposal Company in 1927 to acquire struggling creameries did not bring a marked improvement in affairs. In lieu of promoting rationalised development, it operated in parallel lines to the co-operative movement and proved equally inefficient. There was also the persistent suggestion of fraudulent accounting in all elements of the business.[41] The industry faced collapse in the wake of the great depression. Between 1929 and 1931 the average price of Irish butter fell from 164s 9d to 95s 4d per cwt. In an attempt to salvage the industry the Dairy Produce (Price Stabilisation) Act, 1931 effectively prohibited import and allowed for the payment of export bounties in an attempt to restore the dairy farmer's return to an economic level. A further stabilisation act in 1935 fixed a minimum price for butter. The following year a Milk Act regulated the supply of that product to Cork and Dublin, and allowed the minister to prescribe the price to be paid to producers.[42] The export market continued to pose problems and British butter importers noted that while Irish butter could be excellent there were a number of major marketing difficulties, not least of which was the failure to maintain regular supplies of first-class butter.

Irregularity of supply was due in large part to technical failings. From the foundation of the state there had been a series of reports recommending the use of milk records – this was not undertaken on a comprehensive basis before the 1960s.[43] National breeding policy favoured the dual-purpose shorthorn based on the premise that dairy farmers could sell their surplus calves to graziers – the profits created by this demand for calves encouraged dairy farmers to breed as much for beef as for milk, thereby lowering yields.[44] Inevitably, the greater profitability of the beef trade ensured a bias towards beef characteristics. Yields were further diminished by the abject failure to ensure a substantial, continuous supply of winter feed. This capitulation forced the import of butter through the winter as milk supplies from dairy farmers all but disappeared. Paucity of winter feed was the "greatest of all defects in our methods of production," which resulted in "winter starvation ... The losses from it are enormous. When growth of grass ceases in the autumn, milk production ceases. The dairying industry is active only during a short summer season."[45] Further questions existed over hygiene in the

---

[41] Michael Neenan, 'A popular history of Irish agriculture' (unpublished manuscript), p. 233. Neenan, an official of the Department of Agriculture, wrote an incomplete, idiosyncratic account which proved insightful in some parts. It is housed in the Department of Agriculture.

[42] Hoctor, *The department's story*, pp 179, 181.

[43] Smith and Healy, *Farm organisations*, pp 71–2.

[44] *Ibid.*, pp 71–3; Daniel, 'Griffith', p. 63; Desmond Gillmor, *Agriculture in the Republic of Ireland* (1977), p. 116.

[45] CIPEAP, *second minority report*, p. 181. The *Irish Farmers' Journal (IFJ)* later editorialised: "The weakest link in the Irish farm economy is the winter feeding position. Each winter almost two million cattle are forced on to a most expensive diet, that of beef consumption from their own backs. In creamery areas after a winter of short rations and moderate hay, cows are not in the best form for milk production until well into lactation in June." *IFJ*, 28 May 1955.

[46] In 1946 there were a mere 1,000 milking machines in Ireland, while most farmers did not have a supply of running water on their farms. In 1945 only 2 per cent of rural homes had electricity (compared with 85 per cent in Denmark and 98 per cent in Holland) and until 1960 only 12 per cent of rural homes had running water. See Michael Shiel, *The quiet revolution: the electrification of rural Ireland 1946–76* (1984), pp 222, 178–9.

industry.[46] By the outbreak of war, loss of market and low yields suggested an industry in terminal decline.

In November 1945 the Department of Agriculture argued that the best way to redeem the dairy industry was through a guaranteed market for butter with minimum prices fixed in advance. The subsidy would be decided by calculating the difference between cost of production and the price it realised on sale. It proposed a five-year scheme subject to adjustment as the cost of production varied and with an estimated annual cost to the exchequer of just over £1m.[47] The proposal brought immediate criticism from other departments. The Department of Finance complained the subsidy would have to be met from taxation at precisely a time when it was vital to cut taxation to stimulate recovery and that price guarantees were not a vital factor in stimulating production but would encourage inefficient producers and delay implementation of improved techniques. Finance added that plans to improve yields and cheapen production should be formulated instead and that, at very least, the timeframe should be reduced from five to two years. The Minister for Industry and Commerce, Seán Lemass, was also opposed to the proposal. Arguing that the price guarantee could provoke a vicious cycle leading to higher prices and higher wages all around, he noted that the public were looking for a reasonably early decline in prices which was undoubtedly one of the factors giving stability to the present situation and keeping labour interests from clamouring for wage increases. Lemass pointed out that "actual data from which the average costings of production of milk supplied to creameries throughout the country could be calculated are not in existence." He further argued that the existing method of fixing butter prices by reference to average costs of creameries was inappropriate but should be based instead on the most efficient units and that "if it is necessary to encourage creameries in depressed areas this should be done by some method other than fixing a universally higher price for butter."

More pointedly, Lemass complained that a guaranteed five-year price for butter would create a dangerous precedent for other areas of agricultural production. This lack of any sense that the move towards dairy price support was conceived in the context of overall policy particularly irked Lemass who disapprovingly commented:

> An important post-war agricultural measure like the present should not be submitted to the government without reference to its relation to other branches of agriculture and to any measures which it may be intended to introduce in regard to such other branches. It is obvious that unless all such measures are formulated as part of a general plan for post-war agriculture they may well be found to work contrary to one another, and this might possibly lead to frequent amendments or alterations in the different proposals with consequent upset to the

[47] NAI, D/T S12888 B, D/A memo to govt., 15 Nov. 1945 and 20 Nov. 1943, D/F memo to govt., 15 Nov. 1945, and D/IC memo to govt., 13 Nov. 1945.

economy of the country in general. This is highly desirable to avoid.

The Department of Agriculture was not to be turned. It argued that price was a vital factor in production, even if it was not the only influence, and that a guaranteed price would not induce inefficiency as the margins were too low to facilitate that, but it would provide the opportunity to make more money by being efficient. The Department argued that, in terms of the lack of data on the cost of milk production, it

> would be absurd to attempt to compile such data for this country where conditions vary so much between county and county, parish and parish. The detailed costs supplied by the Department of Agriculture were prepared by practical agriculturists as representing the costs of efficient farmers in creamery districts who make tillage and other arrangements to feed their cows to yield 500 gallons of milk per annum. These costings would be accepted as fair and reasonable by any unbiased person with a knowledge of the subject and they have been so drawn up that they can be used as a basis for determining fluctuations in costs of milk production year by year.

Noting that it would "take a considerable time," to formulate a general plan for agriculture, the minister was acting on the urgent need to produce more milk and more butter and the best way to do that was to give farmers confidence in their industry through a guaranteed price.[48]

The government approved the minister's proposals in principle and agreed to the preparation of a white paper which was published in January 1946.[49] The white paper proposed a five-year guaranteed price, with a two-year notice of withdrawal of guarantee. It also proposed that any surplus would be taken over by a butter marketing organisation and should the price of export sales be lower than the home price, the difference would be made good by subsidy from the exchequer. Drawing on the price which had existed from 1943, the standard price was set for the following five years as 10½d per gallon from 1 April to 30 November, and 1s per gallon from 1 December to 31 March. The initiative had little impact during 1946. There was no apparent increase in production, rather a fall, and "the risk of a further decline in the industry in 1947, which would make its re-establishment in subsequent years all the more difficult, was, it was thought, too great," so the Department of Agriculture sought further price increases. Despite the objections of the departments of Finance, and Industry and Commerce, the government sanctioned price increases of 35 per cent to 1s 2d per gallon from 1 May to 31 October and 1s 4d per gallon from 1 November to 30 April. To help pay for this increase, the retail price of butter was increased from

---

48 NAI, D/T S12888 B, D/A memo to govt., 15 Nov. 1945 and 20 Nov. 1943.

49 NAI, D/T S12888 B, cabinet minutes, 27 Nov. 1945 and 1 Jan. 1946.

50 NAI, D/T S11762 B, D/A memo to govt., 28 Mar. 1947 and cabinet minutes, 15 Apr. 1947; S14627 A/1, D/A memo to govt., 2 Nov. 1949.

2s 4d to 2s 8d per pound, but this was not nearly sufficient and by the end of the year the state was subsiding the industry to the tune of £1,950,000.[50]

Longer term proposals to improve breeding and yields included increasing the value of premiums of dairy bulls, modified cattle registration schemes to require progressively higher standards of milk yields, the establishment of a register for designated cows of high milk yields, payment of a cash bonus for the mating of designated bulls with designated cows, and the expansion of cow-testing. Similarly, Department of Agriculture licensing of artificial insemination plants suggested a fundamental reappraisal of breeding policy. Artificial insemination stations were established across the country and were welcomed by farmers as "a real breakthrough."[51] Yet, if this technique promised much, there was enduring criticism of the continued adherence to the dual-purpose shorthorn which appeared an attempt to buck the trend towards specialisation evident in advanced agricultures. One commentator noted that Ireland was about to "spend another generation in Monte Carlo – gambling with a 'dual purpose cow' to secure a high milk yield and a first class butcher's beast. By the same breeding principles – by mating a thoroughbred with a Clydesdale – we should expect the progeny to win the Derby and plough the 'Rocks of Bawn.'"[52] He predicted: "The dairy industry had no future."

With improved breeding at best a long-term prospect, the reliance on price supports to revitalise dairying was almost absolute. It was not a reliance which inspired confidence. Ministers feared that farmers would interpret the introduction of dairy price supports as the opening gambit in an overhaul of agricultural policy which would see the introduction of cross-sectoral price support. Moreover, although guaranteed prices were an increasingly central aspect of world-wide endeavours to stimulate production, debates flourished in Irish ministerial circles on the benefits of price supports as a means to improve output.[53] For certain ministers, such support was a fundamental prerequisite of increased production; for others, it achieved little beyond the sustenance of inefficient farmers. For still more, price supports not only failed to increase production, but almost encouraged that failure. The whole debate was suffused with the notion that Irish farmers sought to earn to a certain level which, once reached, ended their pursuit of prosperity.[54] High prices could never lure them into decadence.

The efficacy of price supports in a food-exporting country with an insubstantial industrial base was equally open to question.[55] Accordingly, the fact that farmers were consumers themselves would leave them suffering from the very price increases designed to raise their profits. Further, the haphazard manner in

[51] Smith and Healy, *Farm organisations*, pp 71–2.

[52] T.J. McElligott writing in *The Standard*, 7 Sept. 1945.

[53] R. O'Connor, 'Implications of Irish agricultural statistics', in Bailie and Sheehy, *Irish agriculture*, pp 16–43, esp. pp 22–3.

[54] See debates in NAI, D/T S13101 A, especially D/F memo to govt., 1 Nov. 1944 and D/IC memo to govt., 24 Jan. 1945. See also UCDA, Seán MacEntee papers, P67/264 (5), D/A memo to govt., (n.d.).

which price supports had been administered in the past had done little to encourage confidence in their worth as an instrument of policy. For wheat, barley and sugar beet, supports provided reasonably successful incentives to farmers to increase their production of such commodities, but this had been at the expense of a decline in production of other commodities rather than as part of an overall increase in output. Alternatively, minimum prices for butter and pigs were introduced to salvage industries lurching dangerously towards disaster. Nowhere, though, was there evidence of a clarity of application or a vision extending beyond the limits of expediency.

The *Reports of the commission of inquiry on post-emergency agricultural policy* had divided on the merits of price supports. Although agreeing that guaranteed prices should be used in the short term to raise dairy production to meet the requirements of the home market, the majority report recommended that subsidies be given to reduce the costs of production rather than as price subsidies which afforded "neither incentive to economy of production nor encouragement to organisation." It noted that while subsidies could be justified to prevent the collapse of an industry, their use on a long-term basis would entail application over the entire market or the pattern of production would be distorted. It further pointed out that, in Ireland, price supports had tended to discriminate against the smallholder in the poorer regions.[56] On the other hand, the first minority report recommended "a long-term policy of fixed prices on the home market for certain agricultural commodities." It argued that the ensuing profit would stimulate production and drive the industry towards greater prosperity, although it would be impractical to apply it to the cattle and sheep trades.[57]

With the reports unable to offer clear guidance through the debris of present political disagreement and past incoherence of policy, the relationship between price and agricultural production in Ireland was one of case unproven. Nonetheless, spurred by its agricultural advisory committee, the Department of Agriculture began moves towards a policy where price support would hold a more central role.[58] It received the approval of the government to draft a bill establishing a permanent agricultural prices tribunal. As well as advising the minister on the appropriate prices to pay producers, this tribunal was to have the

---

[55] John W. Mellor and Paisuddin Ahmed, 'Agricultural price policy – the context and the approach,' in John W. Mellor and Paisuddin Ahmed (eds.), *Agricultural price policy for developing countries* (1998), pp 1–10. See in particular the authors' contention that the "determination of agricultural prices is intensely political because of its profound influence on equity, income distribution, consumption, production, and economic development. Thus agricultural price policy occupies a major place in political debate, the deliberations of government bureaucracies, and the decisions made by consumers and producers." The authors also noted "the extraordinary complexity of agricultural price policy arises from the immense magnitude of the economic forces involved, the large fluctuations in agricultural prices and their profound implications for the distribution of income and power, the small size of production and consumption units for food in low-income countries, their wide geographical dispersion, and the peculiar limitations imposed by land and other natural factors." *Ibid.*, pp 1–3.

[56] CIPEAP, *majority report*, pp 58–64, 70, 71.

[57] CIPEAP, *first minority report*, p. 139.

[58] NAI, D/A AGI G 928/1946, J. Mahony, chairman of agricultural advisory committee to sec., D/A, 11 Jul. 1946.

power to inquire into the organisation and running of industries concerned with the production and disposal of crops, the breeding, rearing, maintenance and disposal of livestock and poultry, and the production and disposal of milk, butter, cheese, eggs and meat.[59] In proposing the bill, the Minister for Agriculture argued that in order to introduce an element of stability into the industry it

> will be essential to fix a just price for a certain range of commodities so that the farmer may be afforded an opportunity of earning a fair livelihood from his business even though, for reasons outside his control, the return from some lines of production may prove unremunerative. The price necessary to induce a given volume of production, while only giving producers generally a modest return, may be regarded as too high for the mass of consumers. In that event, the question of subsidising consumers' prices will arise and policy in this regard must be settled as soon as producers' prices are fixed.

Moreover, the Minister considered the cost of production was not a complete guide to a fair price as it was also necessary to take into account the returns obtainable from alternative forms of production and "the cost and price of a particular agricultural commodity cannot be considered apart from agricultural costs and prices generally. The farmer's position as a whole must be taken into account." It was argued that the best manner to assess the farmers' position was through a permanent agricultural prices tribunal whose recommendations the state could accept or reject as appropriate. This was viewed as more desirable than direct price fixing by the state which could "give rise to political agitation by producers with the result that the question of agricultural prices be removed from the plane of objective consideration." Previously prices had been fixed in an empirical manner based on the best opinion that could be formed to induce the volume of production required but in the post-war era

> such a method would be subject to constant criticism and could not be justified ... Moreover, it is not desirable that a department charged with numerous functions in relation to which the goodwill of the farming community is essential, e.g. agricultural education, administration of various improvement schemes and acts etc., should be regarded by farmers as the organisation for advising on the fixing of prices.[60]

The proposals elicited a muted response from the Department of Finance as being of uncertain necessity. The Department of Industry and Commerce objected to any suggestion of the tribunal holding the power to investigate wholesale and retail pricing but did not object to a tribunal determining producers' prices.[61] It later raised a series of objections to safeguard its role as prime arbiter of the food processing industry.[62] By February 1947 a draft of the bill

---

[59] NAI, D/T S13930 A, cabinet minutes, 25 Oct. 1946 and 24 Jan. 1947.

[60] NAI, D/T S13930 A, D/A memo to govt., 2 Oct. 1946.

[61] NAI, D/A AGI G 928/1946, D/IC memo to D/A, 21 Sept. 1946.

[62] NAI, D/A AGI G 928/1946, D/IC memo to D/A, 19 Nov. 1946 and 28 Nov. 1946

was ready, but two months into his role as minister, Paddy Smith, declared it would be best if the commission was limited in function to investigating costs and not advising on prices.[63] The reformed bill was presented to cabinet by Smith who outlined his "reconsideration of the matter."[64] Objections from cabinet led to the decision that Smith should consider criticisms of the bill and submit a further memorandum.[65] Following a summer of contemplation the minister decided to withdraw the proposals from the cabinet agenda and now favoured the establishment of a costings branch within his own department.[66] The government further decided that its approach to the rising level of wages and prices in the country would be to attempt to control farm price increases and to relate them to proved increases in farm costs.[67]

The announcement that the proposed price commission had devolved to a proposal to establish a departmental costings branch provoked a furore in the Dáil. Deputies demanded to know why the minister had promised them the previous January that he would establish an agricultural prices commission, to which Smith replied: "I was young and foolish then." Further questioned on his *volte face*, Smith remarked that when walking home from a céilí in his youth a strange object had frightened him as he passed across the hills. Initially fearful that it was a ghost or a wild animal, he discovered on closer inspection it was instead a rush bush: "That often happens. I had proposals for the establishment of this tribunal roughly framed. They were perhaps casually examined by me. As I made a closer analysis of them as to how they would work ... I failed to find a satisfactory answer."[68] Failure to find satisfactory answers ensured that there would be no change in policy. The minister would rely on the department to advise him on prices and he, in turn, would advise the government. The system which had previously been described as potentially corruptive of "the plane of high policy and objective consideration," and one which "could not be justified," was the chosen way forward.[69] Price fixing as an instrument of policy would be operated in accordance with its application to the dairy industry. The inability to construct a viable policy saw a much-heralded initiative disintegrate and existing modes of operation continue unchecked. For milk prices in particular, the implications proved far-reaching. The "political agitation," "constant criticism" and loss of goodwill amongst the farming community prophesied by the Department of Agriculture plagued policy in the following years.[70]

---

[63] NAI, D/A AGI G 928/1946, minutes of meeting between Minister for Agriculture (M/A) and D/A officials, 27 Feb. 1947.

[64] NAI, D/T S13930 A, D/A memo to govt., 15 May 1947.

[65] NAI, D/T S13930 A, cabinet minutes, 23 May 1947.

[66] NAI, D/T S13930 A, cabinet minutes, 21 Oct. 1947; D/A AGI G 928/1946, newspaper cuttings of *Irish Independent*, 9 Oct. 1947 and *Cork Examiner*, 10 Oct. 1947.

[67] NAI, D/T S13930 A, cabinet minutes, 2 Oct. 1947.

[68] *Dáil Debates*, vol. 108, no. 9, cols. 336–48, 9 Oct. 1947.

[69] NAI, D/T S13930 A, D/A memo to govt., 2 Oct. 1946, D/A AGI G 928/1946, J. Mahony, chairman of agricultural advisory committee to sec., D/A, 11 Jul. 1946.

[70] NAI, D/T S13930 A, D/A memo to govt., 2 Oct. 1946.

III

Attempts to reclaim the British market

With tillage acreage in decline, the pigs and bacon sector in chaos, and dairying showing few signs of revival, the livestock industry and the British market remained the prime focus of agricultural activity. Despite the acknowledged importance of the British market to Irish agriculture there was no immediate post-war stampede to drive forward the Irish position. Nor was there much evidence of sustained preparation for post-war export of produce. The Minister for Agriculture, James Ryan, was questioned in the Dáil in September 1944, whether, in the light of radio reports of long-term trade negotiations between Britain and Commonwealth countries on food policy, the government had sought to secure any such arrangements in respect of livestock or livestock products. Ryan replied that he was "not satisfied in present circumstances any useful purpose would be served by initiating negotiations or inquiries in respect of export trade in agricultural produce in the post-war period."[71] One year later, Eamon de Valera told the Dáil the time had not yet come for full-scale talks as, firstly, a considerable amount of normality would have to be restored to the general conditions governing international trade. The slow restoration of normality allowed talks to take place between Irish and British officials in May 1946. In advance of the talks the Irish submitted a proposal to the British which suggested that a new trade agreement might be considered. The Department of Industry and Commerce noted "the 1938 agreement confers no benefits whatsoever on this country at the moment and, in certain directions, imposes handicaps," as the British had been unable to supply essential commodities while central purchase had kept Irish agricultural prices down. In reply, British officials stated that central purchase and subsidising would continue for a long time and might even become a permanent feature as Britain wished to expand its agriculture. Nonetheless, "reasonable regard would, no doubt, be had to the position of regular suppliers of agricultural produce to Great Britain."[72] Throughout the talks, Britain rejected any suggestion that a new trade agreement be negotiated. As Irish officials later agreed, their initiative foundered as the British were consumed with the international trade talks then in progress and did not want to give any firm commitments to the Irish.[73]

This stasis did not satisfy the livestock industry and the fall in prices on the British market exercised their spokesmen in parliament. A lengthy Seanad debate saw one Senator lament the failure of the government to secure a deal with the British, saying that, in future, Irish officials should bring representatives of the

---

[71] *Dáil Debates*, vol. 44, no. 6, cols. 2079–81, 27 Sept. 1944.

[72] NAI, D/T S11846 B, D/IC memo to govt., 25 May 1946.

[73] NAI, D/T S11846 B, D/IC memo to govt., 30 May 1947.

cattle trade whose renowned trading acumen would shore up the delegation as they were

> just as competent as anybody else to make a good deal with the British officials. The department [of agriculture] may look on me as an old fossil and, possibly, the British ministry officials might think that I would go in with a shillelagh under my coat and give them an exhibition of what is supposed to have taken place at Donnybrook fair. [But] the young cattle traders of the present generation are just as competent as anybody else to carry out negotiations on behalf of the country, particularly in regard to a business in which they are interested.[74]

Rejecting the 'Donnybrook' approach, the Minister for Agriculture, James Ryan, chose more diplomatic channels and intimated to Lord Rugby, the British representative in Ireland, his desire to consider the future agricultural programme for Ireland in the light of the long-term needs of the British market.[75] The British responded with the suggestion that they should send two of their agricultural economists to Dublin to address such issues as the rate of expansion likely, the scientific possibilities of expansion if practical difficulties could be overcome, the requirements necessary to carry out agricultural policy, and the marketing organisation and purchasing arrangements necessary to give producers confidence. The British asked for a statement indicating the Irish government's general economic policy and, in particular, its perception of the role within the economy for agricultural as against industrial development.

The British also requested a statement of agricultural policy indicating the general lines of development and giving "the acreages of crops, number of livestock, agricultural production and exports which would accompany such expansion." It demanded, most pointedly: "Has the Eire government the intention of ensuring that agricultural development takes place?" It asked what factors would retard expansion of production, what the fertiliser requirements would be, were there plans to specialise in agricultural industries such as canning, what other countries would Ireland look for markets in and "what effect will the policies proposed have on the number of Irish workers coming to the UK?" Similarly, "what evidence is there that the past apparently leisurely acceptance of improvements in technique etc. by the Irish farmer will now give place to more speedy technical development?"

The British missive wondered whether grassland and home-grown feed could be increased to improve stocking and to even out seasonality, and whether such increases would mean more fat rather than more store cattle. Regarding the dairy industry, it commented: "As there is doubtless an intention to improve milk yields per cow, is it practicable both to increase cow numbers, cattle rearing and

---

[74] Senator Counihan, *Seanad Debates*, vol. 33, no. 1, cols. 56–90, 13 Nov. 1946.

[75] NAI, D/T S14042 A, H. Broadley, British Ministry of Food to D/A, 27 Feb. 1947.

carry on the selective breeding necessary to improve yields? What policy as to concentration on beef, dairy and dual purpose cattle is being pursued? Are the necessary quality bulls available when required?" It asked "why have cow numbers not increased during the last 30 years?" It wondered what steps had been taken to stabilise prices to producers, whether prices would be guaranteed, on what basis they would be fixed and for which commodities, and whether farm costing and estimates of overall agricultural returns were available? Acknowledging that several factors beyond price impinged on the lines of production, it inquired what Ireland's preference for division on the export of her cattle would be between stores, fats, breeding stock and carcass or canned meats. The missive continued: "Which products would Eire prefer to export? It may not simply be a matter of relative price alone, e.g. butter production might have special attractions because the skim milk provides a basis for pig and poultry production which has a social value in a country of small farms." To that end, it considered: "Will the import of feeding stuffs for bacon production be restricted as a matter of policy? Is it practicable to increase pig production from Eire's own soil?"[76]

The tone and tenor of the memorandum suggested that "Eire's own soil" was something of a misnomer.[77] The request to facilitate a fact-finding mission was duly agreed to and two British agricultural experts, aided by Irish government departments, produced a report in May 1947 entitled *Report on Eire food production and export possibilities*.[78] The report noted that the livestock were of "excellent quality and well-managed," and Irish farming was of a "comparatively high standard and no great increases in total output above pre-war levels are likely to be achieved quickly." From a British point of view it approved of the relatively cheap price for Irish cattle and the general value of increasing export from Ireland to prevent any drain on sterling balances. Further, the report noted that expansion would not influence the number of emigrant Irish labourers coming to work in British factories. The report stated that substantial industrialisation was highly improbable and "the peasant character of the economy is evident from an analysis of agricultural equipment and of size of holding." It suggested the encouragement of expansion of milk products but exports of liquid milk were not feasible due to poor hygiene and seasonality. The report concluded that Britain should offer higher prices for cattle, ensure supplies of fertiliser and maize, supply improved grass strains, help develop ensilage, negotiate firm prices for bacon, exchange research information and personnel, give Ireland priority for farm machinery and equipment, and allow an economist from the Department of Agriculture study British costings and price fixing arrangements. In return,

---

[76] *Ibid.*

[77] Irish economic independence was further questioned in an article written by Prof. G.D.H. Cole, a friend of John Strachey, the British Minister of Food, in the *New Statesman* which referred to 'Britain's Irish larder' and assumed that Ireland couldn't industrialise due to a lack of raw materials and asked that it instead use its land to feed Britain.

[78] Public Record Office (PRO) [London], MAF/40/190; the two experts were Dr A.W. Menzies-Kitchen, School of Agriculture, Cambridge University, and Dr John R. Raeburn, Agricultural Economics Research Institute, Oxford University. *Report on Eire food production and export possibilities* (May 1947).

Ireland should prohibit all beef and bacon exports to countries other than Britain, give assurances of basic levels of exports to Britain in 1948 and 1949, and increase its stocking levels.[79]

A copy of the report was sent to the Irish government but it was first stripped of all contentious comment and of its conclusions.[80] On receiving it, the Department of Agriculture commented to the government that the report dealt "fairly and scientifically" with the agricultural situation and, drawing what suited from the gutted document, suggested it could serve as the basis for discussion with a view to securing more equitable arrangements with the British.[81] The British, for their part, utilised the report as a base for their own preparations in advance of proposed talks between Eamon de Valera and British Prime Minister, Clement Attlee, in the autumn. A preparatory memorandum for the talks noted it should be remembered through the talks that a report had shown there was only the slight possibility of an increase in food exports from Ireland.[82] The de Valera–Attlee talks had emerged from an invitation to Irish officials to visit London to discuss the sterling crisis. De Valera took the opportunity to broaden the issue to matters of trade and, in a meeting with Lord Rugby, sought meetings at ministerial level as "public opinion here was already very critical of his government for leaving these matters to officials"[83] Fine Gael crowed that Fianna Fáil had completely reversed their traditional policy and that de Valera's initiative was an "acknowledgement that the economic interests of both countries are inexorably bound together and that we must export or perish."[84]

Lord Rugby opined that, while de Valera was sincere in his desire for agreement, he still

> fights shy of any correlation of interests which would hitch Eire tightly to our wagon. What I described to him as a heaven-sent market for their agricultural produce he regarded as a scheme for putting a chain round their necks ... Mr. De Valera has not himself got a clear grasp of the practical factors which govern international trade in general, nor of the special factors which condition the complementary trade between our two islands. He has frequently stated to me his strong objection to any plan which would establish the supply of the United Kingdom of food and farm produce as the vital element of the economy of Eire. Again and again he has reverted to his government's determination to get manufacturing interests more fully developed here without delay ... He is against intensive farming, and upholds the

---

[79] *Ibid.*

[80] PRO, MAF/40/190, departmental note, 6 Jun. 1947.

[81] NAI, D/T S14042 A, D/A memo to govt., 15 Jul. 1947.

[82] PRO, PREM 8/824, note by deputy secretary of the cabinet, 19 Sept. 1947.

[83] PRO, Dominions Office (DO) 35/3907, Lord Rugby to Commonwealth Relations Office (CRO), 15 Sept. 1947.

[84] UCDA, Richard Mulcahy papers, P7/C/122, James Hughes, Fine Gael agricultural spokesman, speech at Muinebeag, 21 Sept. 1947.

small farm system as best suited to this country. He will strongly defend
the thesis that the prices paid to the Irish farmer should not be lower
than those afforded to the British farmer as the conditions of work are
comparable. He is in favour of reducing the export of store cattle and
increasing the export of fat cattle.[85]

The hope, according to Rugby, lay in the other members of the delegation
"who know that Mr. De Valera's gaelic sanctuary is not viable and who, while
rendering lip-service to Sinn Fein doctrine, will take a realistic view of concrete
proposals."[86] Duly informed, the Commonwealth Relations Office took the view
that the negotiations would be difficult but appeared "to provide an opening for
approaching the mutual problems of the two countries with realism and of laying
down a long range policy."[87]

At the meeting between de Valera and Attlee in London, de Valera insisted
that Ireland did not wish to remain a predominantly agricultural country whose
economy revolved around food exports, but then commented that one of the
main questions at issue was "the best method of dovetailing the agricultural
policies of the UK and Eire in order that they might be pursued to their mutual
advantage." To this end, de Valera stressed that in the forthcoming talks between
officials on both sides there should be a directive that Irish producers receive the
same price as British ones. Attlee sidestepped pressure to give such a directive.[88]
As the talks moved from ministerial to official level there was some disagreement
on the British side. Some of the British representatives thought it would be
desirable to accept parity of price, but the Commonwealth Relations Office
believed the principle should not be conceded, rather price increases should be
given to ensure that all available Irish stock came to Britain.[89] The Ministry of
Agriculture strongly opposed parity which might provide "formidable trouble in
the future," and Rugby, predictably pronounced that parity would be disastrous
for political reasons.[90] Despite Rugby's analysis that Ireland saw that the "United
Kingdom, hitherto free to spurn Eire's small contribution to our large larder is
now looking for the crumbs that fall," the British government decided that there
was no necessity to "concede the principle but suggests that our negotiators should
be as generous as they can on price discussions."[91]

---

[85] PRO, DO 35/3907, Lord Rugby to CRO, 16 Sept. 1947. Rugby further noted that de Valera believed it
was in this manner that the population of Ireland could be doubled: "The Eire government find it
disconcerting that, with the achievement of political independence here, the exodus of the Irish seeking
employment outside the country has increased rather than diminished. It was customary and comforting
to blame the English for this tendency. The idea now is that the Irish can be kept at home by establishing
local industries." The Commonwealth Relations Office, for its part, believed that the timing of the
initiative was clearly political as de Valera "thinks this is a suitable moment to re-enter the international
arena and considers that it would strengthen his position with his own people if he were to do so." See
PRO, DO 35/3907, CRO memo to cabinet, 15 Sept. 1947.

[86] PRO, DO 35/3907, CRO memo to cabinet, 15 Sept. 1947.

[87] PRO, DO 35/3907, CRO note, 19 Sept. 1947.

[88] PRO, PREM 8/824, minutes of Attlee–de Valera meeting at Downing St., 19 Sept. 1947.

[89] PRO, DO 35/3907 memo, 18 Oct. 1947.

[90] PRO, DO 35/3907, Rugby to CRO, 9 Oct. 1947 and MAF memo, 18 Oct. 1947.

[91] PRO, PREM 8/824, Rugby to CRO, 28 Oct. 1947 and PRO, DO 25/3907, cabinet office memo, 27 Oct.
1947.

Irish negotiators, meanwhile, were being advised that the purpose of the ministerial conference at the end of the month was to "receive the proposals of the British side," and that no agreement was to be reached on financial issues unless trade arrangements were "reasonably satisfactory." Irish negotiators were to press for economic prices, without discrimination, for agricultural produce and an adequate supply of fertilisers, seeds and agricultural machinery.[92] When little progress was made de Valera flew to London for secret talks where the Taoiseach pronounced himself disappointed that the negotiations had

> developed into haggling about particular concessions ... He had come over to London almost in a spirit of despair at the number of difficulties which seemed to be arising ... Irish officials felt that their opposite numbers in the United Kingdom were hard bargainers. He felt there should be some clearer instruction to them to work with more sympathy for the expansion and development of the Irish economy.[93]

Again in London in November 1947, de Valera complained to Attlee over the price offers for livestock and other agricultural commodities. Accompanying him, Paddy Smith noted with some disappointment that the price for stores was good but not the price for fats and that clearly the British government were intent on driving an ever-increasing disparity between the two.[94] They found a sympathetic ear in Ernest Bevin who complained that not enough consideration had been given to the political considerations of a failure not to go far enough to meet the Irish. Sympathy did not extend to meeting Irish demands, however, and the eventual agreement was a disappointment to the Irish. The principle of parity was not conceded, price increases favoured store rather than fat cattle and the price increase for fat cattle would be 5d. until 1 March and would then fall by 1d per lb unless a better price was negotiated in the meantime. The Irish also agreed that the "total number of cattle to be exported from Ireland to continental countries as from 1 February 1948 will be the subject of consultation between the Irish government and the British Ministry of Food."[95] More farm machinery and a limited increase in fertilisers was agreed, but no quantitative assurances were given. No agreement was made on sheep or bacon, as there was no likely Irish surplus. Final decisions on carcass meat, canned meat and eggs were left to future discussion.

For both short- and long-term prospects, the outcome offered no cause for celebration and its eventual terms were dictated as much by Irish political necessities as by Britain's economic want. In pushing for ostentatious ministerial summits rather than more discreet negotiations through officials, the Irish made

---

92 NAI, D/T S14042 A, D/T memo to officials, 23 Oct. 1947.

93 PRO, DO 35/3907, board of trade minutes, 25 Sept. 1947.

94 PRO, PREM 8/824, minutes of meeting at London, 3 Nov. 1947.

95 NAI, D/T S11846 A, summary of results of negotiations between Irish and British governments in agriculture, Sept.–Nov. 1947.

a tactical error. The reappearance of de Valera on the world stage raised expectations which the paucity of Irish preparations for negotiations were unable to fulfil. The proximity of a general election in Ireland placed added pressure on the Irish. Failed engagement with Britain did not sit easily with the sensibilities of the Irish electorate. In the political arena, even an inadequate accord which could be dressed up as more than the sum of its parts was better than no accord at all. Conversely, the British were under no outstanding pressure to reach accord and were well acquainted with the truism that Ireland was unlikely to raise quickly its levels of production. The resultant agreement lends eloquent testimony to just how deeply the British understood the Irish economic malaise. And as if to rub salt into the wound, in the month that the agreement was reached extracts of the confidential Menzies-Kitchen report outlining the reasons why Ireland was unlikely to expand was leaked to the press. British embarrassment over the leak paled beside Irish embarrassment at its content. The report had set the tone for British rebuttal of Irish demands but what must have pained most was its accuracy.[96]

One potential source of relief from unrelenting gloom came from a side accord signed with Britain for the poultry industry. The government contracted to export a minimum of 2,062,500 great hundreds of eggs to Britain in 1947/8 and 1948/9.[97] Irish attempts to revive the poultry industry in the immediate post-war years had proved singularly unsuccessful. Attempts to use price-fixing as a means to increase production had not proved valuable and were opposed by the Minister for Agriculture as liable "to postpone, for years perhaps, an improvement in output."[98] By the end of 1947, Irish exports had fallen well below the level promised, but Britain agreed to extend the contract to 1951. The British had considered from the beginning that the Irish would be unable to meet their promises. J.A. Peacock, Director of Eggs at the British Ministry of Food, told an Irish official he understood

> that 97 per cent of the hatching with us takes place on the farm and if this figure proved to be correct, it would how the enormous development necessary on this one point alone ... He reminded me that ... on the proposals put forward by the Department of Agriculture, there was no provision for obtaining the necessary supply of eggs to implement the contract other than what was agreed to be a genuine belief that the eggs would be available ... With great respect he submitted that this could not be done on the sole foundation of higher prices and an optimistic outlook on the future.[99]

There seemed little prospect of Ireland meeting the British requirements, however, as "the industry is in urgent need of rehabilitation and a radical scheme

---

[96] NAI, D/T S14042 A, D/EA memo to govt., 19 Nov. 1947

[97] NAI, D/T S13347 A/2, cabinet minutes, 1 Oct. 1946.

[98] NAI, D/T S13347 A/2, D/A memo to govt., 17 Aug. 1946.

[99] NAI, D/A 6/29/12, report of meeting with Peacock forwarded to D/A by Dulanty, 12 Jun. 1947.

is necessary."[100] The British stressed the need to back bold measures with substantial investment. Propaganda, instruction, technical development, better packing cases, and a single board to control both home and export markets were cited as prerequisites. Previous failure to complete these tasks ensured that the "quality of Irish eggs is at present very poor."[101]

Chastened, the Department of Agriculture moved to convince the government of the need for immediate action. Noting the unlimited scope for expansion and the suitability of the industry to the agricultural economy of Ireland, the Department of Agriculture remarked that unless it could rid the industry of it seasonality through the introduction of improved breeds, it had "no future". A revitalised poultry industry would necessitate a move away from the mentality "amongst Irish farmers of keeping mainly for household use a few hens around the place which have to depend for the greater part of their keep on such scraps and odds and ends of grain as can be picked up in the farmyard." The Department of Agriculture proposed a scheme of 100 commercial hatcheries, each with ten attendant supply farms, coupled with the expansion of existing poultry stations and support for pedigree breeders. The project cost was estimated at £1,350,000. Discussions with the British brought agreement to pay a bonus on Irish exports which amounted to £400,000 per annum. The Fianna Fáil government agreed to the scheme and the future looked bright for the poultry industry.[102] This would later prove to be the falsest of dawns.

The November accord, and the subsequent poultry agreement, were among the last major acts of the Fianna Fáil administration. In office for more than fifteen years, its agricultural policy had evolved from protectionism and self-sufficiency to open acknowledgement of the importance of 'dovetailing' with the British market. Stripped of its dynamic radical agrarianism, its agricultural policies had descended into a mire of chronic irresolution.[103] Post-war attempts to revive various sections of the industry had not proved successful; its land policy had failed abjectly to counteract the flight from the land; and, now, its belated conversion to export-driven, livestock-centred agriculture had brought only the most modest of agreements with Britain. The electorate were disenchanted – the revolution was over.

---

[100] NAI, D/T S13347 B, D/A memo to govt., 14 Jan. 1948.

[101] NAI, D/A 6/29/12, J.A. Peacock quoted at report of conference at Ministry of Food in London, 24 Sept. 1947.

[102] NAI, D/T S13347 B, D/A memo to govt., 14 Jan. 1948.

[103] Witness the following exchange in the Dáil between Fine Gael agricultural spokesman, James Hughes and the Minister for Agriculture, James Ryan, on a programme for post-war agricultural development in the light of the *Reports of the commission of inquiry on post-emergency agricultural policy.*
Hughes: 'When does the Minister propose to give us comprehensive proposals as a whole?' Ryan: 'It is hard to say. I hope to be able to do it from time to time.' Hughes: 'Can the Minister give us any idea at all?' Ryan: 'From time to time: the greatest part of it, I am sure, next session.' See *Dáil Debates*, vol. 98, no. 8, cols. 1675–6, 12 Dec. 1945.

IV

Agriculture and the 1948 Trade Agreement

The extended January 1948 election campaign which brought the first inter-party government to power was played out, in large part, over agricultural policy. Fine Gael stressed that, in government, its focus would be on extending "agricultural production on the lines most suitable for Irish conditions and Irish opportunities."[104] The party's agricultural spokesman, James Hughes, outlined a policy of raising productivity through extensive soils analysis, reclamation schemes, vastly increased fertiliser usage, all backed by a grassland institute. Livestock farming and its products were "the most vital activity in our economy," and improved grasslands "the only method by which we can exploit to the full our high rainfall and humid conditions." Breeding policy and the veterinary services would be refined to aid livestock farmers. Small farms would be equipped for poultry expansion "and arrangements made to give farmers' daughters institutional training to inculcate big ideas in production." The pigs and bacon industry would be reformed: "There is no room for two interests in this industry, namely the producers' and the curers' interests. The curers' interests must be acquired and curing will be done co-operatively by the producers."[105] In contrast to the dictatorship of Fianna Fáil's "state manager … dressed in the garb of Wolfe Tone," Fine Gael promised consultation rather than compulsion while "state interference with farmers and others – if at all necessary – should be reduced to a minimum."[106] There would be unabashed pursuit of the British market which was inextricably linked to the prosperity of Irish farmers. Although Hughes noted there was a very favourable trade in livestock to mainland Europe, "if these continental countries have not a long-term interest in our livestock then their trade is of little use and may in fact do harm because of its upsetting effect on the economy of British farms, where Irish stores are normally purchased."[107]

The post-election construction of government brought the selection of James Dillon and not James Hughes, who died in a car crash weeks before the election, as Minister for Agriculture.[108] Dillon, a member of Fine Gael until 1942 but, at that juncture, an independent, was joined in cabinet by an unlikely alliance of republicans, socialists, and small farmer representatives, as well as his old

---

[104] UCDA, Richard Mulcahy papers, P7/C/121, Mulcahy speech at Nenagh, 7 Dec. 1947.

[105] UCDA, Richard Mulcahy papers, P7/C/121, Hughes speech at Kilkenny, 7 Dec. 1947.

[106] UCDA, Richard Mulcahy papers, P7/C/122, Mulcahy speech at Charleville, 12 Jan. 1948.

[107] UCDA, Richard Mulcahy papers, P7/C/122, Hughes speech at Muinebeag, 21 Sept. 1947.

[108] According to Hoctor, Dillon's political career was marked by "independence and individualism" and "as an orator had few, if any, equals in his own generation … and when he took the floor in Washington or Rome delegates came rushing into the conference chamber to hear and applaud him." See Hoctor, *The department's story*, p. 204.

comrades from Fine Gael.[109] Beyond pursuit of the British market and Marshall Aid money, the inter-party government had no definite programme of government, rather "policy would follow power."[110] The union was due more to pragmatic politics than coherent policy and within its loose coalition the various elements applied their distinctive philosophies. With Clann na Talmhan and Clann na Poblachta intent on protecting the rights of small farmers, Fine Gael's large farmer ethos was never likely to be given free reign. The ensuing compromise brought an approach largely similar to the policies which Fianna Fáil had accepted as inevitable by the end of its period in office. There were attempts to embark on new initiatives but, in its ultimate expression, policy was defined by continuity not change. The fall-out from the trade discussions of November 1947 committed the Irish government to consult with the British on the number of cattle to be exported from Irish shores to continental Europe from 1 February 1948. The outgoing Minister for Agriculture, Paddy Smith, had argued that this consultation should be linked with the British proposal to reduce the price paid for fat cattle from 1 March. Smith considered that an early resolution to the issue was crucial as continental countries were pressing to purchase cattle and the Irish needed to know how many they could sell them so "trade talks can be arranged at an early date with such countries for the purpose of obtaining supplies of essential scarce supplies from them in return for cattle." Smith accepted that sales to the continent had been of great advantage to Ireland bringing better prices, providing a useful bargaining tool for talks with Britain and helping to secure imports. He was unconvinced that it would last, however, saying there was little doubt that, from the long-term point of view, the British market for cattle would "overshadow in importance all other markets, not only because of the very large British demand for meat but also because the finishing of our store cattle is an essential feature of the British agricultural economy."

Smith wrote that almost 60,000 cattle had been exported to Europe in the previous year and they should agree with Britain to reduce that number to 40,000, if a satisfactory price was paid for fat cattle.[111] The government refused the advice and sought, if possible, to avoid linkage of the two issues of sales to continental markets and price on the British market. If, however, linkage was unavoidable, the bottom-line for fat cattle exports to Europe should be 50,000 cattle.[112] A further contribution from the Department of Agriculture in February 1948 stressed the need to remove the differential between fat and store cattle for structural reasons, and that the issue was "more than a mere matter of hard bargaining between a supplier and purchaser. What is at stake is the whole future of Irish cattle production and the supply of store animals and beef to Great Britain."[113]

---

[109] The parties included in the cabinet were Fine Gael, with six seats at cabinet; the Labour party with two; the National Labour party with one; Clann na Poblachta with two; and Clann na Talmhan with one. The independent TDs who supported the government were represented in cabinet by James Dillon.

[110] Maurice Manning, *James Dillon: a biography* (1999), p. 225.

[111] NAI, D/T S14042 A, D/A memo to govt., 28 Jan. 1948.

[112] NAI, D/T S14042 A, D/T memo to D/A, 10 Feb. 1948.

[113] NAI, D/T S14042 A, D/T memo to govt., 17 Feb. 1948.

After negotiations between officials failed to bring agreement, an attempt to resolve the impasse came at a meeting between Irish and British ministers on 24 March. In a dispute over the purpose of the meeting, James Dillon described the British record of the discussions as the product of "the supercilious impudence of junior British civil servants."[114] Dillon claimed he saw the purpose of the meeting as Ireland fulfilling the requirement of consultation before it allocated to continental buyers. The British saw it as intended to discuss the question of differential payments – an interpretation supported by the subsequent agreed press communiqué. Whatever about context, the content was clear. Dillon told British ministers he was prepared to sell fat cattle to them at a lower price than to the continent and "we desired to do this: (1) because the British were old and valued customers, (2) because we believed they needed the meat, (3) because we foresaw that continental purchasers might not continue to purchase after their stocks had been replenished in four or five years." Dillon continued that in order to sell this long-term view to the Irish producer they needed to receive a guarantee that the discrimination in price between fat and store cattle would be ended.[115] No agreement was reached, except that, at the suggestion of the Irish, the cattle talks would now be absorbed into wider trade talks.

Britain's willingness to countenance new trade talks evidenced a change of policy in Whitehall which was related to the sterling crisis and loss of convertibility. The Treasury produced a draft report on the possibility of economic union between Ireland and Britain. It noted that in the November 1947 talks, Britain had preferred an ad hoc arrangement to de Valera's suggested "dovetailing of the two economies", but the subsequent emergence of the European Recovery Programme had committed Britain to a radical review of economic co-operation and "this may involve departures from pre-conceived ideas and prejudices which will need courage and disinterestedness." In terms of Ireland, it was "essential to work as far as possible within the framework of Western Union in order to minimise ancient suspicions and jealousies which would otherwise interfere with direct deals between Eire and UK." It was agreed that new planning should give Ireland a full opportunity to increase wealth but, for all the talk of transcending prejudice and economic suspicion, it was claimed:

> The 'natural' function of Eire appears to be to maximise her agricultural production, and in particular to exploit her natural advantages in the production of meat and dairy products (including bacon and eggs) rather than cereals ... Such a policy will mean an unwelcome reversal of the wheat production policy of Mr. De Valera, which was based not only on the idea of self-sufficiency, but also on the desirability of increasing the amount of labour needed on the land by putting an end to the system of great grazing ranches. [116]

---

[114] UCDA, Patrick McGilligan papers, P35b/32(10), Dillon to MacBride, 3 Apr. 1948; C.H. Spicer, Treasury to J.E. Fox, Office of High Commissioner, Ireland, 19 Apr. 1948; and Lord Rugby to MacBride, 29 Apr. 1948. See also, NAI, D/T S14042 B, minutes of meetings between Irish and British ministers, Mar.–May 1948.

[115] UCDA, Patrick McGilligan papers, P35b/32(10), Dillon to MacBride, 3 Apr. 1948.

[116] PRO, MAF 40/446, Treasury draft report on economic union with Eire, 25 Mar. 1948.

The Treasury outlined what it considered should be the British aims in the forthcoming talks. The need for Ireland to reduce its call on the gold and dollar reserves of the sterling area was to be backed by the assertion that it was imperative for Ireland to maximise its agricultural production through greater efficiency. It was agreed that for this to happen Ireland would require more fertilisers and seeds, but "we must be satisfied – and this is in doubt – that, taking everything into account, if supplies of these requisites were diverted from UK agriculture to Eire they would yield higher dividends than if utilised by our own farmers." It believed that the Irish government probably could not agree to economic integration due to political considerations but wondered whether, once talks commenced, the value of effectively pursuing this possibility and "quite frankly invite them, if they concur in the general thesis of closest integration with the United Kingdom, to suggest how best to utilise 'Western Union', as a cover for action which both governments agree would be in the common interest." Ultimately, though, the primary goal should be to reassert the importance of agriculture in the Irish economy and to do so "it might be necessary, in order to assist a swing away from industry to agriculture, to offer prices and contracts for agricultural products which would make agriculture more attractive than industry, and so enable it to draw itself labour and other reserves which would otherwise tend to flow into industry." At the same time, there was to be no question of price parity as "any increase in prices might discourage effort bearing in mind Eire's national characteristics."[117] This was a point reinforced by another British official who wrote:

> The easier money would be more likely to result in small farmers eating more and doing less ... The Irish are nearer to subsistence mentality than we are, and have yet to learn the attractions (or alleged attractions) of farming to make money for the purpose of buying things that the farm cannot produce. This means a fairly lengthy process of education. The Irish farmers – and more particularly their wives – have to acquire a taste for things than money will buy ... My short point is that higher prices will simply be a waste of money."[118]

If the doctrine of 'frugal comfort' had not been enough to get Fianna Fáil re-elected, its rhetoric had proved more persuasive in Whitehall.

Not that Irish ministers were doing much to sway British perceptions of Irish priorities. MacBride wrote to the Commonwealth Relations Office that trade talks should be delayed for one month to allow more preparatory work. He suggested that the only issue of urgency was the differential rate on cattle prices: "Frankly, unless your government is in a position to remove the differential against our cattle we will have to sell elsewhere."[119] His threat was somewhat undermined by Taoiseach John A. Costello's comments in the British press that although they

---

117 PRO, MAF, 40/446, Treasury memo on Eire, 10 Apr. 1948.

118 PRO, MAF 40/446, L.P. Thompson-McCausland to K. McGregor, Board of Trade, 24 May 1948.

119 UCDA, Patrick McGilligan papers, P35b/32(8); PRO, MAF 40/446, MacBride to CRO, 10 Apr. 1948.

could get higher prices on the continent, "from the long-term standpoint Britain will always be our best customer ... Obviously, we want to do the best we can for our own farming industry, but we know that we shall be better off in the long run by reaching agreement in London."[120] The British replied that price differential talks could only be linked to wider trade talks. The Ministry of Food supported the view that an interim arrangement on cattle prices should be agreed before full trade talks, but the Ministry of Agriculture noted: "This is typical M[inistry of]/F[ood] proposal – food now at any price, whether we are fatally compromised in the future or not."[121] The Ministry of Agriculture argued that they should not allow themselves to be blackmailed into granting extensive price concessions which would be "momentarily attractive" but, ultimately "completely unnecessary," as "the Eire representatives know full well that their only hope of a permanent market for cattle lies in the United Kingdom and provided that the prices are sufficient to make it profitable to rear cattle – and those prices need not be at the same level as UK prices – they will continue to produce cattle for export."[122] This truism underpinned the British negotiating position and although MacBride again threatened to sell elsewhere, both sides agreed to further talks.[123]

Meetings at official level on 4 and 5 May did not resolve the difficulties. Prior to the talks the British embassy in Dublin had suggested price concessions to the Irish as a long-term project to further the cattle trade with Ireland. Such a move would help Dillon out of his political difficulties and this was crucial as "he believes that the cattle trade is the backbone of Irish prosperity, and he is working for a reversion to the old order of things."[124] At the talks, though, there was no sign of concessions. British officials told Irish representatives that if Ireland sold 100,000 cattle to the continent it would do nothing to help the forthcoming trade talks and that, as there seemed no scope for getting the Irish to limit their exports to the region of 40,000 head, it was pointless to continue discussions. The Irish argued that, in terms of fertiliser supplies from Britain, they were being given "very little and very grudgingly." The Irish noted they had received applications from the continent for 107,000 head but "it might yet be possible to come to an arrangement if they could arrive at a figure somewhere between the 40,000 desired by the UK and the 90,000 which it seemed was the present commitment to continental countries."[125]

With officials unable to reach agreement, Lord Rugby was summoned to meet Costello and Dillon. Costello informed Rugby that they could not impose narrow restrictions on export trade in the hope of getting a satisfactory outcome from the London talks in June and, Rugby recalled,

---

[120] PRO, MAF 40/446, cutting from *News Chronicle*, 14 Apr. 1948.

[121] PRO, MAF 40/446, Ministry of Food to Cabinet Office, 13 Apr. 1948. The note from the Ministry of Agriculture was pencilled into the margin of the same document.

[122] PRO, MAF 40/446, Ministry of Agriculture memo., 21 Apr. 1948.

[123] NAI, D/T S14042, Rugby to MacBride, 17 Apr. 1948 and MacBride to Rugby, 22 Apr. 1948

[124] PRO, MAF 40/446, Rugby to CRO, 22 Apr. 1948.

[125] PRO, MAF 40/446, minutes of meetings between Irish and British officials, 4/5 May 1948.

he said there was no question of their holding a pistol at our heads. As a government they could not expose their cattle trade to the risk of getting the worst of both worlds. They would look foolish if they came back from London having turned away the continental buyers now knocking at their door, and being forced to accept a differential factor in the United Kingdom price.

Dillon rowed in with the promise that if he was given an "off-the-record indication" that the differential would go he would stand his ground and hold up continental cattle exports to the lowest possible limit.[126] No evidence exists of an off-the-record guarantee but, on 26 May 1948, Rugby informed London that Dillon had agreed to hold down cattle exports to the continent pending the June talks.[127]

Irish preparations for the talks saw the Department of Agriculture outline its ambitions as the right to permanent duty free entry for Irish agricultural produce, the continuation of preferences accorded under article 2 of the 1938 agreement, an undertaking by the British government not to regulate quantitatively imports of Irish agricultural produce, and the payment of prices which would "bear a reasonable relationship to the prices paid to British producers."[128] Further, the British should be pressed to abolish permanently the price differential between fat and store cattle, and not to increase the difference between the price of British and Irish cattle beyond 5s per live cwt. In return, the Irish would limit cattle exports to the continent to 50,000 head. Long-term contracts for sheep, pigs, mutton and pig meat might be discussed on the assumption that such will be available for export within a few years. The British should agree to supply specific quantities of fertilisers, machinery and other production requisites over a period of years. According to the department, the main object

> must be to conclude satisfactory long-term contracts, especially in the case of cattle. The Ministry of Food has a bad record in regard to the price fixed for Irish fat cattle and the result of its policy (which has in fact been dictated by the Ministry of Agriculture) has been to reduce cattle rearing in this country. Cattle production is the most important of all our industries and every effort must be made to put our export trade on a satisfactory basis.

Similarly, quantitative restrictions and poor prices for fresh meat had plagued the fresh meat trade and this would have to be rectified. A satisfactory long-term market for canned meat would also be useful, even though there were alternative markets on the continent for that particular product.[129] Tempering the

---

[126] PRO, MAF 40/446, Rugby to CRO, 20 May 1948.

[127] PRO, MAF 40/446, Rugby to CRO, 26 May 1948.

[128] The prices being paid for cattle in Britain at the time were: (a) UK-bred fat cattle: 18 ¾–19 ¼d per pound; (b) UK-fattened Irish stores: 17 ¾–18 ¼d per pound; and (c) imported Irish fat cattle: 17 ¼d per pound. See PRO, MAF 40/447, Ministry of Food memo, 10 Jun. 1948.

[129] UCDA, Patrick McGilligan papers, P35b/34(1), D/A memo to govt., 27 May 1948.

optimism of the Irish delegation, the Department of Finance was worried that Ireland would be unable to increase significantly its food production and, as a result, "we were asking a lot from the British but had little to offer in return."[130] It was prescient comment – the British were not impressed by the list of demands. The Ministry of Agriculture remarked that Ireland wanted parity of price for whatever quantity of goods it could send and "if these are the demands, there is not even the beginning of an attempt to obtain agreement."[131]

In the opening session of the June 1948 talks, the Taoiseach, John A. Costello, said they had come looking for a fair price, not a scarcity price, for their agricultural produce. He said they were prepared to sell to the British at a lower price than could be obtained on the continent but, in the absence of a long-term agreement, they would have no choice but to go abroad. The preference was for the "old and valued customer … The Taoiseach said that the Irish government was prepared 'to put all their eggs in the British basket', but they would 'watch that basket very carefully.'"[132] He said that the existing differential between store and fat cattle should be abolished, but stressed they did not expect the same prices as British-bred cattle, rather "that the prices for Irish fat cattle were pegged rigidly to the prices of British fat cattle." The Irish delegation further asked that no quantitative restrictions against Irish agricultural produce be imposed. In response, Chancellor of the Exchequer, Sir Stafford Cripps, said there were some products, such as potatoes, for which there would not be unlimited demand but others where Britain could take a large surplus. He said that Britain required all the fertiliser it could get for its own farmers, and noted "the problem of the cattle prices was a serious problem for Ireland but a matter of detail for the British government, and he would prefer if it were discussed by the British Minister of Food and the British Minister of Agriculture." He further asked whether Ireland could give a guarantee on the future volume of agricultural exports "so as to relate its expectations from Ireland to the British plan. It was minimal figures that Britain wanted – guaranteed minima."[133]

As the meetings continued, Britain agreed that prices per pound of top-grade Irish fat cattle would be equal to that paid for Irish stores, and that the price paid for Irish cattle would not fall beneath 5s of that paid for British cattle. Britain then introduced heads of agreement in agriculture which proposed the revival of cattle exports to pre-war levels, that a minimum of 75 per cent of these exports would be stores, that continental exports would be 50,000 in 1948 and not more than 10 per cent of total exported headage thereafter, that carcass meat would not exceed 200 tons per week or 3,000 to 4,000 tons per annum, that Britain would take up to 10,000 tons of canned meat in 1948 and 1949 but would prefer the meat

---

[130] Quoted in Ronan Fanning, *The Irish Department of Finance* 1922–58 (1978), p. 424.

[131] PRO, MAF 40/447, Ministry of Agriculture memo, 11 Jun. 1948.

[132] UCDA, Patrick McGilligan papers, P35b/37(2), notes by the secretary to the Irish delegation at the Anglo-Irish talks, 17 Jun. 1948. There is a complete record of both Irish and British minutes of meetings in NAI, D/T S14042 C.

[133] UCDA, Patrick McGilligan papers, P35b/37(2), notes by the secretary to the Irish delegation at the Anglo-Irish talks, 17 Jun. 1948.

in any other form, and that Britain would accept the present number of eggs and whatever more became available. It was further stated that Britain would take Irish butter, bacon and fat sheep or lambs at pre-war levels and beyond, with prices related to those earned by the British producer and "to be discussed further as soon as the possibility of exports arises." It was on these terms that agreement was eventually reached.[134]

In terms of price, the Irish effectively secured their objectives. Similarly, the goal of a four-year contract was achieved. Reaction in Ireland was mixed, but generally positive. Lemass derided the agreement as "unsatisfactory from every angle" and "a partial surrender of Irish economic freedom."[135] Inevitably, the *Irish Press* said the agreement was "an anti-climax" which confirmed acceptance of Ireland's position as "Britain's home farm."[136] By contrast, and equally predictably, the *Irish Independent* hailed it as a considerable achievement which should be "of great benefit."[137] The more detached *Irish Times* said that the agricultural provisions were a considerable achievement and that Dillon had "succeeded in everything that he set out to secure."[138] Dillon, himself, was voluble on the worth of the agreement, telling the Dáil that the country stood "on the threshold of the greatest period of expansion in the agricultural industry. Over the next five years we can increase the volume of output by 25 per cent and up to 100 per cent in the volume of exports."[139] In a letter to Cripps, John A. Costello pronounced himself "pleased with the manner in which the Agreement has been received here. It is generally recognised as a valuable contribution to better trading relations between our two countries, to the benefit of both, and it is seen in its proper setting in relation to the economic recovery of Europe."[140]

The sense remains that, in securing their contractual and price targets, the Irish were pushing an open door. Unlimited access for produce was almost guaranteed given post-war scarcity. Equally, the decision not to push for scarcity prices, and not even for parity of price, ensured the ready acceptance of British negotiators. In return, Ireland received the vaguest of assurances rather than a quantitative commitment on the provision of fertilisers and farm machinery, viewed by the Food and Agriculture Organisation (FAO) as so critical to Irish

---

[134] UCDA, Patrick McGilligan papers, P35b/37(4), notes by the secretary to the Irish delegation at the Anglo-Irish talks, 20 Jun. 1948.

[135] *Irish Independent*, 29 Jun. 1948.

[136] *Irish Press*, 23 and 24 Jun. 1948.

[137] *Irish Independent*, 23 Jun. 1948.

[138] *Irish Times*, 22 Jun. 1948.

[139] Manning, *Dillon*, p. 237. He also told the house: "If I never achieve anything else in public life the comparatively trivial part I played in negotiating this agreement is quite sufficient to justify the fifteen years I spent pottering around this House. There is no job I would prefer in this wide world than to be Minister for Agriculture in this country ... This agreement provides for the farmers of this country a sure and certain market at remunerative prices for every conceivable product that the land of Ireland can produce." Manning conceded, though, that "the results were hardly earth-shattering in their consequences." *Ibid.*, pp 237–8.

[140] PRO, DO 35/40002, Costello to Cripps, 15 Jul. 1948.

agricultural progress.[141] The promise of unlimited access lost its allure without the means to increase production. Ultimately, the agreement committed Ireland to develop its agricultural economy in line with British needs, to such an extent that the entire economy revolved around the export of one commodity – cattle. More than that, the 1948 agreement defined the precise nature of that export. The acceptance of a limit of 10 per cent on export of cattle to non-British markets and, particularly, the agreement to transport a minimum of 75 per cent of cattle exports as stores, set the parameters for agricultural development over the following decade. A British official commented:

> The Eire ministers went away with practically everything they wanted … Our advantages, on the other hand, are all in the future and thus, to some extent, remain to be seen, i.e. increased food supplies from Eire, and an improvement (which is so necessary to us) in the Eire balance of payments not only with the UK but with the world generally. Nevertheless, there can be no question that the general lines of the arrangements made were wise from our point of view, and that we stand to gain greatly from them if the Eire ministers live up to their promises, as there is every reason to believe that they intend to do.[142]

V

Marshall Aid and agriculture

Ireland also looked beyond Britain as it strove to find a place in the new world order. The past could not be entirely forgotten, though, and admission to the United Nations was refused in 1946. In that same year, however, Ireland had been admitted to the FAO which compiled a number of reports on the most profitable policy paths at the disposal of the Irish. Indeed, certain Irish ministers embraced re-entry to the world stage with exuberance. Minister for Agriculture James Dillon's grandiose strut and his talent for hubris saw him take centre stage at a variety of international gatherings. Speaking in Washington in 1948, Dillon proposed the economic union of Great Britain, the US, Australia, Canada and Ireland – later to be opened to other European countries – saying that the free passage of money and goods "between these nations was essential for the preservation of democracy."[143] Disappointingly, before other nations could

---

[141] NAI, D/T S15062 A, *Ireland: programme and progress report*, FAO, 1948. The FAO was established by the United Nations in Rome in 1945 to work out a programme for achieving adequate world distribution of food.

[142] PRO, DO 35/4000, Eric Machtig, CRO to Rugby, 28 Jun. 1948.

[143] *Irish Times*, 16 Nov. 1948.

respond to the generosity of the Gael in deigning to consider them worthy of cohabitation, the Taoiseach moved to state that Dillon was not outlining government policy.[144]

With Dillon's proposal in abeyance, attempts to restore economic prosperity centred on European Recovery Programme (ERP), or Marshall Plan. Appalling weather, and persistent food and fuel shortages had reversed immediate post-war gains to such an extent that the imminent collapse of European states seemed a distinct possibility. In this context the US moved to counteract political, economic and social instability which threatened to undermine trade between the two regions and leave Europe open to communist insurgency.[145] Irish neutrality through World War II had raised questions over its inclusion, but incorporation was determined by its potential as a source of food for Europe and its membership of the sterling area pool. Despite Department of Finance objections, Ireland accepted an invitation to participate in ERP and attended a Committee of European Economic Co-operation (CEEC) meeting in Paris in July 1947 designed to draw up a programme covering the needs and resources of Europe for the following four years. Ireland contributed to the report which outlined European needs in the post-war era and was a founding member of Organisation for European Economic Co-operation (OEEC), which allocated Marshall aid funding in conjunction with the US Economic Co-operation Administration (ECA).

Initially, Ireland looked for a grant of $25.7 million for the first quarter of the ERP programme and the government, particularly Seán MacBride, who had championed the cause as Minister for External Affairs, were somewhat shocked when merely offered a loan of $10 million. On 11 June 1948 the government decided to refuse the loan but, following consultations with the British government during the Anglo-Irish talks in London, changed its mind and decided to accept.[146] By the end of the year, it had accepted $60 million in loans, while simultaneously campaigning for more money in the form of grants in Washington. Having secured the money, the government then had to decide what to do with it. No more than in Britain, the tendency to view Ireland as primarily a food-exporting country prevailed amongst Americans and Europeans.[147] In its study on Ireland, the US State Department concluded:

> Ireland's principal problem is the restoration of agricultural production, and Ireland's main contribution to the European

---

[144] *Dáil Debates*, vol. 113. No. 2, 24 Nov. 1948. Whatever about other parties, the *Irish Times* offered enthusiastic support for Dillon's "imaginative and constructive suggestion." Noting that Dillon appeared to be modelling himself on Churchill, the paper did frown on his inclination "to become intoxicated by the exuberance of his own verbosity." See *Irish Times*, 17 Nov. 1948. Dillon's colleagues in government were not always taken by his grandiloquent oratorical flourishes. The deputy leader of Clann na Poblachta, Con Lehane, suggested to Dillon in the Dáil in 1948 "that a little less volatility and a little less flamboyance might serve him better in the conduct of his Department." Quoted in Kevin Rafter, *The Clann: the story of Clann na Poblachta* (1996), p. 120.

[145] Bernadette Whelan, 'Ireland and the Marshall Plan," in *IESH*, vol. xix (1992), pp 49–70.

[146] *Ibid.*, pp 51, 56, 60; UCDA, Seán McEntee papers, P67/593, note, Jun. 1948.

[147] Meenan, 'Agricultural policies', p. 49.

recovery will take place through the production of more food for export ... To expand its exports of agricultural products, Ireland needs to mechanise its agriculture, obtain more fertilisers and animal stuffs, increase its imports of fuel and overhaul its transportation system.[148]

Fulfilling an essential requirement of involvement in the ERP, the government produced *The European Recovery Programme – Ireland's Long Term Programme (1949–1953)*. Masquerading as a dynamic programme of development, it was less than a coherent vision for the Irish economy and far more a product of MacBride's haste to get US aid. T.K. Whitaker, one of MacBride's leading officials in the ERP campaign and later secretary of the Department of Finance, commented that it "was never conceived of as a programme for policy. It was conceived as something to satisfy the Americans so we could get Marshall aid. It did not have, as far as I can remember any commitment of the government to do any of the things."[149] This is largely true in literal terms but the programme did confirm the view of agriculture as almost the sole means for Irish economic expansion. MacBride accepted as much, telling OEEC members: "Our principal contribution to European recovery is to be made in the field of agriculture."[150] The programme envisaged a four-year increase in the value of agricultural output of 22 per cent over 1947, and assumed an increase in the volume of agricultural production of more than 100 per cent over the same period.

How these goals might be achieved was not documented beyond the traditional bland generalities of land reclamation, increased use of fertilisers, reforestation and mechanisation.[151] There was no definite plan of action and this, MacBride acknowledged at the time, had restricted Irish chances of receiving grants in lieu of loans: "Perhaps the chief argument in favour of a grant has not yet been advanced, namely, a sound constructive programme for its use."[152] Throughout the process, MacBride had sought meetings with the British government to ensure a common approach to ERP.[153] The British were thoroughly unconvinced by Irish ambitions saying that increases in output on the scale envisaged by Ireland were "a task of the greatest magnitude. It must be doubtful whether increased supplies of fertilisers and feeding stuffs can and will in fact be effectively utilised by an agricultural community which, to the lay mind at least, appears distinctly backward." More importantly, though, was the programme's context rather than its content:

[148] Cited in John McCarthy, 'Ireland's turnaround', in John McCarthy (ed.), *Planning Ireland's future* (1990), p. 18.

[149] *Ibid.*, p. 20.

[150] Historical Archives of the European Community, Directorates, OEEC 405 8/2, MacBride to OEEC, 13 Jul. 1950.

[151] *The European Recovery Programme – Ireland's Long Term Programme 1949–1953* (1948).

[152] UCDA, Patrick McGilligan papers, P35c/2, D/EA memo to govt., 16 Dec. 1948.

[153] See PRO, MAF 40/446, Rugby to CRO, 30 Mar. 1948: "Mr. MacBride said he felt that the approach to the Marshall Plan should be fully agreed as between the UK and Eire so that we did not find ourselves at cross-purposes in pursuing interests which are obviously common."

It is refreshing to find that the programme is firm in recognising that agriculture is the key Eire industry and that the country stands or falls on its success or failure in rehabilitating it. The programme also flatly recognises that the United Kingdom is and must remain virtually the sole market for Eire agricultural produce ... The Eire government deserve good marks for their realistic attitude; it may not be an easy one for them to maintain; we should do nothing to discourage them.[154]

There remained concern over the precise nature of that agricultural progression, however, and British officials sought to pressurise Ireland to focus on the production of cattle and sheep rather than on pigs and poultry. It was agreed that they would do so by asking Ireland to cut their dollar deficit, thus necessitating a drop in the purchase of imported feed, rather than through outright assertion: "By this means we should try to drive the pattern of Irish agriculture into the lines we wanted." Noting that the Irish seemed likely to revert to "traditional methods of feeding imported maize 'out of the bag', a system which has been largely replaced in progressive countries," the officials recognised that "pigs and poultry are very suitable for a peasant economy," but "Eire is seeking to tread the primrose path towards agricultural prosperity by the simple process of securing more than her due share of the world's supplies of coarse grains."[155] With typical sensitivity, the Treasury outlined the bind in which the Irish found themselves as they sought the most propitious way to use ERP money. Treasury officials argued that beyond the actual Irish proposal there was no

> alternative which would be either economically or politically acceptable. It would be politically inexpedient, for example, to argue that Irish peasants, instead of rearing pigs and hens, should emigrate to work in British factories under the pressure of poverty at home; or even that the government of Eire should abandon a small-holding policy which ranks second only to religion in the hearts of the people. No-one seriously suggests such a development of secondary industries in Eire as would absorb more than a few of the peasant population. And, if they did, we should immediately argue that it would be uneconomical to supply them with imported raw materials. There is left, therefore, the alternative employment of raising cattle and sheep.[156]

The ramshackle nature of the Irish approach to seeking alternatives to cattle farming was borne out by a note passed by Dillon to Costello at a cabinet meeting in February 1949.[157] Responding to queries on the efficacy of maize importation, Dillon confided:

---

154 PRO, MAF/40/190, Rugby to CRO, Nov. 1940.

155 PRO, MAF/40/190, minutes of meeting of cabinet European economic co-operation committee working groups on long-term programmes, 11 Feb. 1949.

156 PRO, MAF/40/190, Treasury memo, 10 Feb. 1949.

157 PRO, MAF/40/191, minutes of meeting of British and Irish officials, 10 May 1949.

Requests for ECA authorisations for 50,000 tons maize and 40,000 N[or]th. D[a]k[ota] Spring Wheat (USA) were put forward by Dept. of Ag., not on market considerations primarily, rather in disregard of them, but in consideration of necessity to utilise ECA dollars before end of ERP year, ie 31/3/49. All market indicators suggest that wheat and coarse grain prices will decline during the next six months.[158]

This necessity to dispose of dollars in such an uneconomic manner was caused, in part, by the obstructionism of the Department of Finance which had plagued Irish involvement in the Marshall Plan from the beginning.[159] When MacBride suggested that the bulk of the money should be used for land reclamation, reforestation, land fertilisation, and agricultural training and education, Department of Finance objections heightened. The departmental secretary, J.J. McElligott, wrote to his minister, Patrick McGilligan, saying they should not commit to such an ambitious programme: "It is no business of the Americans what we do with the loan counterpart funds and they should be told that distinctly. It is generally recognised now that one of the advantages of being a loan country is that you are subject to less 'snooping' by the Americans."[160]

Similarly the Department of Finance objected to Dillon's proposal that land reclamation should be paid for by a fund at his disposal drawn directly from ERP money. Acceptance of such a proposal, wrote McElligott, would be "the negation, and I think the end, of a very limited degree of financial control which this department at present exercises."[161] Finance continued to disapprove of the ERP proposals: "Practically all of these projects are non-productive in a short-term and cannot be prosecuted on any material scale without adding to the inflationary tendencies already strongly evident in our economy. Mr. Dillon's new estimate of £1 million discussed yesterday in the Dáil is a striking example of this."[162] It was almost as if the mandarins' scepticism implied their inviolable right to hold the purse of power was the most critical issue at hand, even if it required refusing American aid. Nonetheless, a substantial portion of Irish funds were invested in land reclamation and drainage, along with smaller amounts in fertiliser purchases, reforestation and maize. Richard Mulcahy, the leader of the largest government party, Fine Gael, announced in February 1950:

We have always accepted the supremacy of agriculture in the nation's economy. Emphasis has been given to this by the government's decision to do what no other government in Europe has undertaken, namely to invest almost the whole of the funds available as a result of Marshall Aid in the rehabilitation of the land of the country.[163]

---

[158] NAI, D/T S14206, Dillon note, 8 Feb. 1949.

[159] Whelan, 'Marshall Plan', pp 52–3.

[160] UCDA, Patrick McGilligan papers, P35c/2, McElligott to McGilligan, 17 Dec. 1948.

[161] UCDA, Patrick McGilligan papers, P35c/4, McElligott to McGilligan, 13 Apr. 1949.

[162] UCDA, Patrick McGilligan papers, P35c/7, McElligott to McGilligan, 7 Jul. 1949.

As the rest of Europe strove to create prosperity, the likelihood of the Irish joining them rested on the success of the land rehabilitation scheme.[164]

VI

Impact of inter-party government policy

The use of ERP money to rehabilitate the land was a logical extension of the 1948 trade agreement which had focussed so much attention on a thriving cattle industry. The key elements of domestic agricultural policy were directed towards improving Irish grasslands. G.A. Holmes, a New Zealand grasslands expert, was employed to prepare a report outlining a programme for substantial improvements of the country's pastures. In his report, Holmes seemed stunned, almost overwhelmed, by the scale of the problems. Ultimately, his patent humanity prevented him from entirely excoriating the ineptitude he encountered and led him to temper his criticism with reference to the enormous potential for development. Nonetheless, Holmes's transparent disbelief that any country's principal industry should be in such a state of neglect underpins all that he wrote. Overworked to the point of cliché, his remark that he saw "hundreds of fields which are growing just as little as is physically possible for the land to grow under an Irish sky," remains the most apt commentary on the failings of Irish agriculture. Putting this travesty in context, he wrote: "there is no area of comparable size in the northern hemisphere which has such marvellous potentialities for pasture production as Eire undoubtedly has," and that Ireland had "ideal natural conditions ... for raising and fattening livestock."[165] The report stressed that, for optimum development of the Irish agricultural economy there would have to be a

---

[163] UCDA, Richard Mulcahy papers, P7/C/123, Mulcahy speech to Fine Gael Ard Fheis, 14 Feb. 1950. Seeking refuge in the inherited politics of spite and spleen, Fianna Fáil took a more jaundiced view of the entire initiative, as evidenced by a 1952 Seán MacEntee speech in Limerick: "The coalition plan ... was to throw Irish agriculture back to 1931 and to have more bullocks, but fewer men, on the land ... This was one of the reasons why American dollars were sought. It fitted in with the policy of Great Britain and it gladdened Mr. Dillon's heart. With American dollars to fling around like pennies, he could buy foreign wheat and sugar and coal ... With American dollars he could eradicate Fianna Fáil wheat and Fianna Fáil beet, he could kill tillage and drive the farmers into beef ... It is not good for a small state to be in the pocket of a great one." See UCDA, Seán MacEntee papers, P67/593, MacEntee speech in Limerick, 1952.

[164] In contrast, Norway, for example, launched an export-based industrialisation drive, which the country's farm spokesmen worried would reduce the importance of the traditional basic industries of farming, fishing and forestry, and turn Norwegians into a "poverty-stricken people, and our country merely into an object in the economic struggles between the great powers of the world beyond." See Helge Pharo, 'Norway, the United States and the Marshall Plan, 1947–52,' in Richard Griffiths (ed.), *Explorations in OEEC history* (1997), pp 73–85, esp. pp 74–5.

[165] UCDA, Richard Mulcahy papers, P7/C/106, Holmes to D/A, covering letter with report, 19 Sept. 1948.

thorough reassessment of policy. As well as direct schemes for land and livestock development, the government would have to create an overall framework of integrated policies incorporating market, education, transport, price policy and co-operative development. More specifically, he outlined initiatives to improve pasture involving drainage, soil analysis, seed policy, and fertiliser application.

Between 1840 and 1940 there had been three significant programmes of arterial drainage amounting to 450,000 acres but much of the work was allowed fall back into chronic disrepair for lack of maintenance.[166] More recent drainage schemes were criticised by Holmes, who noted that the scheme to drain the River Barrow had begun in the middle when it was imperative to start at the mouth. This had produced serious flooding on the lower reaches and even those farmers who should have benefited had taken no steps to profit through cultivation, re-grassing or manuring.[167] The drainage commission report of 1941 had led the government to adopt, in principle, recommendations for a central drainage authority, a comprehensive review of arterial drainage, and the preparation of an arterial drainage bill.[168] When this bill passed into law in 1945 it was estimated that the programme would take 30 years to complete at an annual expenditure of £250,000 per annum.[169] The failure to commit adequate resources, as well as the traditional clientism of Irish politics, brought an unseemly regional scramble to secure a position of priority. Unfortunately, as Paddy Smith explained, "Everybody cannot be first."[170] Responding to suggestions by Holmes, the government used Marshall Aid money to fund field drainage, watercourse construction and improvement, improved fencing, hill land reclamation, and the removal of scrub and boulders though extensive grants and loans. The Land Project was designed to ensure that, while arterial drainage was in progress, farmers could begin the work of reclaiming their own land. Operating initially in eight counties in 1949, the project was extended to the whole country in June 1950. The state would pay two-thirds of reclamation costs, subject to a maximum of £20 per acre. If the farmer did not do the work himself, he could employ the newly-established Land Project Organisation to do it for him, with the state paying two-fifths of the cost, up to a maximum of £12 per acre. The *Irish Independent* reported Joseph Carrigan, the head of the ECA mission in Ireland, telling a Boston press conference that, within ten years, huge areas of Ireland's "swamplands" would be reclaimed.[171]

Reclamation, though, would be pointless in itself. The soil had been "mined of its fertility" through years of inadequate fertiliser application. Holmes commented that "in any attempt to estimate the fertiliser requirements of Irish grasslands, one is dumbfounded by the magnitude of the problem."[172] The

---

[166] Richard Bruton and Frank J. Convery, *Land drainage policy in Ireland* (1982), p. 6.

[167] *Holmes report*, p. 12.

[168] NAI, D/T S11198 A, cabinet minutes, 17 Jun. 1941.

[169] NAI, D/T S11198 A, D/F memo to govt., 27 Jun. 1941.

[170] UCDA, Donnchadh Ó Briain papers, P83/116 (16), Smith to Dr James O'Brien, Newcastle West (n.d.).

[171] *Irish Independent*, 2 Sept. 1949.

[172] *Holmes report*, p. 24.

government embarked on a fertiliser scheme which enabled farmers to have land tested and to receive fertilisers with a 10 per cent cash payment, the remainder to be paid on a long-term loan. As with the *Reports of the commission of inquiry on post-emergency agricultural policy*, the Holmes report stressed the absolute importance of vastly increased fertiliser use, yet the difficulties in negotiating the import of more than a paltry supply of fertilisers undermined that desire. The stuttering attempts to establish an Irish fertiliser industry continued and the government even considered a scheme which would have refined urban sewage for use as farm fertiliser.[173] It remained a singular commentary on the prevailing attitude that in a country with serious lime deficiencies across its provinces, the kilns of bygone eras lay idle or overgrown. Nonetheless, there was a reticence to import at world prices large quantities of fertilisers, even when such became available, in the fear that this would annihilate such vestiges of the native industry as did remain.

Further, in the absence of a soil survey, it remained unclear what the exact nature of fertiliser demands were. What was clear was that fertiliser application alone would take so long to rejuvenate the countryside that it would prove entirely uneconomical. Indeed, Holmes estimated that "about two-thirds of the land under grass is so lacking in species worth manuring as to make the regeneration by this means alone much too slow."[174] He recommended an extensive programme of ploughing and reseeding, yet many farms did not have the necessary heavy implements to satisfactorily complete that work. There was also some doubt over the quality of the seeds and fertilisers at the farmers' disposal. Despite legislation introduced in 1906, there was almost no analysis of the products sold by merchants ensuring they could, with comparatively little risk, dispose of inferior or adulterated wares. A Department of Agriculture scheme to right this problem was held in abeyance, although it did occasionally resurface on the cabinet agenda.[175] The requirements seemed endless:

> Well-drained land, sufficient lime, ample fertiliser and good-strain seed would produce good pastures everywhere in Eire, but unless management and utilisation are properly carried out the results will prove disappointing. The more obvious faults at present are that unfertilised pastures are being over-grazed, particularly in early spring; that too high a proportion of land is being saved for hay, but that the yields of hay are far too low so that stock must be turned out much too early, continuing the cycle of overgrazing. Also the stock are turned out in very low condition, having existed through the winter off their 'kidney fat' and therefore try to make up their loss in weight by close and continuous grazing of whatever fields they are on.

Silage, then "quite a novelty in Ireland," was seen as the "master key" to right the problems of winter feed, and propaganda to advance its use was yet another

---

[173] NAI, D/T S11898 B, D/LG memo to govt., 9 Jan. 1950.

[174] *Holmes report*, p. 50.

[175] NAI, D/T S13684 A, D/A memo to govt., 13 Jun. 1948 and cabinet minutes, 21 Dec. 1954.

imperative.[176] Holmes stressed it was impossible to lay down a programme for pasture *per se*, but it required integration with increased tillage (at least as fodder supplement), better breeding policy and the eradication of animal diseases. He concluded "there is no magician's wand which can be waved over the poor pastures to transform them into first class grazings. There is no royal road to an all-round state of higher farming."[177]

The belief in magic wands, though, was crucial in a country starved of investment and reliant on isolated individual schemes to transform society. The nature of politics ensures that those in power must maintain at least the illusion of access to preternatural power. Accordingly, the Land Project was heralded as the salvation of Irish farming and, in the rush to acclaim its healing powers, the other requirements of pasture improvement which did not fall within its ambit were somewhat marginalised. Although the Land Project has been described as "spectacularly successful," this would appear to represent something of an overstatement.[178] Immediate interest was certainly high amongst the farming community with 28,000 farmers involved by 1951 and the average reclamation rate was four acres per farm. Its long-term operation was the subject of much criticism, however. There was a shortage of suitably skilled engineers and tradesmen, and difficulties in securing the necessary equipment. To this end, it was later complained that the project "was not based on research, and modern scientific methods of drainage layout were ignored."[179] Failure to establish the mooted national drainage board compounded problems in co-ordinating the work of the many departments engaged in the project.[180] Although the Office of Public Works (OPW), the Department of Agriculture, the Land Commission and the Department of Local Government were all involved in drainage, co-ordination was minimal, even undesired: "As far as the Land Commission are concerned, closer co-ordination with other departments would not result in greater efficiency and would cause inevitable delays and additional expenditure."[181]

The expense of the project also provoked great criticism. Over two decades, the Land Project received 18 per cent of state capital spending on agriculture. The Department of Finance opposed the enterprise from the beginning and one of its survey teams would later contend that 37 per cent of the schemes did not cover their costs, and 14 per cent would not have been worthwhile, even if farmers had exploited their lands to the full. It was even claimed "the cost of the drainage exceeded the improved market value of the land. Indeed, in many cases, exceeded the full post-drainage value of these lands."[182] Finance posited that the project became "a social service," and even that was in doubt as large farmers benefited

---

[176] *Holmes report*, pp 57, 61.

[177] UCDA, Richard Mulcahy papers, P7/C/106, Holmes to Dillon, 17 Sept. 1948.

[178] Manning, *Dillon*, p. 250.

[179] James Dooge, of the Electricity Supply Board (ESB), speaking at a land drainage symposium in University College, Cork. See *IFJ*, 15 Mar. 1958.

[180] NAI, D/T S11198 D, OPW report, 10 Sept. 1951. *Holmes Report*, pp 15–16.

[181] NAI, D/T S11198 D, Land Commission note to D/T, 11 Jul. 1951.

[182] Bruton and Convery, *Land drainage*, pp 19, 63, 41.

disproportionately to small ones. And, significantly, "with regard being had to the desirability of absorbing workers in agriculture," the project was intended from the outset "to provide alternative employment for workers disemployed as a result of the discontinuance of the production of hand-won turf."[183] With the exception of the Land Project, few large-scale programmes emerged. It would be many years before most of the requirements of improved grasslands were put into place, even if the Holmes report marked an important step on the path to recovery. The government did not commit the resources and the farmers would not commit themselves to schemes when they remained unconvinced there would be an economic sale to justify increased inputs. Holmes, himself, had argued that even the achievement of a 100 per cent increase in productivity was only justified if the expenditure required to do this was in proportion to the returns.[184] Extensive experience had taught both state and farmer that the market was a fickle suitor.

Indeed, even allowing for the immediate implementation of all the above proposals and the certainty of profitable sale, there were some lands which were beyond use for agricultural purposes and could be more effectively used for forestry. One of the key electoral platforms of Clann na Poblachta, and a pet project of its leader, Seán MacBride, was a greatly expanded reforestation programme. Attempts to expand forestation through the avowed departmental policy of "peaceful penetration" had largely failed as "in this country land has a value, meaning and significance that it has not elsewhere. The ownership of land for immediate economic gain is the primary aim of the majority of our people. The small farmers and graziers have little or no affection for the cultivation of trees for their timber value." From 1948 the forestry division of the Department of Lands began to mechanise through the purchase of three tractors and a bulldozer, but tree-planting had been retarded by the lack of rabbit netting. More importantly, the lack of a land survey meant that analysis of soil suitability for forestry was "mainly guesswork." Forestry received a definite impetus from MacBride's sponsorship. Finnish and Canadian experts were invited to advise operations, mechanisation was accelerated through the purchase of ten further tractors, rotavators and compressors, and the forestry division's inspectorate completed a rough survey. Planting gathered pace but the traditional reluctance of farmers to agree to "the surrender" of even the poorest of land retarded progress.[185]

A 1951 FAO report on forestry remarked that there was no overall definition of forestry policy and recommended that one be devised comprising two categories: a commercial programme and a social one. It noted that the existing forestation programme "is not endorsed to an equal degree in all government departments. If the programme is to succeed, a general acceptance in all government circles is obviously the first requirement." The report pointed out that

---

183 NAI, F 88/10/48, D/T to D/F, 23 Mar. 1948 and D/F to D/T, 8 Apr. 1948.

184 *Holmes Report*, p. 61.

185 NAI, D/T S15066, D/L memo to govt., 15 Jan. 1949.

large forestation programmes required stability of funding which had not been the case in Ireland. Also, to overcome "innate conservatism, suspicion and hostility," the programme would have to be sold to the public and "general experience is that this is where the forestry authorities proper fall down."[186] The report concluded that only a separate department could establish forestry to a position of strength. The Department of Finance attacked the report as being too long-term in its goals which "are almost all in the distant future" and did not satisfy any short-term needs.[187] The Department of Lands did not believe a separate department was warranted and after consideration by a cabinet sub-committee the only action taken was to publish the report.[188]

Cattle were not fed on timber, however, and even had government action on forestry been forthcoming, convincing farmers to recant their monotheistic idolatry of the bullock was inconceivable. With every encouragement – at least verbal – from the government, farmers attempted to recapture the British market. Although export figures never reached the levels predicted, increased numbers of cattle were sent to Britain as stores and these exports were the primary reason for the rise in the volume of agricultural exports during the years of inter-party government (see appendix). Beyond the improvement in the cattle trade, there were few positive developments in Irish agriculture. Overall output increased, as did the volume of exports, but progress was marginal. In a review of the 1948 trade agreement in November 1950, British officials noted that expectations of supplies from Ireland had been unfulfilled virtually across the board.[189] The fact that no definite quantitative assurances on export levels had been provided prevented exact specification of the Irish inability to respond to market access allowed by the agreement, but there was no doubting that failure. It was no consolation that the British, in return, were struggling to fulfil their coal commitments.[190] Rarely, in these years did the Irish seem likely to expand production on a large scale. Dillon's awareness of the precarious standing of attempts to redefine the nature of Irish agricultural production clearly demonstrates the scale of the problem. One British official recorded:

> My talk with Dillon was wholly one-sided. It consisted almost entirely of a remonstrance by Dillon, in histrionic terms, against my hint or suggestion that some limits might have to be set on the expansion of Irish agricultural production in the longer term ... and [he] said that any suggestion of doubt would 'drive the Irish back at once to subsistence farming.'[191]

Yet, many Irish farmers had still to emerge from the culture of subsistence farming.

---

[186] NAI, D/T S11555 C, FAO *Report on forestry mission to Ireland* (1951). The report cited Department of Finance obstructionism as a limiting factor.

[187] NAI, D/T S11555 C, D/F memo to govt., 3 Dec. 1951.

[188] NAI, D/T S11555 C, recommendations of cabinet sub-committee on forestry, 15 Nov. 1951.

[189] PRO, DO 35/4003, CRO memo, 8 Nov. 1950.

[190] PRO, PREM 8/1465, minutes of meeting between MacBride and British Prime Minister, 24 Jan. 1951.

[191] PRO, DO 35/4004, Frank Lee, Ministry of Food to Sir Percivale Liesching, CRO, 30 May 1949.

Amongst the poorer farmers of the west, poultry and pigs had often seemed the most likely route to a better livelihood. The poultry industry prospered for a time under the stimulus of agreement with Britain, and the number of birds increased from 17.4 million in 1947 to 22.1 million in 1949. Despite price assurances given to producers, the bottom fell from the market and as prices collapsed so did the size of the Irish poultry flock. By 1962, there were fewer than 12 million poultry in Ireland.[192] Low prices and high subsidies in Britain, and the high price of feed in Ireland were the immediate problem. In the long run, though, the inability of the Irish smallholder to compete with the application of modernising techniques by large-scale operations in Britain, Europe and America, completely undermined the trade. The Irish had admitted as much to their British counterparts in 1949 when they lamented their inability to increase egg production in the winter months regardless of the price on offer as "the innate conservatism of the Irish farmer made any change from one type of production to another extremely difficult, whatever the incentive."[193] Exports fell away and the poultry industry never threatened to confirm the potential for expansion which had appeared so vast in the immediate post-war years. In the wake of decontrol in Britain, the government decided to abandon any attempt to centrally regulate prices. It accepted a Department of Agriculture proposal that exporters should pay a price for eggs in accordance with their market price. The motivation behind the move was to "remove the odium at present incurred by the Minister in announcing lower prices for eggs and poultry, and transfer the matter from the political into the private commercial sphere."[194] The export trade in poultry and eggs was still worth £7.5 million in 1952, but within a decade had fallen to less than £600,000.[195] By then, newspapers were referring to "Ireland's lost industry" and Dillon's confident assertion that they would 'drown Britain in eggs' was one more empty political slogan echoing across the landscape.[196]

The pigs and bacon industry fared little better. In the wake of the 1948 trade agreement, a further arrangement allowed the Irish receive equality with Danish bacon in the British market. Although Ireland produced a bacon surplus in 1949 and 1950, the general import price into Britain proved unprofitable and exports ceased in the summer of 1950. A new agreement in mid-1951 allowed for the

---

192 Crotty, *Agricultural production*, p. 170.

193 NAI, D/T S13347 B, minutes of meeting between Dillon and John Strachey, British Ministry of Food, 4 Feb. 1949.

194 A Donegal letter writer made his feelings on the loss of the poultry trade very clear: "Why don't yous do what the British government is doing – give all turkey rearers a bonus. No yous wouldn't do that. Yous would rather give it to those big officials, schoolmasters and doctors and so on that is doing very little for it. Yous are acting as bad as old Lord Lietrem done in olden times with the poor people ... Only for America and England and so on, we poor people would die of hunger. Well now we must say goodbye to rearing turkeys and its time we done it." See NAI, D/T S13347 C, letter writer to D/T, Dec. 1960.

195 Hoctor, *The department's story*, p. 231. The *Irish Farmers' Journal* later recalled wistfully in an editorial on 9 February 1957 how the industry once held such promise: "In the days of his ebullience, Mr. Dillon promised to drown the English in eggs. The threatened victims have reacted violently. They quickly sank our pitiful efforts by heavy home production. Now they do not merely promise; they are on the verge of drowning us with eggs, and poultry too, for good measure."

196 *Irish Press*, 24 Jun. 1948. *IFJ*, 13 Jun. 1959.

export to Britain of live pigs at a price closely tied to the British price for their home-produced pigs. Under the agreement, live exports had to be accompanied by exports of bacon at the original import price, but the Irish aspiration was that an average between live pig and bacon prices would prove economic for pig producers. No exports were forthcoming, however, and in March 1952 the Department of Agriculture reflected that it was "not possible to say when exports under the agreement might commence but it could be quite soon."[197] It was the porcine *Waiting for Godot*.

By contrast, there had been improvements in dairying which appeared ready to emerge from its extended slumber.[198] Nonetheless, Dillon believed that Fianna Fáil policies had created the initial problems – "the generally insane agricultural policy obtaining for some years was the real cause of the ruin of the dairying industry" – and that its attempt to revive the industry had been fundamentally flawed. [199] He agreed that the sector had shown marked signs of improvement under the guaranteed prices offered since 1947, but those improvements had been at a prohibitive cost, however, as subsidies had increased from £1,950,000 in 1947/48 to an expected £2,600,000 in 1949/50. Dillon noted that butter production would be in excess of home requirements in 1950 and a market would have to be found for the surplus. He contended that, due to the guaranteed price paid to producers for milk, the price at which Irish butter was produced rendered it impossible to sell on the export market unless the government introduced an export bounty.[200] As the world price for butter continued to fall, the increased butter production would require further subsidisation and place an intolerable burden on the exchequer.

For that reason, Dillon called for a revision of policy and stated that

> the first essential is that the value of milk delivered to creameries should be lowered. It is inevitable that this step will have to be taken sooner or later, and in order to avoid successive reductions in years to come ... the price should be reduced to 1s. per gallon, this price to be applicable in both summer and winter, but that a guarantee should be given by the government that the price will be maintained at that level for five years from that date.

---

[197] NAI, D/T S12846 C/2, D/A memo to govt., 26 Mar. 1952. Farmers chose to be creative in their pursuit of exports and smuggling northwards over the border increased. It was, wrote an *Irish Farmers' Journal* columnist, "all a question of getting those Republican pigs to alter their politics and allow themselves to be driven to market on the right side of the subsidy curtain. That way each little porker enhances his value by five or six pounds." *IFJ*, 19 Dec. 1953.

[198] The number of milch cows and heifers-in-calf had grown from 1,239,825 in 1947 to 1,287,900 in 1949, production of creamery butter had gone from 364,696 cwt. in 1947 to 497,267 cwt. in 1949, and the volume of milk available for the manufacture of chocolate crumb, cheese and dried milk had increased considerably. See *ibid.*

[199] NAI, D/T S14627 A/1, D/A memo to govt., 2 Nov. 1949.

[200] *Ibid.* New Zealand butter was retailing at 252s 6d per cwt., while under the Anglo-Danish agreement, the price for butter would be 271s 6d per cwt. from 1949 with the possibility of a 7.5 per cent annual decrease over six years. In Ireland creamery butter cost 339s 4d per cwt. in summer and 382s 8d per cwt. in winter.

This would reduce the cost of the milk content of butter appreciably and, in tandem with more efficient creamery production, the total cost of butter production would work out at 290s per cwt. Accordingly, the minister signalled his intention that that should be the maximum price payable for creamery butter from 1 April 1950. All restrictions on the distribution of butter should be removed and the retail price increased by 2d to allow the retention of profit margins. In supporting the proposal to have a single year-round price, the minister noted that the quantity of milk produced from December to January was only 6 per cent of total production so a higher price in this period had proved of little incentive and was of little value: "Moreover, the minister's policy is to promote the production of milk from growing grass by extending the pasture season both at the beginning and the end, and by encouraging the use of grass silage, rather than the more expensive concentrated foods, for the winter maintenance of cows." Dillon agreed that the government should subsidise the export of butter through the butter marketing committee should a surplus arise which individual creameries were unable to dispose of. The fixed price paid to the creameries would remain 290s per cwt. but the government "in an effort to equate production with demand, shall reserve itself the right to restrict production of butter in the event of the world market for butter collapsing and production in this country tending to expand indefinitely." It could order the diversion of milk into chocolate crumb or dried milk manufacture should it see fit. The minister concluded that the advantages of his overall plan were the elimination of the £2 million dairying subsidy, the potential to sell abroad at a competitive price and, although farmers would get a lower price, it would be an assured one and production of extra milk per cow would cover them.[201]

Although initially intended for discussion by government on 4 November 1949, cabinet consideration of the proposals was postponed on nineteen occasions, temporarily withdrawn from the agenda while the minister was abroad, before being eventually referred for discussion to a cabinet committee established to examine the draft estimates for the public services for the year ending 31 March 1951.[202] No action was taken and in December 1950 the minister restored his proposals to the cabinet agenda and noted that favourable weather had induced expanded production with the resultant increase in the unsubsidised export of surplus stocks to France and Germany at prices ranging from 364s to 372s per cwt. but it might not always prove possible to dispose in external markets.[203] The original proposals were again referred to a cabinet committee for discussion. The committee roundly ignored the suggested initiative and chose, instead, to recommend price increases to producers to stand for five years. With the agreement of the government, the guaranteed price was raised to 1s 3d a gallon from 1 May to 30 October, and 1s 4d from 1 November to 30 April, while the price paid to milk suppliers in Dublin and Cork was increased by 1d a gallon. To help

---

[201] *Ibid.*

[202] NAI, D/T S14627 A/1, cabinet minutes, 3 Feb. 1950.

[203] NAI, D/T S14627 A/1, D/A memo to govt., 8 Dec. 1950.

meet this guarantee the price of retail butter was increased by 2d a pound.[204]

Dillon's call for a radical revision of dairy price policy foundered, yet he never sought an alternative approach to the problem beyond the grasslands drive of the Land Project. Criticism of the low yields of Irish cows remained undimmed. While the rest of the world's leading agricultural countries refined their breeds and moved towards increasing specialisation, Ireland's loyalty to the dual-purpose shorthorn remained steadfast. "Surely everybody is not out of step, except our Johnnie," asked Henry Kennedy of the IAOS, who believed that breeding policy was "a cruel joke."[205] A veterinary surgeon noted: "Although we have the most suited country in the world to dairying, we harbour and handsomely subsidise the world's most uneconomic cow as the basis of our livestock economy."[206] Criticism of breeding policy mounted throughout Dillon's period in office, but he remained unmoved and referred to proponents of change as "those who preach heresy."[207] He derided those who championed other breeds as "a lot of old maids and cranks," and believed that if the dual-purpose shorthorn was well fed, it was the most suited to Irish conditions.[208]

The cabinet chose to follow the price policy initiated by Fianna Fáil in 1946. The political difficulties of abandoning price support once entered upon proved insurmountable, but nor could it be pursued to its utmost. Stripped of the capacity of other countries to divert industrial profits into farming, the state was unable to follow an extensive price support policy or to allocate significant resources to agricultural development. Enduring crises in sterling continued to have a negative effect and the Department of Finance persistently harangued the Department of Agriculture on the need to curb its expenditure. This constant attention exasperated Dillon who described the intrusions as "the maunderings of an economic outlook long since abandoned by every rational being who has not voluntarily ceased to think," and deplored the reluctance to call on the country's sterling reserves as the currency was "no longer capable of backing a torn newspaper." For Dillon, the Department of Finance were negating the policy initiatives of his department and had been since the government took office:

> This practice of returning to the melting pot, every six months, government policy decisions should stop. It is not becoming or indeed tolerable that government should be perennially harassed with very thinly-veiled diatribes on its profligate disregard for all the 'wise cautionary rebuke' which Department of Finance deems it proper to dole out.[209]

The disillusion increased as policy initiatives failed. In an article entitled "Nation on eve of great advance" in the *Irish Farmers' Journal* in January 1950,

---

[204] NAI, D/T S14627 A/1 cabinet minutes, 27 Apr. 1951.

[205] *IFJ*, 16 Dec. 1950.

[206] *Ibid*, 16 Jun. 1951.

[207] *Ibid.*, 22 Jul. 1950.

[208] Manning, *Dillon*, p. 239.

[209] UCDA, Patrick McGilligan papers, P35c/20, Dillon to McGilligan, 14 Dec. 1950.

Dillon had written that Irish agriculture was "on the threshold of what can be made the greatest advance since 1879."[210] As the inter-party government stumbled into the 1951 election with the dynamism of its first year a dank memory, there was little evidence of advance.

In January 1949 the government had decided that all departments should furnish progress reports. This series of reports – seasonal, half-yearly and annual – detail the activities of the Department of Agriculture in rigorous detail. Initially, the reports were laced with optimism, enthusiasm and were almost dismissive of failure. Over time, the ability of the department to conjure images of progress and prosperity began to wane. By 1951, the formulaic accounts of departmental programmes, had lost this early glow. The inescapable sense that agriculture was stagnating, if not actually regressing, left official propagandists struggling to maintain even the illusion of progress.[211] The problems which would plague post-war agricultural policy were already manifest. Ireland was unable to compete on the export market except with its livestock. The failure to invest in scientific, efficient systems of production was compounded by the inability to overcome political obligations. The incapacity to design a coherent, progressive policy framework subverted expansionist ambitions. Global trends did nothing to ease Irish worries. James Dillon had announced the doubling of the productivity of 80 per cent of the state's land and the increase of agricultural exports by 40 per cent as "the modest aim of the agricultural policy of this government."[212] That aim seemed as distant as ever by 1951 and for all the furore which attended the arrival of Marshall Aid and the signing of the 1948 trade agreement with Britain, agricultural development was intractably elusive. As with Fianna Fáil four years previously, the inter-party government arrived at an election seemingly bankrupt of policy initiatives beyond the assertion of traditional pieties. And those assertions inspired little hope.

---

[210] *IFJ*, 7 Jan. 1950.

[211] NAI, D/T S15062 A-C, Department of Agriculture progress reports, 1949–1956.

[212] *Ibid.*, 17 Jun. 1950.

Chapter

3

The most contented of peoples ... 1951–57

Before leaving office in 1951, the Taoiseach of the first inter-party government, John A. Costello, observed: "The material progress of the Irish nation would be but an empty vanity if it meant that all the real qualities of the Irish character were impaired – the qualities of resourcefulness, independence, endurance and integrity."[1] The speech rests in the long tradition of political orations stressing the spirituality of the Irish nation, as against its materialism, and was directed at the great bulk of the electorate who were as likely to be visited by deity as by wealth.[2] It was not that the Irish did not covet riches, rather they proved incapable of attaining them – at least, in their native country. In the 1950s, the collective national failure to create material wealth ensured the departure of hundreds of thousands of Irish men and women whose 'real qualities' were transferred to the cities of Britain and America. Mass migration from rural areas was the logical, though unintended, outcome of the policies of successive governments. With industrialisation accepted as unsustainable except on the most limited scale, those who fled the land also had to flee the country. In flight, they were joined by their urban contemporaries as the cities were, themselves, denuded of large sections of idle workers.

Beyond its burgeoning trade in human exports, Ireland had effectively accepted its role as an agricultural exporter which could not realistically expect to compete on the international industrial market. As the need to export was governed by the imperative of earning money to pay for the requisite raw materials which Ireland did not hold for either industry or agriculture, the nature of agricultural export was dictated by trade agreements with the British government. By 1961 cattle, beef and veal comprised 70.2 per cent of Irish agricultural exports – an increase from 50.8 per cent at the time of the 1938 trade agreement.[3] Agreements with the British enshrined as dogma the inviolability of the livestock trade and defined the precise nature of that trade by stipulating that Ireland

---

[1] UCDA, Patrick McGilligan papers, P35b/75 (5), John A. Costello speech, 11 Jan. 1951. Writing on this speech in the *Irish Farmers' Journal* on 9 Aug. 1952, Pa. F. Quinlan, sometime president of Macra na Feirme, commented that Irish farming was more a national sport than an industry as "its operatives are expected to give of their very best while being closely guarded against contamination from the attractions of filthy lucre."

[2] From the other side of the political fence, de Valera's legendary St. Patrick's Day broadcast from 1943 sang a similar refrain. See Arthur Mitchell and Pádraig Ó Snodaigh, *Irish political documents, 1916–1949* (1985), p. 231. He claimed, in 1948, that there was "probably not in the whole world at the present a country in which there is such a decent standard of living as there is in this part of Ireland." Quoted in Foster, *Modern Ireland*, p. 568.

[3] Foster, *Modern Ireland*, p. 578.

would export, in most instances, live store cattle for finishing in Britain. This acceptance of the least profitable form of livestock export, for the state if not for the individual grazier, constricted the development of food processing businesses which offered greatest prospect of industrialisation and urban employment. That the agreements further committed Ireland to export its livestock to Britain, even when higher prices could be attained elsewhere, emphasises the almost absolute national dependence on the export of one commodity to one country.

The prioritisation of agriculture in the pursuit of prosperity was not a phenomenon unique to Ireland. Countries as disparate as Australia and Denmark chose the same route.[4] What distinguished the Irish position as particularly bleak was the extent of the failure to industrialise and the inadequacy of the agricultural policy pursued. The inability to secure substantial markets outside Britain need not have been quite so critical. Notwithstanding the fact that a fundamental of the British economy was its low-cost food policy, it still represented a large-scale market to which the Irish had relatively easy access. What condemned Irish agriculture to stagnation was the failure to devise and implement policies to foster revitalisation and ensure greater efficiency. Indeed, it is difficult to avoid the conclusion that government policy at this juncture effectively determined that progress beyond the realms of the cattle industry was, at best, unlikely. Breeding policy, price policy and gross inefficiency retarded the dairy industry; the pigs and poultry industries were regarded as moribund, at least in terms of exports, with policy directed at attempting to satisfy home needs; and the framing of a progressive, sustainable tillage policy remained elusive. Wheat yields rose and fell in response to price and climate, but the overall tillage acreage remained stubbornly low (see appendix). Even in the livestock trade, poor marketing and widespread loss of stock to disease greatly diminished profits. For an economy so dependent on the profitable sale of agricultural produce, subsistence remained the defining characteristic of large sections of the farming community.

That policies pursued by government effectively undermined each other is, perhaps, best illustrated by the manner in which trade agreements revolving around profitable export of livestock conflicted with land division policy which created farms of such dimensions as to render livestock farming the least suitable form of production. For most of the 1950s there were few attempts to remove such fundamental anomalies. In the years following the return to office of Fianna Fáil in 1951, agricultural policy showed little change. Neither did three years of inter-party government between 1954 and 1957 bring any appreciable redirection of policy. Government reports, departmental papers and ministerial memoranda almost invariably acknowledge the flaws in existing policy and the need for change. Unable to find the means to promote such change, successive governments floundered in a policy vacuum. The convergence of policy signalled in the late 1930s was confirmed two decades later. This was not a consensus born of success.

---

[4] L.A. Clarkson, 'Agriculture and the development of the Australian economy in the nineteenth century', in *Agricultural History Review (AHR)*, vol. 19, i (1971), pp 88–96. Hans Christian Johansen, *The Danish economy in the twentieth century* (1987).

I

Fianna Fáil's renewed tillage campaign

Three years in opposition had done nothing to revitalise Fianna Fáil. The new government was not new at all. The old warriors who had served most of the sixteen years in cabinet between 1932 and 1948 returned en masse with de Valera as Taoiseach and Seán MacEntee as Minister for Finance. Only Thomas Walsh, newly installed as Minister for Agriculture, presented a new face in cabinet.[5] There was no fund of new ideas, no new perspective, no imaginative initiatives. Even Seán Lemass did not relish the return to power: "I did not welcome the prospect of coming back into government in the conditions of 1951 at all ... We had not really got down to clearing our minds on post-war development."[6] This acknowledgement that the six years after the war had been squandered in a miasma of confusion defined the inability to arrive at a coherent programme of action to promote economic development. There would be no genuine reappraisal of policy. Proposed new remedies were grafted onto old ones, and, in turn, failed themselves.

Thomas Walsh purported to outline his government's agricultural policy in the *Irish Farmer's Journal* in July 1951. It was a vague assertion of aspiration. The government would promote mechanisation, modernisation, the extension of agricultural instruction, greater use of fertilisers, reclamation and land drainage, and new trade agreements to secure better export prices. At the core of the policy lay a reassertion that greater tillage production was required and the promise to assist agricultural production through guaranteed prices for milk, wheat, beet and "such other products as after investigation may prove to be practicable."[7] The following month, the call for tillage was revived as a means to greater self-sufficiency and more livestock production.[8] Walsh argued that any substantial increase in cattle numbers could only come through the production of more winter feed. He argued a big increase in the tillage acreage was "vital not only for internal economic and social reasons, such as the promotion of employment and the desirability of slowing down emigration, but it is vital to the continued production of basic foods for consumption at home and for export."[9] Walsh concluded, apparently without irony: "Our position gives cause for no complacency."

[5] Hoctor wrote of Walsh: "Big farmer, little farmer and cottager shared equally in his friendship. If any man ever deserved to be described as 'a man of the people' he did." Hoctor, *The department's story*, p. 232.

[6] Bew and Patterson, *Lemass*, p. 74.

[7] *IFJ*, 21 Jul. 1951.

[8] *Ibid.*, 15 Sept. 1951.

[9] *Ibid.*, 18 Aug. 1951.

Conditions in tillage farming alone would have shaken any tendency towards complacency. In 1949, following the removal of compulsory tillage, wheat production fell by 30 per cent despite the presence of a guaranteed price.[10] Although in 1950, wheat production temporarily stabilised, the total area under tillage fell by 134,658 acres to 1,768,876 acres.[11] In 1951 the area under tillage fell by 51,593 and this included a decline in wheat production.[12] The continued decline prompted words rather than action as Eamon de Valera made a series of public speeches, including one to representatives of the County Committees of Agriculture:

> Unfortunately, agricultural production here is low compared with other countries and the government are disturbed about it. The key, it seems, to improvement in the agricultural position generally is increased tillage. More tillage can lead to increased cattle stocks, increased numbers of poultry and increased pig production ... Better agricultural methods call for more winter feeding. Anybody who looks at the lower prices of cattle sold in the autumn will see what a loss it is to our people not to have food to carry cattle over the winter to get the higher spring prices. The same applies to milk production. One of the reasons why our milk production is not higher is that cows are not properly fed during the winter time owing to shortage of home-produced feeding stuffs. The cure for that is increased tillage and increased production of crops.[13]

De Valera called for a 50 per cent increase in the area under crops with the cry: "We must take time by the forelock."

In a radio broadcast, the Taoiseach restated wartime appeals for national sacrifice to secure self-sufficiency and stressed the urgent need for increased wheat production: "There is only one way for safety and that is to grow the supplies ourselves."[14] The farmers were unimpressed and the *Irish Farmer's Journal* remarked: "Patriotism is no substitute for a well-balanced programme of agricultural production. This has been lacking for years, though its absence doesn't seem to be noticed in government circles."[15] The *Irish Times* was even more scathing:

> Vague appeals on these occasions have long proved their worthlessness. What the farmers require is some indication of a constructive policy to put agriculture on a business-like footing. Mr. de Valera, however, contented himself with the usual appeal to the farmers to grow more wheat. He made no concrete proposal for their

---

[10] *Nineteenth annual report of the Minister for Agriculture*, 1949–50, p. 3.

[11] *Twentieth annual report of the Minister for Agriculture*, 1950–51, p. 2.

[12] *Twenty-first annual report of the Minister for Agriculture*, 1951–52, p. 2.

[13] NAI, D/T S15282, de Valera speech, 23 Jan. 1952.

[14] NAI, D/T S15282, de Valera speech, 20 Feb. 1952.

[15] *IFJ*, 26 Jan. 1952.

benefit. The arguments that he used were so naïve that it is hardly to be credited that they could be used by the head of a state over the national radio system.[16]

Eighteen months into Fianna Fáil's term in office, there was no improvement in the tillage area despite de Valera's broadcasts. Again meeting with representatives of the County Committees of Agriculture, the Taoiseach expressed "keen disappointment at the very poor results of these appeals ... The increase in the area tilled was negligible and, in fact, the acreage under all the major crops, with the exception of barley, decreased." Saying his recent visit to Holland confirmed just how undeveloped Irish agriculture was, he noted that 19 of 24 European countries had a greater gross output per acre than Ireland, several four or five times higher, principally due to intensive tillage production. The Irish farmer was a peculiar case, however:

> I must not be taken as implying that the farmer will only respond to economic arguments; his magnificent response during the Emergency is sufficient to disprove any such implication. But the farmer has to make his living from the land and naturally he is mainly concerned with making that living as profitable as possible. What we have to do is convince him that in increased tillage lies his best hope of achieving this object. By increased tillage I mean not only an extension of the existing acreage but also an even greater increase in output by stepping-up the yield per acre through a greater use of fertilisers and lime.[17]

The formulation of policy to secure increased tillage area and yields proved as troublesome in the 1950s as it had done in the 1930s. Confusion reigned as self-sufficiency in wheat for bread production and the perceived desire to increase tillage acreage to produce fodder for cattle proved mutually incompatible goals. The tillage acreage actually fell through the 1950s, even though the acreage devoted to particular crops oscillated wildly as the production of barley, oats and wheat alternatively rose or fell. Inclement weather clearly impacted on yields but this only partially explains the fluctuations of the decade. The failure to devise a coherent policy framework consistently plagued the various initiatives which were undertaken. Production levels of certain commodities rose in any given year only to fall in the next as farmers responded to short-term stimuli or constraints. In this respect, the use of fertilisers fell in 1951 due to price increases forced by higher freight and raw material costs, only for usage to rise again the following year through the greater availability of cheap limestone.[18]

The approach to wheat production clearly exemplifies the ill-conceived nature of much of agricultural policy. Despite the rhetoric which constantly

---

[16] *Irish Times*, 23 Feb. 1952.

[17] NAI, D/T S15282, de Valera speech, 22 Jan. 1953.

[18] *Twenty-first annual report of the Minister for Agriculture, 1951–2*, p. 11 and *Twenty-second annual report of the Minister for Agriculture, 1952–3*, p. 10.

stressed the desirability of increased wheat production and the operation of a guaranteed price and marketing system which duly brought increased production, the agricultural economy was ill-prepared when the wheat acreage did actually rise. Storage facilities, for instance, were entirely inadequate. In 1953 the area under wheat increased by 99,458 acres to 353,879.[19] Depression or uncertainty in other areas of the industry had inspired farmers to turn to wheat as the Minister for Agriculture noted:

> Wheat is now regarded by many farmers as their main cash crop. There is a guaranteed market and guaranteed price for all the wheat produced. The prices obtainable by growers for oats and barley (except barley grown under contract for malting) will depend to a large extent on the price obtainable on the export market for livestock and livestock products, and cannot be stabilised as in the case of wheat, all of which is used in the country.[20]

Accordingly, the minister proposed that the government seek to fulfil the country's entire requirements of wheat amounting to 500,000 tons annually.

The Department of Finance objected strenuously in claiming that the costs to millers per ton of dried Irish wheat was £40 8s per ton, while that of imported wheat was £34 1s 9d per ton. This higher cost of Irish wheat, as well as the high percentage of Irish flour which government decreed millers should use in their grist, would necessitate a subsidy of £8,270,000 in 1954–5 to maintain the prices of flour and bread to the consumer.[21] The Department of Industry and Commerce was equally opposed. It pointed out the logistical problems involved in the artificial drying of every barrel of Irish wheat, saying this would necessitate the construction of greatly expanded facilities. Similarly, storage facilities for 500,000 tons would require a 100 per cent expansion of present capacity. Moreover, bakers were adamant it was impossible to make a palatable loaf solely from native wheat.[22] After some debate, the government decided the general aim of policy should be the production of an annual mill intake of 300,000 tons and that adequate facilities should be provided on a permanent basis to handle an annual intake of that volume.[23]

Attracted by price stability from a cash crop and a guaranteed market, the farmers cared little for what would happen with wheat once a profitable sale was assured. They moved out of other tillage crops and into wheat, and, by June 1954, the wheat yield was expected to reach 400,000 tons, just 30,000 tons short of the expected national requirements for that year. By then the inter-party government under John A. Costello had returned to office and the increases were not

[19] *Twenty-third annual report of the Minister for Agriculture, 1953–4,* p. 4.

[20] NAI, D/T S11402 E, D/A memo to govt., 18 Jan. 1954.

[21] NAI, D/T S11402 E, D/F memo to govt., 18 Jan. 1954.

[22] NAI, D/T S11402 E, D/IC memo to govt., 22 Jan. 1954.

[23] NAI, D/T S11402 E, cabinet minutes, 22 Jan. 1954. Yields were also improving through the provision of better strains, increased mechanisation and greater use of fertilisers.

welcomed by the Taoiseach's department. It noted that imported wheat was £10 per ton cheaper and pushed the price of a two-pound loaf from 6¾d to 8¾d. It further noted that the cost of flour and bread was inflated by the problem of "antiquated and uneconomic drying and storage plants." Nonetheless, the department asserted: "Assuming relative stability in other agricultural prices, it is difficult to see how a reduction in the present native wheat output can be secured other than by (a) a reduction in price or (b) a system of contracts."[24] Neither of these options were pursued and, despite its instinctive aversion to Fianna Fáil's wheat fetish, the new inter-party government opted for minimal change in policy. On the proposal of James Dillon, reinstated as Minister for Agriculture, it was agreed that a guaranteed price and market for home-grown wheat should be maintained for the following five years.[25] The problems of how to store and dry wheat, and how to use it were not addressed. Despite a 1951 initiative providing grants and loans for the erection of storage facilities, little progress was made. Potential investors, forewarned by temporary surges in production in other commodities, feared that any such facilities would invariably stand as hollow shrines to a past when wheat had proved profitable and popular. Similarly, investigations on the use of native wheat in the baking of an all-Irish loaf were greatly delayed. An initial request by the Department of Industry and Commerce to the Institute for Industrial Standards and Research in April 1954 on the potential for such a loaf, led to the establishment of an advisory committee in February 1955, the receipt of adequate equipment to perform the tests in the spring of 1956, and the eventual production of an interim report in 1957. The report was inconclusive.[26]

By then other events had intervened. Poor weather in 1954 had diminished yields significantly. The possibility of Irish farmers filling the entire requirements of the home market had seemed certain to cost the exchequer a large sum of money. As the Taoiseach's department noted in relief, "it was only the accident of exceptionally bad weather which prevented this from happening." As the weather could not be relied upon to so conspire every year, the government seized the opportunity in March 1955 to reduce prices, arguing that for every acre under wheat the farmer was receiving a bonus of £8 above the world price whereas the average gross output of agricultural land was £15. Similarly, farmers were paying "fancy rents" to get land on which to sow wheat as the price subsidy was thoroughly excessive. It concluded:

> it was never contemplated that the system of guaranteed (and inflated) prices, would result in virtual sufficiency in wheat production. Policy aimed, through the mechanism of guaranteed prices, at producing at home a sizeable proportion of our wheat requirements – not all, or virtually all our requirements. This policy had been thrown out of gear

[24] NAI, D/T S11402 F, D/T notes, 9 Jun. 1954.

[25] NAI, D/T S11402 F, cabinet minutes, 19 Oct. 1954.

[26] *Milling and baking quality of Irish wheat: interim report covering the 1956 harvest* (1958).

by the inflated level at which the price was guaranteed in recent years. The recent reduction is an attempt to restore the lost balance.[27]

Farmers reacted against the reduction in price and, in an open letter, the editor of the *Irish Farmers' Journal*, Paddy O'Keeffe, wrote: "In recent years the prevailing good price for wheat has done more to provide capital for farm development than any other single factor ... We maintain that a lucrative cash crop is essential if our numerous capital-starved productive farmers are to move in a reasonable manner into good grass, properly-stocked."[28] The reduced price prompted farmers to renounce their devotion to wheat and the acreage under that crop fell by almost one-third. Senator Patrick Cogan sarcastically congratulated Dillon on his first year in office which saw him preside over a decline of 129,100 acres in the total production of wheat, while the number of cattle also had fallen by 48,400 and the number of pigs by 153,500: "In those distinctive achievements he was, no doubt, ably assisted by his parliamentary secretary, deputy Oliver Flanagan, but if he had been assisted by Oliver Cromwell he could not have done much worse."[29]

For all the rhetoric, Dillon was actually attempting to implement policy as originally envisaged by Fianna Fáil. That party had not intended the country become self-sufficient in wheat as it understood the insufficiency of facilities to deal with such self-sufficiency and could not afford to maintain the subsidies required to promote it. Fianna Fáil misjudgement of the appropriate level at which to pitch the price of wheat had forced it into a price support system which had unduly distorted production. This thwarted the intent to increase wheat production as part of a balanced general increase in tillage usage as a means to secure general agricultural development. In reducing the price, and thereby reducing the wheat acreage, Dillon was seeking to recast national tillage policy in the original image presented by Fianna Fáil in 1951.[30]

Returning to office in 1957, Fianna Fáil made no attempt to reverse Dillon's actions. In July 1957 it agreed that the aim of policy should be the production of 300,000 acres per year, the equivalent of 75 per cent of national requirements. Cognisant of the fact that farmers had abused previously high payments in ill-conceived rotations and through a desire to secure immediate riches, the Minister for Agriculture, Seán Moylan, was asked to submit proposals for "confining wheat-growing so far as may be practicable, to persons farming by proper husbandry."[31] Further, the minister was asked to announce a minimum standard of wheat, in

---

[27] NAI, D/T S11402 F, D/T memo to govt., Mar. 1955.

[28] *IFJ*, 16 Oct. 1954.

[29] *Ibid.*, 28 Jan. 1956.

[30] Dillon also promoted the introduction of new strains of feeding barley to provide more winter fodder for cattle and this policy was one which ultimately reaped rewards.

[31] NAI, D/T S11402 F, cabinet minutes, 12 Jul. 1957. For Hoctor, Moylan was "one of the greatest and most chivalrous leaders in the War of Independence ... With high national ideals, inherited from his Fenian grandfathers, he linked a practical turn of mind which could turn dreams into realities." Hoctor, *The department's story*, p. 234.

terms of moisture content and bushel weight, in an attempt to resolve the ongoing tensions between millers and farmers on what constituted acceptable quality. This dispute had worsened in the autumn of 1957 when, due to bad weather, farmers had been left with sprouted wheat which had been rejected by the millers. Nonetheless, the 1957 harvest amounted to 370,000 tons and the Minister for Agriculture opined that this level was too high.[32] He noted that the combined acreage under wheat, barley or oats remained constant at 1,100,000 acres, but the relative amounts of each depended on price. He considered that some system was required to limit the production of wheat and suggested the possibility of contractual arrangements.[33] Ultimately, the government decided to reduce the price by 6s per barrel and to reduce the extraction rate on flour for Irish wheat to 72 per cent from 80 per cent. The decisions were strongly opposed by farmers who blamed the millers' cartel for the continued inefficiency in the storage and processing of wheat, and complained that tillage policy since the 1930s had been governed by ill-considered motives:

> The decision to encourage wheat was political and emotional rather than economic. Now, 25 years later, the question of wheat is still bedevilled by many of the lunatic ignorances of the 1930s. In particular, the farmer's position has been bedevilled by the attempt, started also in 1932, to preserve and revive the milling industry which was on its last legs.[34]

There was no escaping the conclusion, however, that through the 1950s, tillage acreage had fallen and that that acreage was dependent on crops whose prices were determined by political rather than economic factors (see appendix).[35] Regardless of the fact that the tillage acreage had been left at an artificially high level in the wake of the compulsory orders of the 1940s, the falling acreage was emblematic of the priorities of Irish farmers. The construction of a balanced tillage programme proved beyond the capabilities of policy makers. Similarly, farmers remained committed to a short-term determination to extract the maximum profit from any given year regardless of long-term viability. Salvation was sought in solutions which could only prove temporary. The capacity to float in and out of the production of various commodities did not so much suggest an industry responding to free market forces as one struggling desperately to stay afloat from year-to-year, reliant upon subsidies for buoyancy. If, by 1958, the introduction of better strains of feeding barley promised a move towards a more appealing future, it was a positive feature hewn from a decade of upheaval. The sums misspent on wheat production was money the country could ill afford to squander in a decade pock-marked with the most austere budgets in the history of the state. Most pointedly, other sections of the industry were not performing so spectacularly that such support of wheat was a tolerable indulgence.

---

[32] Moylan died in November 1957 and Paddy Smith returned as Minister for Agriculture.

[33] NAI, D/T S11402 F, D/A memo to govt., 30 Dec. 1957.

[34] *IFJ*, 8 Feb. 1958; and 'Farm Economist' writing in *IFJ*, 2 Nov. 1957.

[35] Crotty, *Agricultural Production*, p. 174.

II

Crisis in dairying

Fuelled by price incentives, the dairy industry had enjoyed something of a renaissance in the late 1940s as milk production and herd numbers rose. This proved an unsustainable ascent as structural flaws continued to produce at all levels gross inefficiencies which undermined the viability of the industry. These flaws were not addressed. Through much of the 1950s, Irish dairy produce was unable to compete on the export market. Even the proximity of Britain brought no relief as the greater efficiency of Denmark, the Netherlands and New Zealand accorded them a dominant role.[36] Indeed, in 1953, exports of Irish rabbits were six times the value of butter exports.[37] Even more alarmingly, for several years in the 1950s, a combination of insignificant exports and seasonality made Ireland a net importer of butter. So great were the structural flaws in the Irish dairy industry that the government was obliged to import New Zealand or Danish butter as Irish farmers found it more profitable to keep their low-yielding herds on subsistence rations through the winter months than to engage in dairying.[38] Attempts to remedy these flaws through the 1950s proved largely unsuccessful for three principal reasons. Firstly, the price policy which had once appealed to farmers now created a major bone of contention between them and the government; secondly, breeding policy was perceived as a constant restriction on increasing output; and, thirdly, systems of processing and marketing dairy produce were chronically inefficient.

The price policy which the government had used in the 1940s to breathe life into the dairy industry enjoyed initial success but was ill-founded. No scientific approach was taken to determine the most appropriate price and there was no sustained campaign to complement price increases with an efficiency drive. The state's approach to price policy was thoroughly unstructured and was rooted more in immediate political necessity than any long-term programme to foster prosperity. Dairy price policy had a number of anomalies, not least of which was that, as all butter exports required a subsidy to compete on the export market, any surplus was a burden on the state rather than an opportunity to earn money. To this end, it was effectively preferable to the state for dairy produce to remain static at a level around total home consumption needs. Ireland simply could not afford high-level price supports.

The avowed wishes of dairy farmers stressed somewhat different priorities. As with tillage, farmers' production depended to a large extent on the prices on

---

[36] For example, in 1930, Ireland had exported 473,000 cwt. of butter to Britain, but in 1955 it managed to export a mere 3,100 cwt. of butter. Smith and Healy, *Farm organisations*, p. 37.

[37] Smith and Healy, *Farm organisations*, p. 71.

[38] NAI, E 22/3/28, D/A memo to D/IC, 28 Jan. 1953.

offer. Dillon's failure to increase milk prices in accordance with the wishes of producers during his first term in office had left an undercurrent of ill-feeling – it also helped to bring down the inter-party government. On its return to office, Fianna Fáil raised milk prices by 2d par gallon in 1951 but this was seen as entirely inadequate by producers who became progressively more agitated. Southern dairy farmers formed the Irish Creamery Milk Suppliers Association (ICMSA) to further their claims.[39] The Minister for Agriculture, Thomas Walsh, unused to lobbying from farm organisations, deplored the agitation of the ICMSA despite the granting of a 2d per gallon price increase saying they had "adopted a most dictatorial attitude on the question of milk prices with a view, it is believed, to forcing the government to increase existing prices."[40]

Nonetheless, the decline in production through 1952 forced a rethink of policy as the dairy industry slipped into recession and the government was forced to import up to 5,000 tons of butter. As the ICMSA continued to agitate for better prices, the Minister for Agriculture wrote to the government in November asking that milk prices be increased by 2d a gallon as part of an overall package which would raise the gross receipts of farmers by £3 million as "anything less than this would have little effect." He proposed that these price increases would be announced as part of an overall programme:

> It is desirable that an announcement on agricultural policy should be made at an early date … It should clearly indicate the Government's long-term intention to maintain prices at a reasonable level and to raise the income of the agricultural population gradually until it bears some reasonable relationship to that of the rest of the community.[41]

Then, in December, Walsh reiterated that he had

> no doubt that the basic cause of the present milk situation and outlook is that the basic price paid for milk is much too low … It is a very serious situation that we have to depend for our full butter requirements on being able to draw on such quantities of butter as Denmark and New Zealand are not obliged to send to Britain under their contracts with the Ministry of Food.

The Minister argued that farmers had no incentive to feed cows through the winter as "at present price levels it would not pay farmers to do it," and the proposed increase would be paid for by an increase in butter prices.[42] He noted in passing that he remained fully alive to the need to raise milk yields through better feeding and reorganised milk recording but that an immediate increase in price was of fundamental importance. He stated that the country required "an injection

---

[39] The organisation was originally known as the Creamery Milk Suppliers' Association

[40] NAI, D/T S15255 A, D/A memo to govt., 19 Dec. 1951.

[41] NAI, D/T S13930 B, D/A memo to govt., 11 Nov. 1952.

[42] NAI, D/T S13930 B, D/A memo to govt., 11 Dec. 1952.

of confidence and money if it is to hold its own and begin to expand. This applies with particular force in the case of the dairy industry."[43] The Department of Finance disagreed saying that any increase in the price of basic commodities would only result in a series of wage increases to the detriment of the economy as a whole.[44] At a meeting of the government on 7 January 1953 the cabinet opted for a holding operation and the Minister for Agriculture was instructed to announce that he would not be in a position to announce a decision on price for several weeks. Farmers were appalled and by the last week in January were blockading the sale of milk to urban areas.

The milk strike was condemned in emotive terms, not least by the Minister for Finance, Seán MacEntee, in an hysterical speech to a Fianna Fáil meeting in Mount Merrion, Dublin: "Precious food, for want of which children might die, had been wantonly wasted ... The leaders of this campaign seemed to be obsessed with the idea of 'total war', war without limitation and without restraint, war such as Stalin and the late Adolf Hitler believed in ... but where did it leave him and his country in the end?"[45] He continued: "No class in the community ... has more to fear from invoking the forces of disorder than the farmers, because their property is particularly vulnerable to attack. Similarly, none has more to fear from the abrogation of its functions by the government." For MacEntee, farmers should ask themselves "whether the measures to which they resorted could be justified by Christian men in a Christian country." The *Irish Times* was scarcely less shrill is proclaiming that the farmers had waged war on the city and had resorted to the "low policy of bringing pressure to bear on the innocent. It is almost as if soldiers should advance to battle, carrying women and children before them as a defence against the enemy's bullets. The policy is unhappily not new but who would have thought that Irish farmers would stoop to it?"[46]

The ICMSA responded with full-page newspaper advertisements claiming: "Never were men more goaded into action – never was a cause more just."[47] Although some members of the Fianna Fáil party agreed with MacEntee that they should face down the leaders of "this disgusting strike," others noted the widespread support for it amongst farmers, including many of the party faithful.[48] One senator wrote to de Valera saying the farmers seemed justified in their calls for a price increase and that "something like a mad strike fever seems to have swept over the entire farming community ... Practically all our farmer supporters seem to have caught the fever."[49] For sixteen days there was stalemate in the trenches until the strike ended on 11 February 1953 when the Taoiseach met the ICMSA. Shortly afterwards the government agreed to raise the price of milk by less

---

[43] NAI, D/T S11762 C/2, D/A memo to govt., 15 Dec. 1952.

[44] NAI, D/T S13930 B, D/F memo to govt., 16 Dec. 1953.

[45] UCDA, Seán MacEntee papers, P67/597, MacEntee speech, 29 Jan. 1953.

[46] *Irish Times*, 26 Jan. 1953.

[47] *Irish Press*, 28 Jan. 1953.

[48] Donnchadh Ó Briain papers, P83/224(1), Paddy Smith speech in Cootehill, Co. Cavan, 25 Jan. 1963.

[49] NAI, D/T S11762 D, Senator Martin O'Dwyer, Kilmallock, Co. Limerick to de Valera, 26 Jan. 1953.

than 1d and to extend by two months the period when the optimum price for milk was paid.[50] It was not victory for either side but an uneasy compromise with renewed hostilities dependent on the expected report from a milk costings committee which had been established two years previously.

In an attempt to place dairy price policy on something of a rational foundation, and to deflect political criticism, Walsh had proposed, in December 1951, the establishment of a milk costings committee: "The minister is satisfied that the only means by which producers can be convinced as to what is an economic price and an end put to the present agitation is to have a comprehensive investigation of the cost of milk production throughout the whole country carried out by an impartial authority."[51] The Minister for Finance opposed the suggestion arguing that it was theoretically impossible to work out the cost of any one agricultural product in a mixed farming system. Further, the proposal to work out a fair price by arriving at an ascertained cost, and then adding a sum which would stand as profit effectively condoned inefficiency.[52] In January 1952 the government approved the establishment of a milk costings committee under the control of Professor Michael Murphy of University College, Cork (UCC) which would investigate the cost of producing milk on representative farms supplying creameries, farms supplying milk for liquid production and farms supplying milk for home butter making.[53] The terms of reference proved impossible and in November 1952 the government were forced to remove the caveat that the inquiry be carried out on 'representative farms' as almost half of the individual 200 farms selected withdrew from the investigation.[54] The move offered no expeditious solution and in Spring 1953 James Dillon taunted from the opposition benches that the committee members "have evaporated more or less into thin air and have suspended themselves like Mohammed's coffin."[55]

The committee had not dissolved but was riven with internal disputes over the most appropriate route forward. The *Irish Times* reported in April 1953 that the committee was to meet again after a four-month break and would attempt to resolve outstanding points of contention. The delays provided something of a buffer for the government who refused ICMSA requests to set up permanent machinery to enable producers to negotiate an economic price for milk. It argued that such a body would be operating in the dark without the reliable information which the milk costings committee would provide. In May 1953 the committee suffered a further blow when its director, Professor Murphy, was forced to resign due to ill health. Professor T.A. Smiddy, economic adviser to successive Irish governments, then assumed control of the operation, acting as chairman to a

---

[50] NAI, D/T S13930 B, cabinet minutes, 25 Feb. 1953; Healy and Smith, *Farm organisations*, p. 37.

[51] NAI, D/T S15255 A, D/A memo to govt., 19 Dec. 1951. The milk costings initiative was variously styled as a committee, a commission and an inquiry.

[52] NAI, D/T S15255 A, D/F memo to govt., 21 Dec. 1951.

[53] NAI, D/T S15255 A, cabinet minutes, 8 Jan. 1952.

[54] NAI, D/T S15255 A, D/A memo to govt., 28 Oct. 1952 and cabinet minutes, 3 Nov. 1952.

[55] *Dáil Debates*, vol. 137, no. 1, cols. 29–36, 11 Mar. 1953.

committee which theoretically laid down the costing principles and general lines of investigation for civil servants to act upon. The committee was not accorded the power to change the actual report which might eventually emerge. In the background, the ICMSA lobbied for increased prices as the dairy industry continued to stagnate. Other impulses were pointing more towards a reduction in price, however. In June 1954 the newly returned inter-party government desired to reduce the cost of butter to the consumer by 5d a pound and considered passing on the loss to the producer before deciding to meet the reduction through exchequer subsidy.[56] In December of that year the Minister for Agriculture, James Dillon, told producers he would not grant price increases as he "was not prepared to raise the cost of a valuable foodstuff which is consumed by the less well-to-do sections of our people."[57] Dairy farmers considered themselves amongst such sections and returned to the streets in a protest march in the spring of 1956 "as a measure of indignation at the shameful way they have been treated by the Milk Costings Commission, a body that is functioning – or supposed to be – since 1952, at public expense."[58]

Expectations that the costings committee would salve wounds were shattered in September 1956 when the first section of its report was produced. It provoked uproar with the implied suggestion that a reduction in the price of milk by 2d was justified. A member of the committee immediately denounced the report as "a departmental fabrication."[59] The *Irish Farmer's Journal* condemned it as

> a 400-page volume of historical fantasy ... These figures are not representative of farmers. They are not, as gathered, fairly apportioned for size and district, nor are they complete or numerous enough to justify confident conclusions. What they really do, on analysis, is to describe statistically the paralysis and progressive impoverishment of Irish agriculture, a process manifesting itself in a growing inertia and a general relaxation of effort, partially offset by the adoption of modern techniques. The figures assembled show the extraordinary low costs of 3¾d. a gallon made statistically possible by the return of the lands and buildings to a state of nature. So long as old fertility and ancient effort can be exploited, slave labour costs can be shown. Silent bankruptcy can show wondrous costings.[60]

The *Journal* accused the Department of Agriculture officials of deciding on the desired result and working backwards. It further saw the debacle as typical of efforts of the state to regulate Irish agriculture: "Not that state intervention is necessarily wrong ... But in this country it is largely perverse, mostly wrong-headed

---

56 NAI, D/T S11762 G, D/A memo to govt., 9 Jun. 1954, D/F memo to govt., 8 Jun. 1954, and cabinet minutes, 14 Jun. 1954.

57 NAI, D/T S15255 B, Dillon to John Feely, ICMSA, 26 Nov. 1954.

58 NAI, D/T S15255 B, Charles Fletcher, ICMSA to Taoiseach, 6 Mar. 1956.

59 *Irish Times*, 17 Sept. 1956.

60 *IFJ*, 8 Sept. 1956.

and where not entirely vitiated by politics, completely uninformed by realities ...
The demeaning and contemptible intrigue of the milk costings committee will
provide no real cure for the ills of the dairying industry."[61] The intrigue was far
from over. The committee continued its work through 1957 in an attempt to
produce a final report and in November 1957 Smiddy presented the document
produced by civil servants, consisting of 40 pages of commentary and 600 pages of
tables, to the committee. There was considerable outcry and the internal rupture
was complete. The Minister for Agriculture advised the government that "serious
differences of opinion" had emerged within the committee and that further delays
were inevitable.[62] The minister was instructed to write to all members of the
committee asking for their respective opinions, while Professor Smiddy resigned
in December 1957.

As the dispute rumbled on. Smiddy noted the tedious nature of the work,
the continual staffing problems, and "futile argument" and "protracted
controversy" about details of little significance.[63] Dan Hoctor, a Department of
Agriculture representative, agreed there were grave methodological difficulties in
compiling the report and John Feely of the ICMSA criticised the chosen
methodology. Various members condemned the "excessive control" exercised by
Smiddy whom, it was claimed, had not consulted the committee on a wide range
of issues. Even when they were consulted some members believed that the
investigation was deliberately biased to suit the Department of Agriculture policy
of maintaining a low price for milk and that its officials had "violated and
changed" principles laid down by the committee. The *Irish Farmers' Journal*
repeated its earlier disregard of the final report and James Dillon condemned the
entire exercise as "a dirty fraud."[64] After six years and an expenditure of more than
£30,000 the report made no impact on dairy policy and was condemned
immediately to irrelevance.

---

[61] *IFJ*, 8 Sept. 1956. See also *IFJ*, 15 Sept. 1956.

[62] NAI, D/T S15255 B, cabinet minutes, 13 Dec. 1957

[63] NAI, D/T S15255 B, D/A memo to govt., 1 Apr. 1958.

[64] *IFJ*, 8 Mar. 1958; NAI, D/T S15255 B, extract from Dáil Debate, 26 Feb. 1958.

III

Revitalising the dairy industry

The costings shambles was but one aspect of the dairy industry's malaise. No fundamental attempt was made to restructure the industry and remove inefficiencies which all accepted were rife. Twenty per cent of the butter produced in Ireland was still home-made on farms.[65] Many of these farms were small-holdings where dairying potentially should have offered a higher return per unit area than other forms of farming. The size of Irish herds was so small, however, that they struggled to compete on an economic footing with the larger continental herds. The total number of milch cows in the country when first counted in 1861 numbered 1,200,000 and this figure remained remarkably constant until the 1950s. Similarly invariable was the milk yield. In 1920, Irish cows were producing an estimated 420 gallons per year. By 1953, the estimated annual milk yield had risen to 445 gallons per cow, although it was claimed that this figure was an overestimation and it was still less than half that of cows in leading dairy countries.[66] Such low yields were the product of inadequate nutrition, poorly developed grasslands, paucity of winter feed, failure to adopt a scientific approach to milk recording, and a much-maligned breeding policy. By 1953 the Minister for Education, Seán Moylan, believed the failure of the dairy industry stood at the very core of a national failure to generate prosperity: "The various features of production are so interlocked that it is difficult to make proposals for one without impinging on the other. It is not, therefore, a question of dealing with the dairying industry alone but rather of providing means of advancing agriculture generally."[67] Moylan argued that regardless of the success of any tillage initiatives the vast bulk of land would remain under grass and the most profitable grassland production was through dairying. Despite the fact that the existing state of Irish dairy farming was "decadent" the industry was "of the utmost importance." He pointed out that dairying offered the potential of a much higher cash return per unit of food than beef – 2d as against 1s 2d per unit – and that export was an absolute imperative. This would require the industry to move to greatly improved levels of production and efficiency to make it competitive, something which would require "reforms of quite a revolutionary nature." He attributed the "growing defeatism" amongst dairy farmers "to the lack of progress in developing a technique of dairying which is designed to lower production costs and to increase output per acre and per man."

Moylan cited three factors crucial to reorganisation of the dairy industry: a better breed of cow, better feed, and improved labour economy on the farm.

---

[65] Hoctor, *The department's story*, p. 259.

[66] Healy and Smith, *Farm organisations*, p. 71.

[67] NAI, D/T S15428, Moylan memo to govt., 13 Feb. 1953.

Lamenting the livestock policy of the past fifty years which had focussed on the "so-called dual-purpose beast," Moylan claimed: "There can be no doubt that in regard to dairy production this policy has been fatal ... There can be little doubt that the present discontent is due to the results of the breeding policy of the past." He continued that there was "plenty of evidence available that even on government and institution farms, cows adequately fed failed to give economic milk yields." He rejected all suggestions that any departure from the dual-purpose beast would jeopardise the beef economy as real change in breeding would be a slow process and would, indeed, permit the establishment of highly-desirable specialist breeds. In the interim, there would be no difficulty in retaining the output of beef animals and the exercise would, in fact, act as a catalyst for positive restructuring:

> The traditional system of beef production in this country is wasteful in the extreme. The calf leaves the dairy farm at various ages and passes through several hands – dealers, farmers, etc. – before he reaches the age of 3½ to 4 years as a butcher's beast. In a rational system of beef production the animals should be finished at from 2 to 2½ years of age and the wastage in food requirements would be eliminated. The farm economy of large landowners is mainly based upon the purchase of 3 year old cattle brought to that age in such a wasteful manner. There is no reason why on these large farms beef cattle should not be raised from the beginning from cows suckling beef calves and perhaps suckling the surplus calves of the dairy districts also.

Moylan stated categorically that Irish dairy produce could not hope to compete abroad if a change was not made to Friesians or Jerseys through the importation of bulls in the specialised dairy districts. Indeed, in three Irish herds where Friesian bulls had been introduced milk yields had increased from 550 gallons to 950 gallons per cow. He said that the veterinary-related dangers of importing animals were not insuperable and together with enhanced grassland development, where output could be at least doubled from the existing 1,000-1,2000 lbs starch per equivalent acre, would produce a distinct improvement in Irish milk yields. Better grasslands would facilitate higher stocking levels which, in turn, would help to overcome the "considerable prejudice against machine milking." This mechanisation had quickened in the last few years but "it is quite common for the use of some of these machines to be discontinued after a comparatively short time. The reason is that there has been no provision for proper and adequate instruction on the use and care of the machines."

Proper mechanisation would be part of an overall scheme to improve the hygiene and quality of milk produced: "One has only to travel through the dairying districts in the early Spring to get an idea of the unsanitary and unhealthy conditions under which cows are kept not only in the houses, but in the 'pounds' where they spend most of the day knee deep in mud." For Moylan, the key to the solution of this problem lay in the extension of advice, education and research, directed by a board who would advise the government and regulate the functioning of bodies to improve agricultural production. In passing, he commented that poor advice in the past had engendered in farmers a deep distrust of government. For this broad policy programme of improved breeding, better grassland management, modernising efficiency and improved education, Moylan stressed the importance of large-scale investment. Improved breeding could be secured for £100,000 while pasture development would cost £20,000,000 over five years. He concluded: "It is no more possible to raise the level of production in agriculture than it is in industry without the infusion of considerable quantities of new capital."[68]

A meeting between de Valera, Walsh and representatives of all sections of the dairying industry to consider the future of the industry was held within a fortnight of Moylan's memorandum. Government representatives stressed the way forward was not through continued price rises. In a rambling debate on the future of breeding policy, there were suggestions that the Livestock Act be suspended. That act had made it illegal to own or possess a bull without licence. There was general agreement that more freedom was needed but no concrete proposals emerged and the chronic indecision was captured in de Valera's closing rhetorical questions: "What is the department to aim at? Is it going to aim at giving the individual farmer the greatest opportunity to try and help him to do whatever he wishes to do himself or to try and induce the farmer to pursue certain lines?"[69] In December 1952 the cabinet considered breeding policy and instructed the Minister for Agriculture to submit proposals which would establish a committee to investigate suggested means of improving breeding policy.[70] The department was not to be easily shaken from its well-worn path, however, and policy remained unchanged. The committee was never established and requests for progress reports in April and July 1953, and August 1954 produced no information from the department.[71] Eventually, on 31 August 1954 the Department of Agriculture outlined its strategy. It recounted that following the initial request from government, it was thought necessary to hold a meeting of the Livestock Consultative Council, a body founded in the 1930s but one which rarely, if ever, met for two decades. Revived in January 1953, an exhaustive discussion produced no unanimity so a second meeting was called in August and "there was again a marked division of opinion on such questions as whether we should concentrate on improving the foundation stock of shorthorns or encourage purely dairy breeds." It did agree that Friesian bulls should be located at artificial insemination stations – a proposal which was enacted.

A third meeting in November 1953 proved equally devoid of clarity leading the department to observe that

---

[68] *Ibid.*

[69] NAI, D/T S11762 E, minutes of meeting, 24 Feb. 1953.

[70] NAI, D/T S15428 A, cabinet minutes, 30 Dec. 1952.

[71] NAI, D/T S15428 A, D/T memos to D/A, 29 Apr. 1953, 17 Jul. 1953 and 4 Aug. 1954.

all aspects of breeding policy in respect of cattle, pigs and sheep have been exhaustively discussed at very representative meetings attended by all the interests concerned. The minister can see no point in setting up another committee to examine the same matters again. The same divisions would certainly arise, and there would be no other results than those of the three meetings of the Livestock Consultative Council. The Minister considers that the livestock policy he is pursuing is best suited to the country's needs. He is fully satisfied that there would be no justification for setting up a new committee and he, accordingly, does not propose to make any such proposal to government. [72]

Within a week the Taoiseach's department replied to acknowledge that the matter could be left to rest.[73] Effectively, the Department of Agriculture were determined, at all costs, to do nothing to jeopardise the livestock trade with Britain. Not alone was the breeding of the shorthorn dual purpose beast biased towards beef and away from dairy farming, but avoidance of any risk of importing bovine diseases into the country was deemed to be paramount. The legal import of livestock from the continent was impossible as there was no quarantine station in the country. The department sought a compromise of sorts. Veterinary officers from the Department of Agriculture travelled to London and met with British officials in December 1953. An Irish official commented that the government was under heavy pressure to arrange the import of up to twenty Friesian cattle from Holland to improve the milk yield and this was "causing the Irish Ministry of Agriculture considerable embarrassment since they were most anxious to avoid creating a precedent by direct importation from the continent of live animals."[74] The Irish official said that an order from the minister allowing the import of cattle would be required but this option had never been exercised and they wished to avoid exercising it as it might set an odious precedent. In that respect, they asked the British officials if their minister would make the order, quarantine the animals and then facilitate their passage to Ireland. Although recognising the value of Ireland retaining a complete prohibition on the import of animals from the continent, Britain rejected the request as "for a virtually negligible advantage to this country our Minister would be exposed to strong pressure from potential importers here if he made an order."[75]

The pressure from Irish interests did not disappear as the dual-purpose beast came under repeated attack. In an attempt to deflect criticism the department asked Dr John Hammond of Cambridge University to advise on breeding policy. The department decided that the best route would be to set a series of questions and for Hammond to present his report as a series of answers formulated on the

---

[72] NAI, D/T S15428 A, D/A memo to govt., 31 Aug. 1954.

[73] NAI, D/T S15428 A, D/T to D/A, 6 Sept. 1954.

[74] PRO, MAF 40/452, minutes of meeting between T.P. Marten, Animal Health Division and Mr Hartnett, Deputy Chief Veterinary Officer, 19 Dec. 1953.

[75] PRO, MAF 40/452, MAF internal note, 19 Dec. 1953.

strength of his week-long stay in the country. In the ensuing report, the department added their own commentary to Hammond's observations.[76] Even the slightest criticism of existing policy brought a tetchy reply from the department. Hammond's remark that he felt dairy exports were "rather too low for a country with dual-purpose type cattle," and consequent recommendation of increased Friesian use where milk yields were low – a policy previously successful in England – was not well-received. The department stated: "While encouraging the maintenance of the existing good-quality dual-purpose Shorthorns as the country's foundation stock, the department has not opposed some grading up with Friesians, but has condemned indiscriminate crossing, i.e. without a steady and consistent policy." Equally, there was "no conclusive evidence" that Friesians would improve matters as the problems lay in poor feeding and management so it was more advisable to stay with Shorthorns. The department did accept Hammond's suggestion that a personal advisory service to herd owners was desirable and they hoped to recruit staff for the purpose as "this would not be practicable with the Department's existing small livestock inspectorate staff who are fully engaged on existing important work." Overall, though the department welcomed Hammond's expression that he was very much impressed by the good organisation of the livestock industry and, ultimately, "no basic change in policy arises."[77]

Yet an earlier report by a British official in 1953 had offered a fundamentally different appraisal:

From the standpoint of an outside observer the Irish agricultural economy as a whole seems distorted and out of balance. Whether as some contend, beef producing interests are unduly favoured because they earn foreign currency, or, owing to their proximity to Dublin, they can more easily gain the ear of the Government departments, one cannot presume to judge. But it does appear that the Department of Agriculture's policy of compromise between the two interests, manifested by the development of dual-purpose cattle, is not in accord with the industry's potentialities or the nation's interests. There seems reason to believe that the country is large enough, and the respective areas sufficiently defined and distinctive, to warrant a greater specialisation among herds than official policy now favours.[78]

As the world's leading dairy countries moved towards refined specialisation

---

[76] UCDA, Patrick McGilligan papers, P35c/112, *Hammond report*, Sept. 1955 and D/A memo to govt., 25 Jan. 1956.

[77] UCDA, Patrick McGilligan papers, P35c/112, *Hammond report*, Sept. 1955 and D/A memo to govt., 25 Jan. 1956.

[78] PRO, MAF 40/452, H.A. Silverman report entitled *Irish food supplies and trade with Britain*, Jan. 1953. Silverman's report was conducted on the basis of visits to Ireland in September and October 1952, and he was assisted by General M.J. Costello of the Irish Sugar Company and, from various Irish universities, Professors Johnston, Busteed and Lyons.

with soaring milk yields, Ireland remained wedded to a policy abandoned elsewhere as inefficient. Inevitably, inefficiency on the farm was replicated off it. Far from aping the rationalisation of European countries, the Irish creamery system was chronically wasteful. Large-scale co-operatives had never flourished in Ireland where the aims of creameries were social as much as economic. Small-scale creameries pocked the landscape using antiquated technology to produce badly-wrapped, poor quality, unhygienic ware in a business further impaired by incompetent or fraudulent management.[79] Moreover, although government effectively directed the co-operative movement through its funding of the IAOS, its contribution was scarcely dynamic. In 1933 the cabinet gave the Department of Agriculture authority to prepare a bill to restructure the movement.[80] Almost a quarter of a century later, in 1957, Eamon de Valera was moved to inquire of the Department of Agriculture why such a bill had not been proceeded with.[81] The department replied that

> examination of the proposal and the preliminary drafting of the bill had been proceeded with, intermittently, from 1933 up to 1949 in which year the Minister for Agriculture decided to request the IAOS for their views on the type and scope of a bill which the co-operative movement considered to be necessary. In transmitting the request the Department brought to the attention of the IAOS the scheme of the bill on which it had been working. So far, the IAOS has not furnished their observations, although the matter has been brought to their notice on a number of occasions.[82]

Indeed, events in 1954 suggested relations between the IAOS and the government were not exactly harmonious. The department noted that it provided £11,000 per year but that, apart from its expansion in the later years of the nineteenth century, the co-operative movement had made few inroads:

> It seems that the society has accepted its present position as the limit of its endeavours. The minister considers that the society should now be informed that unless it takes active steps to fulfil the primary objects for which it exists by means of a vigorous campaign for agricultural co-operation and the organisation of farmers on co-operative lines, reduction of the state grant to the society will have to be seriously considered.[83]

Far from expansion through the years the co-operative movement had focussed on survival.[84] The many *bon mots* floated airily across agricultural circles

---

79 Neenan, 'History of the department', pp 236–7.

80 NAI, D/T S6471 A, cabinet minutes, 24 Oct. 1933.

81 NAI, D/T S6471 B, D/T note, 30 Nov. 1957.

82 NAI, D/T S6471 B, D/A memo to govt., 30 Nov. 1957.

83 NAI, D/T S1206 B, D/A memo to govt., 15 Sept. 1954.

84 Smith and Healy, *Farm organisations*, p. 17.

on the worth of co-operative expansion were theoretical rather than practical. The politically powerful paid homage through rhetoric but made only the most paltry of efforts at realisation. Farmers believed that the Department of Agriculture's attitude to the co-operative movement was "real indifference if not antagonism."[85] Nonetheless, the attitude of the farming community was at least as obstructive. A columnist in the *Irish Farmers' Journal* wrote: "There are many causes for the failure of the Irish co-operative movement to expand, but the most fundamental and important is the apathy of the general body of farmers."[86] It was an apathy which restricted the movement to the operation of creameries and retail shops, and discouraged its involvement in areas where it could make a real contribution. And even within the creamery operations, its involvement was characterised as often by malaise as by progress, moving commentators to remark on "the small, timid and static societies that undoubtedly exist today."[87]

Government attempts to improve the creamery system were unsuccessful. The Dairy Disposal Company Ltd had been founded in 1927 in an attempt to rationalise the industry by purchasing creameries, whether proprietarily or co-operatively owned, and closing down redundant operations or transferring viable ones to existing or new co-operative societies. It had been intended to close down the company as soon as all creameries had been disposed of but, not alone did its creameries operate in parallel lines to the co-operative movement, it also became a repository for all manner of enterprise. Over the years it acquired a complex of companies and became active in cheese making, condensed and dried milk factories, toffee making, cattle breeding, artificial insemination, broiler production, butter storage, as well as the drying, storage and milling of grain. By 1960, it owned businesses in all the above areas and also retained 17 central creameries and 132 separating stations. Far from promoting rationalisation, the government-owned company had contributed to increased inefficiency. Although intended as a temporary holding company, it acquired permanency largely because, in the words of the department, it became "difficult to visualise the circumstances in which it would be possible to dispose of to co-operative societies all the businesses operated by the companies." As well as its side operations, the company offered the sole creamery outlet to one-quarter of milk producers with assets of over £2 million and an annual turnover of £9 million.[88] In essence, the company was one of many interests in an industry which by the end of the 1950s consisted of 157 central manufacturing creameries and 444 separating stations.[89] It was viewed by dairy producers' representatives as a malignant presence in whose shadow the co-operative movement had not thrived:

> The Dairy Disposal Company ... was intended as a temporary expedient. It has, contrary to its purpose, been favoured and used as

[85] See for example editorial comment in the *IFJ*, 24 Oct. 1953.

[86] Tom Duffy in *IFJ*, 9 May 1953.

[87] Editorial in *IFJ*, 7 May 1960.

[88] NAI, D/T S14627 A, D/A memo to govt., 19 Aug. 1960.

[89] *Gillmor, Agriculture*, p. 112.

the means for extending state control over the dairying industry, and the expansion of its activities has been marked by stagnation in the field of co-operative farming enterprise. The IAOS has, in practice, been limited in function, reduced to dependence on the state and to the status of a technical and advisory body. Contrary to sound social policy, the department has through the board arrogated itself in an empirical manner, the control of a large section of the dairying industry, making rural serfs without say, representation, or means of airing a grievance, of a large section of the creamery producers.[90]

The road from serfdom was not readily apparent. Inefficiency at all levels of the dairy industry effectively negated any long-term benefits which might have accrued from price policy. The conflict over prices deflected attention from the fundamental need to restructure and resulted in a series of insubstantial, piecemeal measures backed by insufficient resources. Failure to improve milk yields and herd numbers, and failure to develop adequate processing mechanisms, emasculated the industry. For many of the 'rural serfs' there seemed no prospect of a future in dairying. Only the British market with its emphasis on live cattle exports offered anything approaching a substantial profitable outlet.

IV

Trading with Britain

The overriding influence of the trade agreements of 1938 and 1948 further elevated the traditional importance of Britain for Irish agricultural exports. Cattle exports to the continent had peaked at 70,000 head in 1947 but a combination of government control and falling prices had seen them almost halve by the early 1950s. This was not a situation which unduly concerned the Irish government – indeed, it was one which they had conspired in creating. A 1951 Department of External Affairs review of the 1948 agreement remarked that the agreement was generally satisfactory and "that it is neither necessary nor desirable to seek to replace the existing agreements by an entirely new trade agreement." Indeed the review proposed that any improvements which government departments saw as desirable should be sought on an individual basis without reopening the whole question of trade and providing Britain with the formal opportunity to propose modification to Ireland's disadvantage. On agriculture the report noted that the Department of Agriculture believed that while the agreements were not perfect, the

---

[90] NAI, D/T S14627 A/2, ICMSA memo to govt., Sept. 1951.

arrangements that emerged in practice are actually much better than might have been originally intended on a strict interpretation of the formal agreement of 1948. To a substantial extent this position appears to be attributable to the relatively good relations and close contacts which have prevailed between the Department of Agriculture and the British Ministry of Food.[91]

For their part, the British were also content with the agricultural conditions. In February 1952 the British Ministry of Agriculture had written that it did not agree with the Ministry of Fuel and Power's request to reopen negotiations with Ireland with a view towards reducing their coal obligation as they did not wish to upset the existing Irish commitment to allocate 90 per cent of meat exports to Britain.[92] Nonetheless, the 1948 agreement did stipulate that there be a formal consultation after four years on the agricultural provisions of the annex which regulated prices and accessibility. The Ministry of Food in Britain wrote that there needed to be some renegotiation of the agricultural section as "much of the present text is now a dead letter and the rest needs modifying in the light of changed circumstances."[93] In Dublin, the Department of Agriculture argued that the consultations should be used to seek improvements in the existing arrangements governing agricultural exports, particularly in respect of dressed beef and egg prices. It further alluded to the possibility of some form of contribution from the British towards the eradication of bovine tuberculosis.[94] The Irish were aware that the British would probably seek the restriction of carcass meat sales to countries other than Britain but, while certain ministries in Britain wished to do this, the Treasury argued that the trade should be encouraged as it improved Ireland's balance of payments position.[95] The Irish acknowledged that their developing meat trade with the US had pushed total meat exports to non-British markets to 15 per cent but argued that, in the 1948 agreement, the percentage stipulation related only to live cattle and that no mention had been made of the dressed meat trade.[96] That trade was causing concern in British circles. In July 1952 an official of the British embassy in Dublin wrote that two new factories for meat processing had opened in Dublin and "what may well amount to a silent revolution in the local cattle trade is described by exporters as 'merely a trend which has been long overdue' since the Republic is one of the last countries in the world still to exploit its beef cattle on the hoof."[97]

For British officials, the move towards food processing had "a slightly sinister ring. It is industrialisation in the name of agriculture ... Our real interest lies in

---

[91] NAI, D/T S10638 B, D/EA memo to govt., 24 Jan. 1952.

[92] PRO, MAF 40/448, MAF note, 6 Feb. 1952.

[93] PRO, MAF 40/448, M/F memo, 4 Apr. 1952.

[94] NAI, D/T S14042F, D/A memo to govt., Jul. 1952.

[95] PRO, MAF 40/448, overseas negotiation committee report, 23 May 1952. The Ministry of Agriculture and the Ministry of Food both wanted the trade to be limited and argued that Ireland's total meat exports to non-British countries be limited to 10 per cent as against the treasury's proposal of 20 per cent.

[96] NAI, D/T S14042 F, D/A memo to govt., Jul. 1952.

[97] PRO, MAF 40/448, Dublin Embassy to CRO, 22 Jul. 1952.

fresh meat from the Republic and not in canned meat."[98] In an attempt to undermine that trade, they had given only the most meagre of assurances that Irish processed beef would find a market in Britain in the belief that the Irish might be dissuaded from investing in it without some certainty of profitable sale: "It remains to be seen whether in fact people are sufficiently confident in the future of this trade to sink the large amount of capital needed."[99] The British recognised that the carcass meat trade was, as yet unimportant, but they did not wish it to develop in stature.[100] Accordingly, it was agreed between departments that the British approach in the talks would be to seek a guarantee that Ireland would send 90 per cent of all cattle and beef to them – for which they would offer slightly higher prices than were previously paid.[101]

Talks commenced between agricultural officials of both governments in August 1952 in Dublin. The British reported that they had offered increased prices for cattle and meat, provided the Irish agreed to a 90 per cent clause but: "The Irish Department of Agriculture said that they were not anxious to see any such increase go into the pockets of their farmers; they would prefer the money to be used to finance part of the cost of a scheme for the eradication of bovine tuberculosis" Indeed, the Irish "freely admitted" that existing prices were good enough for the farmers and that unless a tuberculosis eradication scheme was enacted quickly there would be long-term problems. Irish officials asked for a contribution of £200,000 per annum to a scheme which they envisaged would cost £500,000 per annum and resisted British suggestions that the best way to pay for such a scheme would be through a levy on exports as Eamon de Valera had given a public assurance that no such levy would be introduced.[102] The proposal took the British somewhat by surprise. The Ministry of Agriculture broadly supported the idea, but wondered whether the scheme would be of adequate standard and commented that "the appropriate course of action is for the Irish Government to pass on to the farmers the increases in prices which we offer and to finance the TB eradication scheme out of their own internal resources. These things are, nonetheless, a matter of governmental policy."[103]

That, in itself, was a moot point. The British officials had noted of their original discussion with the Irish in August:

---

[98] PRO, MAF 40/452, MAF note, Oct. 1953.

[99] PRO, MAF 40/448, MAF note, Feb. 1952.

[100] PRO, MAF 40/448, M/F note, 31 Jan. 1952.

[101] Similar contractual agreements existed between Britain and other agricultural importers. For example, in 1952, there was a limit of 20,000 tons placed on the import from New Zealand of processed meat. The New Zealand authorities were unhappy with the limit and sought to have it raised to 30,000 tons in the dying months of 1952. See NAI D/A 10/10/1/1, part ii, newspaper cutting from The Grocer, 5 Jul. 1951. Danish farmers also accepted a commitment to higher prices in an attempt to tie them almost exclusively into the British market. See The Times, 25 Oct. 1951.

[102] PRO, MAF 40/448, British notes of talks, Dublin 25–29 Aug. 1952.

[103] PRO, MAF 40/448, MAF memo to govt., Oct. 1952.

The Irish delegates had not sought any instructions from their Ministers before the talks began; and although it was easy to get them to criticise our proposals, it was not easy to extract from them any full statement of what they themselves wanted. Moreover, there were some indications that what the Irish Department of Agriculture wanted was not necessarily quite the same as what their Ministers would ask for.[104]

This lack of unity and direction in the Irish proposals was manifest throughout the discussions of the following nine months which often seemed as much a struggle for supremacy within the Irish side, as an attempt to secure better trading arrangements with Britain. The inability to formulate a coherent response to British proposals to place a 90 per cent limitation on export to non-British markets offers a case in point. In September 1952 the Department of External Affairs wrote to say that rather than commit Ireland to a percentage, they should choose a base year, say 1951–2, and promise a basic quantitative number for guaranteed export so that "any increase in cattle production over existing stocks should be free of any treaty limit and open to competition on equal terms by the whole world."[105] The Department of Agriculture replied that in the past specific quantitative arrangements had failed and, regardless of that, after "a conscientious appraisal" of export markets "we cannot reasonably hope for any appreciable expansion in their demand." Moreover, "increased cattle production is inevitably a long and slow business … [and] a substantial increase in the total output of cattle seems unlikely in the next few years."[106] In general, the Department of Agriculture retained an ambivalent attitude to food processing. Enquiries by British firms on the possibilities of setting up in Ireland met with less than enthusiastic response.[107] The talks stalled as, in the absence of de Valera through illness, the Irish were unable to obtain clear direction.

In the interim, a report was published by a group of American consultants, Ibec Technical Services Corporation, commissioned by the Industrial Development Authority (IDA) and backed by Economic Co-operation Administration (ECA) funding, which was deeply critical of the extent of the dependency of Ireland on the British market and, particularly, of the fact that the vast majority of exports were live cattle. One section of the report was entitled: "In the Irish economy cattle is king." It opined that it appeared to outside observers

> that the overall pattern of the Irish cattle industry has been organized
> in a fashion that serves the convenience of the economy of the United

---

[104] PRO, MAF 40/448, British notes of talks, Dublin 25/29 Aug. 1952.

[105] NAI, D/T S14042 F, D/EA to D/A, 30 Sept. 1952.

[106] NAI, D/T S14042 F, D/A to D/EA, 20 Oct. 1952.

[107] See, for example, NAI, D/A 10/10/1/1 part ii, exchange of letters in summer of 1951 between D/A and Pre-Cooked Hygienic Foods, Ltd. That company had a licence to import frozen pre-cooked meals into Britain and wanted to explore the possibility of setting up a company in Ireland. The company proposed to produce quantities of meals substantially greater than the combined total which Irish firms managed to export but the Department was decidedly unenthusiastic about the proposals. Far from encouraging investigation of the worth of the scheme, the Department outlined, at length, the potential difficulties entailed in a project of its nature.

Kingdom ... [I]ts persistence for so long a period after the Republic of Ireland had won its political independence is somewhat of an enigma. There can be no doubt that the organization of Ireland's cattle industry is exceptional in the degree to which its product is disposed of through export shipments of live cattle and, consequently, in the meagerness of its meat production from cattle in Ireland relative to the size of its cattle industry.

The report stressed that the 1948 trade agreement was a disaster for the Irish government and that, if the Irish economy was to prosper, it was an imperative that the food processing industry be greatly expanded: "every practicable effort should be made to modify the terms of the Treaty to allow Ireland to ship carcass meat instead of live cattle, or at least to increase radically the proportion of carcass meat that Great Britain agrees to receive." Ultimately,

> the essential fabric of Ireland's cattle policy has been weak, based on a warp of pessimism crossed by a weft of timidity. It could only be justified, and we have heard a variety of such justifications, by an appraisal of market outlook sufficiently dismal to warrant adherence to a pattern that has proved devoid of dynamic growth, on the ground that a meager certainty is better than the most promising hazard.[108]

The British Board of Trade responded to the Ibec report with the criticism that it was founded on "an unreasonable prejudice against the dependence of Irish agriculture on exports to the UK."[109] Nonetheless, the Ministry of Agriculture commented that in the course of the discussions with the Irish no mention should be made of the report "lest they begin to take an interest in it which they do not seem to have."[110] The Ibec report had had a deep impact on some Irish ministers, however. The *Irish Times* reported that Seán Lemass had not just been influenced by the report, but had begun preaching from it. Lemass, it was noted, "is taken with the American idea of adding to the national income by processing the home-produced raw materials, and is in complete accord, apparently, with the view that foreign markets should be developed more and more, if only as a bargaining weapon in Britain." Ominously, though, the paper continued: "There is a sober stratum of opinion in this country, however, which believes that foreign opinion may be quite a good thing to have, but recognises that it cannot escape the defect of being simply too logical!"[111]

The Department of Agriculture continued to argue that the 90 per cent limitation was not "disadvantageous in any practical sense to this country, in weighing against it the solid advantages offered in return," and considered that "a settlement on the lines proposed would be decisively in favour of this country."[112]

---

108 *Ibec report: Industrial potentials of Ireland: an appraisal* (1952), esp. pp 70, 73, 75, 76.

109 PRO, MAF 40/449, Board of Trade (B/T) memo, 27 Jan. 1953.

110 PRO, MAF 40/449, MAF to CRO, 9 Mar. 1953.

111 *Irish Times*, 24 Nov. 1952.

112 NAI, D/T S14042 F, D/A memos to govt., 8 Sept. 1952 and 20 Nov. 1952, and D/IC memo to govt., 20 Nov. 1952.

The proposed agreement offered a clear path to favourable treatment in the British market: "There is little doubt that the continental demand is inherently marginal and that the purchases are largely a matter of closing a relatively small gap between consumption and domestic supplies. There is no market for store cattle on the continent and the fat cattle purchased are for the most part of secondary quality." It commented: "It should not be thought that there are any markets on the continent which have not been explored." Equally, the US market offered, at best, a potential export of 10,000 tons due to Mexican and Canadian imports, while there was the possibility of winning sizeable sales with the British who had now promised they "would bind themselves to make specific arrangements to ensure that the prices offered for beef would enable very substantial exports to be made." To that end, the department had "no doubt that the balance of advantage in the proposed new annex is decisively in Ireland's favour and that no concession of practical significance falls to be made on the Irish side." All told, the offers from Britain "clearly outweigh the largely theoretical restriction which would represent the quid pro quo ... It would be highly disadvantageous to have no agreement with Britain on the off-chance that some time or another a temporary market may turn up elsewhere."

Under Lemass, the Department of Industry and Commerce was fundamentally opposed:

> British interests are different from ours. It is the British aim to ensure the maximum supply of meat from Ireland in the form most suitable to Britain's own economy and at the lowest price. British preference is for the supply of the bulk of our cattle in the form of stores and, presumably, for obtaining the balance in the form of fat cattle rather than meat. The British government, being the purchaser of our fat cattle and meat, also the body which determines ultimately the price of our stores, is in a strong position to influence the trend of our trade ... It is in Ireland's interest on the other hand to develop, as far as possible, alternative markets to Britain and to aim at the export of meat rather than live cattle.

Ultimately, the Department of Industry and Commerce argued, it was essential that any Irish agreement with Britain would preserve the right to develop other markets, and secure unlimited markets in Britain at prices which would favour carcass meat rather than cattle exports. In opposition to this, it claimed the arrangement which the Department of Agriculture proposed would confirm virtually complete dependence on one market, limit Ireland's export potential to British requirements and discourage any pioneering efforts to open new markets. The Department of Agriculture derided the contribution from Industry and Commerce as "suggestive and tendentious rather than factual and cannot be said to reveal a full grasp of the actual points arising ... It is of course very easy to set out the ingredients of an ideal Agreement but a point that should not be overlooked is that there are two parties concerned."[113]

---

113 *Ibid.*

In February 1953 the Irish government moved to reopen negotiations. Its officials were finally given definite instructions, clearly influenced by the Department of Industry and Commerce's stance. The British proposals of the previous August were deemed to be unacceptable and the Irish avowed they would not accept limitation on export to any third country. Further, the officials were to seek admittance for all Irish agricultural produce free of duty and without quantitative restrictions, that all Irish produce would be bought so long as bulk purchase remains, that after decontrol there would be no price discrimination against Irish produce, that Irish producers would receive equality of price with their British counterparts, and that the British should pay the Irish a sum equal to the existing 5s differential in price towards the cost of a TB eradication scheme.[114] The Irish embassy in London was instructed to inform the British government that they were not prepared to accept any limitation on export to third countries as "it is better that the destinations of meat and cattle exports should be determined by price and trade considerations. If satisfactory prices and an assured and permanent market are available in Britain, it is certain that the great bulk of Irish exports will be directed to Britain."[115] In Dublin, de Valera informed the British ambassador that any undertaking on a 90 per cent limitation was now politically impossible.[116]

Negotiations resumed in April 1953 and the British reacted against the Irish demands by saying that without either a percentage or quantitative guarantee from the Irish over cattle, all existing arrangements where Irish prices are related to British ones would be brought into question. Equally the British proposed that, in the event of continued deadlock, they would just go for a one-year deal rather than the four-year one sought by the Irish.[117] The Irish negotiators viewed the risk of this happening as too great. The government in Dublin capitulated and decided to resume negotiations on the basis of the British proposals of the previous August which had effectively promised higher prices in return for the maintenance of a 10 per cent limitation.[118] On 27 April 1953 the Irish announced to the British that they were now accepting the original offer. The British

> were considerably surprised that they should feel able now to revert in view of all that has been said publicly and privately in the meanwhile … The Irish negotiators were themselves rather abashed by their revised instructions which they had clearly won only after prolonged discussions in Dublin – discussions which they described as involving burning boats on streams flowing uphill under broken bridges.[119]

On 17 May 1953 the two governments announced they had reached agreement on a three-year accord which reduced the differential on Irish cattle

---

[114] NAI, D/T S14042 G, D/A memo, 19 Feb. 1953.

[115] NAI, D/T S14042 H, D/T memo to Irish embassy in Dublin, Mar. 1953.

[116] PRO, MAF 40/449, MAF note of meeting, 17 Mar. 1953.

[117] NAI, D/T S14042 H, Irish embassy in London memo to govt., 9 Apr. 1953.

[118] NAI, D/T S14042 H, cabinet minutes, 21 Apr. 1953.

[119] PRO, MAF 40/448, British embassy in Dublin to CRO, 4 May 1953.

from 5s to 4s 6d per live cwt. and which committed Ireland to send 90 per cent of its meat to Britain, without any definite commitment on the internal relationship between stores, fat cattle and processed meat.[120] The *Irish Farmers' Journal* welcomed the agreement as bringing a good increase in price and said it would lend "highly desirable" safeguards to the cattle trade.[121] The *Irish Times* believed that the new deal was a welcome one but wondered: "How many of the farmers will, in fact, take advantage of it is another matter. Agricultural production has increased so slowly in recent years that there is little cause to expect any desire among the farmers for their economic betterment. One is impelled to ask whether, if they got ten times the present prices for their produce, they would be interested."[122] The Department of Agriculture claimed the deal "constitutes a significant advance in the arrangements governing the export of our most important agricultural commodities to Britain."[123]

Nonetheless, it is difficult to see the Irish approach to the talks as anything other than a shambles. Initially, officials entered the negotiating process without definite ministerial instruction. The absence through illness of de Valera facilitated a level of inter-departmental disagreement which delayed the potential to reach any settlement. In the hiatus which absorbed the middle months of dealing, the publication of the Ibec report decrying dependence on the British market and the pronouncements of Seán Lemass in support of this view, suggested a definite move away from absolute reliance on live cattle exports to Britain. It was clear, though, that the Department of Agriculture was more concerned about the practicalities of price and contract duration than what it perceived as mere theoretical restrictions on percentage sales to non-British markets. The threat of losing its position in the British market cowed the Irish and the brief rebellion was over. The earlier emphasis on duration of contract seemed somewhat futile, however, during further discussions in the early months of 1954. The Irish sought a meeting over impending decontrol of livestock and meat in Britain in the wake of the British announcement that, in the following summer, the Ministry of Food would cease to be the purchasers of livestock and meat and that there would be some return to free market conditions.[124] The Irish government accepted as their starting point for discussions a Department of Agriculture memorandum which proposed that the Irish seek the extension to their livestock of the minimum price guarantees paid to British farmers and to seek to either remove or relax the possibility of the imposition of quantitative restrictions on agricultural imports.[125]

A series of meetings saw the Irish proposals countered by British officials who said they would be unable to extend price guarantees and claimed that they would have to extend the residential period obligatory for Irish store cattle to

---

120 PRO, MAF 40/450, MAF note, 17 Jun. 1953.

121 *IFJ*, 14 Jun. 1953 and 27 Jun. 1953.

122 *Irish Times*, 19 Jun. 1953.

123 NAI, D/T S14042 H, D/A draft speech for Minister for Agriculture, 17 Jun. 1953.

124 NAI, D/T S14042 I, D/A memo to govt., 22 Jan. 1954.

125 NAI, D/T S14042 I, D/A memo to govt., 27 Feb. 1954 and cabinet minutes, 1 Mar. 1954.

qualify for subsidies from two to three months.[126] Irish officials were unable to make any progress as the British reiterated the impossibility of the extension of price guarantees for all produce beyond livestock as other countries would want the same concession.[127] Ministers Lemass and Walsh flew to London to salvage the Irish case. Eventually, the British agreed that the price differential would continue at 4s 6d per live cwt. and that the two month period would remain, although this would be reassessed the following year. There was no extension of price guarantees beyond livestock.[128] Lemass pronounced himself very satisfied with the outcome and the *Irish Times* crowed that "Irish agriculture ought to be set fair on the road to prosperity. Whether it achieves the goal depends on itself."[129]

Although in 1954 Irish lobbying had prevented the extension of the period of residence necessary for Irish store cattle to qualify for guaranteed prices from two to three months, the following year it was back on the agenda. The Ministry of Agriculture was determined to press the matter forward and indications that Britain intended to extend the residency term and end guaranteed payments for sheep and lambs were received with dismay by the Irish. M.J. Barry wrote from the Irish embassy in London to British officials that it marked "a complete departure from the spirit of the arrangements which have operated between us over many years and would, if pursued, raise questions of the highest policy on our side."[130] On negotiation, guaranteed prices for sheep and lambs were not terminated but the Irish were unable to deflect British aims on store cattle residency. It was agreed in November 1955 that the three month period would come into force from March 1956 and that the abatement on collective guarantee to British-bred cattle would be dropped by 1s per live cwt. In an attempt at damage limitation the Irish had sought a guarantee that these arrangements would not be changed for three years, but the British only gave a qualified assurance on that point.[131] The Irish government accepted James Dillon's argument that the new disimproved arrangements were "in the circumstances, satisfactory."[132] Dillon publicised the new arrangements in December saying "on this foundation we can procure for all our people the best standard of living enjoyed by any agricultural community in the world."[133] The hyperbole was unjustified. The Irish had succeeded only in preventing a serious deterioration of their position – not in creating the conditions for leaping forward.

Irish economic circumstance continually weakened the Irish hand in the negotiating process. In January 1956 the British government considered breaking the 1948 trade agreement by cutting the exports of coal due to be delivered to

---

[126] NAI, D/T S14042 I, D/A memos to govt., 16 Mar. 1954 and 22 Mar. 1954.

[127] PRO, MAF 40/450, MAF note, 13 Mar. 1954.

[128] *Irish Press*, 15 Apr. 1954 and *Irish Times*, 19 Apr. 1954.

[129] *Ibid.*

[130] PRO, MAF 40/360, M.J. Barry to MAF, 13 Jun. 1955.

[131] PRO, MAF, 40/360, MAF note, 2 Nov. 1955.

[132] NAI, D/T S14042 J, D/A memo to govt., 3 Nov. 1955 and cabinet minutes, 25 Nov. 1955.

[133] NAI, D/T S14042 J, D/A note, 8 Dec. 1955.

Ireland. A draft minute by the Ministry of Agriculture acknowledged the importance of Irish store cattle to the British livestock economy but noted:

> From time to time the Southern Irish have tried to find alternative outlets for their products but ... they remain almost wholly dependent for their livelihood upon their exports to this country. If, therefore, we break the agreement and the Southern Irish wish to retaliate, there is little that they could do so far as our major food interests are concerned which would not hurt them more than it would hurt us. But they could be tiresome in small ways.[134]

By the time the minute was sent its tone was refined somewhat but its core remained the same. Ultimately, though, the British decided not to press the matter in case it disturbed the existing arrangements which they viewed as favourable.[135]

Farming interests in Ireland continued to press for a new agreement in the second half of the decade. A columnist in the *Irish Farmers' Journal* commented: "Our trading relations with Britain are now almost entirely governed by the 20-year old agreement made in 1938. This agreement is now obsolete and Irish farm prices are suffering as a result."[136] The paper noted that agricultural policy had been to integrate as closely as possible with Britain but that the agreements now effectively hindered that desire.[137] Throughout this period Britain resisted any desire to renegotiate the existing agreements and Ireland did not press for substantial review. There were intermittent discussions on specific agricultural products but, as the British Board of Trade pointed out, there was no provision for a general review of the agreement. For agriculture, it was the arrangements on prices and access contained in the annex to the agreement which determined its worth and the British believed "with the end of state trading for the products in question this provision has become virtually a dead letter."[138]

With the failure to renegotiate definite agreements, market forces dictated that livestock remained the only truly viable Irish export.[139] This is reflected in the increasing dependence on the sales of store cattle despite the unfavourable readjustment on price and residency through the era (see appendix). Some viewed the dependency in apocalyptic terms, including a correspondent to the *Irish Farmers' Journal:*

---

[134] PRO, MAF 40/471, MAF draft minute, 18 Jan. 1956.

[135] PRO, MAF 40/471, B/T memos 23 Jan. 1956 and 13 Feb. 1956.

[136] *IFJ,* 30 Mar. 1957.

[137] *Ibid.,* 24 Aug. 1957.

[138] PRO, MAF 40/471, B/T memo, 23 Jan. 1956.

[139] The pigs and bacon industry, in contrast, only managed to compete on the export market in 1956 with the help of significant government subsidies. Subsidy cuts in 1957 further depressed that industry and left it struggling to export competitively. See NAI, D/T S12846 D/1, cabinet minutes, 24 Feb. 1956 and 31 Dec. 1957.

Because we have tried and failed in the past does not absolve us from trying again to shake off this blight, this cancer that emasculates the Irish people, and makes of them a more pitiable object in the eyes of the nations than they ever were in the worst days of oppression; for then we could blame our misfortunes on others; now we have none but ourselves to blame. Why are we so faint-hearted when we have never really made a bold attempt to cart off the beef economy?[140]

An *Irish Farmers' Journal* columnist was more practical in his analysis: "An economy which is largely dependent on cattle for its export earnings cannot be easily adjusted to the demands of a relentless outside pressure. An agricultural policy – if there be such – based upon it is hopelessly inadequate."[141] It was impossible to disagree with the British official who noted that, for Ireland, "political separation from the United Kingdom has not been accompanied by any economic separation."[142]

V

Land policy

The chasm between aspiration and reality in Irish society has rarely been more evident than in the interaction of land, people and politics in the 1950s. The veterans of the struggle for independence still held power through the decade and most remained faithful to a vision which inherently contradicted the prevailing forces in western society. The second half of the twentieth century brought 'the death of the peasantry' across the industrialised world. By contrast, the ideological inheritance of Irish political leaders emphasised the social worth of a thriving agrarian society and this found continuous expression in the political rhetoric of the era. But not only were international market forces aligned against this vision, government policy effectively undermined any possibility of realising it. By the 1950s there were no new initiatives to rally round, rather old ones were pursued with a distinct lack of conviction. Nonetheless, continued loyalty to the old romance of the comely maiden at the cross-roads was not merely the delusional fantasy of a Celtic cabal bound immutably to an imagined past. Beyond the woolly idealists who dreamed of rural idyll from the comfort of suburban streets, there remained a popular passion for land rooted in the perception of its potential as a

---

[140] Tom Duffy in *IFJ*, 5 Feb. 1955.

[141] 'Farm Economist' in *IFJ*, 21 Jul. 1956. More than a year earlier, on 4 Jun. 1955, the paper had warned of the "grave weaknesses in an agricultural policy that centres wholly on beef."

[142] PRO, MAF 40/448, A.M. Hillis letter to Chancellor of Exchequer, 5 Feb. 1952.

conduit to economic security. This manifested itself in different manners at different levels but, in its essence, it continued to reflect post-famine agrarianism: those who had land wanted more and those who had none wanted, at least, a few acres to farm.

Acute land hunger was an ever-powerful dynamic in the Irish political process. Elected representatives continually received demands from constituents seeking to exploit the parochial clientism of the brokerage system. Old tensions were never far beneath the surface. Limerick TD, Donnchadh Ó Briain, was only one of many who received a series of pleas to intervene in the workings of the Land Commission. In 1946, Ó Briain received a letter asking: "Will you please let me know what the Land Commission are going to do with the land of Mrs. Westropp. Are they going to divide it or no? Let me know as soon as possible for if she is not going to give it up we will talk to her and make her give it."[143] More common were demands in respect of land already acquired by the commission. A Fianna Fáil cumann chairman, Dick O'Donnell, wrote to Ó Briain in support of an old comrade seeking lands at Caherguillemore, Co. Limerick which were due to be allocated:

> I spoke to you some time ago about getting a holding or portion for Batt O'Brien ... He is an uneconomic holder and an old IRA man and vice-chairman of the Grange Fianna Fail cumann ... On the same occasion I informed you that a James O'Loughlin of Grange was also looking for a holding there and you told me to send on the particulars of his case. This man was the leading light of the Blue shirt campaign in Grange and is still a leading light in the Fine Gael party ... I am informed that he is leaving no stone unturned. Should this man succeed in his effort to obtain a holding it will mark the end of Fianna Fail in this locality. Even if our nominations are turned down, the blow will fall lightly so long as O'Loughlin does not beat us.[144]

Other requests were borne of sheer desperation. One Co. Limerick supplicant mentioned his war wounds in passing and told Ó Briain: "If I got a decent farm even in the hills of Wicklow I'd grab it."[145] Another informed Ó Briain that he owned two acres of land which he supplemented with four cottage plots to keep two cows, six heifers, four sows, two chicks and some barley, and asked for a few acres of a nearby estate to enable him to expand his operations.[146] Even as the 1950s passed into the 1960s the demands continued to flow. One woman wrote on

---

143 UCDA, Donnchadh Ó Briain papers, P83/116(8), John O'Brien, Kilcornan, Co. Limerick to Ó Briain, 1946.
144 UCDA, Donnchadh Ó Briain papers, P83/124(88), Dick O'Donnell, Grange, Killmallock, Co. Limerick to Ó Briain, 7 Dec. 1953.
145 UCDA, Donnchadh Ó Briain papers, P83/144(10), Stephen Ryan, Limerick to Ó Briain, 7,8 or 10 Mar. 1953 (the author of the letter wrote that he was unsure of the date). Ryan commented: "There is one thing I notice about the Minister of Lands and the Land Commission, and that is that it is absolutely necessary to keep pressing them and reminding them all the time."
146 UCDA, Donnchadh Ó Briain papers, P83/134(86), Dermot Cregg, Croom to Ó Briain, 4 Dec. 1953.

behalf of her son who was married with one child and farmed "eight acres of craggy land which you may understand is hard to make a living on ... I wonder if you could do anything for him to get a few extra acres."[147] Land assumed a quasi-religious importance. A columnist in the *Irish Farmers' Journal* wrote in 1950: "I still believe that a man will rise from among our own to take us in hand and to divide the people until every acre has its man."[148] Warming to his theme the following week, 'Agricolae' wrote that "the whole aim of the coming of the People's man will be to divide the people over the land so that eventually every acre will be a hive of production and the Republic of Ireland will have a population of 12 to 15 millions, where today she has less than 3 millions. The programme will take 75 to 100 years from his coming."[149]

In the apparent absence of any land messiah, the Department of Lands was forced to operate through the more prosaic medium of the Land Commission. The commission's operations in the 1930s had been characterised by a singular vigour and bore all the hall marks of an agent of social revolution. The war years had cooled its ardour significantly. In the year ended March 1938, the area of land divided was 63,302 acres but ten years later that total had fallen to 12,615 acres per annum.[150] There were several causes of the dramatic decline. The principal immediate reason was the secondment of a large number of officials to other departments during the war, yet even before the Emergency, Eamon de Valera had acknowledged the extent of the difficulties faced by the Land Commission. The most ardent of visionaries could not avoid the assertion that continued redistribution on a 1930s scale was impractical. For many others, it was now viewed as undesirable. Resources were not again committed on a large scale amid a tacit acceptance that the original project was unfeasible, however desirable it may have been.

Radical agrarianism was not a central aspect of post-war policy but it was never conceivable for political reasons that all aspects of the doctrine would be laid to rest. The Land Commission continued to operate and, in the years 1945 to 1972, distributed 341,000 hectares in land settlement operations, created 2,300 new farms, enlarged 23,500 existing farms and spent £16.5m on estate management.[151] Effectively, the policy from 1948 was to attempt to relieve the problems of the congested districts of the west. The arrival as Minister for Lands of Joseph Blowick of Clann na Talmhan brought a new impetus to land initiatives. In April 1948 the government agreed with the Department of Lands that it could recommence operations in acquiring land outside the congested districts to assist in

[147] UCDA, Donnchadh Ó Briain papers, P83/175(2), Madge Ranahan, Askeaton, 15 Feb. 1961.
[148] 'Agricolae's Corner' in *IFJ*, 11 Feb. 1950.
[149] *Ibid.*, 18 Feb. 1950.
[150] Sammon, *Land Commission*, p. 17. By the 1950s, farmers had lost all faith in the commission as a western farmer commented: "The Congested Districts Board were the greatest men to ever help the small farmer. This damned Land Commission is not worth a curse." See Irish Folklore Archives, Ms. 1506, James Delaney interview of John Naughton in 1950s.
[151] Gillmor, *Agriculture*, p. 42.

the relief of the appalling conditions still prevalent in those districts. There are very many over-crowded areas, with the tenants' land in rundale patches and with inferior, unsanitary housing, for which nothing can be done until lands are found to which some of the landowners, large or small, in the congested places can be migrated.[152]

One month later the government moved to reverse this decision and asked Blowick that division of untenanted land be ceased as an economising move with the proposal that the departmental budget for land improvement be cut from £254,000 to £100,000. Blowick's response was uncompromising: "The Minister is convinced that he as minister, and the government, could not stand over a decision which would bring a stop to the work of the Land Commission for the relief of congested tenants – the 'have-nots' of our farmers."[153] This thinly-veiled resignation threat brought agreement from the government that its original decision stood but in October 1948 the Department of Finance again requested that land division cease outside the congested districts. Finance believed that the division of land reduced the labour available for agriculture, lessened the likelihood of mechanisation and lowered output.[154] Again, the Department of Lands withstood the assault from Finance, but at the same time it was agreed that the desirable size of holding should be increased from 25 to 33 acres of good land, or its equivalent in land of lesser quality.[155]

Originally, an attempt had been made to increase the size of holding in 1947 when the Department of Lands had argued that:

The small standard farms of £20 P.L.V. or 25 acres of good land which present policy allows the creation outside the badly congested areas are only subsistence holdings which add little to the agricultural wealth of the country, provide little or no exportable surplus and allow no appreciable cash margin, even under favourable circumstances, out of which the ordinary allottee could hope to assist his children to find places in the world. These holdings are not economic and unless situated close to good markets are more than likely ... to lead to the impoverishment of their owners in a time of even partial depression.

The Department of Agriculture agreed and opined that "unless a holding is such as will maintain two working horses it cannot support a family from generation to generation." The Department of Agriculture further argued that landless men should not be given land as the results of their efforts were "unsatisfactory and disappointing, often shamelessly so," rather that farmers' sons should be the recipients of reallotment. In a telling commentary on social priorities in post-war Ireland, the Department of Lands argued that it should

---

152 NAI, D/T S6490 B/1, D/L memo to govt., 25 Mar. 1948 and cabinet minutes, 25 Mar. 1948.

153 NAI, D/T S11980, D/L memo to govt., 20 May 1948.

154 NAI, D/T, S6490 B/1, D/F memo to govt., 28 Oct. 1948.

155 Sammon, *Land Commission*, pp 26–7.

continue to allot small accommodation plots of three to seven acres to clergy, teachers, doctors and shopkeepers who "require a plot of land to keep a cow or two," but that the allocation of such plots to Board of Health cottiers who already held one acre be discontinued as it was "more than they can manage" and was "a very serious waste of land and expenditure and is in fact a cause of discredit to the state and to the locality."[156] The government considered these and other proposals through the summer of 1947 but in the end decided to do nothing.[157] In the immediate post-war years, the Land Commission struggled to fulfil the task expected of it principally because of paucity of resources. It had been hoped to clear the backlog of 7,500 unvested holdings within five years but the task remained uncompleted by the end of the 1960s.[158] The tortuous nature of the work was not improved by the absence of any training officer, rather experienced staff were expected to assist new recruits and stringent legal requirements left all involved fearful of errors which could forever blight a civil service career. Apart from administrative difficulties, the persistent and growing questioning of the actual role of the Land Commission did nothing to facilitate its activities. A sense of demoralisation pervaded its operations in the post-war era.[159] Even within the commission itself there was no unanimity of purpose and its directors divided on the primacy of social as against economic concerns.

Attempts to revitalise operations in the 1950s brought the ongoing division into stark perspective. Although the government agreed to raise from £250,000 to £500,000 the amount of money spent annually on acquisition and resumption of land, the use of this money was fundamentally contested. The Department of Finance had condemned the manner in which land acquired by the state was improved and passed on to tenants at a large loss. This view was accepted by one Land Commissioner, M. Deegan, who stated that loss on resale of land was indefensible and claimed that they should only give land to those who could reasonably be expected to pay back its full cost as "the area might not be as large as we could handle but it would still be of reasonable extent and it would have this great value, that the work done would be good, unhurried, unflustered work on which staff, Land Commissioners, Minister and Government could look back with satisfaction in the years to come."[160] Three other Land Commissioners offered a fundamentally different appraisal of the manner in which the budget should be spent and regarded any losses incurred as fundamentally justified:

> These losses are merely temporary losses and are more than balanced by the great benefits accruing to the nation from the creation of more farmsteads and the establishment of more families on the land ... It is an investment that, in a remarkably short time will yield a rich and abundant return in its outlay; not perhaps in cash dividends from

---

[156] NAI, D/T S6490 B/1, D/L memo to govt., 26 Jun. 1947.

[157] NAI, D/T S6490 B/1, cabinet minutes, 1 Jul. 1947, 29 Jul. 1947 and 9 Sept. 1947.

[158] Sammon, *Land Commission*, pp 29–30.

[159] *Ibid., passim.*

[160] NAI, D/T S6490 B/2, M. Deegan memo to govt., 15 Oct. 1951.

investments in the Far East and other places nearer home, but in citizens, in stock and food supplies, to say nothing of increased internal markets. Each little rural homestead that the Land Commission creates is a permanent factory for producing human and animal stock turning out its valuable quotas of the former every generation, and of the latter every year.[161]

In the end, the government swayed toward the latter approach and requested the commissioners to ensure that losses be kept to the minimum but gave no explicit directives on the matter.[162]

Throughout the 1950s the Land Commission operated schemes to relieve congestion in the congested districts, to bring holdings there up to a £10 rateable valuation, and to migrate families to midland and eastern counties. It was a thoroughly challenging task as one official noted: "In the vast majority of schemes, the area of land available was so limited and the number so great, that the best that could be done was to bring them some way towards the £10 R[ateable].V[aluation]. standard."[163] Migration proved equally laborious and between 1947 and 1952 the number of families migrated from the west to better lands averaged 52 per annum.[164] Most were ill-equipped to meet changed circumstances. The *Irish Farmers' Journal* noted: "These men are well-versed in the traditional western methods but when they try to apply them on a limited amount of Meath soil, they will hardly pay the rent."[165] There were no resources available to smooth the transition: "You might as well be in a leper colony as far as visits or advice go," complained one migrant.[166] By 1952, the department was stressing that "land alone can never completely solve the problem of congestion. Any general improvement of economic conditions in the congested areas must, to a large extent, be effected by other means."[167] In the absence of other means, the Land Commission was a convenient scapegoat for the many whose economic situation did not improve. The commission was continually attacked for being bureaucratic and politically biased. A Clann na Talmhan TD claimed the commission was "bound hand and foot in red tape and had been a failure" since its inception doing "more harm than good."[168] Claims that the work of the commission had been dictated by political influence was supported by Clonmel-based Fine Gael senator, Denis E. Burke: "The only people I know who were interfered with by the

161 NAI, D/T S6490 B/2, K. O'Shiel, D. de Brún and E. Herlihy memo to govt., 15 Oct. 1951.

162 NAI, D/T 6490 C, cabinet minutes, 31 Oct. 1951.

163 Sammon, *Land Commission*, pp 26–7.

164 NAI, D/T S6490B/2, D/L memo to govt., 14 Oct. 1952.

165 *IFJ*, 31 Mar. 1956.

166 *IFJ*, 7 Apr. 1956. Inevitably, the migration schemes were also seen as a means to spread the Irish language and the tradition of government initiatives attempting to fulfil a myriad of purposes – to such an extent that the original aim was obscured – continued. The migration of Irish speakers brought to mind Castro's adage: "Who should manage a farm? A revolutionary. What are his prerequisites? That he be a revolutionary." See Frederic L. Pryor, *The red and the green: the rise and fall of collectivized agriculture in Marxist regimes* (1992), p. 220.

167 *IFJ*, 7 Apr. 1956.

168 Bernard Commons, quoted in *Irish Independent*, 4 Jun. 1948.

Land Commission are hard-working and progressive farmers whose only fault appears to be that they have been continual supporters of the Fine Gael party."[169] Allegations of political interference in the work of the commission around Clonmel were supported by a local solicitor, James Shee who commented that "the manner in which land has been allotted up to the present is nothing short of a political bribery. Holdings which have been divided and houses built on them have been allotted to persons with absolutely no capital to work them. They could not buy a pitch-fork." Shee argued that the land should be given to farmers' sons who had a knowledge and affection for the land which "no road worker or the general run of 'hangers-on' of Fianna Fáil have."[170]

Land Commission officials strenuously denied they were politically biased and argued that it was merely a political myth propagated by TDs who sought to elevate their own status as brokers. An official recalled the attempt by one Minister for Lands to insist that every TD inform constituents who sought intervention in support of applications for land that elected representatives had no function in the selection process. This was abandoned within weeks as "the public representatives did not want the fiction that they had some hand in the decision as to which applicants would be approved for parcels of land to be brought to an abrupt end."[171] Another official stated in 1960: "It is the most utter nonsense for anyone to suggest that we would be subject to political influence." It is impossible to reach any definite conclusion on the extent of political interference in the distribution of land except to suggest tentatively that an independent TD may have been most accurate in suggesting: "The Land Commission have been made the scapegoats of politicians for years. Everybody knows they resist strongly any attempts to force people on them. But they do not always get away with it, no matter what they say. If a man can put up a reasonable claim for land and is backed by a member of the ruling party, or parties, the gun is put to the heads of the Land Commission men".[172]

Whatever about determining the selection process, there can be little doubt that the division of land was not part of any coherent agricultural policy. Almost all other impulses in Irish farming suggested the need for consolidation of farm size, not least the extensive farming hegemony which defined Irish agricultural exports. The manner in which various government departments undermined each other through the decade was a matter of frequent comment. An editorial in the *Irish Farmers' Journal* in 1952 commented: "It is most surprising that a Land Commission which for 30 years is committed to a policy of increasing the number of small farms has never applied itself towards developing a system of farming that would give the 25 to 35 acre man a decent living."[173] The paper called for the creation of farms of sixty to one hundred acres and one of its columnists noted:

---

[169] UCDA, Richard Mulcahy papers, P7B/117, Burke to Mulcahy, 26 May 1954.

[170] UCDA, Richard Mulcahy papers, P7B/117, Shee to Mulcahy, 30 Jun. 1954.

[171] Sammon, *Land Commission*, p. 126.

[172] *Sunday Review*, 10 Apr. 1960.

[173] *IFJ*, 15 Nov. 1952.

"It would be an inexcusable waste of scarce resources to continue the creation of rural slums with 30 acres of land, which, most likely, will have to be united a few years later with other holdings ... What happens here is just one more case of government departments acting in disregard of each other's existence."[174] Through the years, farmers and government alike accepted that land distribution was not economically motivated. A Department of Finance official noted "the work of the Land Commission is of a social nature," while a farm leader defined it as "a social adventure."[175] There was a singular failure to reconcile that adventure with the economic aim of maximising agricultural profit through the export of livestock. The small farms created were too small to accommodate the economic demands of extensive pastoral farming and many slid into disrepair at an early stage.[176] The parameters of what constituted a viable farm steadily increased and, in this, the Irish experience was not a unique one, rather part of a global trend.[177] If the social motivation of land division limited the maximisation of agricultural production, the failure to expand production ultimately brought social decay. The inability to supplement social policy with economic progress brought disaster in the 1950s. The vision lingered, so did the scent of impending disaster.

VI

Leaving the land

The convergence of social and economic use of land within agricultural policy was not confined to Land Commission endeavours. Eamon de Valera had long sponsored a dower house scheme which would have seen the erection of a second dwelling house on medium or large farms where farmers' sons could reside with their young wives until their fathers were ready to bequeath the farm. This, de Valera believed, would greatly alleviate the problem of late marriage in the countryside and stem its loss of population. He reiterated a long-held belief in the scheme in 1943, telling the Agricultural Science Society of University College,

---

174 *IFJ*, 23 Jun. 1956 and 'Farm Economist' in *IFJ*, 23 Jun. 1956.

175 NAI, D/T S14550, D/F memo to govt., 11 Jun. 1949 and Larry Sheedy writing in *IFJ*, 14 Apr. 1956.

176 Scottish land settlement initiatives, to cite just one example, suffered a similar experience. See Leah Leneman, 'Land settlement in Scotland after World War I', in *AHR*, vol. 37, i (1989), pp 52–64.

177 Farm sizes grew across the globe. One historian has noted that probably the most extensive exercise in land reform was the Mexican one of the 1930s. He noted, though, that "it was a huge political success, but economically irrelevant to subsequent Mexican agrarian development." Eric Hobsbawm, *Age of extremes: the short twentieth century, 1914–1991* (1994). Robert C. Stuart wrote in *The collective farm in Soviet agriculture* (1972) that from the early 1950s the size of Soviet collective farms grew substantially. In Denmark, where legislation preventing the amalgamation of small farms had been enacted, the shift away from small farms gathered such pace that in the years 1959 to 1972 the labour force halved and the number of farms fell by one-third. See Johansen, *Danish economy*, p. 137.

Dublin (UCD) of "his pet scheme," although acknowledging in passing that the trouble "would be two households on the farm and in order to make it practical you would have to convince the farmer that he was going to get some economic value apart from the social value of it."[178] De Valera received a number of letters supporting his scheme and wrote back to one of his correspondents that he "has always been surprised that farmers seemed to care for it so little. The matter is being reconsidered."[179] The cabinet set up an interdepartmental committee to consider de Valera's proposal. At its first meeting the committee proposed that its terms of reference be broadened to consider other means to encourage earlier marriage than the provision of a separate house on its own plot of land. De Valera did not agree and stated that the business of the committee was to "ascertain whether the idea that a second house should be provided on farms is a sound one and, whether sound or not, to propose a scheme."[180] The committee reported in November 1944. The report noted the tendency towards fewer children in rural schools, later marriage and single life and commented that

> farm holdings are rarely handed over until the old couple have reached 70 years, and become independent with the grant of the old age pension. When the land is given up at an early age the annuity and other pre-requisites available to the old couple under the marriage agreement are frequently not in themselves sufficient to ensure them an independent living.[181]

The report also included comments from Land Commission inspectors who were almost unanimously of the opinion the scheme would not be availed of. The inspectors believed the scheme would undermine their work through promoting subdivision, would dilute resources and prove a fruitful source of domestic friction.[182]

Some inspectors saw the scheme as desirable but impracticable: "The project would be suitable for a farming community in a high state of economic and social advancement, but appears premature in a country whose essential farm buildings only provide one-fifth of the elementary amenities necessary for production of clean wholesome food at the present rate of progress." Others were more scathing and wrote with acidity: "The only advantage I can see in the provision of a dower-house on the ordinary farm would be as a 'love nest' for the newly-weds, so that they could spend a protracted honeymoon billing and cooing until such time as they realised they had also to earn their living."[183] On receipt of the report, de Valera let the matter lie with the proviso that a more appropriate time for its

---

[178] *Irish Press*, 4 Dec. 1943.

[179] NAI, D/T S13413 A, D/T to D. Clavin, Youghal, Co. Cork, (n.d., 1943)

[180] NAI, D/T S13413–1, minutes of inter-departmental committee on early marriages, 17 Apr. 1944 and 24 Apr. 1944.

[181] NAI, D/T S13413 A, cabinet minutes, 21 Dec. 1943 and inter-departmental committee report, 17 Nov. 1944, esp. p. 12.

[182] NAI, D/T S13413 A, inter-departmental committee report, 17 Nov. 1944, *passim.*

[183] NAI, D/T S13413 A, inter-departmental committee report, 17 Nov. 1944, questionnaires.

pursuit might one day arrive.[184] If the Land Commission's inspectors were resolute in their opposition, others were more supportive. The *Irish Press* deemed the initiative worthy of serious consideration and, with its analysis assisted by the prospects of sectional gain, the *Irish Builder and Engineer* said the plan was eminently desirable and its emergence saw de Valera "displaying an unusual and welcome sense of reality."[185] In opposition, the *Evening Mail* believed that, whatever advantages accrued, would be lost as "family feuds would be multiplied and civil land wars would get into full swing and never end."[186] De Valera told the Dáil that the dower house scheme was shot down by various departments as neither wise nor feasible, and remarked wistfully:

> If I were a dictator, I would implement my idea irrespective of the objections and difficulties ... I first mentioned this 20 years ago at a convention in Cork, and I was laughed at. I have been laughed at practically every time I mentioned it ever since. Nevertheless, despite all the laughing, I believe it would be a good thing for the countryside ... I am told by critics that one of the difficulties is not so much that the people could not get married, but that the girls do not want any longer to marry the farmers. I doubt that. I would like to see it tried, anyhow. I would like to see a young, eligible farmer getting a good farm and a nice house and I would like to see that put up as an attraction in the countryside and then see whether the young man would get a girl or not.[187]

Yet, for women as much as for men, the hold of the land, regardless of its conditions, remained a powerful draw. Although a letter to the *Irish Times* lamented the absence of women from many farms as "a sorry loss to man and beast," others remained faithful to the traditions of farming life.[188] Even up to the late 1950s, almost 90 per cent of all male married farmers wed farmers' daughters and for every son who remained at home on the farm, at least one daughter also stayed.[189] In contrast to trends in most other western countries, the proportion of female farmers in Ireland increased through the twentieth century and by 1951 had reached 15.8 per cent.[190] Almost invariably this was not by way of female empowerment or the assertion of economic independence, rather it was that women had been left in possession through the death and emigration of all male relatives. Accordingly, the proportion of female farmers over 65 years of age doubled from 3.6 per cent to 7.3 per cent in the course of the century.[191] For

---

[184] NAI, D/T S13413 B/2, D/T note, 16 Jan. 1945.

[185] *Irish Press*, 5 Jul. 1947 and the *Irish Builder and Engineer* quoted in the *Irish Times*, 12 Jul. 1947.

[186] *Evening Mail*, 12 Jul. 1947.

[187] NAI, D/T S13413 B, extract from Dáil debates, 2 Jul. 1947.

[188] *Irish Times*, 6 Apr. 1944.

[189] Diarmaid Ferriter, "'A peculiar people in their own land". Catholic social theory and the plight of rural Ireland 1930-55' , (Ph.D., UCD, 1996), p. 163.

[190] Crotty, *Agricultural production*, p. 105. This total had risen from 13.5 per cent in 1881 and stood in marked contrast to other countries such as England and Wales where it dropped from 9.2 per cent to 6.7 per cent.

[191] *Ibid.* Conversely, in England and Wales the number of women farmers in that age group halved in the corresponding period – 1881 to 1951 – and by the later date stood at a mere 1.5 per cent.

women who did not marry or inherit, emigration was the most likely option. Perversely, it was seen as deplorable that these women should be forced to undertake menial tasks on foreign shores, but were nonetheless expected to acquiesce in a life of drudgery and sufferance at home where they received little if any remuneration for their labours. Gaelic poverty, it seemed, lost its spiritual essence removed from the sanctity of its rural haven.

Beyond decrying emigration from farming areas, government policy was unable to prevent it. A de Valera speech in Galway in 1951 condemning the conditions endured by Irish workers in English cities brought angry responses from the mayors of Wolverhampton, Coventry and Birmingham who might justifiably have noted that conditions must have been appalling in Ireland for its people to seek sanctuary in English ghettos.[192] A 'Commission on emigration' sat in the 1930s, reported in the 1940s and had its findings considered by a government committee which was established to co-ordinate formal action.[193] It was never acted upon but without the emergence of meaningful proposals, and inspired by a sense that something had to be done, the dower house scheme resurfaced occasionally through the 1950s. It engendered mixed emotions, especially among the farming community.[194] Again, though, no attempt was made to implement it.

Indeed, no conceivable proposal seemed capable of restraining the torrents of human tide that flowed from the country (see appendix). The director of the Central Statistics Office, R.C. Geary, lamented the lack of science which shrouded the Irish policy process:

> How does one kill specious or dangerous fallacies? Silliness gets a far better press than seriousness. The Irish population problem is not one for amateurs. The views of economists, demographers and statisticians are entitled to respect in regard to it. Our scribes and orators, prone to bright ideas, could do with the exercise of a little humility. Bright ideas are never new and rarely right.

Geary commented bleakly that there were a fixed number of jobs in the Irish economy, that that number was far less than the number entering the job market and that there seemed little prospect of the scenario altering in the foreseeable future. Noting that "neither capital nor labour as such is patriotic, and we have no

---

[192] PRO, DO 35/3917, Newspaper cuttings from *Manchester Guardian*, *The Times* and *Sunday Press*.

[193] Ferriter, 'Peculiar people', pp 240–1. Flann O'Brien's tales of incessant rain, poverty and misery offer a parody not just of the folklore of hardship, bad luck and perfidious Albion used to excuse so much of Ireland's plight, but also the mindset which acknowledged the inevitability of that status. Instead of acting to resolve their plight, the Gaels of Ireland could be seen "sitting together on the brow of a hillock discussing the hard life and debating the poor lot which was now (and would always be) Ireland's." See Flann O'Brien, *The poor mouth* (1972), p. 89.

[194] De Valera again mooted the scheme in October 1953 and it was the subject of argument in correspondence in the *Irish Farmers' Journal* in April 1954. See NAI, D/T S13413B, D/T note, 2 Oct. 1953 and *IFJ*, 17 Apr. 1954.

right to expect it to be so," Geary remarked that the Irish standard of living was only as high as it was because of the low density of population, but given the relative income of small farmers and British factory workers "one is more surprised at the number who stay than at the number who go." Geary concluded: "The Irish people are like the people in every other country in that they want to obtain the highest material rewards with the least effort ... The people collectively regard emigration as an unqualified evil, and national instincts are to be respected, but in their individual capacity they are not prepared to do anything about it."[195]

For farm labourers, emigration contributed to the further decline of a class in freefall since the famine (see appendix). The protracted demise of agricultural labourers accelerated after World War II. The appalling conditions endured were apparent and seemingly inevitable. The Department of Agriculture informed the Department of Finance in December 1947 that "it is clear that agricultural wages here are in general below the minimum subsistence standard." But McGilligan replied from Finance that a wage increase "would, to say the least of it, be most injudicious at the present time ... We are, as you know spending millions of pounds to stabilise food prices and we hope to prevent further rises in the cost-of-living index. This, in itself, rather deprives the agricultural labourer of any sound case for an increase just now on the basis of cost-of-living."[196] McGilligan further argued it was not justified to compare the relative incomes of industrial and agricultural workers, not least because it was vital to keep agricultural costs as low as possible to facilitate export – whereas industry operated with the benefit of "a closed highly-protected market."[197] This inequality of treatment was emphasised when agricultural labourers were specifically excluded when the Labour Court was established in 1946. Instead, they had to rely on the politically-loaded Agricultural Wages Board to regulate their income.[198] By 1965, a succession of amendments to the Agricultural Wages Act, 1936 and to the Agricultural Workers (Holidays) Act, 1950 entitled employees to a minimum wage of £8 per 50-hour week and 12 days' annual leave (with church and public holidays left at the discretion of both parties). Through it all, farmers continually argued that, however much they wished to do so, they could not afford to pay higher wages.[199] Factories in urban

---

195 UCDA, Richard Mulcahy papers, P7/C/139, speech by R.C. Geary to People's College Summer School, Drogheda, Co. Louth, 9 Aug. 1956.

196 UCDA, Patrick McGilligan papers, P 35 c/35, Ó Broin to McGilligan, 19 Dec. 1947 and McGilligan to Ó Broin, 3 Jan. 1948.

197 UCDA, Patrick McGilligan papers, P 35 c/35, McGilligan to Ó Broin, 3 Jan. 1948 and 6 Jan. 1948. McGilligan continued his arguments with the statement that "no increase in agricultural wages that could at all be entertained will retain workers on the land to the same extent as in the past, and any increase that could conceivably be given in wages will not affect the drift from the land." More than a decade later, J.C. Nagle made the point that the income gap between industrial and agricultural workers was large and "it seemed very doubtful whether this gap would ever be closed." See PRO, MAF 379/34, minutes of Anglo-Irish economic committee meeting, 13 Dec. 1961.

198 The chairman of the Agricultural Wages Board for the first two decades after its establishment in 1936 was former Fianna Fáil TD, William O'Leary.

199 This view was stressed by the *Irish Farmers' Journal* which, in an editorial on 22 Nov. 1952, claimed a prospective bill to reduce the farm labourers' working week was "just another step at socialising the agricultural industry." It claimed that farmers had no objection to better conditions for their workers but that they had not the money to pay for it – and any additional cost would have to be passed on for the consumer in the price of milk, butter and bread.

Ireland and on foreign shores could – the labourers turned their backs on an industry and a lifestyle which could no longer sustain them.

This sense of a society in decay pervades much of the farming attitudes of the 1950s. The leader of Macra na Feirme, Pa Quinlan wrote that the status of the Irish farmer had been "whittled down to a level not a whit higher than the livestock with which we work."[200] Stagnation was almost attractive:

> The man who sticks to the dual-purpose Shorthorn, the Large White pig, gets married late, lives a poor life, and sends his surplus children abroad, will never go broke and need never be evicted ... Is it any wonder that ... most of us chose the easier way, and just drift along, accepting such slight variations in production we get from year to year as being mostly a matter of weather? A happy enough position for those with sufficient hundreds of acres of land to provide a decent living, and for those in comfortable, and preferably state or semi-state jobs, but not so happy for your average 30-acre man or his children.[201]

The children of the 30-acre man were leaving in their droves. With the farm to be handed on intact regardless of circumstances and with few non-farming opportunities available, many had no option but to leave.[202] Others left by choice. Even the inheriting son was questioning the life which lay ahead of him. The tradition of being called 'boy' even at the age of fifty can never have been alluring, but more than ever before, the land was no longer seen as the only option. One prospective inheritor wrote, in 1956, of his life on a small farm: "I have worked on and off it as required, but now, as it is coming to the time when I shall inherit it, I am wondering what shall I do ... Shall I accept my father's farm and go on as my father did before me keeping the farm that should keep me, or leave it and step aboard the emigrant ship?" It was in this context that a farmers' son was brought to court in 1954 for stealing nineteen fleeces of wool from his father's farm in Clondalkin, Co. Dublin. The farmer "who pays his son, aged 29, £1 a week as wages was told by District Justice Reddin at Kilmainham that he was living in Victorian times and that young people nowadays would not stand for such treatment."[203]

---

[200] *IFJ*, 26 Sept. 1953. Earlier that year Quinlan had claimed that the failure to provide a decent standard of living was paving the way for communism which, one suspects, was seen as a step below a life as livestock. See *IFJ*, 25 Apr. 1953.

[201] Tom Duffy in *IFJ*, 15 Aug. 1953.

[202] "The inability to counteract the losses in agriculture by the provision of alternative employment was particularly obvious in the western parts of the country; we can illustrate this with statistics relating to three 'problem' regions – the West, North-West and Donegal. During the 1926–61 period, these regions lost a total of 96,704 agricultural jobs and gained 4,861 jobs outside agriculture – representing a net decline in employment of 91,483." P.J. Drudy, 'Land, people and the regional problem', in P.J. Drudy (ed.), *Ireland: land, politics and people*, p. 204. This is in marked contrast to the Danish experience where, for example, in the 1945–50 period, the 12 per cent decrease in agriculture employment coincided with a 58 per cent increase in industrial employment. See Peder J. Pedersen, 'Post-war growth of the Danish economy', in Nicholas Crafts and Gianni Toniolo (eds.), *Economic growth in Europe since 1945* (1996), pp 541–75, esp. p. 552.

[203] *IFJ*, 3 Jul. 1954.

Decrying the "genocidal blood-letting" of emigration created by politics of "futility, indecision and subserviency to outmoded shibboleths," the *Irish Farmers' Journal* claimed: "The people trying to work uneconomic small holdings with poor soil, without the benefit of advice, education or marketing arrangements, have thrown in the sponge and, realising the meagre pittance they can hope to earn, have bid goodbye to reservation penury."[204] Throughout the second half of the 1950s, the apocalyptic tone of most contemporary comment is striking. The claim that Ireland was "a land half-farmed, a people fleeing in despair," was echoed in most sectors of the media.[205] The population of the twenty-six counties declined by 5.2 per cent between 1926 and 1961.[206] By the mid-1950s, emigration amounted to an average of more than 45,000 per annum, the equivalent of 75 per cent of the birth rate.[207] The vast bulk of this number came from rural areas. In the 35 years between 1926 and 1961, the numbers employed in agriculture declined by 272,303 to 648,575.[208]

Emigration helped ensure an ageing farm population. A substantial number of farmers had no direct heirs and those who did tended to maintain control until late in life. Ownership was often retained even when sale of land would improve economic status. As only 13 per cent of farms in the country were purchased on the open market, the vast majority were passed on through inheritance or by means of a gift.[209] Given the relationship between age structure and economic development, there was an inevitable sense of disillusion around the deterioration of the age structure in Irish farming.[210] In areas of high emigration, small farmers were so demoralised that they

> do not want to even listen; of those who do listen, there are large numbers who either sneer at or sympathise (through ignorance) with the man on the radio or in a hall who is speaking what they like to call 'book knowledge'... They are too busy farming in the most unprofitable way (in an effort to make ends meet) to read the weekly newspaper, much less listen to lectures or read farming journals. Agriculturally speaking, the devil you know is better than the devil you don't know.[211]

---

204 *IFJ*, 9 Jun. 1956.

205 *IFJ*, 11 Jan. 1958.

206 M.J.B. Bannon, 'Urban growth and urban land policy', in P.J. Drudy (ed.) *Ireland: land, politics and people*, pp 296–323, esp. p. 300.

207 Garret Fitzgerald, 'Foreword', in John F. McCarthy (ed.), *Planning Ireland's future – the legacy of T.K. Whitaker* (1990), p. 6.

208 Drudy, 'Land', pp 203–4.

209 *Ibid.*, p. 201.

210 Gillmor, *Agriculture*, p. 43.

211 NAI, D/T S16326, anon. to de Valera, Oct. 1957. This viewpoint was supported, in part, by the economist, James Meenan, who pointed out that experience as well as age was critical to this conservatism: "The average age of male farmers was 55 years in 1946. The average farmer would thus have been 23 years old when the First World War broke out in 1914. Since then he has lived through two world wars, the Anglo-Irish war and a Civil war; two collapses in price including a major depression; four devaluations of currency, the 'Economic war' and all the business of reconstruction after 1918, 1922, 1938 and 1945. It is perhaps not a matter of wonder if farmers today take short views and are reluctant to embark on improvements that, however excellent they may be in theory, are only hostages to the fortunes of prices and to the political and economic events that control prices." Quoted in Shiel, *The quiet revolution*, p. 116

Demoralisation ran through the generations as

> in the opinion of the rural schoolboy of 14 years, his father's farm is a
> place or state where a boy suffers before he emigrates – some having
> to suffer longer than others. If asked in a rural school what occupation
> he would like to take up, it will be found that only the 'wag' or
> 'character' will say farming. He is usually a boy who will take a joke.

The writer of the above could offer little in the way of concrete measures
except to call for a "peaceful agricultural revolution" and for a campaign which
would be launched by ringing church bells for two days – an act which would "do
more to create an enquiring mind than if guns were fired for a week from
O'Connell bridge." The campaign would be aimed at raising the educational
standards of farmers with teachers in local national schools inculcating a spirit of
enterprise in the young which the parish priest would attempt to imbue in the
elders. The aim would be to produce an atmosphere to ensure that "the horse was
not only brought to water, but drank as well."[212]

For their part, policy makers seemed as demoralised as the public they
sought to serve. Government officials believed the failure of a large section of the
farming community to adopt modern efficient systems of farming was rooted in an
innate conservatism emanating, at least in part, from the demographics of rural
decline. Customs and traditions clearly played a central role in Irish farming and
there was a fatalism which suffocated progress. But the failure of farmers to
innovate seems often to have served as a convenient device as policy makers
sought exculpation from all blame. The underlying ethos in government circles
suggested that farmers would, if presented with the wheel, attempt to box it into
corners.[213] Yet, it was not merely farmers who stood exposed to accusations of
being rooted in the past and bereft of imagination. For want of resources and
ideas, advisory and educational bodies failed to have new methods accepted on a
wide scale. More pointedly there was a persistent failure to develop coherent
policy in a multitude of areas. Attempts to provide farms for young farmers was a
case in point. A 1957 initiative by Joseph Blowick, Minister for Lands, to increase
the powers of the Land Commission to acquire poorly-run farms and give them to
young farmers foundered on objections from several quarters. Land
Commissioner, Kevin O'Shiel, agreed that there were many inefficient farmers
due to a variety of reasons "such as the greater facility of moving around, now that
our farmers have 40,000 motors between them, the temptation to distraction is
larger for going to races, football matches, dances, and getting non-farming
employment in town and England."[214] O'Shiel recognised the worth of placing a

---

[212] NAI, D/T S16326, anon. to de Valera, Oct. 1957.

[213] This view was summarised in an article in *The Irish Times* on 6 Jan. 1954: "The Irish farmer is
notoriously conservative in his methods. He is so proud and jealous of his rights as a peasant proprietor
that he regards any attempt by the authorities to improve his position as an unwarranted imposition."

[214] NAI, D/T S16105 A, D/L memo to govt., 21 Feb. 1957. The memo contains an account of
correspondence over two years on attempts to resolve a scheme to improve the possibilities for small
farmers to get their own farm earlier in life.

young farmer of verve and aptitude on a hitherto inefficient farm which would allow him "to marry Mary, a girl of corresponding efficiency and love of the land, to work that farm well and to rear a family on it." Nonetheless, any imposition of an outsider would only stir up the land trouble that was such a dominant aspect of Irish history: "The locals would think nothing of burning the house and driving the cattle of the beneficiary. And from attacking non-local landless men, it would be but a short step to attacking migrants from the West or elsewhere; and we would have the whole trouble all over again, and in even more violent form."

An official of the Department of Agriculture was not quite so dramatic but while recognising the worth of a young farmer scheme noted "serious consideration must be given to the extent to which we could implement such a policy and to the reaction which it might have on our present general activities." The problem of raising expectations was deemed serious and the official was wary of "the flood of applicants whose hopes will be excited by our new policy and the consequent disappointment when it is realised that we can satisfy but a tiny trickle of this flood." The debate generated much heat but in the end the overriding feeling that, while it was feasible to use the relief of congestion in the west as a grounds for compulsory acquisition of land, the application of those powers as a means to establish an élite corps of vibrant young farmers across the country would provoke extreme opposition.[215] The proposal was never seriously considered – and no more viable alternative fell readily to hand.

In this policy vacuum, electoral fiefs and bailiwicks prospered.[216] Unable to disagree over policy, politicians competed in the pork barrel of personal favours. The shame of the politician unable to win his own area fuelled a transactional system of politics founded in dealing and strokes – or, more importantly, in the perception of access to power.[217] TDs were expected to arrange expeditious premium and grant payments, the loan of Department of Agriculture tractors, or jobs for constituents. Donnchadh Ó Briain attempted to influence the awarding of a position as horticultural instructor in Meath for a relation:

> I don't know the boy himself but I know his parents very well. His mother is a distant relation of mine and was born in my native parish in Co. Limerick. His father is a sergeant in the gardai, if he has not retired by now. Last year Neal Blaney helped another brother to get a job as agricultural instructor in Co. Donegal. They are a good decent family and I would appreciate any help you could give them.[218]

---

215 *Ibid.*

216 A.J. Parker, *Localism and bailiwicks: the Galway West constituency in the 1977 election* (1977), p. 34.

217 For example, in his memoirs Monsignor James Horan noted that the independent TD Jack McQuillan was perceived by his constituents in the west to be all-powerful as "local people believed that the government departments were afraid of him and his word was law." Quoted in Monsignor James Horan, *Memoirs* (ed. Fr Séamus McGréil) (1992) p. 84.

218 UCDA, Donnchadh Ó Briain papers, P83/165(44) and (45), Ó Briain to Michael Hilliard, 30 Oct. 1957.

Equally, when the party did not hold the majority on a County Committee of Agriculture charged with awarding the position there was little point in lobbying.[219] Nothing was considered too trivial. One constituent introduced himself as the brother of a man who had received a special allowance in 1948 on the back of Ó Briain's efforts and wrote:

> I have a girl going for the butter making examination. She went for it last year and didn't get it. So I am asking you for a favour now. Would you see the Minister for Agriculture to know would she get the examination. She is notified for the 13th November. I am sitting in the chair with fifteen years [sic] but nevertheless when the time comes I don't forget you.[220]

It was a request for assistance rooted in an aspect of the national psyche epitomised by one Limerick man who noted: "Everybody is aware that whatever job is offering in this country the two foremost qualifications are push and pull."[221]

Attempts to dignify the pushing and pulling of public representatives, invariably rested on continuous allusion to the value and moral purity of rural life where material gain was not a primary ambition. Speaking in 1954, the leader of Fine Gael, Richard Mulcahy claimed: "The fact is that Ireland is one of the most contented countries in the world only for the reason that the aspirations of the people are so low. Contentment is measured by the ratio between realisation and aspiration. In relation to the general aspirations of the people we have nearly what we want."[222] This perception was thought risible by such commentators as Flann O'Brien whose mock-hero Bonaparte O'Coonassa proclaimed: "I was sunk in poverty, half-dead from hunger and hardship; yet I failed to think of any pleasant object that I needed."[223] As the rustic mysticism of political and vocational visionaries seeped ever deeper into cant, the sense of national disillusion deepened. The land was losing its people. Bleak drudgery in unremunerative fields offered little attraction against the stories floating home from the thriving cities of prosperous nations where the 1950s brought the biggest boom in history. Irish poverty was not consequent to its reliance on agriculture, however. The performance of the industrial sector was utterly abject and the problems experienced by agriculture were, at least in part, caused by the ongoing malaise in industry. Through the 1950s industrial growth reached 3.5 per cent in Denmark and 8.5 per cent in Spain. In Ireland, industrial output increased by just 1.3 per cent per annum between 1950 and 1959. Crucially, in those same years, employment in industry fell by 38,000, equivalent to 14 per cent of the industrial

---

[219] *Ibid.* Ó Briain wrote advising one individual against making any advance to a county committee: "Ní mór duit dul ag caint le comhaltaí uile an Choiste Talmhaíochta mar ná fuil dar liom an breis ag Fianna Fáil ag an gCoiste sin."

[220] UCDA, Donnchadh Ó Brain papers, P83/166(13), J.D. to Ó Briain, Oct. 1957. On this occasion, Ó Briain was forced to reply that he could not assist.

[221] UCDA, Donnchadh Ó Briain papers, P/83/168(82), Pierce Rowsome to Ó Briain, 18 Mar. 1961.

[222] UCDA, Richard Mulcahy papers, P7/c/135, Richard Mulcahy speech, 8 Feb. 1954.

[223] Flann O'Brien, *The poor mouth*, p. 113.

labour force.[224] Total employment in the country fell by more than 12 per cent between 1950 and 1958 – during which time the volume of GNP expanded by just 6.5 per cent.[225]

Agriculture was unable to bear the burden. Successive 1950s governments were incapable of devising policies to bring prosperity to the agricultural community – and that community was unable to step beyond the subsistence mentality which conditioned a large swathe of its ageing members. And yet, the need for change was accepted throughout the decade. In 1952, the Minister for Agriculture, Thomas Walsh, commented:

> It is impossible to expect marked progress in agriculture so long as this industry – our most important from all points of view – is kept at the bottom of the social and economic ladder. There cannot be the slightest doubt that the general effect of the policies in operation has been to subordinate farmers' interests to those of other classes ... It is of course perfectly true ... that agriculture is capable of considerable expansion but this will be largely dependent on a considerable shift in policy in this country. It will be necessary for those in charge of the formulation of policy genuinely to accept agriculture as deserving of the first consideration among all the economic activities carried on.

Warming to his theme, Walsh continued that, because of the wide disparity between the incomes of those in agriculture and those in industry, "it is not ... in the least surprising that the number of people on the land has been declining so rapidly." He stressed the need to alter the position where agriculture had almost 50 per cent of the workforce but only 29 per cent of the national income. Ultimately, change was imperative:

> In framing agricultural policy for the future we should take into account both long-term and short-term aspects. As regards the long-term, much could be achieved in due course by means of a really effective advisory and extension service which so far is only in the initial stages of development in this country. This will mean a lot more staff, a lot more money, and a lot more organisation. It is certain that in the long run this would raise the productivity of agriculture and thus the income of those engaged in it. In the long run however, as the late Lord Keynes remarked, 'we are all dead.' Long before that stage is reached, agriculture will need an injection of confidence and of money if it is to hold its own and begin to expand.[226]

There were injections of neither confidence nor money. Agricultural policy, whether short-term or long-term, remained largely unchanged through the 1950s. A report by British official H.A. Silverman on the position of Irish agriculture in

---

224 Liam Kennedy, *The modern industrialisation of Ireland* (1989), p. 9.

225 Kennedy *et al.*, *Economic development*, p. 62.

226 NAI, D/T S13930 B, D/A memo to govt., Nov. 1952.

January 1953 had compared Ireland with Denmark, Holland and Belgium, and
said that there "must be cause for disquiet ... These three countries were far more
gravely disorganised by the war than was Ireland, yet their production is much
superior."[227] Ireland failed to cope with the global shift in trading patterns and the
progressions of its agricultural competitors. It did not hold an industrial sector
capable of extending financial support to smallholders who were languishing in
farms too small to produce efficiently. Farmers were expected to generate their
own supports through export earnings but the social and economic elements of
policy operated in opposition to each other. Policy sought unsuccessfully to deny
the world-wide decline in agricultural employment but, in its efforts, succeeded
only in diminishing its own commercial capacity. Bemused, Erskine Childers
wondered in the mid-1950s what could be done to improve output, yields and
investment in agriculture: "Could not the ideas mooted from time to time be
examined at special government meetings?"[228] Between 1951 and 1957, both
Fianna Fáil and inter-party governments examined a range of ideas but few found
their way towards official policy and Ireland continued to lag far behind its
competitors. Such was the stagnation in policy and performance that, towards the
end of the decade, Childers, by then Minister for Lands, commented that the mass
of unresolved problems was enormous and that solutions remained singularly
elusive. He concluded: "Farmers have every right to wonder what on earth their
successive governments have been up to during the past 35 years."[229]

---

[227] PRO, MAF 40/452, *Irish food supplies and trade with Britain*, Jan. 1953. Silverman noted with dismay the
lack of agricultural education, "the inadequate, sometimes primitive, methods, not only in production but
in the general manner of organisation and in the systems of collection and distribution," "the over-zealous
policy of [land] reform," "the common practice of withholding independence from the grown-up sons
[which] tends to breed frustration, and to weaken their vigour and enthusiasm by the time they come to
farm on their own account." Again, the report highlighted the huge potential for expansion and noted
that some progress had been made, but that there did not seem to be a great likelihood of increased
supplies in the immediate future. The Department of Agriculture said the report was a "rather specious
effort, showing confused thinking and ignorance of basic facts."
[228] NAI, D/T S12888 D, Erskine Childers to D/T, 9 May 1952.
[229] *IFJ*, 11 May 1957.

Chapter
4

Supplying beef to John Bull ... 1958–61

Politically, survival may be the ultimate achievement of any newly-independent state but, for the Irish, that survival did not come without grave concessions. The upheavals of the 1930s were interpreted as a historical lesson that the pursuit of economic independence was an enterprise fraught with too great a peril. Far from standing free and independent, Ireland remained economically subservient to Britain and, through the 1950s, the economy was effectively in thrall to British requirements. The formal declaration of the Republic of Ireland in 1949 had not signalled a nation on the brink of a great advance, proclaiming genuine freedom with confidence and spirit. It was almost as if the proclamation was a political gesture designed to deflect attention away from the singular failure of the state to prosper in its newly won independence. Political independence was not quite a charade – as demonstrated by neutrality in World War II – but it was attended by a degree of economic dependency unrivalled between other European states. Ireland remained an economic annex to the houses of Westminster.

The very nature of the dependency, intertwined inextricably with the export of live cattle, proved a root cause of Ireland's flirtation with economic ruin in the 1950s. The entire agricultural economy gravitated towards the need to export cattle to Britain to pay for imports of such raw materials and products as Ireland did not possess or could not produce. Yet, a coherent policy which recognised the *de facto* bovine hegemony on which trade was predicated was never enacted – nor could it be. The demands of politics and of social and cultural commitments dictated that policy was inevitably compromised away from maximising profits from the livestock trade. Policy making is invariably bound to the need to compromise, but it is upon the successful resolution of these compromises that progress depends. In Ireland, compromise brought irresolution, contradiction, decline. The individual and collective trauma of emigration and poverty was the logical consequence of the inadequacies of social and economic policy in post-independence Ireland. That this related not merely to agricultural policy but to all sections of the economy was no comfort. Indeed, it exacerbated the inadequacies of the agricultural economy. It was not that the vision which inspired the leaders of the state was necessarily invalid, rather it was increasingly clear that to devise a policy to achieve anything approaching its realisation was beyond the state's capabilities. As J.J. Lee commented, the crisis lay in the conundrum that "de Valera not only had no idea how to move the existing reality in the direction of his ideal, but that many of his policies directly subverted it."[1] De Valera had

---

1 J.J. Lee, *Ireland, 1912–85: politics and society*, p. 334.

conspirators from all parties in this subversion which, though born of good will, not malice, had effects no less damaging for that.

The policy hiatus eventually provoked an economic tailspin so drastic that not even the vast array of self-delusional talent at the disposal of the Irish political élite could continue to gyrate in ignorance of social and economic realities. Indeed, these realities, which had previously curtailed attempts to realise an imagined rural nirvana, eventually forced the progressive abandonment of that vision. And, paradoxically, the very factors, particularly emigration, which led some to question the future viability of the state were emblematic of real change underway in Irish society, particularly agriculture. Farm sizes grew and the numbers working on the land fell. In the second half of the 1950s, the number of 5/15 acre farms fell by 20 per cent and those of 15/30 acres fell by 12 per cent. Through the 1950s the total farm labour force fell by 17.5 per cent.[2] This land clearance ensured the level of productivity per man rose by 50 per cent, a rate faster than industry. Incomes also rose by 30 per cent, yet this was from such a low base level that "despite the improvement average farm incomes towards the end of the period were still very low." Most crucially, over the period 1953 to 1959, agricultural exports increased by less than 0.5 per cent and the output of the industry as a whole increased by less than 2.5 per cent.[3] Agriculture was shedding underemployed workers but this was change as the antithesis of expressed policy objectives.

It was also change which forced a reassessment of policy. The tides of history are pulled by both short- and long-term forces, and the particular circumstances of their draw on Ireland saw the state embark on a process of substantial societal change. The legitimisation of innovation most often comes when traditional societies see their rigid normative framework of the past strained to breaking-point and unable to function properly.[4] And so it was with Ireland. But, if traditional policies and external forces had produced the long-term drift towards the need for innovation, the more immediate impetus came from the actions of a coterie of civil servants and the revitalisation of the political process overseen by de Eamon de Valera's replacement as Taoiseach and leader of Fianna Fáil, Seán Lemass.[5] This revitalisation brought a fundamental reassessment of economic priorities and of the policy process which carried deep consequences for farming interests. A shift in policy saw agriculture ostensibly retain its primordial status in the Irish economy but the crucial acknowledgement that it alone could not be expected to drive the economy was made explicit.

The late 1950s saw Irish agriculture further emerge from the subsistence culture which had long retarded its expansion. The research, education and

---

[2] E.A. Attwood, *Ireland and the European agricultural market* (1963), p. 17

[3] Robert O'Connor, 'Implications of Irish agricultural statistics', in Bailie and Sheehy (eds.), *Irish agriculture*, pp 27, 15.

[4] Eric Hobsbawm, *On history* (1992), p. 16.

[5] Although the *Programme for economic expansion* was prepared and published in de Valera's last months in office, Lemass was its driving force in political terms.

advisory services played a key role, though not always an effective one, in that process and offer a valuable insight into the policy processes which dominated the mindset of those who controlled the state. It would be risible to suggest that the later years of the 1950s saw Ireland begin to walk from the dark ages – economic, social, cultural or political. Such a perception is based on the fundamental assurance that what followed was necessarily superior to what went before. Nonetheless, as the decade turned, Ireland embarked on a process which fundamentally redefined the state. It was not necessarily a watershed, but the currents did begin to move the economy towards safer waters. It was a fraught journey, though, and nowhere were the ends more frayed than in agriculture.

I

Programme for economic expansion

Much has been written of the importance of the 1957 white paper, *Programme for economic expansion*, and its predecessor, *Economic development*, as a defining moment in the revitalisation of the Irish economy. There were significant differences between T.K. Whitaker's study, *Economic development*, completed in May 1957, and the *Programme for economic expansion* which was published in November. The broad thrust, though, was complementary. Taken together, the importance of the documents, in one form or another, to the development of Irish industry is accepted by all commentators.[6] Equally, it is accepted that agriculture did not come close to achieving the results desired of it by the *Programme*. One analyst wrote of how industry had reached the targets set for it but agriculture "was not nearly so successful ... Growth was very slow, and indeed between 1957 and 1963 the net [output] index increased by less than 1.6 per cent. It is difficult to explain this stagnation."[7] Nonetheless, in the immediate aftermath of the joint publications, the *Irish Farmers' Journal* had pronounced its pleasure that almost half the content was dedicated to farming and argued that the "entire work may be taken as the clearest and most satisfactory statement on agricultural policy that has so far come from official sources."[8] At the same time, the *Journal* was worried that, of the £53.4m extra investment promised in the programme, only £14m would go to agriculture, which was "deplorably small." There was further concern that a

---

[6] Buoyed by foreign investment – though scarcely by native firms – the industrial sector led the economic growth rate of 4 per cent over the five years from 1958. In the first six years after the commencement of the *Programme* 80 per cent of private investment came from foreign capital. From 1960 to 1969, 350 new foreign companies were established in Ireland. See Foster, *Modern Ireland*, p. 579.

[7] R. O'Connor, 'Implications of Irish agricultural statistics, in Bailie and Sheehy (eds.), *Irish agriculture*, p. 27.

[8] *IFJ*, 29 Nov. 1958.

possible weakness was its avoidance of specific proposals in favour of a more general nature, but, overall, the *Journal* believed that the documents showed "a progressive level of thinking on agricultural problems: far higher than we have seen in the past."[9] The *Programme* was also considered by the National Farmers' Association (NFA) who welcomed it as broadly in agreement with its own proposals.[10]

The *Programme for economic expansion* concluded its agricultural section with a brief outline of its self-professed "constructive and realistic programme which if vigorously pursued will lead to a substantial expansion of agricultural output on a sound economic basis." This outline stated as its main objectives:

1. A steady increase in agricultural output and exports based on increased productivity, which in turn will be fostered mainly by a policy of grassland improvement related to increased use of lime and phosphates in particular and to the introduction of improved methods of management.

2. Eradication of bovine tuberculosis in the shortest possible period.

3. A considerable further improvement of agricultural education, advisory services and research (in association with An Foras Talúntais).

4. Improved agricultural marketing and the further development of trade relations with the countries where we market our agricultural products.

5. To apply state aid so as to secure expansion of output at lower unit cost, leading to competitive selling prices and, through higher turnover, to an increase in net agricultural incomes. A measure of price support will be maintained for wheat, beet, milk and pigs.

And in a pithy statement of policy, the *Programme* noted: "the aim of policy will be to direct expenditure to the progressive reduction of production costs and thus enable agricultural produce to be sold abroad on a profitable basis." Effectively, the entire policy rested on a dynamic grassland improvement drive, which through the greater use of fertilisers, backed by research, advice and education, would allow Irish farmlands stock more cattle for export. Further, there was to be a more constructive approach to breeding policy and a more modern approach to winter feeding. Equally, more credit would be made available to farmers and export produce would be better marketed. Ultimately, "the test of agricultural policy is ... whether in the long run it enables output to be increased at costs which make exports profitable without subsidisation. On this depends not

---

9 *Ibid.*, 15 Nov. 1958.

10 *Ibid.*, 29 Nov. 1958.

only the possibility of a higher income for the agricultural community but the future development of the whole economy."[11] The open acknowledgement that the future prosperity of Irish farmers lay in cattle and the avowed pursuit of a policy to prioritise the unfettered export of livestock and livestock products, marked a sea change in Irish politics. Writing in the *Irish Times*, a former Minister for Local Government and Public Health in the inter-party government, Seamus Burke, noted Fianna Fáil's conversion to livestock farming as the way forward and commented that it was "a truly breath-taking advance that our rulers have at last become aware of this simple truism, which has never been obscured from the eyes of the babes and sucklings of economics."[12] The radical smallholders' organisation Lia Fáil was not quite so enamoured with this conversion and believed it was "a clear statement of Fianna Fáil's diabolical policy to banish the Irish people from the land of Ireland and put the bullocks in their place to supply beef to John Bull."[13]

Supplying beef to John Bull was not simply a matter of outlining vague objectives, however, and it was noted that the only definite target set in the *Programme* was to increase the number of cows in the country from 1.2m to 1.5m by 1964.[14] It was one thing, though, to formulate a statement of intent on the desired main lines of development, and altogether another to secure that development. In truth, neither *Economic development* nor the *Programme for economic expansion* represented a dramatic new departure for agricultural policy, even allowing for Fianna Fáil's symbolic public affirmation of the primacy of the livestock trade. Significantly, Whitaker's proposal in *Economic development* that the agricultural grant be redirected was largely absent from the *Programme*. Use of the agricultural grant to offer a relief of rates on agricultural land had been constantly criticised by the Department of Finance, yet political sensibilities dictated that such a move could not be contemplated.[15] Far from redirection of the grant, moves to increase the rate of relief dominated the agenda.[16] Indeed, relief on rates was such a permanent issue that between 1946 and 1969, twelve temporary acts

---

[11] *Programme for economic expansion* (1958), pp 26–7, 11.

[12] *Irish Times*, 19 Nov. 1958.

[13] Brian S. Murphy, 'The land for the people, the road for the bullock: Lia Fáil, the smallholder's crisis and public policy in Ireland, 1957–60', in Tim O'Neill and William Nolan (eds.) *Offaly: history and society* (1998), pp 889–928.

[14] *Programme for economic expansion* (1958), p. 15.

[15] The Rates on Agricultural Land (Relief) Act, 1946 provided for the abatement of rates on agricultural land to: (a) primary allowance of three-fifths of the general rate on land valuations not exceeding £20, and the first £20 of higher valuations, (b) supplementary allowance of one-fifth of the general rate on land over £20; (c) employment allowance at rate of 10s in £ on land valuations above £20, subject to the allowance not exceeding £6 10s per man. Crotty argued: "Very probably the economic effect of the grants in relief of rates was to reduce total agricultural output. Although they did represent a transfer of wealth from the community as a whole to agriculture, the manner of distribution of the wealth transferred could hardly be justified on social grounds. As the grants were based on valuation, the largest went to the people with the most property." See Crotty, *Agricultural production*, p. 129.

[16] See NAI, D/T S11042 E/95, D/F memo to D/LG, 7 Jan. 1959, which claimed that the grant "as well as representing a heavy burden on the Exchequer, can hardly be said to have any appreciable beneficial effect on agricultural production while it is clear that its effect in increasing or maintaining employment on the land is negligible."

had been grafted on, expanding the original relief act.[17] Considerable insight was offered into existing policies, but there was no formal planning methodology applied in constructing new ones.[18] Its successful impact on Irish agriculture would be dictated by the ability of the Department of Agriculture to find the resources or the wit to either inspire or impel the farming community towards much-cherished increased output. Ominously, the Department of Agriculture did not envisage any substantial revision of policy. It agreed that the aim of policy should be to reduce dependence on price subsidies but noted that the extent to which this could be done was limited. The department stated its opposition to any diversion of funds from beef to dairy farming, argued against radical change in breeding policy, and said that existing educational policy was adequate in that it was complementary to Department of Education schemes.[19]

The central aspect of the agricultural section of the *Programme* was grassland improvement and greater fertiliser application. The provision of fertiliser subsidies was the only agricultural policy instrument specified in the *Programme for economic expansion*. One of the great mantras of Irish society was an exhortation to farmers to use more artificial fertilisers. Through the decades a number of schemes had resulted in the same outcome – farmers used an inadequate amount of fertilisers, and used them inconsistently. This was compounded by wastage caused by failure to conduct soil tests. In 1957, attempts by the Minister for Agriculture to encourage the ACC to offer credit facilities to farmers who wished to purchase large quantities of artificial fertiliser brought a rebuff from the ACC, through Pa F. Quinlan who wrote that the scheme was

> based on the popular fallacy that the application of vastly increased quantities of artificial fertiliser to grasslands is synonymous with increasing both agricultural output and agricultural exports … Our farmers are still being exhorted to go into debt so that they may waste fertiliser growing bigger and better weeds on their old pastures.[20]

---

[17] NAI, D/T 99/1/442, M/A note on 2 May 1969 which noted that "most of the temporary acts gave some measure of rate relief and this has undoubtedly fostered an air of expectation that each succeeding Act will give further concessions."

[18] Des Norton, *Problems in economic planning and policy formation in Ireland, 1958–74* (1975), p. 12.

[19] NAI, D/T S16066 A, D/F memo to govt., 4 Jul. 1958. The difficulties in revitalising agriculture were exemplified by problems in breeding policy. The Irish based their breeding methods on the British model and implacably followed the moves of their neighbour. Only when it was clear that the British had sanctioned the importation of Charollais did the Irish agree in principle to follow suit. Even then, the importation of the French cattle was delayed when it seemed that American objections for fear of foot-and-mouth disease would cost the Irish a £7 million boneless beef deal. Only, in 1963, when the US government lifted its objections did the Irish move towards controlled importation with the establishment of a quarantine station on Spike Island. That station was functional by the end of 1964, more than six years after the publication of the *Programme*.

[20] NAI, D/T S7901 C, ACC to M/A, 11 Apr. 1957.

In response the government set up an interdepartmental committee to examine how to improve soil fertility.[21] The committee faded quickly into obscurity.

As the *Programme* was being formulated and throughout its implementation, however, there was an ongoing debate within cabinet on a Department of Industry and Commerce proposal to build a nitrogenous fertiliser plant. Although the Department of Agriculture effectively removed itself from the argument, the Department of Finance opposed the scheme, arguing that farmers would "derive no benefit," and "neither could the factory be justified on employment grounds."[22] Yet, in July 1961 the cabinet authorised the establishment of a state company to negotiate tenders for the construction of such a factory, although it did not agree to Department of Industry and Commerce suggestions to use the agricultural grant to pay for the enterprise.[23] The NFA strongly opposed the move, although the ICMSA backed it.[24] In a final attempt to stop the scheme, the Department of Finance claimed that the capital involved was committed "without economic benefit even if the investment is a success, but with serious disadvantage to agriculture and the economy generally, if it is not."[25] Eventually, the Nitrigin Éireann Teoranta (NET) factory was built despite the avowed intention in the *Programme* to ensure that the supposed new approach to agricultural expansion was rested on reducing costs to a minimum. In its operation, the NET factory proved to be a huge disappointment and throughout the latter part of the decade the government was forced regularly to reorganise its financial operations.[26] Indeed, it was crises in the fertiliser industry which forced the government to agree to price increases which went someway towards negating the subsidies on offer.[27] In this respect, the Department of Agriculture noted that although fertiliser consumption increased steadily up to 1964, it then declined with "price increases being a contributory factor."[28] Indeed, backed by state subsidies which increased from £866,000 in 1957/8 to £3,645,000 in 1962/3, fertiliser usage increased by two-thirds.[29] The failure to increase subsidies in line with the increase in price contributed to the decline in the consumption of fertilisers after 1964,

---

[21] The cabinet asked the same committee to examine whether the agricultural grant could be altered "to ensure that the assistance provided to farmers by means of the grant will be more directly related to the encouragement of increased agricultural production." See NAI, D/T S7901 C, cabinet minutes, 26 Apr. 1957.

[22] NAI, D/T S7901 G/61, D/F memo to govt., 20 Jul. 1961.

[23] NAI, D/T S7901 G/61, cabinet minutes, 28 Jul. 1961. The contract was eventually awarded to the German firm, Lugi, in October 1962.

[24] *Irish Independent*, 16 Jul. 1962

[25] NAI, D/T S7901 H/62, D/F memo to govt., 7 Sept. 1962.

[26] See NAI, D/T 99/1/68, D/IC memo to govt., 19 Nov. 1968.

[27] See, for example, the 7.5 per cent increase agreed in February 1968 in NAI, D/T 99/1/67, cabinet minutes, 27 Feb. 1968.

[28] NAI, D/T 98/6/67, D/A memo to govt., 11 Oct. 1966.

[29] Raymond Crotty argued that the increase in the growth of fertilisers was small in relation to the subsidies provided and that the increased use of fertilisers was part of a general trend already existent by the close of the 1950s, independent of the existence of subsidies. Crotty, *Agricultural production*, pp 194–5, 196.

however. Considerable advancement was made but, even in 1966, the Department of Agriculture commented: "Grassland is, in general, grossly under-fertilised."[30] Even more critically, the increased use of fertiliser was dependent in itself, and in relation to its overall worth, upon a comprehensive programme for the development of the agricultural economy. This was intrinsically related to a better comprehensive management policy for grasslands, which was, in turn, fundamentally dependent upon an improved research, educational and advisory service. Welcome though any increase in fertiliser usage would be, it was only one element in an equation which demanded inclusive resolution. The four years after 1958 saw Irish agriculture move towards the objectives outlined in the *Programme* but to understand why it moved so slowly, it is imperative to assess the modernising process at work in farming circles; the attempts to reform the education, research and advisory services; the use of credit; and, ultimately, efforts to improve the operation of the livestock industry.

II

Research and the Agricultural Institute

The isolated nature of projects such as the fertiliser subsidy scheme, heightened the importance of assisting farmers generate their own progressive initiatives. Fostering a culture of self-advancement was an imperative, yet the inadequacy of research, education and advisory facilities was, by common accord, the gravest deficiency in Irish agriculture. Although this was an unwanted accolade bestowed, at one point or another, on many aspects of the industry, in this instance it marked a deficiency which undeniably limited the progress of the entire agricultural economy. A multitude of commentators and a raft of reports decried the failure to expand a system of advice which would have facilitated the dissemination of knowledge of the most modern techniques and the most recent research to educated farmers.[31] In post-independence Ireland not one element of this holy trinity of research, education and advice even approached what was

---

[30] NAI, D/T 98/6/67, M/A memo to govt., 11 Oct. 1966 and 16 Dec. 1966.

[31] The Recess Committee of 1896 had recommended that a new type of post-primary school for agriculture and practical industry be introduced to Ireland. See Marie Clarke, 'Vocational education in a local context, 1930–1997' (Ph.D thesis, UCD 1999), p. 11. Eight years later, Horace Plunkett wrote that much of the development work needed in Irish agriculture "must consist of educating adults into their business concerns the more advanced economic and scientific methods which the superior education of our rivals in agriculture and industry abroad has enabled them to adopt, and which my experience of Irish work convinces me our people would have adopted long ago if they had had similar educational advantages." See Plunkett, *Ireland in the new century*, p. 177. Both report and commentator made remarks that were echoed through the decades.

deemed acceptable in leading European countries. It was not just that Ireland did not meet the standards of progressive, modernising agricultural countries, it had not even laid the foundations on which to develop an effective system. Holmes had stressed the imperative need to "use all possible means of experiment, demonstration, education, and propaganda."[32] He was writing on grassland improvement but his exhortation carried relevance to many sectors of Irish agriculture.

The very officers employed by the state to further research, education and advice led the criticism of the service provided. These officers formed the core of the Agricultural Science Association (ASA) which sent a pamphlet of its analysis of the Irish agricultural advisory services to the government in 1946. The pamphlet spoke of the need to centralise operations, to use more modern means of instruction, and to redesign the entire operation of agricultural research, education and advisory services. To this end, the first requirement was a higher level of general education as "the want of adequate continuation education in the past has been a serious limitation to the progress of agricultural education, and we strongly recommend that the scheme for the provision of continuation education in all parts be completed without delay." This would go some way towards improving the prospects of the agricultural instructors who continued

> to suffer from at least three severe handicaps, namely, insufficiency of agricultural instructors, inadequate accommodation for the holding of classes, and, except where the students have received post-primary education, a standard of education which is too low to enable the agricultural instructor to proceed directly with his course of agricultural instruction.[33]

Of crucial importance was the development of a progressive programme of research.

The following year, in the absence of any apparent action, the ASA resubmitted its memorandum and informed Taoiseach, Eamon de Valera that it was

> so fully conscious of the shortcomings of the existing schemes for agricultural education, the inadequacy of facilities for research and of the urgency, in view of the condition of agriculture for development in this connection, that the recommendations are again brought to your notice in the hope that they will be implemented without delay.[34]

Again, little evidence of progress encouraged the ASA to resubmit its plea in 1951, noting that

---

[32] *Holmes' Report*, p. 57.

[33] NAI, D/T 99/1/485, *Memorandum on agricultural education and research*, Agricultural Science Association (1946).

[34] NAI, D/T 99/1/485, ASA to de Valera, 24 Sept. 1947.

on the criterion of production the record of the first half of this century cannot, in comparison with progressive agricultural countries, be interpreted as progress ... Re-organisation of agricultural education and research, and of the agricultural extension services is imperative ... An effective scheme must provide the machinery for the full co-ordination and co-operation between the various sections engaged in education and research. This is regarded as fundamental. The establishment of a single authority charged with the control of higher agricultural education, education at agricultural school level, advisory services, and research is considered the only means of securing the ends in view.[35]

The Minister for Agriculture, James Dillon, was not moved by the plea and, embittered by divisions with the ASA over other matters, condemned the organisation as "the refuge for middle-aged incompetents."[36] Refusing demands to apologise, Dillon warmed to his theme and decried the ASA as "the most poisonous organisation."[37] Relations between the minister and his officers did nothing to improve the advancements of the schemes attempted in the following years. It lends eloquent testimony to the failure to achieve any substantial improvements, that, in 1955, the ASA once more felt compelled to circulate unaltered its memorandum of nine years previously.[38]

The inadequacy of agricultural research was the subject of continual criticism. That a country with such an overbearing dependence on agriculture for its income could devote such meagre resources to scientific research in its principal industry was a singular commentary on, first, the mores of Irish society and, second, the status of agriculture within the economy. What nature could not provide, the state would not presume to impose. By the 1950s, the volume of criticism of the state's research facilities was incessant as all agreed the critical importance of the establishment of a research institute. Significantly, it was there that the unanimity ended. On its eventual inauguration in 1958, the Agricultural Institute was "blessed by the church and honoured by the state," but this was a momentary island of calm in a tempestuous sea.[39] In the acrimonious debate which preceded its official opening in 1958 and in its subsequent turbulent relationship with the Department of Agriculture, the Agricultural Institute was attended by an intemperate clamour of some magnitude.

The government agreed in principle to a scheme for an agricultural and veterinary institute, both for research and teaching purposes in May 1950.[40]

[35] NAI, D/T 99/1/485, ASA to D/T, Apr. 1951.

[36] NAI, D/T 99/1/485, ASA to D/T, 5 May 1951 and Dillon to Cosgrave, 7 May 1951. The ASA did not offer the support which Dillon believed was due his plan for an Agricultural Institute (A/I) and was opposed to the minister's parish plan for agricultural advice.

[37] Ibid.

[38] UCDA, Patrick McGilligan papers, P35d/100, ASA to McGilligan, Jun. 1955.

[39] IFJ, 3 May 1958. In the years after its establishment, it was known alternatively as the Agricultural Institute or An Foras Talúntais.

[40] NAI, D/T S14815 A/1, cabinet minutes, 12 May 1950.

Although the initiative derived support from the ECA and was propounded by the Minister for Agriculture, James Dillon, it was not welcomed by Department of Agriculture officials who sensed a threat to their status. Initially, the suggestion of the institute was made by Joseph Carrigan but "instead of acting on the advice of a well-meaning man, the department went on the defensive ... In reality the Department of Agriculture was vehemently against the idea, and in the internal correspondence of the Department, one comment was 'the less said about this matter the better.'"[41] Nonetheless, James Dillon was determined to establish the institute and embarked on a consultation process with a range of interested parties, including the universities and the Catholic church.[42] This was a tortuous process. All involved sought to at least preserve their existing share of facilities and in so doing, the debate entered the darkness of sectional squabbling. Discussion focussed on the role of the institute, the definition of its tasks, the manner in which it should be run and where it might be located. For almost a decade vested interests locked horns in a parochial rutting-match while politicians failed to provide much that could pass for leadership. With the Marshall Aid plan having evolved into a Grant Counterpart Fund and necessitating the agreement of the government of the United States on how the money should be spent, the Irish government needed to present a coherent framework for development of the institute. This did not easily happen.

When it became clear that the Institute was more a certainty than a possibility, with the broad agreement in 1954 that £1.84 million of Grant Counterpart money should be expended on its establishment, debate focused on control of the new body. The Department of Agriculture fought a rearguard action to preserve its existing status. Having attempted to strangle any movement towards a new institution through inertia, the department now focused on ensuring that it retained control over the institute's annual budget. The church was similarly determined to assert its authority over the new body. Writing from Daingean Reformatory in the mid-1950s, a priest claimed that the Department of Agriculture was entirely divorced from the farming community and that its attempt to deny autonomy to the Agricultural Institute was "precisely what happens in totalitarian countries. Our attempt to assert our democratic rights is intended to safeguard our country from the menace of state control whether it be exercised by a self-confessed dictator like, Hitler, Peron or Mussolini, or by a benevolent but misguided department of state."[43] Equally, there was disagreement on where the new institute would be sited. Both the *Irish Independent* and the *Irish Times* argued that it should not be in Dublin and, across the country, various counties forwarded their claims as the ideal home for the proposed institute.[44] In this fracas over place and power, it was once again demonstrated just how limited government investment in agriculture remained – and just how crucial it was to secure the major portion of that investment.

---

[41] Neenan, *Popular history*, pp 204–16.

[42] The debate surrounding the project is minutely detailed in NAI, D/T S14815.

[43] UCDA, Patrick McGilligan papers, P35d/103, Letter from Very Rev. T. Reidy, to unnamed newspaper, (n.d.).

[44] *Irish Independent*, 26 Sept. 1953 and *Irish Times*, 18 Jun. 1954.

Back in office, James Dillon proposed in 1955 that the institute would not just conduct research but would also reorganise agricultural education in the universities. For Dillon, the dispersal of facilities across Trinity College Dublin (TCD), UCD and UCC was a further unwelcome dilution of already paltry resources which was more conducive to poverty of achievement than decentralisation of service. He proposed that the institute would have the autonomy of a university with its governing body nominated by universities and farming organisations. Both the universities and the farmers opposed the proposal. It was, they argued, unnecessarily expensive, would remove students from the cultural environment of a university leaving them with a purely technical training, would concentrate students in one centre thereby ignoring the regional variations in Irish agriculture, while government financial control would be used to strangle initiative and dominate application.[45]

Even within cabinet, though, there was disapproval of Dillon's scheme. Patrick McGilligan opposed the proposal to supersede the universities in agricultural education as being against world-wide trends. For McGilligan, a viable institute could not be achieved "by flaunting all accepted canons of scientific education ... It can be definitely asserted that no consultations worthy of the importance of this great project, on which our whole future depends, have yet taken place." Overall, the proposal had not been approved by even one scientist or educator and was wrongly rooted in the Department of Agriculture's "pantheistic adulation of science."[46] Nonetheless, the draft bill proposed by the department was welcomed by the *Irish Farmers' Journal*: "There are many favourable aspects to this bill. The governing body has a good representation of farmers and the principle of an autonomous institute has been accepted." For the paper, though, the failure to link research with advice and the fact that the Department of Agriculture retained control of the budget was a great worry.[47] The *Irish Times* was fully supportive and believed that the scheme "would work if it is given a chance to work."[48] Opposition to the scheme, with UCD President, Dr Michael Tierney leading the charge, was so great, though, that early implementation proved impossible. The failure to act decisively led the *Cork Examiner* to contrast the failure to establish an agriculture institute with the resources diverted to the revival of Irish and to the Dublin Institute of Higher Studies:

> It would be of greater utility to investigate the elimination of cattle diseases or the control of farm pests than cosmic rays. There is now fairly general agreement that a large portion of the money, time and energy spent on the revival of Irish as a spoken language has been wasted. Some of the money and energy might be more profitably applied to the teaching of agriculture. It remains to hope that the promotion of agriculture under the aegis of the new Institute will not be made the shuttlecock of faddists or fanatics of any school.[49]

[45] J.H. Whyte, *Church and state in modern Ireland, 1923–79* (1984), pp 307–11.
[46] UCDA, Patrick McGilligan papers, P35d/98, notes for speech, n.d.
[47] *IFJ*, 20 Aug. 1955
[48] *Irish Times*, 8 Sept. 1955.
[49] *Cork Examiner*, 16 Aug. 1955.

Through Macra na Feirme and the newly founded NFA, farmers continued to demand that the institute, and not the Department of Agriculture, should have complete control over all research and would also regulate the advisory services.[50] This belated entry into the debate by organised farmers did nothing to speed the decision-making process but moved the *Irish Times* to support their proposal as "inasmuch as the whole idea behind the institute is that its services shall be utilised enthusiastically by the Irish farmers, Mr. Dillon will be wise to abandon the Government's scheme in favour of the other." Most emphatically, the paper stressed the need to end the delays: "This matter of the Institute had been on the stocks for a long time before the Department of Agriculture showed sufficient interest in it to formulate a positive scheme; and now the Department has appeared to have lost interest again. The matter, however, is of supreme importance to Ireland. If the institute is established on sound lines, and makes itself acceptable to the farmers of this country, it may turn out to be the decisive influence on our agricultural progress."[51] Ultimately, in the absence of anything approaching consensus, the idea of passing all university teaching under the auspices of the institute was abandoned, as was the proposal to absorb the advisory services. A correspondent to the *Irish Times* was not impressed:

> To separate the institute's research from the advisory services is absurd. It must re-invigorate, co-ordinate and expand the advisory services, and feed it all the time. The two belong together. Our present advisory services are merely skeletal … But the Institute could unify and animate the pathetically small network of county committees.[52]

In its eventual form, the institute's role was defined as to "review, facilitate, encourage, assist, co-ordinate, promote and undertake agricultural research." As well as the £1,840,000 ECA establishment grant, the institute was provided with state aid for £146,000.[53] Tom Walsh was seconded from the Department of Agriculture to serve as director, and John Litton, a working farmer, was appointed chairman at the institute's home in Merrion Road, Dublin.[54] Five divisions – soils, animal science, plant science, and rural economy – were set out, each comprising a number of departments. At one point, the research staff reached 160, but it generally stood at 100.[55] The *Irish Farmers' Journal* initially believed that the scope was so limited that it would be a supreme achievement to make "this emasculated institute of some slight value to the farmers of the country."[56] Under Walsh, however, progress proved reasonably swift, at least according to the *Journal*, and by the end of 1958 the paper was commenting that the institute "appears now to be

---

[50] *Irish Times*, 31 Dec. 1956.

[51] *Ibid.*, 21 Apr. 1956.

[52] *Ibid.*, 3 Jan. 1957.

[53] Hoctor, *The department's story*, p. 247.

[54] Tom Walsh was an official of the Department of Agriculture and should not, of course, be confused with his namesake, Thomas Walsh, Minister for Agriculture.

[55] Neenan, *Popular history*, p. 222.

developing in a highly promising way ... It is vital that it should maintain this momentum and become the arch-contriver of technical and planning progress."[57] Not all parties were quite so enamoured with the initial moves of the institute to establish itself. The secretary of the Department of Agriculture, J.C. Nagle, wrote:

> Making full allowance for the natural desire of a new body to show action, I feel that the course which An Foras Talúntais has begun to follow could, if accepted, ultimately lead to what in many respects would be akin to a second Department of Agriculture but much less subject to financial and policy control than a department of state. The general tone of written and oral communications from An Foras Talúntais is such that to pursue detailed discussions with them at departmental level on policy questions might lead to a certain amount of friction. This has been avoided up to the present, but not without some difficulty.

According to Nagle, the institute would be better served concentrating on co-ordinating and reviewing existing research functions and on filling the existing gaps "and less on their assuming control of every activity of the Department of Agriculture which has any relationship to research or experimental work." Nagle further stressed that the institute should not expect to merely submit a wish-list of financial demands with guaranteed positive results.[58]

Nagle wrote to the institute offering suggestions for lines of co-operation between the department and the new body through regular consultations.[59] The Minister for Agriculture, Paddy Smith, also wrote to the institute noting that the department had been as generous as possible to date and had acceded to requests to hand over research operations at such locations as Johnstown Castle, but the future would require the institute to show a "certain degree of flexibility."[60] Flexibility was not to the forefront of the institute's agenda and its director, seeking to bypass the Department of Agriculture, wrote directly to the Taoiseach asking him to receive a delegation of its members in view "of certain fundamental differences of opinion between the Department of Agriculture and An Foras Talúntais in matters relating to functions, work and responsibilities of An Foras Talúntais."[61] By then, relations between the department and the institute were in free fall in the wake of discussions between representatives of both parties over attempts by the institute to expand its budget for 1959/60. Nagle was to comment:

> I cannot remember any negotiations which were so trying and unsatisfactory ... We feel that the basic difficulty arises from the rather

---

[56] *IFJ*, 3 Apr. 1958.

[57] *Ibid.*, 27 Dec. 1958.

[58] NAI, D/T S16647 A, J.C Nagle to M/A, 30 Dec. 1958.

[59] NAI, D/T S16647 A, Nagle to Tom Walsh, 3 Feb. 1959.

[60] NAI, D/T S16647 A, M/A to John Litton, Chairman of the A/I, 3 Feb. 1959.

[61] NAI, D/T S16647 A, Walsh to govt., 18 Feb. 1959.

extraordinary attitude of An Foras Talúntais to its task and to this department. Their outlook seems to be monopolistic and, so far as this department is concerned, I would say even dictatorial. They seem to think that once they make decisions, everyone must conform, and their general policy is certainly not what one would expect from a reading of the Act and of the speeches made by the Taoiseach and Ministers when the bill was going through Dáil and Seanad.

Nagle called for a firm attitude to be taken, something which "will be to the ultimate advantage of An Foras Talúntais," and noted disappointment at the rejection of his suggested procedure "for co-ordination of their activities and those of this department which we believe to be essential if there is not to be hopeless overlapping, confusion and extravagance."[62] For the institute, there was no sense of confusion, no ambiguity. In September 1958 Tom Walsh wrote that the Minister for Agriculture had agreed to the transfer of all agricultural research facilities then under the remit of the department but "since then there has been a constant questioning at conferences and in correspondence by the Department of Agriculture, of the responsibility for national agricultural research." Walsh complained that in the previous months the Department of Agriculture had embarked on research programmes which "conflict fundamentally with the objectives and purposes for which An Foras Talúntais was established." Indeed, according to Walsh, while the institute "was preparing its plans for the development of its research programme, plans for the development and expansion within the department of agricultural research on matters which were clearly the function of the Institute were being developed."[63]

For his part, Nagle argued that the institute was taking a distorted view of its function:

It may be that the Institute genuinely believe that they are destined to revolutionise our agriculture and that they are justified ... in aiming eventually at taking over functions which neither the Act nor the government contemplated for them. I, myself, think that progress in agriculture is much more likely to be achieved if the Institute can be made to remember what their statutory functions are and why they were set up and how important it is that they should co-operate very closely with the department on a basis of mutual understanding.

He claimed it was "proving almost impossible to establish a working relationship," and that the institute was attempting to "isolate this department and to reach a position in which they can afford to ignore this department altogether." He decried the efforts of the institute to assume control of all agricultural research:

How can there be any hope of research yielding really valuable results

---

[62] NAI, D/T S16647 A, Nagle to Maurice Moynihan, secretary to the govt., 20 Feb. 1959
[63] NAI, D/T S16647 A, Walsh to Moynihan, 27 Feb. 1959.

here or anywhere else if it is to be subjected to a monolithic and monopolistic type of control stifling any element of liberty or spontaneity? I do not think that the Institute's philosophy in these matters would be approved in any country in the world, with the possible exception of some of the Iron Curtain countries. This does not mean that anarchy must reign if the human mind is to have full expansion.

Nagle agreed that lively co-operation was an imperative but that the institute appeared not to realise that there were extensive borderlands between research, education and developmental work, with the result that it was on course to turn such borderlands into "a jungle."[64] When an Agricultural Institute delegation came to see the Taoiseach, de Valera maintained the Department of Agriculture line. He insisted that the enabling act did not give the new body direct control over all agricultural research, but

> stressed that there was plenty of work for the Institute to do and suggested that it should concentrate on those matters where procedural and other difficulties did not arise leaving over until later any matters where difficulties were anticipated. Where it was thought essential to take action in a particular matter not covered by this formula, he suggested that such might be dealt with as a special case. Time solved many problems.[65]

A series of meetings between departmental and institute officials saw the emergence of an uneasy truce and while relations were not warm, the combatants had reached something of an accommodation by the autumn of 1959.[66] The sensitivities of both parties flared again in a dispute over the proposed inclusion of references in the institute's annual report to inadequate government funding and an oblique reference to disputes with the department. Further division emerged when Walsh professed his disappointment in March 1960 at receiving only a £170,000 state grant – a sum which covered only two-thirds of anticipated costs and imposes "a severe restriction on the research activities which our council considers necessary for agricultural development."[67] Interaction between the department and the institute worsened in the early years of the decade and a series of disputes based on autonomy, financial control and personality plagued an already fragile relationship, as did the ongoing confrontations over research control and co-ordination. The Department of Agriculture acknowledged that, for instance, a "satisfactory procedure had not been evolved whereby each side would be kept adequately in touch with the work being done by the other on animal production."[68] Poultry research was a further case in point. Walsh requested information from the department on such research as it was then undertaking as

---

[64] NAI, D/T S16647 A, Nagle to Moynihan, 10 Mar. 1959.

[65] NAI, D/T S16647 A, Minutes of meeting between Taoiseach and A/I delegation, 25 Mar. 1959.

[66] NAI, D/T S16647 A, Minutes of meeting between D/A and A/I representatives, 28 Oct. 1959.

[67] NAI, D/T S16647 A, Walsh to M/A, 9 Mar. 1960.

[68] NAI, D/T S16647 A, minutes of Liaison Committee on Animal Production, 14 May 1960.

he wished to place it under the auspices of the institute where, he claimed, it more properly belonged.[69] Nagle replied that the department had managed to conduct some trials on breeding but such trials "can only be fitted in at times when the facilities primarily provided for the breeding and educational programmes become available for such use." Similarly, feeding trials could only be carried out "using brooder houses during periods when they are not required for the rearing of replacement stock." In total, this dictated that "poultry activities are being conducted at the school farms by technical officers who are mainly engaged in educational or developmental work and are regarded as part and parcel of the Department's educational and poultry improvement work."[70] Through all this correspondence the tone used by Walsh was provocative and unhelpful. His demands, and the manner in which they were delivered, seemed designed to antagonise the department. To wit, he was adamant that the department honour his interpretation of the agreements made as the one undeniable truth. He proclaimed to department officials that "to effectively discharge its statutory co-ordinating function permission be forthcoming for the appropriate officers of the Institute to visit your institutions and examine the research work now in progress under your immediate control."[71] There could be no accusations levelled of excessive diplomacy.

The department particularly resented repeated institute demands for an increase in its annual budget, with Nagle vociferous in his criticism of tactics employed saying they were reminiscent

> of a pressure group rather than of a learned body ... Expenditure on agricultural research has been increasing at a remarkable pace, and ... it is the intention of An Foras Talúntais to maintain, and even accelerate, that pace in the future. The pace so far has probably been much too fast, because in the nature of things, a research organisation is one which should be built up very methodically and comparatively slowly over a period of years. The number of first-class research workers is not unlimited, and everything depends on the calibre of the men recruited.

Noting that the institute was demanding £650,000 grant for the following financial year, Nagle was fundamentally opposed to the provision of an increase of that scale as "a very serious issue of policy arises. If the F[oras] T[alúntais] request is conceded ... they will always consider themselves entitled to receive whatever grant they may request. The consequences of this could be disastrous. Other bodies could follow the same policy and this would mean an end to financial control in all such cases."[72] Following his election as Taoiseach in 1959, Seán Lemass, supported the view that it was the institute rather than the department

---

69 NAI, D/T S16647 A, Walsh to Nagle, 27 May 1960.
70 NAI, D/T S16647 A, Nagle to Walsh, 8 Aug. 1960.
71 NAI, D/T S16647 A, Walsh to Nagle, 27 May 1960.
72 NAI, D/T S16647 B/61, Nagle to M/A, 3 Jan 1961.

which was at fault for deteriorating relations, and considered that "the fault did not seem to me to rest with the Department of Agriculture and was in part attributable to the atmosphere of Empire-building which had surrounded the Institute and to the pressure tactics used to get a larger grant such as the suggestion that staff would have to be laid off if it was not given."[73] Again, a compromise was reached with the exchequer contributing more than the Department of Agriculture considered justified but less than the Agricultural Institute deemed necessary. It was not an enduring compromise, however, and acrimonious budgetary exchanges between the department and the institute were an annual affair.[74]

As well as being disconcerted by budgetary demands, the department railed against the acquisition of building and the expanding staffing levels. The Minister for Agriculture, Paddy Smith noted, in 1962, that the institute now had twenty centres including thirteen farms in eleven counties amounting to 4,700 acres in total, and that the institute's increased demand for a grant of £889,000 for agricultural research would place it entirely out of line with the amounts of £127,500 and £350,000 that the department received annually for university education and advisory services. Smith wrote:

> I think that the Institute is developing at too fast a pace, and if this trend continues, I am scared to think what the salary bill will amount to ultimately. I have doubts also about the ability of any organisation in this country to assemble in such a short time so many men with the very special qualities the Institute's research workers ought to have ...
> It has mounted a tremendously varied and comprehensive programme, and, while I am not in a position to criticise the individual items in it, I feel that many of them are, at best, relatively unimportant. I should feel happier about the future of the Institute if it had leaned more towards encouraging, assisting and co-ordinating agricultural research by other institutions, as the Act empowered it to do, and if it had itself concentrated on a small number of research projects and pursued these to finality before taking on more work.[75]

Through the 1960s relations remained so poor that the institute refused to deal with departmental officials and insisted, instead, on direct communication with the minister. In a 1964 memorandum provided for Seán Lemass, the Department of Agriculture questioned whether the institute had achieved the practical results commensurate with its expenditure and whether it would not be better for it to consolidate rather than expand. The department continued:

---

[73] NAI, D/T S16647 B/61, Lemass note on meeting with Litton, 2 Feb. 1961.

[74] NAI, D/T S17221/62, minutes of meeting between D/A and A/I, Dec. 1961.

[75] NAI, D/T S17221/62, Smith to D/F, 8 Jan. 1962.

It would be useless to pretend that there has existed a really effective and co-operative link between the Institute and the Department of Agriculture. The Department does not claim a monopoly of virtue, but it is a fact that it has never once noticed any genuine move by the Institute to work in close and friendly collaboration with the Department which, after all, is in direct touch with government policy and is responsible for our export trade and for all the difficult trade negotiations that have to be undertaken with other governments – the department which, in other words, must ultimately 'carry the buck'. This is also true of the Institute's relations with the colleges of the National university. It is, perhaps, no wonder therefore, that the question is sometimes asked: 'What is the limit of the Institute's ambitions? Is it research, properly or so-called, or are there other aims of a more far-reaching nature?[76]

At a 1965 meeting between institute and departmental officials, organised on the initiative of newly appointed Minister for Agriculture, Charles Haughey, in an attempt to break the impasse, Nagle opened by saying that "if the end for which the two organisations existed, i.e. to develop agriculture and advance the interests of farmers, was to be properly served, each organisation must understand and accept the position of the other."[77] He then commented that the institute would do well to end its refusal to communicate with departmental officials and to remember that it "was a semi-state body, and, however important its functions, they could not be equated with those of the state."[78] The rest of the meeting was a time-honoured rehearsal of the long-dated lines of an unseemly squabble.

That the squabble should have proved so intractable was due, in no small part, to the flawed and indecisive nature of the founding act. The failure of the Department of Agriculture to formulate a definite scheme in the initial stages allowed a whole array of vested interests claim centre stage and effectively dominate the agenda through the decade. These interests were so entrenched by the time the department eventually unveiled its own proposals that the ensuing battle was a thoroughly destructive war of attrition. The eventual compromise was more rooted in ambiguity than clarity. To this end, the institute was given no compulsory powers over research, rather the task of co-ordinating through consultation. Denied a definition of its role, the institute was forced to fight to establish its own role. It marked the opening of another front in the battle to secure as large a portion of state resources as was possible. The result was a classically petty bout of sniping which became almost ritualistic. This is not to suggest that neither the institute nor the department produced agricultural research of worth during the seven years that followed its inception, rather that

---

[76] NAI, D/T S16647 B/95, D/A to D/T, 15 Feb. 1964

[77] Paddy Smith resigned as Minister for Agriculture in October 1964 claiming that he disagreed with the government's capitulation to sectoral representatives. He was replaced by Charles Haughey who, Hoctor noted, was part of the "new generation born since the Anglo-Irish Treaty of 1921 ... [and] coming to the forefront in politics during the fifties." Hoctor, *The department's story*, p. 235.

[78] NAI, D/T 98/6/508, minutes of meeting, 26 May 1965.

the failure to develop a suitable policy framework within which both bodies could thrive was a limiting factor on development. The institute made a genuine contribution – but that contribution was not worthy of the ambition which inspired its conception.

III

Agricultural education and the advisory service

The positive impact of emergent research work was profoundly limited by the disconnected education and advisory systems which it fed. The poverty of agricultural education at all levels was a critical flaw which undermined many of the policy initiatives pursued by the state.[79] Although agricultural science was introduced into the curriculum of secondary schools as an elective subject in 1943, it did not prosper. In 1964, only 258 candidates sat the subject at the intermediate certificate and 449 at the higher certificate – totals which contrasted sharply with the 7768 and 6530 sitting the equivalent certificates in Latin.[80] An *Irish Farmers' Journal* columnist wrote, in 1962, that every year 7000 farmers' sons left school to go into farming but "probably not more than 200 receive training in an agricultural college."[81] In the mid-1960s, the proportion of students whose education terminated at primary level was 83 per cent for agricultural occupations and 59 per cent for others.[82] Given the structure of the Irish educational system, it was little surprise that agricultural education was so inadequate, as in common with most other facets of society, education suffered from chronic underinvestment. Although Ireland had a well-developed educational system relative to its material wealth, this was because the state abdicated responsibility to the religious orders who economised by running a curriculum of low technical content requiring little costly equipment.[83] The only education not controlled by the religious was the technical or vocational education run by local authorities. Clergy were frequently co-opted onto the ruling committees of these schools, however, and Catholic bishops were given "a written assurance that the vocational

---

[79] In the 1950s, a Jesuit correspondent of Patrick McGilligan called for the establishment of a commission to study "the threefold question of higher agricultural education, agricultural research facilities, and the development and improvement of the agricultural advisory services. In view of the relative lack of knowledge and experience which even the best-informed persons in the country confess to, intelligent discussions or proposals are rendered almost impossible." See UCDA, Patrick McGilligan papers, P35d/101, EJC, Milltown Park to McGilligan, 21 Nov. 1955.

[80] Desmond Anderson, 'Education and rural society in the Irish republic', in *Éire–Ireland*, vol. ii, no. 2 (1967), pp 89–94, esp. pp 89–90.

[81] 'Critic' in *IFJ*, 3 Mar. 1962.

[82] Gillmor, *Agriculture*, p. 39

educational system would stick strictly to its authorised field, and would not be allowed to develop so as to impinge upon the field covered by the denominationally-run secondary schools."[84] Not alone did the state suppress any instinct to interfere, but educational policy was only rarely an issue of debate.[85] Only in the early 1960s did the Minister for Education, George Colley assert the departmental role of "policy responsibility and initiation."[86] Before then the system was not directed towards the encouragement of economic growth and there was "an utter lack of correlation between the curriculum and the subsequent careers of the pupils."

Without the religious orders, most Irish children would have received little formal education beyond national school level, but it is equally true that the role of the church was a restrictive one in terms of agricultural education. In 1835, efforts to establish state-run agricultural schools in each province were successfully opposed by the Catholic church. When the Vocational Education Committees (VECs) were established in 1930 under the Vocational Education Act, the church feared it marked the beginning of state-controlled education and the Minister for Education was moved to tell the Dáil the act was merely intended as a stopgap measure.[87] Most crucially for agriculture, the act initiating the schools did not deal with agricultural training or education which remained firmly within the remit of the Department of Agriculture. It was a provision which went some way towards negating the ambition that the VECs would both reflect and immerse themselves in the development of their local communities.[88] Agricultural education, therefore, was played out in the fault-lines which ran between the departments of Agriculture and Education, and those running between church and state. The role of the church in agricultural education came sharply into focus in the 1930s when a Department of Education official, Seósamh Ó Neill, wrote to Eamon de Valera in 1933 calling for "educational reconstruction," and for an analysis of "the reorientation which I feel is necessary if we are to give our education a direction towards agriculture and the life and work of the vast majority of our people." Ó Neill wrote that rural education was neither bringing students to a necessary standard of education in general subjects nor providing any practical training. Further, any students who do go to secondary schools are intended for the church, the professions or the civil service. With those conditions in mind, it was an imperative to focus on national schools where traditional academic subjects could be taught in such a way "as would be calculated to arouse interest in rural life and the pleasures that surround a rural community if only it is trained to enjoy them."[89]

---

[83] Dale A. Tussing, *Irish educational expenditures – past, present and future* (1978), pp 12–3.

[84] Whyte, *Church and state*, pp 37–8.

[85] *Ibid.*, p. 21.

[86] Ó Buachalla, Seamus, 'Review of *The politics of Irish education, 1920–65* by Sean Farren', in *Studia Hibernica*, no. 29, (1997), pp 247–9. Previous to the 1960s the Minister for Education was occasionally sneeringly referred to as the "Minister without Portfolio". See Tussing, *Educational expenditure*, p. 67.

[87] Tussing, *Educational expenditure*, pp 65, 50, 28.

[88] *Ibid.*, *passim.*

Ó Neill proposed the establishment of 500 schools across the country to take students who left national schools and provide them with training. After interdepartmental consultation, a pilot scheme was devised which envisaged the establishment of an initial twenty schools in Gaeltacht areas to be paid for by the state and jointly managed by the departments of Agriculture and Education. The school would provide "manual instruction, rural science (for boys) and domestic science (for girls), and the aim of the school generally will be to make rural life as interesting and creative as possible." Before submitting the proposal to the government, the department decided to seek the views of the Catholic bishops as if they "were unfavourable to the scheme, it was not considered that it would be desirable to go further with it in view of the great labour and expenditure involved."[90] The bishops reviewed the plans and unanimously reported through the Bishop of Galway that they were concerned that the proposed initiative would be an extension of state control and that the existence of vocational schools suggested the scheme was somewhat superfluous.[91] Moreover, in some of the Gaeltacht areas families were so poor that children had either to work at home or go out and earn which would suggest that any proposed schools should be part-time. While, from the moral point of view, there was danger from boys and girls between the ages of twelve and sixteen coming from long distances without supervision. The scheme was dropped and was not again referred to – apart from brief allusions in 1936 and 1956. That some scheme was needed remained clear to all concerned. In 1951, Professor E.J. Sheehy wrote that the inadequacy of agricultural education was responsible for the

> low standard of agriculture practised by the majority of land holders in this country ... The improvement of agricultural techniques and the raising of the level of agricultural practice depends on the adoption of a long-term policy of education. Short-term methods for the achievement of temporary improvement result in disappointment. A more effective system of agricultural education for this country is long overdue and, in the interests of national economy, is now urgently needed.

In 1952, the Minister for Education, Seán Moylan, was equally emphatic on the importance of education: "I believe our own national welfare can be forwarded in no more effective fashion than by way of the integration of the work in the schools with the work on the land."[92] Moylan cited the example of Denmark as the model for Ireland to follow in this regard – but nothing of substance was changed. In his second stint as Minister for Agriculture, James Dillon, wrote: "I hope that we shall be able to provide a good agricultural reader for the National Schools, and to develop in every Technical School in Ireland an active programme

---

[89] NAI, D/T S9271, Seósamh Ó Neill, Department of Education (D/E) to de Valera, 21 Jul. 1933.

[90] NAI, D/T S9271, D/E to D/F, 30 Dec. 1933. The schools would draw children from a six-mile radius and would cost a total of £68,000 to build with annual salary costs of £26,400 for teachers. A booklet outlining the effectiveness of a similar scheme in England was included in support of the proposals.

[91] NAI, D/T S9271, Thomas Doherty, Bishop of Galway, to D/E, 5 Oct. 1934.

of agricultural education for farmers' sons, which will equip them to apply the most modern methods of agriculture to their own holdings."[93] Agricultural education remained firmly in the world of the aspirational.

The abdication of control of education to the church restricted the state to a marginal role. But even within the margins there was room for self-destructive infighting between government departments. Following the establishment of the Department of Education in 1924, matters relating to agriculture were separated from technical instruction and assigned to the Department of Agriculture.[94] Agricultural education became a field of conflict between two departments intent on retaining as many schemes as possible under their particular control and who were unable to agree a progressive way forward. There were periodic outbreaks of harmony such as in 1956 when the Taoiseach, John A. Costello, announced that a series of minor projects would be jointly run by the departments and that the ministers had been in consultation. The departments were asked to examine how best to establish further co-operation between their departments with regard to providing further facilities for agricultural education in the vocational schools.[95] The number of farmers receiving anything approaching the requisite level of specialised training remained far too few to genuinely impact upon the agricultural economy. However, in co-operation foreshadowed by the *Programme for economic expansion*, the departments of Agriculture and Education combined to establish winter farm schools, offering 200 hours instruction during two winter seasons. Designed to fill the gap between the classes given by agricultural instructors in the evenings and full-time courses, it was primarily aimed at those young farmers who could not leave their farms to go to residential agricultural colleges. This interdepartmental co-operation organised through the County Committees of Agriculture and the VECs demonstrated the potential of a cohesive approach.

Cohesion was the exception, not the norm. Decades of interdepartmental turf warfare with tensions running only slightly beneath the surface occasionally exploded into open conflict. In 1962 the struggle for control of the proposed rural home economics advisory service fanned the flames of discord between the departments of Agriculture and Education. Extension work in rural home economics played a large role in the post-war initiatives to develop the agricultural economies of several European countries and was regarded as a central component in fostering increased output.[96] The Department of Agriculture argued that the service should be integrated into the advisory services run by the County Committees of Agriculture, thus retaining it within its ambit. The department argued that farmers' wives should be offered training to act as genuine partners in the running of farms, and that any course

---

[92] NAI, D/T S9271, D/E notes, 8 Jun. 1936, 5 Oct. 1956, 17 Nov. 1951, 29 Mar. 1952.

[93] UCDA, Richard Mulcahy papers, P7/c/139, Dillon speech, 5 Feb. 1957.

[94] Clarke, 'Vocational education', p. 15.

[95] NAI, D/T S9271, Costello speech at special inter-party govt. meeting, 5 Oct. 1956.

[96] Clarke, 'Vocational education', p. 124.

must teach farm women to do well their appropriate tasks both inside and outside the farm home ... It is, of course essential for the future development of our agriculture that an atmosphere more favourable to farm life be encouraged or inculcated, as already there are indications that, in some areas at least, farmers have difficulty in finding suitable wives.[97]

For its part, the Department of Education argued that, while there was much room for departmental co-operation in a properly integrated scheme, advisory work in home economics to rural housewives must rest under its control as it was

an extension to the rural homes of the education (in domestic science or home economics as it is now commonly called) already provided in the rural vocational schools and has been so defined ... The extension of the scheme should, therefore, logically fall within the province of the Department of Education, through Vocational Education Committees.[98]

In a follow-up note, the Minister for Education wrote of his meetings with County Education Officers under his control who left him

convinced that the entry of Agriculture into this activity will be to the detriment of rural families ... The clear distinction between what the committees are doing and what the Department of Agriculture now propose is the difference between educating human beings to raise their own standards and an attempt to give isolated skills to persons desirous of learning them.[99]

In an attempt to realise a compromise Lemass established an interdepartmental committee chaired by J.R. Whitty of the Department of Finance.[100] The committee sat for three months but by the end of November 1962 the Taoiseach was informed by one of his officials:

There is scarcely any hope of an agreed recommendation from the committee as to who should be responsible for the service. The Chairman has informed me in confidence that the representatives of Agriculture and Education have very rigid instructions. However, the committee are going ahead with the intention of producing a properly-documented report – even if there has to be a majority report as well.[101]

Reports, majority or otherwise, were not forthcoming and in October 1963 officials of the Taoiseach's department enquired why no further details had emerged.[102] No response was forthcoming and in June 1964 Nagle reported that

---

[97] NAI, D/T S17318/62, M/A memo to govt., 7 Jul. 1962.
[98] NAI, D/T S17318/62, D/E memo to govt., 27 Jul. 1962.
[99] NAI, D/T S17318/62, M/E note to govt., 28 Jul. 1962.
[100] NAI, D/T S17318/62, D/F note, 7 Sept. 1962.
[101] NAI, D/T S17318/62, D/T note, 26 Nov. 1962.
[102] NAI, D/T S17318/63, D/T to D/F, 5 Oct. 1963.

in a meeting with T. Ó Raifeartaigh, secretary of the Department of Education it was "agreed to bury the inter-departmental committee which has not met since October 1962 and is bogged down in controversy about the procedure followed."[103] The well-honed bureaucratic tactic of delay again proved insurmountable.

By then there was a renewed attempt to foster co-operation between the two departments. In April 1964 the Minister for Agriculture wrote to the Taoiseach that his department was

> having trouble with Education over the whole field of agricultural education. Their policy is an illogical and ambiguous one which fails to recognise that one institution or service must be responsible for agricultural education – that is the training of young people for the occupation of farming. They appear, indeed, to be almost obsessed with a desire to enter the domain of agricultural education at every possible opportunity, even though this means overlapping and confusion all around ... Agricultural education has been the responsibility of my department since its inception and there can hardly be any question that this is as it should be. Our task would be made much easier, however, if the young people with whom we have to deal received a good continuation education course after leaving primary school. I think that there is great scope for the development of continuation education in rural areas, and I am prepared to do all in my power to co-operate with the Department of Education in creating an interest in this type of education among the farming community.[104]

The need for co-operation was given added impetus by a fractious affair in Shinrone, Co. Offaly where the local VEC initially gave permission for the use of vocational school facilities to the Irish Countrywomen's Association (ICA) for a series of lectures and demonstrations by an instructor allied to the County Committee for Agriculture. After one lecture, the right to use the school was withdrawn and the Department of Agriculture alleged this was done at the behest of the Department of Education.[105] Education vehemently denied this and it would seem that the entire incident was the product of misunderstanding rather than malice, but the debacle moved Ó Raifeartaigh to write that "given a proper spirit between our Departments, this whole affair, with all that it entails, would never have arisen. It is a pitiable state of affairs between two government departments. What an example to those concerned throughout the country."[106]

---

[103] NAI, D/T S17318/95, Nagle note, 13 Jun. 1964.

[104] NAI, D/T S17318/95, M/A to D/T, 20 Apr. 1964.

[105] NAI, D/T S17318/95, D/A note, 20 Mar. 1964; and T. Ó Raifeartaigh to J.C. Nagle, 4 Jun. 1964. By charming coincidence, Shinrone was about to serve as the location for a Teilifís Éireann programme exemplifying what co-operation between people and services could achieve in a community.

[106] *Ibid.*

The Shinrone affair, as well as the impasse on the interdepartmental committee, brought an appraisal of relations between the two departments. Following discussions at official level which brought agreement on the specific functions of each department, Nagle reported that "this demarcation – though a painful and delicate process – was a prerequisite to genuine co-operation. Now that each department would know where it stood, I fully expect that there would be a degree of co-operation that it was impossible to achieve in the past."[107] These lines of demarcation were subsequently given clear expression in the *Second Programme for Economic Expansion* and effectively ensured that the input of the Department of Education on agricultural education was not to stray beyond the classroom. It allowed the Department of Agriculture full control of the rural home economy advisory service, as well as the subsequent farm apprenticeship courses. The decision to hand control to the Department of Agriculture of the rural home economy advisory service has been severely criticised, not least by Marie Clarke who noted that the department did not have a fixed local centre to support the initiative. Moreover, it "had no trained personnel to carry out this scheme" rather its primary motive was "to retain control over all matters agricultural."[108]

Using that control to formulate specific schemes of development proved extremely difficult. A 1957 proposal from Macra na Feirme and the NFA was a case in point. This proposal promoted a farm apprenticeship scheme which proposed the allocation of fifty farms per annum to young farmers who completed a requisite agricultural education and apprenticeship programme. After a five year trial, the selected farmers would be given the opportunity of buying the farm through loans from a reconstituted ACC.[109] The scheme, ambitious but apparently unfeasible, was rejected by the government on the grounds that it involved the provision of farms by the state.[110] Despite three years of modifications, the Department of Agriculture viewed that the scheme's "effects in increasing production, raising farming standards or correcting population trends would be of little significance." Equally, the department believed that the scheme "should not be allowed to take priority over the more pressing problems of relieving congestion and transforming small uneconomic holdings into viable units."[111] The Minister for Lands, Erskine Childers, and the Taoiseach, Seán Lemass intimated general sympathy with the proposals, excepting the provision of farms as it was desirable that such powers should only be used "for very restricted and very special social aims."[112] Lemass doubted if the government could justify making land available when there were still 50,000 farmers in the west whose farms were uneconomic.

Before meeting an NFA/Macra delegation in August 1960 Lemass

[107] NAI, D/T S17318/95, Nagle note, 13 Jun. 1964.
[108] Clarke, 'Vocational education', pp 128, 129.
[109] NAI, D/T S16105 A, NFA/Macra na Feirme memo to govt., 7 Dec. 1957.
[110] NAI, D/T S16105 A, M/A copy of reply to Dáil question, 3 Dec. 1958.
[111] NAI, D/T S16105 A, D/A to D/T, 21 Jan. 1960.
[112] NAI, D/T S16105 A, Minutes of Macra na Feirme/NFA delegation meeting with Taoiseach and M/L, 19 Feb. 1960.

commented that, although the Minister for Agriculture was not favourably disposed to the scheme and it was clear that the Land Commission was not designed for this function, he was "very desirous ... to be able to put forward some constructive idea at the meeting." To this end he asked the Minister for Finance, James Ryan, to assess whether the ACC could play a part.[113] The intervention of Lemass, followed by the promise of every assistance to the joint Macra na Feirme/NFA committee, went some way to raising expectations. The Minister for Agriculture remained opposed, though, and refused a request that one of his officers join the farmers' committee to investigate ways to make the scheme operative, saying that he regarded "this whole Apprenticeship Scheme idea as quite unsound, and I could not, therefore, agree to one of my staff joining the committee."[114]

A further draft scheme from the NFA in November 1960 accepted that the government would be unable to provide farms, but that it should instead look to give scholarships while placing apprentices with suitable tutor farms.[115] The NFA wrote to County Agricultural Officers asking them to draw up a list of suitable tutor farms as there is "considerable hope of obtaining a limited number of farms for allocation to young men who may complete a farm apprenticeship course ... We will not advertise for applicants for apprentices until we are sure that we can hold out the prospect of obtaining farms at the end of the apprenticeship course."[116] Through December, government departments offered their opinions on the redesigned scheme. The Department of Finance argued that not more than £500 be provided per scholarship, of which there should only be five in the first year, rising gradually in the light of experience to a maximum of twenty.[117] The Department of Lands argued that the number of farmers willing to take on apprentices would be few, and, in any event, there were 350 graduates leaving the six state-aided agricultural schools which was "a regular, and not inadequate, flow of good class material into farming, that the flow is gathering rather than losing momentum, and that in time the necessary upsurge will come from that source. The Minister has not heard that these students feel deficient or that they have been clamouring for more extensive courses."[118] The Minister for Agriculture was even more critical than previously, arguing that to offer the scheme "lavish funding" would be "educationally unsound and unwarranted from every point of view." Moreover, the scheme would "have no worthwhile effect in raising our farming efficiency or in the solution of our social and economic problems ... Far more fruitful results would follow if the expenditure entailed in the scheme were devoted to strengthening other existing advisory and educational services."[119] The Department of Education believed that the attendance at classes over the first two years of the proposed four-year apprenticeship should be made compulsory as

[113] NAI, D/T S16105 A, Lemass to D/F, 8 Aug. 1960.

[114] NAI, D/T S16105 A, M/A to Lemass, 2 Sept. 1960.

[115] NAI, D/T S16105 A, NFA to D/T, 9 Nov. 1960.

[116] NAI, D/T S16105 A, NFA to County Agricultural Officerss, 2 Dec. 1958.

[117] NAI, D/T S16105 A, D/F to D/T, 21 Dec. 1960.

[118] NAI, D/T S16105 B, D/L to D/T, 21 Dec. 1960.

"the danger of the young person being used solely as an economic production unit would thus be avoided. There will be a natural tendency to use him, as a farm labourer, to the full extent of the agricultural wages."[120]

Despite these reservations, the government decided to accept in principle the idea of a scheme and organised a committee to consider the most efficacious manner of implementation. In a personal note, Lemass considered: "It may be unavoidable to have this department represented on the committee to ensure that it functions with reasonable expedition and as I have been dealing with the NFA/Macra committee."[121] Indeed, so concerned was Lemass that the Department of Agriculture would obstruct the movement towards the formulation of a scheme that he informed Agriculture that any reservations "it may have in regard to the merits of the Farm Apprenticeship Scheme will not be permitted to result in a negative approach to the matter by the Department's representatives on the committee or in any delay in completing the task which has been assigned to the committee."[122] The secretary of the Department of Agriculture, J.C. Nagle, replied that although his minister "had had some reservations about the scheme … there would be no danger of any lack of a constructive attitude towards it so far as his department was concerned."[123] Shortly afterwards, the department's attitude thawed further with Nagle informing the Department of the Taoiseach that the OEEC had appointed a representative to travel to various member countries to study their respective farm apprenticeship schemes and to discuss the introduction of such schemes where they did not already exist.[124] Nagle suggested that the visitor meet the newly-formed committee and, then, in 1964 the farm apprenticeship scheme was unveiled. With the acknowledged object of producing a corps of élite farmers and farm managers who would combine academic knowledge with practical training on well-managed farms, it was to be administered by a board drawn from the NFA, the ICA, the Federation of Rural Workers and Macra na Feirme. It was a long way from the revolutionary (and most probably unworkable) proposals of 1957 and seven years of dilution radically limited the scope of the exercise. The scheme which emerged was valuable in producing progressive, well-trained farmers but was restricted by the lack of funding which severely curtailed its operation.

For its part, university agricultural education also suffered from the traditional lack of resources. The agricultural faculty at the country's largest university, UCD, produced an annual average of just twenty graduates from

119 NAI, D/T S16105 A, M/A to D/T, 21 Dec. 1960.

120 NAI, D/T S16105 B, D/E to D/T, 21 Dec. 1960.

121 NAI, D/T S16105 B, Lemass note, 29 Dec. 1960.

122 NAI, D/T S16105 B, D/T to D/A, 30 Dec. 1960.

123 NAI, D/T S16105 B, D/A to D/T, 30 Dec. 1960.

124 NAI, D/T S16105 B, Nagle to D/T, (Jan. 1960).

agricultural science between 1925 and 1957. Indeed, in 1945 the number of graduates was a mere five.[125] In 1951, there were no applications in several counties for scholarships to university courses in agriculture. For the *Irish Farmers' Journal*, this was because there were only a few, undesirable jobs awaiting graduates. For those who did graduate there was "a stampede for the few poorly-paid jobs."[126] In the late 1950s there was something of a reorganisation of university courses with economics, farm management, farm machinery and farm buildings given more attention. But increased specialisation did not solve the problem of insufficient resources. Indeed, in 1960, the National University of Ireland, reduced its number of agricultural professorships.[127] Although the number of graduates increased through the 1950s even Hoctor was forced to concede that the courses remained "rather unsatisfactory ... The number of agricultural students entering the University did not keep pace with the rising demand for workers in the advisory and other technical services and the resulting shortage was to slow down progress in later years. In the case of veterinary education there was a similar trend with similar results."[128]

Apart from the failure to respond to a series of pleas to establish a veterinary institute of meaningful scope, persistent problems with veterinary education exemplified the flawed approach to education which plagued agriculture. In the 1940s the Department of Finance repeatedly refused to facilitate Department of Agriculture requests to enable UCD establish postgraduate courses in veterinary medicine by providing an annual sum of £700. At that same point, the Minister for Agriculture responded to a TCD initiative to establish its own veterinary school, and a request that there should be some concession on fees, by saying that he "cannot help in any material way and can only agree that the scheme should proceed with my blessing."[129] In the aftermath of World War II, the development of veterinary schools in TCD and UCD was greatly hampered by poor co-operation between the two universities. Although both used the facilities of the veterinary college in Ballsbridge to teach the core practical element of their course, co-operation on a way forward "seemed to be unobtainable."[130] In essence, the problems stemmed from the desire of UCD to absorb the veterinary college, while TCD wanted to acquire equal rights in the administration of that college with UCD. The pressure to resolve the crisis was heightened by the failure to respond to the changes in Britain in the 1940s which saw alterations in the manner in which veterinary education was regulated in that country, particularly in training and certification. As the British authorities began insisting that a university degree was necessary to obtain a licence to practise as a surgeon, the Irish government was forced to introduce legislation to revamp its system to bring it to a standard which would allow its graduates to practise in Britain should they so desire. In the

---

[125] UCDA, Patrick McGilligan papers, P35d/99, McGilligan note, 1958.

[126] *IFJ*, 1 Sept. 1951.

[127] *Ibid.*, 2 Apr. 1960.

[128] Hoctor, *The department's story*, p. 216.

[129] NAI, D/T S4521 B/1, M/A to de Valera, 7 Feb. 1945.

[130] NAI, D/T S4521 C, A.F. O'Dea, Registrar of Veterinary Council of Ireland to D/T, 26 Jul. 1957.

immediate post-war era, the government was unable to devise a long-term programme to reorganise veterinary education but opted, somewhat inevitably, for a holding operation through interim arrangements in 1947 and 1954. Effectively, these arrangements allowed both Dublin universities to send students to the veterinary college and to confer degrees. The Department of Agriculture acknowledged:

> No-one has ever claimed that these arrangements were ideal from all aspects, but at least they achieved in a simple and practical way the important desideratum of enabling veterinary students from the two universities – these having different traditions and representing on the whole different sections of the population – to obtain veterinary degrees.[131]

Both universities were irreconcilable on how the veterinary college should be run.

The visit of inspectors from the British Royal College of Veterinary Surgeons in November 1958 lent force to a move to resolve the matter of management. That delegation stressed the imperative of bringing the college under university control and noted that assurances given in 1954 that this would be done had not been acted upon. The delegation further noted that the clear acceptance from the 1954 visit that substantial staff increases were vital had not been addressed either.[132] In a report on their visit the delegation commented that, as well as few teachers, there was an almost complete lack of technicians, lengthy delays in procuring even simple drugs and equipment, a little-used field station, and that the level of education was not acceptable, to such an extent that "the RCVS Council, having regard to its statutory responsibilities, could scarcely remain indifferent to a continuance of such a state of affairs."[133] In an attempt to rectify the problem, de Valera took a personal hand in proceedings and outlined a plan which would have seen both universities confer degrees from a college administered by a board of governors drawn from representatives of UCD, TCD, the Veterinary Council and the government. Both universities would be free to appoint staff to work in the college while the students would have shared use of facilities. UCD President, Michael Tierney, was not impressed: "Sooner than go into partnership with TCD in a Veterinary Hospital which, in fact, will remain under Government control, I should recommend that the college give up all part in veterinary education."[134] The hierarchy of the Catholic Church weighed in with Archbishop John McQuaid saying that "it is a matter of grave concern and regret to the hierarchy that the

---

[131] NAI, D/T S4521 C, D/A to D/T, 10 Aug. 1957.

[132] NAI, D/T S4521 C, D/A meeting with Royal College of Veterinary Surgeons delegation, 6 Nov. 1958. A dispute over scales of pay had contributed in no small measure to the problems in adequately staffing the college. Indeed, when the Department of Agriculture advertised posts in the college, the Veterinary Medical Association issued a counter-advertisement advising potential applicants not to take the position. The dispute was not resolved until 1960 when "an uneasy truce" emerged. See *Irish Times*, 1 Feb. 1960.

[133] NAI, D/T S4521 C, W.G.R. Oates, Registrar of the RCVS to Nagle, 18 Nov. 1958.

Government has proposed to settle definitively the professional training of students of University College, Dublin, who are entrusted to our pastoral care, without any consultation of the Hierarchy."[135] At a subsequent meeting between de Valera and McQuaid, the Archbishop agreed that TCD should get equality of treatment with UCD – but that this should be done through the establishment of separate faculties. When de Valera pointed out the duplication of cost, McQuaid argued that "the extra cost would, in the circumstances, be warranted."[136] Subsequent to that meeting, de Valera produced a plan which would have allowed both universities to retain their own faculties and teaching staff, and accorded them the use of separate rooms in the veterinary college. McQuaid commended the new initiative: "This draft plan admirably preserves the principles which I outlined."[137] Of course, the proposed sharing of facilities was not without its rancorous moments. Tierney rejoined the fray to suggest that TCD students be given the top floor and UCD students the bottom, that there should be no sharing of laboratory assistants and that only in limited circumstances should laboratory space be shared.[138] The Department of Agriculture resisted that suggestion but the compromise once more demonstrated the forces limiting progress in agriculture. At the precise moment that the country needed an expansion in the number of graduates in veterinary science to forward the tuberculosis eradication scheme, the educational system was paralysed by inter-university dispute and a political establishment unable to provide direction. The resultant compromise – tortuously extracted, even if it did achieve the goal of continued recognition for Irish veterinary qualifications in Britain – was uneconomic and involved a duplication of expenditure on resources which were already stretched threadbare in the first place.

Those threadbare resources were not unduly strained by farmer pressure to expand the availability of agricultural education. Such resources as were provided remained underutilised. To the great number of farmers, inheriting sons were not to be bothered with full-time education once they had passed the compulsory level. Compulsory education finished at fourteen for children whose labour was crucial to the viability of the entire farming enterprise. Immediate economic survival held distinctly more importance than any potential long-term gain through extended education.[139] It was through this prism that Irish farmers viewed agricultural education. In 1905, Arthur Smith had written of how farmers had viewed specialised education in agriculture as a "palpable absurdity" with supposed students failing to attend Department of Agriculture courses.[140] Little

---

134 NAI, D/T S4521 C, Tierney to De Valera, 2 Jan. 1959.

135 NAI, D/T S4521 D/94, McQuaid to de Valera, 16 Feb. 1959.

136 NAI, D/T S4521 D/94, D/T note on de Valera meeting with McQuaid and Dr Lucey, Bishop of Cork, 27 Feb. 1959. The note also recorded: "In reply to a question by the Taoiseach as to the stage of education up to which His Grace would regard it as essential for Catholic students to remain in an institution with a Catholic atmosphere, I understand that the Archbishop indicated that that stage would be the conferring of a primary degree."

137 NAI, D/T S4521 D/94, McQuaid to de Valera, 5 Mar. 1959.

138 NAI, D/T S4521 F/94, Tierney to D/A, 26 Nov. 1959.

139 Clarke, 'Vocational education', p. 50.

had changed by 1952 when the Bishop of Galway, Dr Browne, commented that "the most serious problem is not simply the lack of agricultural education but the lack of demand for it. While there seems to be an improvement in recent years, there are still too many farmers who just won't be bothered ... Worse still, they won't give their sons a chance."[141] Even in 1957, an *Irish Farmers' Journal* columnist wrote of it "being common to read of agricultural scholarships not taken up, short courses organised by Macra na Feirme in conjunction with the Department of Agriculture are abandoned for want of pupils and ... the recent Folk High School in Skerries was mainly supported by those whose principle concern might be how to occupy their retirement."[142]

It was a state of affairs which moved Raymond Crotty to remark that it was "not uncommon to find in these circumstances that the least educated, least intelligent and least progressive son inherits the farm." This did not augur well for the agricultural instructors working through the countryside and, according to Crotty, the advisory officers were faced with the task of "trying to get unwilling and uninterested farmers to adopt more efficient methods."[143] It was a task for which the advisory service was singularly ill-prepared, even without the sheer inadequacy of the research and education problems which rendered the climate of operations so hostile. Too few advisers were expected to perform too many functions backed by too few resources. Although it was often acknowledged that the advisory service was lamentable in scope and impact, the attempts to improve its aspect were irregular and insufficient. These attempts were not aided by the persistent perception, whether on the farm or in political circles, that advisers were more a luxury than a necessity. To this end, James Dillon commented, in 1950:

> There may be a small minority of farmers who would like to have an inspector to wake them up in the morning, to dress them, to direct their daily work, and to tuck them into bed at night. But the vast majority of farmers of this country are well able to look after their own business, to make their own bargains, to hunt away from their gate anyone who seeks to exploit them, and effectively to make use of a profitable market when it is provided for them. It is to these farmers I look for the efficient operation of the agricultural industry in this country.[144]

Even those with greater awareness of the importance of publicly encouraging the use of advisers and of emphasising their worth, could not envisage substantial development of the advisory system. In 1953, Minister for Agriculture, Thomas Walsh, wrote:

---

[140] Quoted in Ferriter, 'Peculiar people', p. 44.

[141] *IFJ*, 3 May 1952.

[142] *Ibid.*, 3 Aug. 1957.

[143] Crotty, *Agricultural Production*, p. 102.

[144] James Dillon speech to Cork County Committee of Agriculture, quoted in, *IFJ*, 18 Feb. 1950.

During the past 15 years or so, grassland management and utilisation in other countries, have undergone remarkable changes. Unfortunately very few of these improved techniques have been adopted by the majority of farmers in our typically grassland districts ... I depend on County Committees of Agriculture and their advisory staffs to undertake a vigorous campaign.[145]

It speaks volumes for the significance attached to agricultural advice that the system was based upon the ability of County Committees of Agriculture to employ such officers as they believed were necessary or financially sustainable. Although the state paid half the cost of the salaries of the advisory staffs, it was only in the better-off counties where holdings were larger that anything approaching a reasonable service was developed. The comprehensiveness of the service was largely a matter of decision for the county authorities and "in times of financial stringency or occasionally because of political expediency, expenditure on the service has been curtailed."[146] This remained an undiminished feature of the advisory service through the years and the disparity between the richer and poorer counties was great.[147]

When, in 1950, the OEEC organised a survey of the advisory services of European countries, the resultant report noted that while there were commendable aspects of the Irish service, the ratio of one instructor per 4,000 farms was insufficient. The report stressed the need for more agricultural inspectors, more specialist advisers and the provision of vastly enhanced facilities. Further, it stressed the need to co-ordinate research, education and advice.[148] By 1950, there were a mere 83 instructors in agriculture, as well as a further 49 in horticulture and 80 in poultry keeping across the country. Poultry instructresses were also expected to advise on butter and cheese making. To enable the County Committees of Agriculture to better develop effective advisory programmes, to examine and evaluate progress and results, and to assist in supervising and training county staffs, the state was divided into three districts, each under a district inspector. In 1958, in an attempt to expand services, this was increased to six districts. By 1960, the number of instructors in agriculture had increased to

---

[145] Thomas Walsh speech to County Committees of Agriculture representatives, quoted in NAI, D/T S15282, M/A speech, 22 Jan. 1953. In 1954, Walsh told de Valera that, although they required a good many more advisers and a more co-ordinated approach, "the County Committee system has worked admirably," and "suits our conditions." He dismissed all criticism: "In my opinion, such organisations as Macra na Feirme, although they talk very loud, in practice do not so far contribute much to building up the agricultural economy. My experience is that every time they are asked to do something they bungle it." He did note, though, that they "are past masters at slating the department and myself." See NAI, D/T S14815 C, Walsh to de Valera, 8 Feb. 1954.

[146] *Review of the Irish agricultural advisory service* (1967), p. 21.

[147] In 1967, the ratio of advisors to holdings was 1 to 316 in Kildare, but 1 to 1,462 in Donegal. See *ibid*, p. 21. In Co. Louth in 1957, there was only one permanent instructor and he, along with two temporary men, was expected to cover the 6,000 farms in the county. See *IFJ*, 18 May 1957.

[148] *IFJ*, 7 Oct. 1950. The report was produced by Th. Vandelbo of the Danish advisory service, A. Lidtvoit, a director of the Norwegian Ministry of Agriculture, and Paul Miller, director of the extension service in Minnesota. See also Hoctor, *The department's story*, p. 239.

230, with horticulture also rising to 62, although poultry instructors fell to 77.[149]
This expansion of the advisory services in the latter part of the 1950s also saw the
opening of local offices, equipped, for the first time, with telephones.

Yet, even this increase in the number of instructors was so piecemeal and so
painfully realised that its impact was not nearly as positive as it ought to have been.
From the attempts originating in 1949 by Dillon to implement his much
trumpeted parish plan, and through the developments which originated in the
Programme for Economic Expansion, the most striking aspect of the development was
its incoherence. There was no realised framework of progression, no overall plan,
no systematic approach to finding the best possible solution. The parish plan was
devised by James Dillon, in conjunction with the leader of Muintir na Tíre, Canon
John Hayes.[150] It was intended that Catholic parishes would be served by agents
who would offer advice to farmers. Significantly, the agents would be directly
responsible to the Department of Agriculture and would operate outside of the
advisers employed by the County Committees of Agriculture. As ever, the scheme
was conceived as a response to more than one agenda. Not merely was it intended
to promote agricultural advisory work but was also born of a desire to respond to
the vocational movement as the Taoiseach, John A. Costello, later told Muintir na
Tíre members: "I and my colleagues believed so much in this idealism that we
adopted as part of our agricultural policy the parish plan of Canon Hayes."[151]

The proposed direct relationship between the new parish agents and the
department contributed to the controversy which dogged the proposal from the
start. For some, centralised control offered the potential to finally foster close co-
ordination between the various government services, more effective supervision
and a rational distribution of staff throughout the country. Others were equally
convinced that advisers reporting directly to the department would not enjoy the
confidence of the farmers and that the service would duplicate, with equal
ineffectiveness, the existing advisory service rather than offering a path of
progress.[152] The first parish agent was appointed in Bansha, Co. Tipperary in 1948,
and a further two were appointed in 1949 in an *ad hoc* pilot scheme. Yet, by August
1950, Dillon was telling Muintir na Tíre members in Mullingar that the scheme
"had gone up the spout," pushed there by the ASA who had persuaded prospective
agents to refuse positions on financial, and other, grounds.[153] Faced with the
trenchant opposition of the ASA, Dillon was forced to leave the parish plan in
abeyance, and little more seemed likely to come of it until, in 1955, he declared
his intention to restart it.[154] By the end of 1957 there were 24 parish agents
working through the country, but their presence did not solicit universal approval.
Even as the scheme was beginning its new life, a Tipperary farmer wrote to the
Irish Farmers' Journal: "While I do not grudge the lucky men that will be appointed

---

149 *Review of the Irish agricultural advisory service* (1967), pp 12, 13.

150 *Irish Independent*, 17 Aug. 1950.

151 *Irish Independent*, 14 Aug. 1958.

152 Hoctor, *The department's story*, p. 242.

to the soft jobs, I am satisfied that they will not be very busy."[155] That correspondent's disenchantment was rooted in perceptions prevalent in many other countries, notably England. One commentator noted English farmers as hostile to the advisory service as they believed in practice over theory and were suspicious of any purported expert who had not earned his living off the land. Equally, the advisory service was perceived there as evidence of expensive, unnecessary bureaucracy staffed by over-zealous, callow college trainees, while farmers resented the implication they were using ineffective methods which were easily rectifiable. Significantly, these attitudes were common amongst farm leaders as well as ordinary farmers.[156] In Ireland, this attitude was compounded by the belief that instructors could suggest any manner of improvements but the vast bulk of farmers simply did not have the capital to act on the advice. Those charged with overseeing agricultural instruction held other concerns. Con Meany, chairman of Cork County Committee of Agriculture, reacted to the announcement that a parish agent was to be appointed to serve within his domain by saying that "apart from duplication of advisory services, the parish agent would not be under the local committee but would be directly supervised by the civil service."[157] This tension exercised the *Irish Farmers' Journal* in an editorial which argued that

> it would be highly desirable to limit the expansion of this
> 'experiment'. Friction is developing in many cases between the agents
> and the existing advisory service. The farming organisations cannot be
> said to be sympathetic with the venture ... We hold that more would
> be accomplished if the number of county agricultural advisory officers
> was increased and if the undoubted ability of Dr. Spain were used to
> improve where possible the existing services.[158]

The stuttering attempts to enact the parish plan, opposed from the outset by Fianna Fáil, were abandoned in the wake of the publication of the *Programme for Economic Expansion* in 1958 with the announcement:

> The Parish plan will not be developed further; the Plan could be
> operated quite successfully if it were adopted as the only or basic
> advisory system in the country, but to allow two systems to develop, one
> centrally controlled by the state and the other under Committees of
> Agriculture would inevitably lead to friction and confusion. A choice
> had to be made between a centralised system or the essentials of the
> present system, and on the whole it is felt that the present system,

---

[154] In June 1950 the Department of Agriculture announced it was postponing the proposed initiative "because the persons appointed to work the scheme had declined to accept the terms offered." See *IFJ*, 10 Jun. 1950.

[155] *IFJ*, 12 Feb. 1955.

[156] Colin J. Holmes, 'Science and the farmer', in *AHR*, vol. 36, ii (1988), pp 77–86.

[157] *IFJ*, 11 Feb. 1956.

[158] *IFJ*, 19 Nov. 1955. Dr Henry Spain was the Department of Agriculture official charged with organising the parish agents.

subject to certain improvements, should be continued.[159]

Within seven years of the sounding of this death knell, the last of the parish agents had passed into other employment. This scarcely creditable interlude was the extent of government attempts at centralisation of service. In 1962 the interdepartmental report on the problems of small western farms was strongly critical of the poverty of agricultural instruction in the poorer farming regions. In reaction, a new initiative by the Department of Agriculture saw it agree to contribute 75 per cent, rather than the usual 50 per cent, of the salaries of instructors in western counties and within three years the number of instructors in those counties had increased by 50 per cent.[160] Even this increase, though positive, was insufficient. Not alone was the service growing from the most feeble of roots, but the resources fed into it remained inadequate. Instructors were isolated not only by the lack of research and an unreceptive audience but also by the nature of their work. The *Irish Farmers' Journal* noted constant complaints by agricultural instructors that they were forced to spend too much time on soil analysis and sundry administrative tasks, rather than on farm management.[161]

Even if the number of advisers increased, attempts to lend vitality to the advisory service and to make it more responsive to the needs of farmers did not succeed. The 1967 *Review of the Irish agricultural advisory service* confirmed the enduring flaws which policy had singularly failed to address. The decision to relinquish any attempt at uniformity ensured "the comprehensiveness of the service is a largely a matter for decision by the county authorities … In some counties a satisfactory service has been established, but in others the service is either indifferent or inadequate." The imposition of all manner of tasks from grant administration to the organisation of local agricultural shows "means that advisory and educational programmes do not always have the attention that they deserve." The failure of county committees to provide the necessary resources to run a service was exacerbated by the inadequate infrastructure through which it operated. Specialist advisers, the report noted had "no laboratory or other field station facilities to enable them to test out new techniques or initiate investigative work. Unless they can do this they may soon be out of touch with new developments and advancements." Similarly, there were

> a number of instances where three or four officers all worked in one room with no facilities for interviewing farmers on confidential matters nor did they have clerical assistance. There are also in our view too many advisers who are based in their homes and working in isolation from the rest of their colleagues. This in our view is a very unsatisfactory state of affairs and we believe it is a bad practice.

The explicit failing was lack of co-ordination as "for an advisory service to be

---

[159] *Programme for economic expansion* (1958), p. 24.

[160] Hoctor, *The department's story*, p. 240.

[161] *IFJ*, 1 Dec. 1951 and 7 Apr. 1962.

equally effective over a whole country there must be, and be seen to be, a direct chain of command between all levels." The rapid transfer of staff between counties and the fact that some western counties had trouble getting permanent staff was compounded by the shortage of suitably qualified graduates from universities. The solutions suggested were markedly similar to those proposed in 1950. There was the continued need to employ more instructors, to give them a common base from which to work and to provide them with sufficient resources. There was a definite need to strengthen links between the service and the Agricultural Institute without opting for amalgamation. In reality, "no method of improving the present system without any fundamental change in the organisation will provide an effective advisory service ... The improvement and extension of advisory work in Ireland can only come about through the setting up of a National Agricultural Advisory Service." Within that service, management advice should be one of the primary tasks, while the review further stressed the need for a more professional outlook: "Farming is a business and its success should only be judged in the same way as any other business ... we believe from what we have seen that there is a tremendous educational and advisory task facing those who work with farming people in making them aware of the implication of a more business-like approach to their job."[162]

The inability to inculcate a more businesslike approach to the job was critical. The failure of research, education and advisory bodies to initiate, foster or service an efficient, market-orientated culture of business fundamentally undermined the objectives outlined in the *Programme for economic expansion.* As he embarked on his plan to revitalise the advisory service in 1949 through the parish plan, James Dillon wrote:

> The history of the existing educational and advisory system is not one of national growth or development but rather the application as expedients of various supplementary measures to meet particular needs or special circumstances ... The system worked well in its earlier years, however, it has tended to become very complex and unwieldy and control is divided between this department and the County Committees of Agriculture ... Any further considerable expansion of the existing system would, unless the system were at the same time re-organised on a rational basis, greatly increase the difficulties being experienced and fall short of requirements in efficiency.[163]

Dillon's own endeavours, as well as those of his counterparts through the 1950s, served only to exacerbate rather than soothe both requirements and difficulties. Ireland continued to devote little attention to services considered critical to agricultural expansion in its more progressive contenders. It was not merely paucity of funding, though, which limited the formulation of progressive policy.

---

[162] *Review of the Irish agricultural advisory service* (1967), pp 21, 24, 23, 28, 45–6.

[163] NAI, D/T S14477 A, D/A memo to govt., 13 Dec. 1949.

IV

Farm Mechanisation

If the drive to reach the specific and general targets outlined in the *Programme for economic expansion* was clearly undermined by a thoroughly inadequate foundation of research, education and advisory services, an ill-conceived mechanisation process and chronic underinvestment proved similarly detrimental to development. Ireland began mechanising its agriculture on a large scale, only after the majority of its competitors had made considerable progress in that direction.[164] Further, even the stuttering moves to mechanise were limited by social, political and economic dictates defining the pattern and pace of change. Although some Irish farmers embraced with alacrity the new scientific methods sweeping international agricultures in the post-World War II era, many more remained rooted in a subsistence mentality preoccupied with survival. Invariably, and understandably, the adoption of new techniques was not viewed as an integral part of survival. In essence, change conjured connotations of risks too great for those living from hand to mouth to consider. It is convenient to consider the resultant mindset of Irish farmers as innately conservative. Undoubtedly, the small farm structure, the organisation of the agricultural economy, the delayed development of farming organisations and the ageing farm population, were not conducive to radical change. Yet, this portrait of a retarded rump is grossly simplistic. Indeed, it was market forces, as well as structural deficiencies, which dictated that Irish farmers did not pursue mechanisation on the scale of their competitors. It was not that the farming community considered its way of life sacrosanct or without need of improvement, rather it considered that suggested mechanisation brought little guarantee of increased prosperity. The response was typical of a small-farming community. In Germany, where nearly 90 per cent of farms were under 50 acres in 1950, change was "slow and difficult." For the German farmer, "the predominant type of agriculture was not one to which specialisation or mechanisation could be easily applied ... Moreover, he was naturally fearful of the temporary insecurity which might result from changes in existing techniques and methods."[165]

---

[164] See NAI, F 23/39/50, D/A to D/F, 31 Oct. 1949. The Department of Agriculture applied to the Department of Finance for funds (which it duly received) to send an officer to the US to study mechanisation for one year: "The mechanisation of agriculture is expected to assume increasing importance during the next few years and it is highly desirable that this Department should have on its staff at least one officer who will be fully acquainted with all kinds of agricultural machinery." It noted that before the war, Irish agriculture was "seriously undermechanised by comparison with that of other Western European countries," but it was hoped to give a series of public displays which "would help considerably in influencing the farmer towards mechanisation."

There was even the question within government circles on the desirability of far-reaching mechanisation. On taking office in 1951, Thomas Walsh, was reported as saying he did "not believe in mechanisation to an extreme limit. 'Complete mechanisation of cropping, from the combine drill up to the combine harvester can only result in reduced rural employment and that would be a bad thing' ... In the event of war, he went on, the shortage of horses might be serious."[166] The remnants of the old separatist vision of a thriving rural populace retained a hold. It was similar concern over moves to mechanise which brought a demand from the Taoiseach, John A. Costello, to the Department of Agriculture for an appraisal of how employment on the land and in country areas would be affected by any influx of new machinery. [167] The Department of Agriculture noted that in the decade and a half prior to 1954, the number of males who were family members engaged in farm work had fallen by 16.6 per cent and the number of hired labourers had fallen by 21.5 per cent.[168] Within the same time frame, the number of tractors on the land had grown from 2,067 to 19,096, while the number of combine harvesters and milking machines had grown from "just a few" to 539 and 4,540, respectively.[169] Nonetheless, between 1929 and 1954 the number of working horses merely declined from 326,958 to 286,148. The department noted that the reduction in the labour force was least pronounced in those areas where mechanisation had made the greatest advance and that

> mechanisation as such has no discernible effect on the reduction in the farm labour force which is taking place but rather that mechanisation is in some areas the farmer's answer to the difficulty of retaining family or hired labour ... It is widely held both here and in other countries that a very strong factor in the farmer's decision to purchase mechanical equipment is the desire to render himself independent of casual labour at the peak of the season.

The Department argued there "had been some reduction through increased mechanisation in the numbers and work for blacksmiths but this has been more

---

[165] Hubert G. Schmidt, 'Post-war developments in West German agriculture, 1945–53', in *AH*, vol. 29, no. 4 (1955), pp 147–60, esp. p. 147. The German experience was not helped by the fragmentation of farm holdings which ensured that farmers spent, on average, one-quarter of their time travelling between their various parcels of land.

[166] *IFJ*, 7 Jul. 1951.

[167] NAI, D/T 15645 A, D/T to D/A, 28 Jan. 1954.

[168] NAI, D/T S15645 A, D/A to D/T, 18 Feb. 1954. The memorandum enclosed a booklet from the Ferguson School of Mechanised Farming in Wicklow, which carried a message from the agricultural machinery producer, Harry Ferguson: "St. Patrick came south to rid the land of snakes. I am no saint but I am dedicated to ridding your land of power animals."

[169] *Ibid.* The previous year, the Department of Agriculture had noted: "There is undoubtedly some scope for further mechanisation of farm operations but ... tractor numbers in themselves are not the best index either of requirements or of progress. The Report is certainly not correct in assuming that multiplication of tractors will increase agricultural production, in the way that increased mechanization in industry increases industrial production ... However, the Department of Agriculture provides financial facilities for farmers who wish to mechanise, within the limits laid down by the Department of Finance." See NAI, D/T S14042 H, D/A memo to govt., 13 Mar. 1953. The report in question was one compiled by a British official, H.A. Silverman, *Irish food supplies and trade with Britain* (1952).

than offset by the increased employment given in garages and to the makers of
trailers and other ancillary equipment." Further, the department argued that
mechanisation had contributed to increased tillage production and believed that
the "fullest exploitation of grass in present circumstances could only be obtained
through a relatively high degree of mechanised farming." It was also asserted that
the "one factor most likely to make for a slowing down in the drift from the land
is unquestionably growing productivity to which increasing mechanisation could
contribute."[170]

Beyond this acknowledgement of the broad worth of increased
mechanisation, there was little conception of how to foster or assist the process.[171]
Despite the clear acceptance that farmers would need easier access to working
capital to facilitate increased mechanisation, access to credit remained difficult.[172]
Indeed, there remained a belief in the Department of Agriculture that "easy credit
would be the ruination of farmers. The minister regards most of the schemes put
forward from time to time for the grant of credit to farmers as propaganda."[173]
Against this background, the founding of the ACC had not been of great benefit.
Although the ACC was initially welcomed by farmers and, in 1929, 3,239 loans to
the value of £400,531 were issued, by the 1950s this annual figure had declined to
such an extent that only 766 loans totalling £261,254 were issued in 1951.[174] There
was constant criticism of the ACC by farmers, press and public representatives and,
in 1953, according to the Department of Agriculture,

> numerous complaints are made personally to the Minister for
> Agriculture. It would seem that farmers generally are not disposed to
> do business with the Corporation. There can scarcely be any doubt
> that the Corporation is fully aware by now that its policy denies many
> farmers access to the credit facilities for the provision of which the

---

[170] NAI, D/T S15645 A, D/A to D/T, 18 Feb. 1954.

[171] A scheme was introduced in 1948 to speed mechanisation by providing a repayment of 6d per gallon
on petrol shown to have been used in petrol drives, tractors and agricultural machinery. In 1951, the
repayment was increased to 8d per gallon and in 1956 to 1s 1¾d per gallon. By 1960, only 3,900 farmers
made use of it and although it was noted that fraud was not a major issue, "of its nature the scheme is
incapable of wholly effective administration." See NAI, F 22/9/48, D/F note, 1960.

[172] In the bad winter of 1924, *ad hoc* co-operative credit societies were formed to administer assistance to
small farmers hit by heavy losses of livestock. A total of £87,495 was received by 63 societies. By 1950, 44
had repaid in full, nine more had their balance written off. A total of £88,664 was repaid in principal and
interest. Ten societies still owed a total of £11,714. A test case against Gneeveguila Society, Co. Kerry had
ended in the Supreme Court after the society was pursued for repayments by the departments of Finance
and Agriculture. The court had ordered that the individuals involved in the society should make up the
arrears but the Department of Agriculture (having originally pushed the moves) effectively refused to
enforce this order. The secretary to the Department of Finance, J.J. McElligott, wrote in 1950 that "from
the point of view of preserving the morale of the community, there is everything to be said for bringing
it home to borrowers that a debt due to the state must be paid just the same as a debt due to any other
creditor. Having carried the proceedings in the Gneeveguilla case 99 per cent of the way, it would be a
sign of weakness to throw in your hand completely at this stage." Eventually, in 1953, McElligott agreed
that the debts be written off – by then the officially-appointed liquidator had retired. See NAI, F
145/0001/25, D/A to D/F, 30 Oct. 1950, D/F to D/A, 23 Nov. 1950, and D/F to D/A, 7 Feb. 1953.

[173] NAI, D/T S12830, D/T note, 17 May 1941.

[174] NAI, D/T S2643 B, D/A memo to govt., 5 Mar. 1953. The ACC was founded in 1927 to provide loans
to co-operatives and to farmers. By 1938 only eight co-operatives had loans – four of which were in default.

Corporation was formed. Nevertheless, neither the public criticism of its policy nor the comparatively small number of advances made by the corporation in the past 24 years has succeeded in causing the corporation to revise its policy. The Minister for Agriculture is constrained to deplore the relative failure of the Corporation to provide convenient credit facilities for the agricultural community. He feels that it has now become expedient in the national interest that the unduly hampering policy of the Corporation be altered.[175]

To this end, the Minister proposed the reconstitution of the board of directors and the formulation of a policy to allow easier access to credit. Ironically, even the Department of Finance was critical of the ACC's parsimony and had "on various occasions suggested to the Board of Governors the desirability of relaxing its security requirements in connection with the provision of credit facilities for farmers."[176] The government formed a committee to assess the matter and received the views of the ACC which cited examples of recently rejected loan applications, all of which had received the support of public representatives.[177] Some of the applicants had been refused between thirteen and eighteen times due to proclivities for greyhound racing, drinking, gambling, criminal activity and IRA involvement. Others had forged the names of guarantors who were either dead or had never lived. In particular, the ACC cited a farmer who had 28 convictions against him under the School Attendance Act through trying to get his children to run the farm while he "spends his mornings in bed and his nights in public houses."[178]

The government did move to reconstitute the board of the ACC and Pa F. Quinlan, president of Macra na Feirme, was appointed as a director. Yet there was to be no overhaul of farm credit availability. There was agreement that the ACC and the Department of Agriculture would combine in a scheme making loans available to farmers to purchase fertilisers and lime, but this was little more than a limited gesture, not a wholesale restructuring.[179] De Valera told a meeting of bankers in 1954 that "intervention by the state was undesirable both because of the administrative cost and of the government's preference that the solution of the problem should be left to private enterprise."[180] Only through the Land Commission would the government offer large-scale credit facilities – but this only confirmed the notion that it was the ownership of land, not its utilisation, which was the key to wealth. By 1955, the inter-party government moved the matter still further when the Department of Agriculture renounced its involvement in credit

---

175 *Ibid.* See also, for example, the *Irish Independent*, 8 Jan. 1954, whose editorial called for the ACC to be wound up as it was "a useless body ... Quite obviously, this institution has not justified its existence."

176 NAI, D/T S2643 B, D/A memo to govt., 5 Mar. 1953.

177 NAI, D/T S2643 B, ACC memo to govt., 27 Jul. 1953.

178 *Ibid.* The memorandum listed 192 people who had had applications rejected in the previous year, included in which was an eleven-acre farmer who kept two acres of tillage with the remaining nine acres being used to stock one cow. He asked for £150 to feed and dress his wife and children, and to pay for turf until his crops came in.

179 NAI, D/T S15465 A, cabinet minutes, 26 Jan. 1954.

matters and announced that all schemes of loans for agricultural purposes would be centralised in the ACC – a body scarcely changed from the one which it had so trenchantly criticised two years previously.[181] The reasons cited were convenience and the desire to save the state money.[182] Through the 1950s, the ACC scarcely thrived on its new-found responsibilities and its continued lacklustre performance drew the *Irish Farmers' Journal* to remark that it was "a very sour but faithful index of public policy."[183]

Nonetheless, for the majority of farmers over-investment inspired greater fear than underinvestment and they remained largely unaffected by failure to reform the ACC. In 1953, de Valera was told by the assistant secretary at the Department of Agriculture, Tony Dempsey, that the "traditional farming outlook was that money should be lodged in the bank, not invested in the land."[184] That same year the Department of Agriculture asserted that, as well as freeing up the availability of credit, the main problem appeared to be to convince farmers that it would pay them to invest more capital as

> the experience of government or semi-government credit schemes clearly indicates that farmers in general are not availing themselves of the facilities provided … Among a large number of such farmers, there is a deeply ingrained disinclination to incur debts unless they can see in the clearest way that they can discharge the debts in full and reasonably promptly. There does not seem to be much object in providing additional credit until such time as the more progressive farmers are prepared to borrow money to expand their operations. The root of the problem would, therefore, appear to be educational mainly.[185]

Educating the farmer to recycle savings as investment proved an insoluble problem through the 1950s. In 1959, the continued underinvestment in agriculture prompted the government to employ Fred Gilmore, deputy governor of Farm Credit Administration in the US, to produce a report. Gilmore noted that on the smaller farms, particularly those under 15 acres, the issue was how to make a living, and there was evidently no additional debt-paying capacity. More industrious farmers had the potential to use credit in an orderly manner but

> one discouraging factor was the very substantial number of farmers that appeared to lack the will or the incentive to improve their operations. Part of this may be due to the advanced age of many farmers and to the large number of bachelor owners. In discussing this

---

[180] NAI, D/T S15465 A, note of meeting between de Valera and banking representatives, 4 Jan. 1954.

[181] See NAI, D/T S2643 C, D/A note, 12 Apr. 1965, *Irish Independent*, 14 Apr. 1955 and *Irish Times*, 13 Apr. 1955.

[182] See NAI, D/T S2643 C, D/A note, 12 Apr. 1965.

[183] *IFJ*, 19 Sept. 1959.

[184] NAI, D/T S15465 A, note of meeting between de Valera and T. Dempsey, 5 Mar. 1953.

[185] NAI, D/T S15465 A, D/A note, 5 Aug. 1953.

problem with the agricultural advisers they indicated that while progress was being made the majority of the farmers were satisfied to plod along much as their fathers did before them.

Farmers also preferred to use the more costly method of owing money to merchants rather than banks as, while they might not have the money to pay the bank, they would have the milk or grain to send to the co-operative or merchant. Further,

> several farmers took great pride in telling me that they did not owe the bank, but rather 'the bank owes me.' Yet on these same farms there was evidence of a very real need for capital investment, particularly in connection with the use of fertilisers and building improvements ... It was evident in the majority of interviews that there was some social stigma about being in debt.

More critical still, were the number of farmers who wondered whether raised output through use of credit was actually desirable as many farmers worried "what the increased production would do to prices." For Gilmore, a two-pronged solution was required: "Just a plan for the provision of additional credit is not the answer – it would be putting the cart before the horse. The first requirement is to disseminate credit information to farmers ... An attempt to expand credit facilities to farmers without first creating the desire for that credit is doomed to failure." Gilmore stressed the need to use all educational and advice facilities, as well as farm publications, to stimulate farmer receptivity to the use of credit. He also called for the use of legislation to revitalise the ACC. Gilmore argued that the money then loaned by the ACC was "only a fraction of the sound productive intermediate and long-term credit that could be used to advantage by farmers." To this end, he believed that the earning capacity of the farm should be used to determine lending standards, that farmers should be given far greater representation on the board of directors, and that, through the purchase of stock, farmers should emerge as owners of the corporation.[186] In response to this report and to continued criticism the government introduced, in 1961, the Agricultural Credit Act, which increased share capital in the ACC from £300,000 to £2m and the borrowing limit from £8m to £10m, while simultaneously loosening the criteria for credit.[187] The impact was immediate and loans by the ACC to farmers increased from £800,000 to £4m by 1965. Ireland retained one of the lowest levels of indebtedness to total assets in Europe, but a more modern approach to credit was finally underway.

Even beyond poor access to, and use of, credit, the ability to mechanise farm operations was restricted by the need to protect Irish industry. In August 1956 the inter-party government considered a request from the Department of Industry and Commerce to increase tariffs as the only feasible way to allow Irish

---

[186] *Survey of agricultural credit in Ireland* (1959), pp 11–13, 8, 14.
[187] NAI, D/T 97/6/330, D/F memo to govt., 4 Mar. 1965.

manufacturers demonstrate their ability to meet the requirements of the home market and to protect imperilled companies, particularly in Co. Wexford, where serious unemployment was then threatened through prospective closures. The government agreed to the introduction of import duties of 35.5 per cent (25.5 per cent for British manufactures) on imported farm machinery. This was compounded by similar tariffs on fertilisers and chemicals, including weedkillers.[188] The NFA agreed reluctantly to the increase on the promise of the formulation of a joint committee of manufacturers and farmers to supervise the effects of the duties, and to investigate the usefulness and durability of home versus imported machinery.[189] When Fianna Fáil returned to office in 1957, it not only retained the tariffs, but expanded the range of dutiable implements.[190] Meanwhile, the investigative committee collapsed with the NFA claiming that the Department of Agriculture refused to co-operate in machinery tests.[191] The NFA claimed that the duties placed a financial burden on the farming community, limited the choice available to farmers and placed new inventions beyond the reach of Irish farmers.[192] The *Irish Farmers' Journal* argued that it was sufficient "to say that these Irish firms have been established for over 100 years and if after that period they are unable to compete on an open market, then let is be quite honest and straight forward and forget the whole question of that industry."[193] Regardless of complaints from the farming community, industrial concerns held sway and the duties were not removed. As late as 1967, the government ignored the opposition of the Department of Agriculture and agreed to a Department of Industry and Commerce proposal that if Irish manufacturers agreed to build a new plant for the production of muckspreaders, the existing duty of 22.5 per cent (full), 12 per cent (UK) and 10.5 per cent (Northern Ireland) would be retained.[194]

Equally, for all the symbolism of the shining of a new light onto the countryside associated with the rural electrification schemes, farmers were not to the fore in the project. Electricity was often seen as a costly, though admittedly superior, alternative to kerosene, paraffin or candle. A 1953 survey by the Electricity Supply Board (ESB) recorded that, even amongst those farmers who took electricity, usage in the farmyard was low. For this reason, only 25 per cent had put lights in the yard or outhouses, 9 per cent used electric motors for root-pulping, 9 per cent used infrared lights for pig and chicken brooding, and 6 per cent had electrified milking.[195] The lack of education and advice was so critical that "mechanisation has been inadequately planned on some farms and some are undoubtedly over-mechanised." Regardless, the pace of mechanisation greatly accelerated through the 1950s and 1960s. The number of tractors increased from 13,569 in 1950 to 43,697 in 1960, and to 84,349 in 1970. Nonetheless, even in 1960

---

[188] *IFJ*, 25 Aug. 1956.

[189] *Ibid*, 22 Feb. 1958.

[190] *Ibid.*, 8 Jun. 1957.

[191] *Ibid*, 22 Feb. 1958. See also UCDA , Richard Mulcahy papers, P7/C/137, NFA memo, 17 Feb. 1958.

[192] *IFJ*, 22 Feb. 1958.

[193] *Ibid.*

[194] NAI, D/T 98/6/340, cabinet minutes, 17 Oct. 1967.

horses were still in use as beasts of burden on just over half of all Irish holdings.[196] The use of plant machinery and milking machines also showed spectacular increases.

Yet, there remained the persistent suspicion that the entire process was unnecessarily expensive, ill-conceived and was fundamentally undermined by flaws in other departments of the agricultural economy. Through it all, farmers remained sceptical of the rewards they might reap and the lack of trust in such advice as they did receive from agricultural instructors did not improve matters. The *Irish Farmers' Journal* warned that small farmers could not "afford to be the guinea pigs of mechanisation."[197] In this respect, farm leaders condemned the "wasteful over-investment in tractors in Ireland."[198] Significantly, mechanisation was often viewed as a means to replace existing labour in the protection of existing levels of output and not as a means to increase productivity. And, always, the question remained – where would increased production find a remunerative market?

V

Selling and marketing agricultural produce

Faltering attempts to sell in foreign markets such increased production as did emerge further hindered the successful realisation of the ambitions outlined in the *Programme for economic expansion*. It was one thing to state that the aim of policy was to sell in foreign markets at a competitive price the accrued surplus of expanded output. It was quite another matter, though, to actually secure a place in those markets. The agricultural community did not consider the development of new markets as falling within the realm of probability. Even had they been convinced of the effectiveness of new methods of production, farmers retained the belief that producing more would most likely reduce profit as an over-supplied market prompted a fall in price.[199] In tandem with the publication of the *Programme for economic expansion* came the acknowledgement that the Irish approach to marketing its produce on the international market was entirely inadequate. It was inconceivable that Irish agriculture could significantly expand along desired lines without a dramatic overhaul of approach to selling in other

---

[195] Shiel, *Quiet revolution*, pp 152, 299.

[196] Gillmor, *Agriculture*, pp 75, 72, 130.

[197] *IFJ*, 14 Sept. 1957.

[198] Smith and Healy, *Farm organisations*, p. 116.

markets. There may have been a massive market for store cattle in Britain – a trade which demanded no genuine initiatives – but, in the pursuit of a more diverse sale of product, the existing shambolic processes could conceivably bankrupt both farmers and the state.

Expanding agricultural exports was the most severe of tests for any state. Free trade in agricultural products had not existed since the 1920s and was fundamentally incompatible with domestic price support and tariff policies across the globe. Comparative advantage had lost its sheen as protectionism seized the day. With production expanding at a faster rate than consumption, most countries had higher levels of self-sufficiency or increased export surpluses.[200] The freeing of international trade in industry was not replicated in agriculture as many countries feared excessive fluctuation or outright depression in market prices. Further, as developed countries moved towards greater industrialisation, domestic agricultural policies proved increasingly inimical to free trade. The wealth of industry grew allowing support for farmers which remained politically imperative due to the enduring strength of agricultural pressure groups. This support was not conducive to free trade. As one historian wrote: "In every western European country agriculture became the equivalent of a large nationalized industry, managed by interventionist policies which sought to impose macroeconomic objectives in return for exemption from the forces of open economic competition."[201] For Ireland the implications were immense and, as James Meenan, remarked, that, in the light of the *Programme for Economic Expansion*, the proponents of outward-looking, expansionist agriculture "rejoiced to see that their values had been adopted. In the years after 1958 they were to learn that conditions abroad had changed ... and that their policies, however admirable intellectually, were no longer relevant to contemporary conditions."[202]

Openings did remain, but attempts to sell Irish agricultural produce on the European continent and in America were attended by a sense of fatalism which pervaded marketing policy. Effectively, the Department of Agriculture perceived that Irish produce was uncompetitive in foreign markets and, consequently, attempts to develop a presence in such markets were largely perfunctory. Even in the 1930s when the 'economic war' left Irish access to the British market in such peril, the Department of Agriculture viewed the barriers to the continental market

---

[199] Columnist, Tom Duffy, wrote in the *Irish Farmers' Journal* on 21 Feb. 1953 that "it is not at all a self-evident truth today that increased production will bring the reward of increased profits to the farmers." See also *IFJ*, 28 May 1960, where 'Southern Clodhopper' wrote in relation to the fall in price of lambs consequent to increased production: "Increased production is a popular policy and I am all for it provided that a market can be found to give a reasonable profit, but if the market cannot be found, I believe it would be economic suicide for the farmer." Evidence of this came in many ways. On 21 Nov. 1959, the *Irish Farmers' Journal* proudly announced the availability for export of hundreds of tons of Irish onions which were of "superb quality and expert harvesting." The same paper reported barely two months later on 6 Feb. 1960 that over 1,000 tons of onions had in fact been exported but that it had proved an uneconomic venture and the Kerry County Committee of Agriculture were now calling for a guaranteed price.

[200] J.C. Nagle, *Agricultural trade policies* (1976), p. 11.

[201] Alan S. Milward, *The European rescue of the nation-state* (1992), p. 229.

[202] Meenan, 'Agricultural policies', p. 51.

of quantitative restrictions, and high import duties and taxes as insurmountable. Further, according to a report of the Markets Advisory Committee in 1933, the Department not only had "no knowledge or experience whatever of dealing with the export of our produce to Continental countries," but did not seem overly concerned with acquiring it as "the absence of a Department of Agriculture inspector has meant that the work of investigating possibilities for agricultural products and the sending of trial consignments has had to be divided amongst the Higher Executive Officer and the Principal Officer in addition to their other duties." Originally, an inspector had been provided to the committee but he had almost immediately been recalled to the department and inadequate staffing ensured that only the most cursory of investigations could be made of even the main lines of production. The sense remained that there was something unnatural about selling outside of Britain.

Inevitably, farmers proved thoroughly incapable of developing their own marketing systems and, as the Markets Advisory Committee noted, "traders in agricultural produce in the Saorstát were not prepared to explore for themselves the prospects of foreign markets."[203] Even in the 1950s, the approach taken by Irish firms was less than professional. An exhibition of Irish goods in America arranged by J.F. O'Dowd of American Overseas Airlines, which bore the entire cost of the promotion, led the organiser to remark: "It was practically impossible to interest Irish manufacturers in the American market. They appeared to be lackadaisical, and for one reason or another, declined to avail of the opportunities available for exports to the dollar area." More precisely,

> a firm order for Mitchelstown Creamery Company's cheese was secured on the basis of samples brought out privately by Mr. O'Dowd. He passed the order to the creamery which replied asking for detailed particulars of the conditions on which their cheese would be admitted to the American market. Mr. O'Dowd obtained the requisite information from the American Consulate in Dublin and passed it to the Creamery Company which merely replied regretting their inability to do business as they could not conform to the standards specified.[204]

Bereft of any meaningful producer initiative, sales of agricultural produce were won through trade agreements, the activities of individual representatives abroad and the use of fairs and exhibitions to demonstrate the quality of Irish goods. In the post-World War II years, the potential for developing an export market to the continent for the beef industry was restricted by the percentage limitations written into the 1948 agreement with Britain. The effects were psychological as much as practical and exemplify the mindset which considered large-scale sale of agricultural produce to the continent of Europe as unsustainable on even a medium-term basis. That is not to say that there were no

---

[203] NAI, D/T S6511 A, notes of conference between the D/EA, D/A, D/IC and the Markets Advisory Committee, 4 Sept. 1933.
[204] J.F. O'Dowd, quoted in, NAI, D/T 2676 B/1, D/IC memo to govt., 6 Mar. 1950.

attempts to sell in other than the British market, rather they were rarely of much note. The trade with Europe was passed off as a temporary expedient, a way of disposing of produce – often at a loss – that simply could not be sold on the home or British markets.[205] Trade agreements and the activities of individual representatives were fundamentally undermined by the sheer inadequacy of staffing levels. In 1949, James Dillon stressed:

> the urgency of an appointment of a competent trade attaché to cover western Germany and Scandinavia cannot be too strongly emphasised from the point of view of our agricultural industry. I am certain that the want of such an attaché in West Germany has resulted in the loss of a substantial volume of trade in agricultural products during the last six months, the remuneration for which would have been the equivalent of hard currency over the whole period. In regard to Denmark it would be of incalculable value to us to have reliable trade information so as to prepare us for the various developments which transpire from time to time in Anglo-Danish trade, because in almost every branch of agricultural production Denmark is our most formidable rival in the British market, and, as you are aware, under the 1948 Trade Agreement in more cases than one the terms of her Agreement with Great Britain constituted the yardstick by which our price schedules are arranged.

Noting that Dutch and Belgian purchasing agents were making "wildly excessive" profits in selling onwards Irish livestock arriving at their ports, Dillon pointed out that, in contrast, "our efforts at negotiating satisfactory purchase arrangements for fertilisers are perennially embarrassed by the fact that there is nobody in either of these countries competent to give us reliable information as to what domestic price levels for these products are, or what is the machinery of distribution." In all, Dillon believed that without such trade representatives "we shall find ourselves at a reasonably early date in a situation of grave embarrassment on the occupation of these markets by trade rivals who are vigilant to seize any and every opportunity that presents itself of forestalling us where a profit can be earned on agricultural exports."[206]

Little movement was made to develop a coherent team of trade representatives worthy of the name.[207] In 1956, Dillon remarked that a serious weakness "was our lack of up-to-date and accurate information in regard to market prospects abroad. The staff of our Embassies were doing all they could, but they

---

[205] NAI, D/T S12846 E/95, D/A memo to govt., 24 Apr. 1964 and cabinet minutes, 28 Apr. 1964. The government agreed to the imposition of an order restricting the sale of young pigs to France. The trade had developed due to "a shortage of pigmeat on the continent which has been evident for some months past but which informed sources indicate is likely to be of a short-term nature." Amidst fears that sales to France would prevent fulfillment of Ireland's quota of sales to Britain, the order was agreed to, a move which was approved by the *Irish Independent*, on 30 Apr. 1964, as "a sensible one … However immediately profitable it might have been this trade was not likely to pave the way towards a permanent build-up of pig exports to the French market."

[206] UCDA, Patrick McGilligan papers, P35b/51(7), Dillon to Patrick McGilligan, 7 Oct. 1949.

were not really qualified to deal with such highly-specialised matters as the livestock trade."[208] In fact, through the 1950s the Irish government opted to continue on the premise that, in terms of trade, at least, nothing had altered regardless of the declaration of a republic. Although there was no formal arrangement between the governments, the system had developed where Irish interests seeking to export abroad would use British representatives at overseas posts when seeking information on trade matters. Since leaving the Commonwealth, the Irish had avoided any formal arrangement for assistance in consular and diplomatic matters but had continued to refer Irish firms seeking information on foreign matters to the British embassy in Dublin. In respect of these requests for assistance, Brian Walsh-Atkins, the British ambassador, wrote from the Dublin embassy that his staff had

> been struck by the almost total lack of knowledge of export practice, procedure, and requirements of very nearly all manufacturers in the Republic ... They are simply hanging on, getting all the help they want when they want it, without having to commit themselves to the shameful position of formally accepting our assistance in general.[209]

Nonetheless, the Dublin Embassy did not favour a complete cessation of assistance, even if a Commonwealth Relations Office (CRO) official asked if it was not "quite wrong to give the Irish the impression that if they maintain their masterly inactivity long enough we will take on our own shoulders the responsibility which is clearly theirs."[210] Although it was eventually decided to continue to offer advice to Irish exporters in the manner of previous years, the nature of the assistance was clearly evident in a draft Board of Trade missive which considered:

> Although since 1949 the Irish Republic is no longer in the Commonwealth it is not to be regarded as a foreign country. Exporters in the Irish Republic may, therefore, be given certain forms of assistance in suitable circumstances. If overseas officers judge that the exports of the firms in the Irish Republic which approach them for assistance are unlikely to dislodge United Kingdom or Commonwealth exports in the local market they should generally provide lists of importers and they may, at their discretion, supply names of possible agents whom the firm may approach and market reports if suitable reports already exist.[211]

With only a skeleton trade staff of its own and with the British providing understandably tempered assistance, the Irish government sought to use trade

---

[207] To put that failure in context, the *Irish Farmers' Journal* reported in 1960 that the Danes were in the process of increasing the agricultural representatives in their diplomatic service through the appointment of 23 new staff.

[208] NAI, Department of Foreign Affairs (D/FA), 348/55, D/A to D/EA, 3 Oct. 1956.

[209] PRO, DO 35/5689, Walsh-Atkins to CRO, 11 Mar. 1955.

[210] PRO, DO 35/5689, CRO to Dublin Embassy, 31 Mar. 1955.

fairs and exhibitions as a key element of its marketing strategy. It was not the most efficacious of approaches. Through the 1950s, while other countries were developing their brand names and refining presentation and distribution, Ireland was still attempting to base its marketing strategy on infrequent appearances at large commercial fairs. Ireland only participated in four international fairs outside of Britain in the 25 years before 1955. Agricultural interests did not see the worth in participating. Despite government promotion and the belief that sales of bacon and ham could be secured, no Irish agricultural interests took part in the International Food Exhibition in Chicago in 1950.[212] Similarly, although Irish industry filled 21 stands at the Frankfurt Spring Fair in 1953, potential exporters of agricultural produce were exceptionally slow to show any interest and their approach was exemplified by the Meat Exporters Association who "decided not to exhibit at the Spring Fair, as they were of opinion that the considerable expense involved would not be justified and that if their prices suited the German market the trade would flow irrespective of whether they participated in the Fair or not."[213]

The Irish, nonetheless, took a permanent pavilion at the Frankfurt Fair, held twice a year, and it reaped some dividends. In 1955, German interests bought 280 tons of meat and a market for tinned beef emerged as a genuine possibility while there was comment on the "excellent display of agricultural products by the Department of Agriculture."[214] The department committed itself to repeat its exhibit given Department of Finance consent. Within a year, though, the inability to sustain the initiative led a representative of the legation in Bonn to describe the Irish agricultural exposition, which consisted of a fridge filled with cuts of beef, at the Fair as "deplorable … Only people who expected miracles to happen could have hoped for business to come from displays such as these. The manifest indifference to securing business made its impact on the visitor from the moment of entering the pavilion and ensured that there were no miracles." Dr. T.J. Kiernan called for a radical examination of policy regarding trade fairs which, he now believed, were "futile and damaging to the national interest."[215] This call was backed by a Department of External Affairs official who also attended the fair and remarked: "One of the four flag-poles carrying provincial flags had disappeared, having become rotten at the butt. There was no time to get it replaced before the Fair … The palmy days when Fair quotas were allocated to exhibitors and it was not necessary to do a selling job are over."[216]

The necessity to do a 'selling-job' was becoming more acute but, in the light of the deterioration of the Irish experience, it was determined to exhibit at Frankfurt only once a year – for the other staging of the bi-annual show, the

---

[211] PRO, DO 35/5689, Board of Trade draft note, Jan. 1955.

[212] NAI, D/T S2676 B/1, minutes of the Foreign Trade Committee, 18 May 1951.

[213] NAI, D/T S2676 B/2, minutes of the Foreign Trade Committee, 9 Jan. 1953.

[214] NAI, D/T S2676 B/2, F.J. Hegarty report of the Frankfurt Autumn Fair, 1955 and minutes of Foreign Trade Committee, 25 Mar. 1955.

[215] NAI, D/T S2676 C, Dr T.J. Kiernan memo to D/EA, 15 Sept. 1956.

[216] NAI, D/T S2676 C, M.J. Quinn memo to D/EA, 9 Oct. 1956.

pavilion should be sublet, though not to any communist country. In the event, it was decided for spring 1957 to lease the Irish stand to Moroccan and Libyan interests, before reclaiming its use the following autumn.[217] The quality of the stands improved somewhat, but it still lagged behind those of Ireland's competitors. An official reported the results as "rather disappointing," and noted that the unattractive design and poor labelling of the tins displayed at the Irish Meat Packers stand "contrasted very badly with, e.g., the food tins in the Polish pavilion, which gave every indication of advanced industrial design."[218] Further, the paucity of deployed resources and the lack of conviction that European markets could be won deterred the Irish from exhibiting at other than the Frankfurt Fair. A report from the legation in Bonn that the Anuga trade fair, held in Germany every two years, had become the most important food fair on the continent did not make great impact on Department of Agriculture representatives. Responding to the suggestion that it should investigate the 1955 fair with a view towards exhibiting in 1957, the department's officials argued there were very many difficulties in exhibiting at the fair and that the department was already heavily committed to fairs in Britain. Under pressure from other departments, Agriculture eventually conceded that "it was possible that one of the Department's officers might be in the vicinity of Anuga, and he could probably be asked to report."[219] That officer duly attended the 1955 fair and reported it as a missed opportunity for Irish firms who "would have benefited greatly from the packaging and packing sections alone."[220] Nonetheless, Ireland rejected the opportunity to attend in 1957.

Nor was Ireland prospering in the fairs it attended in Britain despite the overwhelming importance of that market for its goods. The problems which beset Irish agricultural produce for decades continued to undermine its position against more progressive competitors. An Irish official reported that for all the competent exhibits at the 1955 Grocers' Exhibition in Manchester and the Olympia Food Fair in London, others "were very poorly arranged and the lack of uniformity and order in the design and dressing of the stands spoiled the general effect."[221] The decline in turkey sales offered a case in point. Despite the production of high quality birds, their transport in over-packed wooden crates drew much comment on "the poor condition in which our birds arrived at Smithfield market. Broken bones and bruised turkeys were common sights amongst the Irish lots at the market."[222]

Even within the all-powerful cattle industry, marketing systems were far from efficient. William Fay, Department of External Affairs official, wrote in 1950 from the Irish legation in Stockholm that continental Europe preferred lean to fat meat

---

[217] NAI, D/T S2676 C, minutes of Foreign Trade Committee, 12 Dec. 1958.

[218] NAI, D/T S2676 C, M.J. Quinn memo to govt., Autumn 1957.

[219] NAI, D/T S2676 B/2, minutes of Foreign Trade Committee meeting, 23 Sept. 1955.

[220] NAI, D/T S2676 B/2, D/A report on Anuga Food Fair, 2 Nov. 1955. The fair involved 1,679 exhibitors from 38 different countries across four continents

[221] NAI, D/T S2676 B/2, minutes of Foreign Trade Committee, 21 Jan. 1955.

[222] *IFJ*, 28 Dec. 1957.

and that it

> was completely hopeless to expect to develop an export trade of any
> size with any country unless we study the demands of that country. If,
> therefore, we are anxious to develop a cattle trade with countries other
> than Britain, we must be prepared ... to provide them with what they
> want. If we do not, our export trade will simply go by default ... If our
> attitude is that under no circumstances must a change be made in our
> age-old cattle trade and that continental countries are lucky to have
> the opportunity of bidding for our very high quality cattle, then we
> must expect to find they may turn to other sources of supply.[223]

Regardless of Europe, farmers professed their bewilderment at the
intermittent failure on the British market of their cattle which they believed were
the best in the world and that only anti-Irish prejudice prevented them from
selling better.[224] Cattle crossed the Irish Sea in huge numbers, yet the profit
earned was not commensurate with the potential of the trade. The delivery to the
market of horned cattle suffering from warbles, liver fluke, bruises, TB and weight
loss, diminished profit, as did the trauma of transport across the sea in ships ill-
equipped for the task. A commission interested in animal welfare investigated the
transport of cattle across the Irish sea to Scotland and reported that "after a bad
crossing nearly every animal is damaged ... It appears that cattle are neither fed
nor watered during journeys of 24 hours' duration."[225] As well as being
detrimental to the welfare of the animals, the transport system also adversely
affected profit margins. Vested interests, restrictive practices and a reliance on
traditional modes of operation rendered the transport of Irish goods
exceptionally costly. Few licences were issued to allow private road hauliers
compete with the semi-state Coras Iompair Éireann (CIE) whose monopoly on rail
transport was effectively extended to the roads.[226] Although farming interests had
long complained about the problem and the Minister for Agriculture in 1952 had
accepted the increasing burden of transport charges as "a problem which would
repay detailed study," the perceived need to defend the position of CIE and other
organisations allowed only minor alterations to the transport network.[227]

Against this stasis, change was underway through the 1950s as Irish farmers
sought to replace the traditional fair with cattle marts. Some towns lamented the
passing of the old world, but most embraced the new system with alacrity. Opening
one such cattle mart in Fermoy, Co. Cork, in 1957, the Minister for Agriculture,

---

[223] NAI, D/FA 348/55, Fay to D/EA, 31 May 1950.

[224] *IFJ*, 9 Jan. 1960.

[225] *IFJ*, 25 Feb. 1950. Even, in 1964, the *Manchester Guardian* reported, in breathless tones, on the Irish
export of cattle: "The terrified animals, driven wildly – and always too fast – by untrained, shouting, and
naturally frightened drovers, charged dangerously about the narrow, crowded quay. Some got impaled (as
on previous occasions) on piles of iron girders stacked on the quay, or ran into a piece of machinery, only
extricating themselves with difficulty; two fell and were trampled over by others."

[226] See, for example, Smith and Healy, *Farm organisations*, p. 111.

[227] NAI, D/T S13930 B, D/A memo to govt., 11 Nov. 1952.

Seán Moylan, said: "Fairs today are an anachronism. The marketing conditions of a former age are entirely unsuitable for the trade of today."[228] Sensing a threat to their position, cattle dealers opposed the change and, in support of its boycott of marts, the Irish Livestock Exporters' and Traders' Association claimed "the fair and not the mart suits the particular pattern of the cattle trade, with most profit to farmers and the Irish people as a whole."[229] In some areas, the fair was not easily abandoned, as a Department of Agriculture official wrote:

> Old customs die hard and despite the fact that many of the marts are co-operative ventures there are still big numbers of farmers who prefer the old-fashioned fair day method of bargaining and in a community such as ours where compulsion in any form is not kindly received, the abolition of the old concept of bargaining cannot be brought about overnight by government decree.[230]

Nonetheless, the change from fair to mart continued apace. By 1960 there were thirty marts as farmers were progressively attracted to public auction above private treaty. Development was inconsistent, however, and every town wanted a mart to replace its fair, even if there was not sufficient livestock in the area to warrant establishment. Warnings were issued on the waste of capital as the *Irish Farmers' Journal* remarked that "positive action by farmers, co-operative marts, private marts and the Department of Agriculture is needed before we have too many vested interests in confusion."[231] The foundation of Co-operative Livestock Marts in 1959 did nothing to ease the problem and by the end of the 1960s there were 140 marts in the country with rationalisation a must.[232] Even genuine widespread support for a modernised marketing system demanded a considered framework of development if it was not to prove as inefficient as the system it displaced.

The quality of the goods, as well as the marketing system, endured continuous criticism. There was official grading for quality of milk and pigs, while in other commodities grading operated for public health or pricing purposes, but typical of the overall approach was the fruit and vegetable trade. A 1943 report contended "it would be rash to introduce a compulsory system of grading, per saltum, but we think that an attempt should be made to bring about a gradual standardisation of purpose.[233] Some growers operated their own rudimentary system but efforts to adopt a binding code failed.[234] In 1952 the *Irish Farmers' Journal* had warned that "this grading business will have to come with all crops and agricultural produce generally if we are to hold our own in time to come. At

---

228 *IFJ*, 22 Jun. 1957.
229 *IFJ*, 21 Feb. 1959 and 31 Jan. 1959. The apparent altruism of the cattle exporters possibly lay in their displeasure at having to pay commission to the cattle marts.
230 NAI, D/T S2392 D/94, M.J. Barry to J.W. Salter-Chalker, National Farmers' Union, 29 Jul. 1959.
231 *IFJ*, 8 Nov. 1958.
232 Gillmor, *Agriculture*, p. 125.
233 *Report of the tribunal of inquiry on fruit and vegetables* (1943).

present with a world shortage of food, it is easy to sell any kind of farm produce no matter state it is in. This will not last for ever."[235] For Irish farmers, though, higher grading standards were something to sidestep or manipulate in the search for a higher price rather than any genuine aspiration towards quality production: "There are too many cases of farmers who have been promised by factories or buyers that improved grading would be obtained by changing from one factory to another, and these promises have been honoured." Equally, grading standards had a tendency to shift according to the relative levels of supply and demand, while more blatant corruption was not unknown.[236]

The poor standard of Irish produce was exemplified by the prices paid for bacon. On the British market, first grade Irish bacon earned 32s per cwt. below Danish bacon, 20s per cwt. below Dutch and British bacon, 13s per cwt. below Northern Ireland's bacon, and earned less than Hungarian and Polish bacon imports. Most gallingly, second grade Dutch and Danish bacon earned more than first grade Irish bacon.[237] More than thirty factories, each with its special secret cure competed to sell Irish bacon ensuring a lack of uniformity whereby the consumer could never be certain what the next Irish purchase could taste like.[238] Distribution across Britain was similarly detrimental to the development of a cohesive marketing strategy. Ireland continued to ship large quantities of commodities on bulk cargo to a diversity of agents. Devoid of uniformity of product, regularity of supply and support advertising, the construction of a network of cohesive, committed agents proved too great a task. Too many agents were badly promoting poor quality Irish bacon in lieu of the required "more modern and direct method of selling."[239] Envious eyes were cast in the direction of Denmark whose system was acknowledged to be thirty years ahead of the Irish one: "The difference in selling techniques is the difference between haphazard bulk consignments of unbranded products and determined shop-to-shop personal salesmanship of branded and well-advertised goods, delivered on time and in a presentable manner."[240] Ongoing failure to increase sales of produce on foreign markets brought what the *Irish Farmers' Journal* termed "the revolutionary admission of the Minister for Agriculture that, after thirty-years of mis-

---

[233] *Report of the tribunal of inquiry on fruit and vegetables* (1943).

234 Rosemary Fennell, 'The domestic market for Irish agricultural produce,' in I.F. Bailie and S.J. Sheehy (eds.), *Irish agriculture*, pp 98–117, esp. p. 113.

[235] *IFJ*, 9 Feb. 1952.

[236] *Ibid.*, 25 May 1957.

[237] *Ibid.*, 30 Aug. 1958.

[238] Smith and Healy, *Farm organisations*, p. 80.

[239] *IFJ*, 30 Aug. 1958. As Smith and Healy wrote: "Irish bacon was of secondary interest to marketing agents. A Danish agent in Britain handled 200 tons a week; Irish agents averaged 15 tons. The Danes had 24 agents to handle 5,000 tons a week, the Irish had at least 38 agents to handle 500 tons." See Smith and Healy, *Farm Organisations*, p. 80.

[240] *IFJ*, 18 Oct. 1958. Evidence fell readily to hand. Exports to America by Castlebar Bacon Co. Ltd. of 152 cans (each weighing 13.5 cwt.) of bacon were refused entry by the American authorities on the grounds they were over-packed. The Irish authorities then attempted to tax the products on re-entry and the company had to apply to the Department of Finance for special exemption from duty. See NAI, F 22/5/57, D/A to D/F, 11 Feb. 1957. The *Report of the survey team on the dairy produce industry* (1962) documented almost identical problems in the dairy export business. Products needed to be improved, standardised, properly distributed and expertly marketed.

government, our marketing systems are antediluvian."[241] It was in the context of the acknowledged failure of existing services that the government launched an initiative to revitalise the country's agricultural marketing system. In the 1957 budget, £250,000 was provided for "not only a thorough investigation of possible openings in foreign markets, but a careful study of such changes as may be necessary to suit consumer requirements."[242] Using this money, and implementing a suggestion made by the Department of Agriculture, the government set up an advisory committee to examine the existing state of marketing arrangements. The committee was chaired by the president of the NFA, Juan Greene, and was authorised to set up small expert groups to furnish reports for various commodities.[243] The project was lent greater urgency by the publication of the *Programme for economic expansion* and, by 1959, had produced its commodity reports and, more importantly, the *Report on general aspects of the Irish export trade in agricultural produce.*[244] This general report left nobody in any doubt of the problems which needed addressing within the Irish marketing system and the manner in which these could be addressed. The report acknowledged the difficulty of selling into the low-cost subsidised or restricted markets of the continent which created "a particularly difficult situation for countries, such as Ireland, which are mainly agricultural and rely on agricultural exports to pay for their imports of industrial products."[245] The report accepted that access to agricultural markets across Europe would be afflicted by the artificial conditions obtaining in international trade and that the "the general development of this country's agricultural export trade requires the adoption of a foreign policy aimed at securing equitable trading arrangements with industrial countries to meet the country's great dependence on exports of agricultural produce." To this end, it was noted that the trade agreements which Ireland made did not involve appreciable commitments on behalf of other countries to purchase Irish products, and that "it must be made clear to the industrial countries on the continent that a country such as Ireland whose exports consist mainly of agricultural items cannot continue to import industrial goods unless it is able to earn foreign exchange by sales of agricultural produce."

---

[241] 'Farm Economist' in *IFJ*, 1 Sept. 1956. The *IFJ* reported on 11 May 1957 the comments of the Minister for Lands, Erskine Childers, that agricultural exports "have been allowed to go their own sweet way with consequences so awful that we do not yet know the full extent of what we have lost. Certainly, it is true that our cattle are valued down by between £5 and £10 per head because we have neglected the details, such as care of hides. Taken over the years this means the loss of a colossal sum to Ireland. Shocking things have occurred such as the export to the continent of old sheep carcasses under the name of 'Irish lamb.' All these things – and many more besides – have got to be put right."

[242] *Export marketing of Irish agricultural produce: statement of the government's policy on the recommendations of the advisory committee* (1959), p. 7.

[243] NAI, D/T S16283 A, D/A memo. to govt., 2 Aug. 1957 and cabinet minutes, 3 Sept. 1957. Originally, General Michael Costello, the head of the sugar company, had been asked to chair the committee but he declined the invitation.

[244] The other reports issued dealt, individually, with dairy produce, bacon, livestock and meat, turkeys, and shell eggs and liquid eggs.

[245] *Report on general aspects of the Irish export trade in agricultural produce* (1959), p. 2.

Nonetheless, the report accepted that Britain, as the only market likely to provide long-term unrestricted access, would remain of paramount importance, even if fiscal matters and the British dalliance with the European Free Trade Area (EFTA) ensured that Irish advantages were continuing to diminish. The report called for the establishment of "a form of association" with Britain which would facilitate the introduction of the price links which had proved beneficial for cattle and sheep to other products, especially pigs, eggs and dairy produce. Further, the report considered that association with Britain would also have to be balanced with involvement in "a larger economic unit in which the economies of the other participants would be complementary, the industrial economies of the other participants providing a market for the expanding exportable surplus of Ireland's agricultural economy." Crucially, it was "necessary to strengthen to the full the country's relative competitive position in all export markets by raising the efficiency of its agricultural production and of its transport and marketing arrangements." To this extent, it was crucial to establish the long-awaited ferry service to Britain, and end the restrictive practices in shipments to the continent and on travel within Ireland itself. The report accepted it had to be decided whether the relative merits of developing a separate brand name within Britain or remaining undistinguished from British produce given that Ireland benefited from British preferences in some lines. Either way, the existing marketing arrangements in Britain were roundly condemned. It was deemed unsatisfactory that Ireland's two agricultural officers in Britain only occasionally left London for the provinces and, even though it was only in Britain that specialised agricultural officers were based, two remained a distinctly inadequate number. Overall, government officials needed to modernise their approach as

> there is no significant amount of organised and scientific market research and that little or no regular use is made of the comprehensive facilities which market research organisations can provide. Even though market conditions and requirements may be altering fundamentally, most Irish exporting interests appear to trade in what has been the traditional manner for the products which they export.

This inattention to modernising processes displayed by Irish exporters was condemned as inept and their lack of initiative was a grave disability. The report noted that

> Irish exporters of agricultural produce are inclined to wait for purchasers to come to Ireland instead of themselves going abroad to seek purchasers. The seller's market for many agricultural products that existed for some time after the war has long since vanished and successful exporting now depends on an aggressive selling approach involving personal contact with potential purchasers.

Nonetheless, all attempts to improve the presentation and distribution of Irish produce, would be founded on the necessity to increase production to allow for continuity of supply. Previously, there had been "little or no continuity of supplies of most Irish agricultural products ... If the development of a thriving export trade is to be taken seriously, continuity of supplies must be maintained and temporary inconveniences and difficulties in regard to supplies for the home market must be accepted." The core problem – and its resolution – were outlined in stark terms:

> Irish farmers tend to have a strong psychological complex about the dangers of increasing production as past experience has ingrained in their minds a fear that, if they increase production to any great extent, prices will decline unduly. It is necessary that the old-established fear should be overcome completely, e.g. by the adoption of a definite long-term policy for agriculture, including where possible the provision of minimum guaranteed prices related to the costs of efficient producers. [246]

The *Irish Farmers' Journal* welcomed the report as "a highly interesting and suggestive document," called for "minimum delay in implementing its proposals," and announced approvingly that the new Danish Agricultural Marketing Board had just received a £5m government bank guarantee.[247] In the light of the publication of the report, the cabinet asked the Minster for Agriculture to submit his views and to elaborate recommendations of proposed action.[248] Amongst the proposals which emerged from the Minister's report – subsequently published as a white paper – were the establishment of 'An bord bainne' to regulate the sale of dairy products and the reconstitution of the 'Pigs and bacon commission'.[249] The difficulty of reforming the marketing of agricultural produce was cast in stark perspective by the reconstitution of the 'Pigs and bacon commission'.[250] The critical importance of revamping the bacon industry was highlighted by the progressive loss of the British market to Danish competitors. Continuity of supply had been disrupted by the failure of farmers to resist "any tendency to move in and out of pig production with each slight movement in prices."[251] The situation required radical action as the "entire machinery for the disposal of bacon in Britain demands drastic reorganisation. Something more than piecemeal repair work is needed and, certainly, it will not be sufficient to bring our sales organisation up to the Danish level thirty years too late."[252] Acting in the wake of his response to the report on export marketing, the Minister for Agriculture proposed recasting the 'Pigs and bacon commission' whose board would carry two representatives each from the farmers, the bacon curers and the Department of

---

246 *Ibid.*, pp 2–3, 6–7, 8–9, 10, 13, 14, 16.

247 *IFJ*, 27 Jun. 1959 and 7 Nov. 1959.

248 NAI, D/T S16283, cabinet minutes, 15 Sept. 1959.

249 *Export marketing of Irish agricultural produce: statement of the government's policy on the recommendations of the advisory committee* (1959).

250 For information on the establishment of An Bord Bainne through the Dairy Produce Marketing Bill, 1960, see NAI, D/T S17005 A.

251 *IFJ*, 4 Jan. 1958.

252 *Ibid.*, 18 Oct. 1958.

Agriculture.[253] The legislation conferred the power to regulate the export and pre-packing of bacon and other pigmeat. The bacon curers objected to the proposed bill but the Department of Agriculture insisted the bill met any fears which the curers might hold and "should not be radically altered by acceptance of the proposals of the bacon curers."[254] Nonetheless, the department agreed to meet the curers and, in the light of that meeting, Smith informed Lemass that he was now willing to alter his original proposal of equal representation as "there is a good deal to be said for the curers' viewpoint."[255] Accordingly, Smith then agreed that the curers could have one of the two departmental places on the proposed board of management.

Farmers reacted forcefully. The ICMSA claimed it was "inadvisable and completely against the interests of the industry ... [A] curer dominated board will not bring into being that healthy pig industry we believe possible and essential."[256] The NFA regretted that the government were refusing the need for the various sections of the industry to sit as equal partners and said it was "a retrograde step – which cannot but jeopardise the chance of building producer-confidence in the industry."[257] Explaining its *volte face*, which the government approved, the Department of Agriculture recalled that, in the light of its original scheme, the bacon curers, through the Irish Bacon Curers' Society Ltd., expressed apprehension towards the exercise of the proposed statutory powers over the bacon industry by a reorganised commission. Eventually, a deal was struck which ensured curer support for the commission, provided they were given the greater share of representatives. In the aftermath of the decision the department duly informed the NFA and the ICMSA of its decision and claimed that the new arrangements were justifiable as the powers of the commission are preponderantly exercisable in respect of bacon factories not pig producers and "the processing and marketing of bacon is primarily a matter for curers, not pig producers."[258] The ham-fisted approach to reconstitution provoked what the *Irish Times* termed "the most undesirable and bitter controversy," and by 1962 the paper was remarking that neither 'An bord bainne' nor the 'Pigs and bacon commission' had "shown real sign of life."[259] Seán Lemass admitted that the new marketing strategy was little better than a holding operation: "This problem is unlikely to be resolved until the European Economic Community's agricultural marketing arrangements are in complete operation on our and British accession to membership. In the meantime, we have set up marketing boards for butter and bacon."[260]

---

253 NAI, D/T S17006 A/61, D/A memo to govt., 27 Feb. 1961.

254 NAI, D/T S16283 B, D/A memo to D/T, 7 Jul. 1960.

255 NAI, D/T S16283 C, Smith to Lemass, 10 Aug. 1960.

256 NAI, D/T S17006 A/61, ICMSA to D/T, 8 Mar. 1961.

257 NAI, D/T S17006 A/61, NFA to D/T, 7 Mar. 1961.

258 NAI, D/T S17006 A/61, D/A memo to govt., 15 Mar. 1961.

259 *Irish Times*, 5 Jan. 1962. The paper's editorial contained a clichéd acknowledgement of the charm of the leisurely Irish approach to life and to material things but commented: "It is becoming increasingly clear that happy-go-luckiness will no longer serve in a competitive world, and, it is, therefore, disturbing to note that the streamlining of agricultural marketing is going so slowly."

Perhaps the continued failure to deal professionally with the demands of modern agricultural trading and the inability to respond through the development of an efficient marketing system to the threat posed by international competitors, was best illustrated by an exchange in the Dáil in March 1962. A Fine Gael deputy, Thaddeus Lynch, asked the Minister for Agriculture, Paddy Smith, how much of the £250,000 which had been voted in 1957 for agricultural marketing had been spent. When Smith replied that only a total of £23,154 had been spent in five years, Lynch and James Dillon combined to condemn the minister and to accuse him of hypocrisy. Lynch's attack was more than Donnchadh Ó Briain could take and, reverting to old lines of conflict as the best way to defend his minister, he proclaimed: "We know where the deputy was when we were trying to get the British out." That briefest of marketing debates ended with a discussion on whether the red complexion which had accompanied Ó Briain's outburst should be described as 'dearg' or 'rua'.[261] The priorities of political discourse had yet to reflect the rhetoric of economic development signalled in the *Programme for economic expansion*. It was not merely agriculturists who were struggling to adapt to the new demands of an evolving society.

VI

Eradicating tuberculosis

Although the output objectives cherished in the *Programme for economic expansion* were pursued with only limited success, the commitment in that document to the elimination of bovine tuberculosis was accorded a pointedly different status in the formulation of agricultural policy. Safeguarding the cattle trade was a cause which the agricultural community could unite behind, at least in some measure. Through the gloom of the 1950s and the uncertainties of the 1960s, the export of cattle to Britain remained the central element of the Irish economy. Although it remains undeniable that over-reliance on livestock played a central role in restricting progress in other sections of the agricultural economy, the country could not afford to do without the earnings from its cattle sales in the British market. Through the 1950s, the profit margins in the export of cattle, combined with the traditional emphasis on the trade, ensured that livestock exports accounted for the vast bulk of sales to Britain by Irish farmers. The trends desired by the British government in settling the 1948 trade agreement duly

---

260 NAI, D/T S16283 D/62, Lemass to M. O'Mahony, Main St., Buttevant, Co. Cork, 19 Mar. 1962.

261 *Dáil Debates*, Vol. 193, no. 7. col. 1044, 7 Mar. 1962. Eventually, the bulk of the balance of £226,846 was distributed between the Pigs and Bacon Commission, and An Bord Bainne.

emerged as by far the most favoured in practice. Not even the cattle trade was immune from risk or from change, however, as exports were threatened by British moves towards TB eradication. Those moves, begun in 1932, took 27 years to reach the stage of near-eradication but, by the 1950s it was obvious to all concerned in the livestock industry that unless some concerted effort was made to combat the disease in Ireland, trade with Britain would be jeopardised. James Dillon had announced in 1950 he believed cattle which were not tuberculosis-tested would be refused by Britain within 20 years.[262] The *Irish Farmers' Journal* was no less concerned: "When are we going to face attestation seriously in Ireland? If we do not do it soon we will be late and we will find ourselves at the bottom of the British market. Attested cattle are fetching considerably more in England today than ordinary stores. Why are we missing this market?"[263] The scarcity of initiatives to remove bovine tuberculosis is scarcely surprising given the enduring failure to commit resources to limit the disease in the country's citizens. The relationship between tuberculosis in humans and in cattle had long been seen as a pernicious one. A Royal Commission in England in 1911 stated that tuberculosis in cows was a hazard to human health and a 1945 Danish report agreed that the amount of tuberculosis in humans was directly linked to the degree of the disease in cattle herds with which they had been in contact as "a few moments' contact with infected animals is often sufficient to set up the disease in man and other animals."[264] The evidence in Ireland was equally assertive. A Clare priest wrote to Eamon de Valera in 1947 that eight hardy young men had died from tuberculosis in his parish of Kilmihil in the past three years, and that small farmers would "remain on the verge of famine," unless steps were taken to remove the disease in cattle.[265] Through the 1950s, the *Irish Farmers' Journal* frequently highlighted the links between the human and bovine forms of the disease and stressed its deleterious effect on society and economy.[266]

Equally, the relaxed attitude of the farming community to the eradication of animal diseases was compounded by the propensity to seek solution in cheap remedies promising immediate salvation. In 1954 the Department of Agriculture lamented that stockowners were buying useless medicines such as a bottle retailing at 3s marketed as a remedy for hoose in cattle which was found to contain commercial turpentine. Still worse were products sold at 2s per bottle as cures for abortion and sterility in cattle. There were no known cures in veterinary science for these conditions and the bottles were found to contain 100 per cent water.[267] This was evidence which finally provoked the government to move legislation implementing proposals signposted in the *Report of the commission of inquiry on post-emergency agricultural policy* that all importers of such products be licensed and that all bottles contain detailed listings of their ingredients.[268] The problem of reliance

---

[262] *IFJ*, 22 Jul. 1950.

[263] *Ibid.*, 15 Dec. 1951.

[264] Robert O'Connor, *A study of the bovine tuberculosis eradication scheme* (1986), pp 1–2.

[265] NAI, D/T S14065, Fr P. Gaynor, parish priest, Kilmihil, Co. Clare to de Valera, 30 Jun. 1947.

[266] *IFJ*, 6 Sept. 1958 and 26 Mar. 1960.

on non-scientific methods saw the *Irish Farmers' Journal* join with the veterinarians in "deploring the large sale of quack veterinary medicines which continues in this country. The sale of such quack substance is furthered by ignorance."[269] Attempts to replace this tradition of elixir idolatry with anything approaching organised, modernised veterinary services only began in earnest in the 1950s. In December 1951 the Department of Agriculture proclaimed "the eradication of bovine tuberculosis is overdue in the interests of public health and of the livestock industry. Human tuberculosis of bovine origin occurs here to a disturbing extent and is responsible for a significant number of deaths." Stressing the immediacy of the need for a scheme, though, the department highlighted economic rather than health concerns: "The disease is a great menace to the country's future cattle exports ... The time is rapidly approaching when the important Irish store cattle trade with Great Britain will depend on the animals being certified free from tuberculosis."[270] The department estimated that an eradication scheme would take 15 years and would cost £15 million. The cabinet approved the proposal that initial funding of £1 million be sought from Marshall Aid.[271] While awaiting sanction from Grant Counterpart funding, the Department of Agriculture proposed in March 1953 that when the funding arrived it be used to back a non-compulsory scheme in Clare and Limerick, two dairying counties with no inward movement of cattle and which supplied large numbers of stock to other counties.[272] The cabinet amended the plan somewhat and decreed it should apply to Clare alone, and the extra money be focused on that county to improve compensation given to reactors and to provide grants for the erection of proper byres.[273]

Continuing to press for the acceptance of a scheme, the Minister for Agriculture, Thomas Walsh, wrote of the serious animal diseases

> prevalent in Ireland which cause losses in meat and milk running into millions of pounds annually; the eradication of such diseases can only be effectively achieved by organised action on the part of the state ... Apart from the direct losses to the farmer who has tuberculous cattle, serious difficulty and loss will be encountered in the export trade in livestock in the fairly near future unless an official scheme is put into operation which will enable exported livestock to be certified free from bovine tuberculosis. If such a scheme is not put into effect, the

---

[267] NAI, D/T S13089 E, D/A memo to govt., 25 Sept. 1954. Non-veterinary traditions of healing and curing played an important role in the methods of Irish farmers. In many localities there were people renowned for their skill in treating animals and for the cures which they produced. See, for example, Irish Folklore Archives, ms. 1845, p. 167 and pp 172–4, ms. 1862, p. 229, and ms. 1837, pp 80–7.

[268] NAI, D/T S13089 E, cabinet minutes, 5 Oct. 1954.

[269] *IFJ*, 9 Apr. 1955.

[270] NAI, D/T S2392 B/1, D/A memo to govt., Dec. 1951.

[271] *Ibid.* and NAI, D/T S2392 B/1, cabinet minutes, 16 Dec. 1951.

[272] NAI, D/T S2392 B/1, D/A memo to govt., 6 Mar. 1952.

[273] NAI, D/T S2392 B/1, cabinet minutes, 29 Nov. 1952.

steadily increasing eradication areas in Britain may be closed to our store cattle.[274]

Walsh proposed that as an attendant to the tuberculosis scheme there would be action to lessen losses through the death of new-born calves, infertility, abortion, parasitic diseases, nutritional diseases and others which have caused losses of more than 200,000 head a year. The continued delay in receiving ECA money as well as the failed attempt to build a contribution towards an eradication scheme into a new trade arrangement with Britain (see chapter 3), brought the proposal that the government should pay for a scheme in Limerick from the national development fund.[275] The Department of Finance objected on the grounds that such a scheme "would definitely prejudice the possibility of the cost of the scheme for Clare and elsewhere being recouped in due course from the Grant Counterpart's moneys."[276] The Department of Agriculture disagreed as "any delay now in going ahead with an eradication scheme would have very serious repercussions on our agriculture and therefore on our whole economy."[277] Only in April 1954 was it recorded that the Taoiseach had spoken to the US ambassador who could not see how the Limerick scheme would in any way influence ECA discussions on the Clare one.[278] In a personal appeal to the Minister for Finance in that same month, Walsh wrote that it was "hard to defend inaction in the face of continuing national losses brought about by bovine tuberculosis and indeed by the other diseases …"[279]

The government finally sanctioned a scheme which was announced on 11 April 1954. The Irish Veterinary Medical Association opposed elements of the scheme, such as the choice of Limerick as the first county as the high number of reactors would discourage farmers and asked that Sligo or Mayo be included as they had a far smaller number. Equally, the veterinarians opposed the free treatment of contagious abortion, blackleg and mastitis as part of the scheme as "undue intrusion on private practice, having regard to the fact that they constitute a most important part of the normal professional work of veterinary surgeons, who, they asserted, are treating these diseases in a competent manner." In the face of this opposition the Minister for Agriculture, James Dillon, agreed reluctantly to remove that "important part" of the scheme which it was now proposed to run in Clare, Sligo and Bansha, Co. Tipperary. The scheme allowed that herds would be tested free of charge, though involvement would be voluntary, and the

---

[274] NAI, D/T S2392 B/1, D/A memo to govt., 6 Jan 1954.

[275] The notion of one country contributing to another's campaign to eradicate bovine disease was not without precedent. In March 1947, the US voted $9m as its share of the expenses in a campaign to suppress an outbreak of foot and mouth disease in Mexico. The countries set up a joint commission to study eradication of the disease, entered a fund-pooling agreement to accelerate the campaign and the US assisted in rehabilitating herds. See William Dusenberry, 'Foot and mouth disease in Mexico, 1946–51', in *AH,* vol. 29, no. 2 (1955), pp 82–90.

[276] NAI, D/T S2392 B/1, D/F memo to govt., 17 Dec. 1953.

[277] NAI, D/T S2392 B/1, D/A memo to govt., 31 Dec. 1953.

[278] NAI, D/T S2392 B/1, D/T memo to govt., 10 Apr. 1954.

[279] NAI, D/T S2392 B/1, M/A to M/F, 2 Apr. 1954.

department would buy cow reactors at an agreed price. In addition, a scheme was installed to offer incentives towards the pasteurisation of fresh milk.[280] Through all this period the Department of Agriculture was in constant contact with its British counterpart. On one such contact the British were told "the regulations are on the same lines as yours and are, at present, awaiting approval and the necessary legislation ... We were very pleased with our visit to you and are pretty familiar with the snags. Our farmers are of course an entirely different body to the average British farmer."[281] But, as the British were told, the department had received no further staff to help with its campaigns despite the departmental assertion that "really satisfactory progress cannot be made generally until the veterinary staff of the Department of Agriculture is strengthened."[282] Ultimately, the failure to strengthen the departmental staff of veterinarians was a critical flaw which greatly hampered the development of the scheme and forced the department to insert proposals allowing farmers to chose their own veterinarians to test their cattle. Moreover, the scarcity of veterinary surgeons persistently limited the scope of the scheme.[283]

The 1954 scheme brought steady progress, but eradication was not proceeding at anything approaching the desired pace. The introduction of an accredited herds scheme in 1956 improved matters to some extent and the committal of more substantial resources gave the initiative badly needed impetus. Irish minds were concentrated by the expectation that Britain would be fully attested by 1961. The Department of Agriculture proposed a scheme which would go beyond the voluntary one then in operation:

> Further development will require statutory authority to ensure that every herd owner will participate and that eradication measures will be fully effective. The proposed bill will, inter alia, give power to enter premises, test animals, direct the slaughter of reactors, pay compensation, control movement of bovines, regulate and control markets and fairs, and deal with such matters as the disinfection of vehicles and carriages and conditions of transit. Power to require the pasteurisation of separated milk at the creameries is included.

The department stressed the need to clear one area of good size as soon as possible and said it intended to make Sligo the first accredited area by 1959. Clare would follow in 1961 and all areas west of the Shannon, together with counties Donegal and Kerry by 1963.[284]

---

[280] NAI, D/T S2392 B/2, D/A memo to govt., 6 Aug. 1954. The choice of Bansha was based on the earlier moves in the parish by Muintir na Tíre under Canon John Hayes towards the eradication of bovine tuberculosis. A pilot scheme had been undertaken in the area from 1950.

[281] PRO, MAF 35/825, D/A to MAF, 10 Nov. 1954.

[282] NAI, D/T S2392 B/1, D/A memo to govt., 6 Jan. 1954.

[283] See NAI, D/T S2392 C, M/A speech, Jul. 1952 which noted that even in 1957 there were fewer than 400 private veterinary surgeons in the country which equated to one for every 11,000 cattle. On average there were a mere fifteen resident veterinarians per county.

Introducing the bill in the Dáil in July 1957, the Minister for Agriculture stressed the economic obligation of eradication: "We in this country have an incentive towards T.B. eradication which did not operate in other countries and which should help us reach success more swiftly. Failure to eradicate means a complete disruption of our economy." The minister called on the farmers to rally around the eradication flag and lamented those "who are reluctant to set about eradication in a positive way. I hope the growth of public opinion will rectify this. It can do so more effectively than any legislation." Moylan asserted: "Each individual farmer must realise that unless he tackles his own problem now and works systematically towards the elimination of T.B. in his cattle he will have on his hands in three or four years time stock that cannot be exported."[285] The *Irish Farmers' Journal* agreed: "The Bovine TB bill passed through the Dáil last week without political dissension. It is now up to us to approach the task of providing TB-free cattle at high speed and with the least possible burden on our limited resources."[286]

The driving force remained the need to satisfy the British market. In March 1957 an Irish official told a British counterpart that, in essence, the "eradication scheme was a scheme to facilitate exports as much as to clean cattle."[287] In May the Ministry of Agriculture recorded that at a meeting in London, the Irish Minister of Lands, Erskine Childers, "hinted off the record that it would not be a bad thing if we pressed them more severely on the urgent need for them to speed up their measures in view of the fact that we are now well within sight of becoming 100 per cent attested. A strong official approach from us would, he thought, do much to help them catch up."[288] Then, in June 1957, the Minister for Agriculture, Seán Moylan, forwarded a detailed outline of their new eradication measures with the promise to "keep in closest touch … on the question of tuberculosis eradication," and the assurance that "nothing will be left undone to further its development."[289] There was understandable British scepticism of this assurance. That scepticism rested at most levels of British agriculture. Noting that Britain needed 500,000 head of cattle from Ireland every year but that in 1956 only 26,000 head were being once-tested, the British Ministry of Agriculture believed that only in November 1956 did Ireland launch anything approaching a proper scheme and "the response as yet is small. Eire cannot afford to give bonus payments and apart from the free-testing facilities, the only inducement to farmers to co-operate is compensation for reactors in the intensive areas and some assistance with the improvement of buildings."[290] A director of a livestock marketing concern in the British midlands wrote that attestation was hampered by "chaotic" distribution systems in Ireland and the lack of resources or expertise, and not least by "the easy-going mentality of the people of Eire, whose outlook in such matters as carrying

---

[284] NAI, D/T S2392 B/2, D/A memo to govt., 21 Jan. 1957.

[285] NAI, D/T S2392 C, M/A speech, Jul. 1957.

[286] *IFJ*, 6 Jul. 1957.

[287] PRO, MAF 35/825, MAF note, 12 Mar. 1957.

[288] PRO, MAF 35/825, MAF note, 30 May 1957.

[289] PRO, MAF 255/978, Moylan to MAF, 20 Jun. 1957.

out the orders of the Department is … very different from that of the average English farmer."[291] Close contact was continual, though, as in the early months of 1958, when Irish officials proclaimed to the British that it was in their "interest to be guided by your people especially as you have so many years of practical experience in the successful eradication of bovine tuberculosis." To this end, "far from being offended by your criticisms we on our side will greatly welcome your opinions as to what is wrong with our T.B. scheme."[292]

Through 1958, definite progress was made as the Irish followed the British advice and concentrated on ensuring that there would be at least one accredited area ready by 1960. Equally, the Irish attempted to follow the British suggestion that they attempt to send boatloads of cattle under accredited designation as soon as possible. The Department of Agriculture believed that by the end of 1958 the Irish would be in a position to export 80,000 once-tested cattle and that that figure would rise to 200,000 in 1959.[293] With Britain adamant that no untested cattle would be admitted after its regions were declared either attested or eradicated in April 1960, the department stressed the need to continue to forward its campaign. The accredited herds scheme was improved and the advisory officers of the County Committees of Agriculture and the NFA joined together with the aim of intensifying farmer support for the scheme.[294] The somewhat haphazard approach to eradication, though, was admitted by the Minister for Agriculture, Paddy Smith, who told a meeting of farmers that "there was no fixed procedure yet available for the limitation of T.B. in the country. They were still trying to find the best approach to the problem and the procedure was varying from week to week."[295] This failure to devise a more coherent policy led the *Irish Farmers' Journal* to lament: "The kind of mentality that tolerates tinkering with the issues in a matter like this is not easy to understand, but it goes a long way to explain the failure of this country to use its independence constructively."[296]

Nonetheless, the eradication scheme was strengthened during 1958 through the establishment of a clearance area extending across most of Connacht with heavy fines for those who contravened its edict.[297] Further, amongst a range of tighter controls, it was announced that cattle sold as once-tested had to be tested not more than fourteen days before sale.[298] The modifications brought immediate progress and the *Irish Farmers' Journal* was moved to comment that "the whole T.B. situation has been radically changed."[299] The Department of Agriculture was able to inform London that, even though they were still reliant on voluntary participation beyond the clearance areas, "the 'climate' here in regard to this

[290] PRO, MAF 35/825, MAF note, 1 Apr. 1957.

[291] PRO, MAF 35/836, A.P. McDougall, Midland Marts Ltd. to MAF, 31 Jan. 1958.

[292] PRO, MAF, 35/387, Irish embassy to MAF, 24 Mar. 1958.

[293] NAI, D/T S2392 C, D/A memo to govt., 2 Apr. 1958.

[294] *IFJ*, 1 Mar. 1958.

[295] *Ibid.*, 24 May 1958. See also NAI, D/T S2392 C, M/A speech to Kildare farmers (n.d.).

[296] *Ibid.*, 31 May 1958.

[297] NAI, D/T S2392 C, D/A memo to govt., 4 Jun. 1958 and *Irish Press*, 13 Aug. 1958.

matter of eradication has improved tremendously in recent months and farmers are now generally anxious to get on with it."[300] British officials remained unconvinced. In April 1958 it was noted that the Republic's failure to keep in step with Britain in the eradication of tuberculosis was due to "the shortage of qualified veterinary surgeons and of the difficulty of winning the farmers over to wholehearted co-operation."[301] Indeed, a UK trade commission report in March 1958 had spoken in bleak terms:

> The eradication scheme would be an immense task even if all concerned were co-operating to the full. It is an impossible one in the existing circumstances of serious unrest in the farming community, open hostility from the creameries and a lack of confidence between the veterinary profession and the government. At the present rate of progress the Republic cannot hope to eradicate bovine tuberculosis in less than ten years. It must face the certain loss of the British market for store cattle and, therefore, for 35 per cent of its domestic exports, if the job is not done within three years. The probability is that none of those who are directly concerned, even the government, really believes that the United Kingdom will finally close the gate against non-attested Irish store cattle in 1961.[302]

Even the British Ministry of Agriculture acknowledged that the demands of its agricultural economy necessitated the contemplation of the importation of unattested Irish store cattle even after Britain was declared a tuberculosis free area. A study group on the problem considered whether the Irish could be given some level of veterinary assistance to speed the campaign, suggested that no hint be made of the possibility of access of unattested cattle after 1961 in case it slowed the campaign, but crucially agreed that the entry of unattested cattle might be allowed in "the very last resort."[303] That same group did argue, though, that if they did allow once-tested, rather than untested, cattle through, the shortfall would be sufficient to cause price increases but not to cause deep-seated problems and "the loss of supplies could no doubt be made good within a year or so," from increased home production and other sources.[304] Ultimately, the group recommended that no untested cattle be allowed in after Britain was declared tuberculosis-free, but that once-tested cattle be allowed through for five years. Its report in August 1958 noted that the Irish government had asked for financial help and agreed that this would be desirable, not through direct assistance, but through manipulation of the differential price paid on imported stores.[305] Overall, though the British

[298] *Ibid.*, 14 Aug. 1958.

[299] *IFJ*, 17 Dec. 1958.

[300] PRO, MAF 35/840, D/A and Irish embassy to MAF, 30 Sept. 1958.

[301] PRO, MAF 40/360, MAF note, Apr. 1958.

[302] PRO, MAF 40/360, UK trade commission report, Mar. 1958.

[303] PRO, MAF 40/360, Study group on the problem of imports of Irish cattle at the final stage of the tuberculosis eradicating plan in Great Britain, 14 Apr. 1958.

[304] *Ibid.* The Fatstock Marketing, Meat Division and External Relations sections of the study group did argue, though, that "it is important to bear in mind that if the Republic did find alternative markets for their cattle exports the United Kingdom might have great difficulty at a later date in getting back these supplies, and in the long term, it is not desirable that there should be any serious diminution in the supply of Irish beef cattle to this country." See PRO, MAF 40/360, Joint paper, Apr. 1958.

remarked that "at long last the authorities in the Republic propose to approach their difficult task of bovine T.B. eradication on an organised basis." [306] The new initiatives brought a progressive increase in the number of once-tested cattle and, in October 1958 the Department of Agriculture trumpeted the first direct shipment of attested store cattle from an accredited Irish herd to Britain.[307] The National Farmers' Union (NFU) in Britain reacted against their government's decision to accept once-tested cattle for a five year period as it would allow the Irish to "sit back."[308] The *Irish Farmers' Journal* warned its readers not to accept the grace period "as a licence to be complacent."[309] Money remained the best guardian against such complacency, the Commonwealth Relations Office proposed that Britain assist the Irish eradication scheme with a grant of £750,000 and, in return, should seek trade concessions. This was swiftly killed by the Chancellor of the Exchequer who said "the proposal amounted to a grant to a foreign government to help them to improve the efficiency of their agriculture."[310]

The eradication scheme was the largest project undertaken by the Department of Agriculture. By mid-1962 the overall incidence of disease in cows had fallen to 11 per cent. A further intensive drive was launched, apparently to clear the country, in 1962 and after four rounds of testing in the southern dairying counties, Ireland was declared attested on 19 October 1965. In the years since 1954 net expenditure on the scheme had reached £37.9 million. Of this, £19.4 million was paid to farmers for reactors, £11 million to veterinarians in fees, and the remainder in modernising grants and sundry expenses. In the overall course of the scheme, 600 private veterinarians were engaged in almost continuous testing, as well as the department's 24-strong veterinary staff, while on the administrative side, 210 officers were employed in seventeen district offices.[311] Ostensibly, the announcement by the Minister for Agriculture, Charles Haughey, that the entire country was attested should have marked a celebration of a policy process which had seen Ireland clear its herds of tuberculosis in a markedly shorter time than other countries. Yet, it was an announcement which was premature to the point of inaccuracy. In the decades after 1965 tuberculosis lingered through the Irish countryside, testimony to "poor administration and the growth of vested interests at the expense of the ordinary taxpayer." T.K Whitaker was later to denounce the scheme as "the greatest single financial scandal since the state was founded."[312] The fact that the incidence of the disease remained so high in Ireland, added to the annual sums which continued to be spent on

305 PRO, MAF 40/360, Report of the inter-disciplinary study group on future imports of store cattle from the Irish Republic in the light of progress in tuberculosis eradication in Great Britain and Northern Ireland, Aug. 1958.

306 PRO, MAF 40/360, MAF to CRO, 30 Mar. 1958.

307 PRO, MAF 40/360, D/A press release, 10 Oct. 1958.

308 PRO, MAF 225/978, National Farmers' Union to MAF, 22 May 1959.

309 *IFJ*, 28 Mar. 1959.

310 PRO, MAF 225/978, minutes of the cabinet economic policy committee, 6 Oct. 1960.

311 O'Connor, *Tuberculosis*, p. 28–31.

eradication, made a nonsense of Haughey's claim. Too many factors proved too limiting for the converse to be true.

Inevitably, fraud was a limiting factor on the progress of the scheme. Reacting to British farmers' claims that Irish farmers were sending over reactors as once-tested cattle, Irish officials agreed that they were aware of the occasional breakdown of procedure and that as a result four veterinarians had been removed from the list of authorised testers.[313] Equally, the *Irish Farmers' Journal* warned of tanglers who continued to employ dishonest veterinarians to fake tuberculosis tests.[314] In 1960 a British official at the treasury wrote to the Ministry of Agriculture: "Those of us with farmer friends in Eire know of the widespread abuse of attestation certificates. They can be had at a price."[315] Despite widespread suggestions of fraud, prosecutions were slow in coming. As a Department of Agriculture official wrote: "little or no assistance from the trade is forthcoming until we ourselves have uncovered the irregularities." Irregularities and malpractice had been effectively dealt with but

> our greatest problem, however, has always been the collection of sufficient evidence to sustain successful court prosecutions. In this we have to say, regrettably, that neither we nor the Garda authorities, who are most helpful, have received much assistance from members of the public despite numerous allegations of fraud and misdemeanour.[316]

In August 1962 the Minister for Agriculture, Paddy Smith wrote to the then justice minister, Charles Haughey, expressing concern that no prosecutions had taken place despite numerous investigations into tuberculosis fraud and referred to public suspicion that "some sinister hand is at work," in preventing any court cases.[317] The discovery of malpractice by a Department of Agriculture official at Dublin port in the autumn of 1962 offered the opportunity to make a stand. Smith wrote to the attorney general:

> I am extremely anxious that this case should get into court with all possible speed; I had indeed hoped that this could have been done before re-assembly of the Dáil. I am convinced that the ventilation of this case is of the utmost importance to our cattle export trade and to the success of the bovine tuberculosis eradication scheme.[318]

A cattle exporter, a cattle drover, as well as the departmental official were sentenced to one year imprisonment, later reduced to a fine of £400, for

---

[312] Sean O'Donnell, 'Vetting the herd', in *Éire–Ireland*, vol. xx, no. 2 (1985), pp 130–2.

[313] NAI, D/T S2392 D/94, Minutes of meeting between D/A officials and Mr Salter-Chalker of the National Farmers' Union Animal Diseases Committee, 24 Jul. 1959.

[314] *IFJ*, 28 Nov. 1959. The paper made no mention of the possibility of farmers exercising the same option.

[315] PRO, MAF 225/978, Treasury to MAF, 5 Dec. 1960.

[316] NAI, D/T S2392 E/62, D/A to D/T, 26 Jun. 1962.

[317] NAI, D/T S2392 E/62, M/A to M/J, 16 Aug. 1962.

attempting to export 59 head of cattle which were not attested but were presented as fully attested.[319]

Yet, the very nature of the scheme as first devised in 1954 contributed to the less than rigorous adherence to the spirit of the arrangements. The scheme was reliant on the absolute integrity of veterinarians, civil servants and farmers. The decision to allow the farmer to name his veterinarian of choice rather than accept the departmental nominee was a critical error. It is unreasonable to expect that, given the nature of the relationship between the two parties, the scheme would not be in some way compromised. Rather than force the farmer to remove the offending beast at somewhat lower than market cost, it was not inconceivable that a veterinarian might facilitate the onward sale of the beast rather than enforce regulations which would substantially devalue the herd. Given the fact that the testing serum was only 90 per cent effective in any case, there was little likelihood of any party being deemed culpable of fraud. Moreover, the fact that the eradication scheme came to employ 1200 civil servants and provided a substantial source of income for 850 veterinarians suggested a certain interest in perpetuating the operation.[320]

Ultimately, the tuberculosis eradication scheme highlighted the importance of store cattle to the Irish economy. A scheme was only contemplated when the trade – and thus the entire economy – was in peril. Public health was not nearly so powerful a motivating factor as the loss of bullock earnings. It is an unavoidable truth that it was the desire to perpetuate the cattle export trade with Britain rather than conviction of the worth of eradication in itself that drove the initiation, implementation and declaration of successful completion of the scheme. Within that truth lies its success and its failure. That eradication progressed so rapidly from 1958 when the prospect of losing the British market seemed real offers ample evidence of the motivations behind the involvement of almost every party. Equally, it was in the knowledge that enough had been done to secure continued access to the British market that attestation was declared. Tuberculosis may not have been eradicated but the scheme had successfully achieved its principal objectives: Ireland could continue selling its cattle in Britain.

---

[318] NAI, D/T S2392 E/62, M/A to Attorney General, 30 Oct.1962.

[319] *Irish Press*, 14 Dec. 1962 and 26 Jan. 1963.

[320] O'Donnell, *Vetting the herd*, pp 130–2. Indeed, Raymond Crotty has argued that it is doubtful if the bovine tuberculosis eradication scheme was economically worthwhile. Crotty believed that while it may have been justified on the grounds of public health, no attempt was ever made to do so and the tenor of the *Programme for economic expansion* stressed that investment of a social nature should give way to productive investment. He further argued that even had the export of live cattle stopped, the move towards live processing and a more intensive form of farming would actually have benefited the country, even if it had meant a transfer of income from cattle producers to beef processors. For Crotty the loss of the live export trade would have been at least counter-balanced by the forced development of the meat processing industry. He offers no suggestion where all the processed meat would have been sold to. Nonetheless, it was undeniable that the tuberculosis eradication scheme did affect the nature of cattle exports as "sales of store cattle to England continuously declined since the summer of 1959. On the other hand, sales of fat cattle increased to a similar degree. When gradually the Irish farming community increased its attested herds, demand for Irish stores rose again." Crotty, *Agricultural production*, pp 197–201.

In this, it was the sole aspect of the agricultural section of the *Programme for economic expansion* which realised its target. Other attempts to meet the ambitions laid down in the *Programme* demonstrated the ongoing difficulty in constructing a dynamic agricultural policy. Essentially, the Programme did not unduly reshape Irish agricultural policy. Without the conviction that markets existed where expanded agricultural produce could be disposed of, there was limited potential for assuring farmers of the worth of increasing their output. By the early 1960s, policy had converged to such an extent that divergence between the major parties was almost wholly rhetorical. That policy was predicated on the export of cattle, but also on the acknowledgement of the growing importance of industry. Significantly, limited investment in agriculture restricted the development of programmes to propel farmers towards expanding their operations. This was reflected in the relative investment levels for the various sectors of the economy. As the 1960s progressed, the displacement of agriculture by industry as the prime focus of Irish economic development continued relentlessly. Ireland was moving in the way of the rest of the world.

Chapter
5

Thinking of farmers as people ... 1962–65

The inability of agricultural communities to innovate or to expand at as precipitate a rate as industry was not peculiarly Irish, but represented, instead, an enduring world-wide phenomenon.[1] The failure to progress significantly in the wake of the *Programme for economic expansion* offered further evidence of the chronic afflictions of Irish agriculture and of the incapacity to devise cathartic policies. Consequently, the sense of a new departure in Irish economic development associated with the *Programme* was less pronounced for agriculture than for other sectors of the economy. Inherent structural deficiencies were never going to dissipate miraculously in the face of the publication of any programme, no matter how revolutionary in aspect, especially when that programme held no proposals to rectify or to alleviate such deficiencies. Previous reports and plans had come and gone with little impact, and even allowing for the apparent intent to actually implement on this occasion, farmers remained unconvinced that the indecision of the past would not continue to manifest itself. In terms of actual expansion, though, the failure to devise policies capable of surmounting endemic structural problems gravely limited the expansionist aspirations outlined in the *Programme*. Despite the initial setbacks occasioned by appalling weather, there was, indeed, an increase in output (see appendix) and the *Irish Farmers' Journal* remarked on the "slow but steady progress in our industry." Commenting favourably on the six-monthly reports published by the government assessing the advances made in the economy under the programme, the *Journal* believed they indicated "an increased awareness in the Department of Agriculture of the main problems of agriculture." This welcome of increased awareness was tempered by the assessment that "as yet there is no real dynamic attempt at meeting the problems."[2] The contrast between the relative fortunes of agriculture and industry was not lost on the paper which saw the sections in the progress reports devoted to agriculture as akin to "dilute skim milk – a little bit of goodness, but a terrible amount of water. Economic expansion, as far as industry is concerned is now well

---

[1] For example, Pedersen documents the manner in which Danish industry expanded far faster in the post-war era than agriculture did. See Peder J. Pedersen, 'Post-war growth of the Danish economy', in Gianni Toniolo and Nicholas Crafts (eds.), *Economic growth in Europe since 1945*, pp 541–75. See also James Simpson, *Spanish agriculture: the long siesta, 1765–1965* (1995). For evidence of the slow response of farmers to adopt specific innovations, see Gilbert Fite, 'Recent progress in the mechanisation of cotton production in the United States', in *AH*, vol. 24, no. 1 (1950), pp 19–28; Schmidt, 'German agriculture, 1945–53'; and Paul Brassley, 'Silage in Britain, 1880–1990: the delayed adoption of an innovation', in *AHR*, vol. 44, i (1996), pp 63–87.

[2] *IFJ*, 27 May 1961.

off the ground and apparently in full flight, but in the field of agriculture we have not yet had an imaginative approach towards Irish farming."[3]

When the imagination did take hold of the Irish agricultural community, Europe loomed large on the horizon. The stirrings of a relationship with the EEC offered the genuine long-term prospect of easier access to non-British markets as well as a measure of price and income support which the Irish state could not contemplate in isolation. Farming organisations were left salivating at the vista of unfettered expansion at guaranteed profit but, for all their desire, this was no whirlwind romance. Indeed, the initial courtship was protracted, even tortuous, and essentially joyless. It is one of the great ironies of Irish history that it was the desire to preserve the intimacy of its links with Britain which eventually moved the Irish government to seek a place at the continental table. Only when it became certain that the British government were to apply for membership did the Irish seriously consider application. The absolute reliance on the British market dictated that Ireland inevitably had to follow the lead of the country to which it remained in economic thrall. It is a singular commentary on the priorities of the Irish government, that failure to join the EEC in 1963 was viewed as welcome, given the simultaneous failure of Britain to accede to the community. In time, of course, there would be no more ardent Europeans than the Irish themselves, particularly when the distribution of structural funds sat high on the agenda, but the original motivation for membership was rooted in perceptions of fear, not of opportunity.

Rejection by Europe pushed the Irish even further into the arms of the British. In pursuit of a policy which he had promoted almost from the first days of his tenure as Taoiseach, Seán Lemass sought a more definite alignment with the British economy. The resultant 1965 Anglo-Irish Free Trade Agreement was a recognition of the prevailing realities of the Irish economy and its intimate relationship with Britain. Almost a half-century after independence, the Irish were more dependent than ever on trade with Britain. The Anglo-Irish Free Trade Agreement recognised the intimacy of the bonds which tied the Irish economy to its larger neighbouring island. The agreement represented the symbolic public acknowledgement by the Fianna Fáil party of the abandonment of even a veneer of devotion to the doctrine of self-sufficiency. There was no longer any suggestion that Ireland could thrive unless it was associated with a larger bloc of countries. Increasingly, there could be no escape from the forces of history or of economics. In the short term, these forces determined the formal acknowledgement of the historic relationship with Britain and, in the long term, fostered the pursuit of economic alignment with Europe, in the event of British accession to the EEC. The Anglo-Irish Free Trade Agreement was both an end in itself and the means to an end. For the agricultural community, the years which preceded the agreement were less than enchanting. Internal and external forces promoted changes which were often painful as the Irish agricultural community developed an acute awareness that modernisation engendered difficulties as profound as those produced by stagnation.

---

[3] *Ibid.*, 30 Apr. 1960.

In 1966, the Minister for Agriculture, Charles Haughey, reflected on these difficulties and on the apparently unsuccessful attempts to devise a policy to improve the living standards of the farming community:

> we must think always of farmers as people. We must not listen only to the economist and the bureaucratic planner who think of agriculture as simply another sector of the economy and who are concerned only with output, return on investment and so on. Agricultural policy cannot be measured by the norms that are applied to policies for other sectors.[4]

Haughey noted the obvious improvement in living standards enjoyed by farmers but accepted that, as a societal sector, they were more dissatisfied at that point than even in the 1930s when conditions had been far worse. This dissatisfaction was because "firstly, farmers compare their situation with that of other sectors and are not at all satisfied with the comparison, Secondly, when, by their endeavours, they acquire some of the benefits and amenities of modern living they want more of them and they want them quickly."[5] Although determined to redress the income position by raising the purchasing power of farmers, he noted: "the lesson of our time is that material progress in itself is not enough. Furthermore, it can bring many new problems, tensions and stresses, in its train."[6] Prophetic words which heralded a decade where these "new problems, tensions and strains" exacerbated existing difficulties in another difficult decade for Irish agriculture.

---

[4] Charles Haughey, 'Rural sociology and Ireland,' in *Éire–Ireland*, vol. 1, no. 4 (1966), pp 63–69, p. 65.

[5] In support of his interpretation, Haughey quoted approvingly (*ibid.*, pp 64–5) from J.K. Galbraith's, *The affluent society:* "It is not the poor but the well-to-do farmers who find onerous the uncertainties of the market. In the mountain country of Kentucky or Tennessee a depression is not a grievous hazard. Farmers have little to sell; their property has small value. They are, therefore, little affected by declining prices and not much concerned about declining property values. In the well-to-do regions things are different. In the nineteen-thirties it was the comparatively rich farmers of Iowa who threatened the judges who presided over foreclosure proceedings. From these farms came the demands for farm relief. Unlike those of the Appalachian plateau, these farmers had something to lose."

[6] *Ibid.*

I

Small farmers and government policy

In the clear understanding of a growth in income disparity between the country's small farmers and other sections of society, government attention turned to addressing the position of the small farmers of Ireland. The small farm structure, with a high prevalence of subsistence farming, was not conducive to the increased output sought by successive governments and the problems of smallholders were further accentuated by the inferior quality of their inadequate tracts of land.[7] In 1954, an *Irish Farmers' Journal* columnist reiterated the view that small farming in the west was "based generally on wrong premises. A community cannot exist by raising store cattle on small farms ... This is subsistence farming on quite an extensive scale and it cannot go on for much longer. Either improvement comes fairly quickly or these small units will all be consolidated into large ranches."[8] There was no assessment in official policy of how to cultivate a prosperous small farming economy, even though the state continued to actively create smallholdings through the Land Commission: "Although we are a nation of small farmers, all too little attention has been paid here to the special problems associated with small holdings."[9] The results were, as the Department of Lands noted, "the increase in agricultural production since 1931 has taken place on farms of over 100 acres mainly in Leinster and Munster; the increase in production on farms under 50 acres being virtually nil."[10]

For some, these problems were assumed to be insurmountable. Writing in the *Irish Farmers' Journal* in 1957, a columnist proclaimed; "Everything points to the conclusion that the small mixed farm will slowly but surely disappear; and we must adapt our farm planning to the realities of the situation."[11] This fatalism was a source of outrage for those who saw that developments such as the *Programme for economic expansion* could not cater for a large swathe of the populace: "An atmosphere hostile to the small farmer is being created by our economists, our industrialists and the lineal descendants of the old landlord class ... What a catastrophe and anomaly, a country without a people," railed Bishop Lucey of Cork and Ross.[12] For all the economic inconvenience it entailed, disappearance was not on the mind of those rooted in traditions of survival. Under Fr John Fahy, parish priest in Lusmagh, Co. Offaly a smallholders' radical agrarian movement, Lia Fáil, was founded in 1957.[13] Evoking the spirit of an earlier age, its members

[7] Gillmor, *Agriculture*, p. 47.
[8] Dr Robert O'Connor writing in *IFJ*, 24 Apr. 1954.
[9] Editorial in *IFJ*, 9 Mar. 1957.
[10] NAI, D/T S6490 C/1, D/L note, 31 May 1958.
[11] Dr P. Moran writing in *IFJ*, 4 May 1957.
[12] *Irish Times*, 20 Nov. 1961.
[13] Brian A. Murphy, 'Lia Fáil', *passim.*

marched under the tricolour, drove cattle off lands and ploughed fields while couching these actions in the classic language of revolutionary fringe groups. It was blatantly sectarian and xenophobic, although it was as willing to target Catholic landlords and graziers, as it was to dispossess Protestant and unionists, the remnants of "the British garrison."[14] Its journal, *Lia Fáil*, proclaimed that small farmers "are neither free nor Gaelic. Our economy has collapsed. Our main exports are our people and our money – our money to the tune of hundreds of millions sterling invested in Britain and elsewhere; our people to the tune of fifty or sixty thousand per annum."[15] *Lia Fáil* faded into obscurity within eighteen months but the conditions which fomented its development were unrelenting. The realities of the impoverished lifestyle of smallholders stood in stark contrast to the steady increase in prosperity across other sections of society. It was not that many smallholders had not come enjoy a higher quality of life than their forebears but this paled against both the reality and the stories of economic successes of those who left the land. For all the pain of emigration "it is arguable that those who left had less to regret than many of those who stayed and who inherited the small farm and the hard grind for survival."[16]

As that grind for survival became more acute, the necessity for action became more compelling. In a letter to the Minister for Finance, James Ryan, in March 1961, the Taoiseach, Seán Lemass, wrote:

In my view the main, if not the only question arising in national economic policy to which we have not yet found a satisfactory answer is how to deal with the problem of the small (mainly western) farms, and to ensure reasonable standards of income for those who live on them. Is it possible to alter the traditional production pattern or to expand the output from these farms so as to raise the income from them? Should the aim be to facilitate their amalgamation into larger units and what would be the social consequences of so doing? Does afforestation offer any solution and if so can it be extended in these areas? Is there any useful channel for further State aid to reduce production costs?[17]

In an attempt to resolve these questions, and acting on the proposal of the Minister for Agriculture, Paddy Smith, the government established an interdepartmental small farms committee.[18] Expanding on the proposed role of this committee in the course of an address to the annual general meeting of the Irish

---

14 *Ibid.*, pp 862–3.

15 NAI, D/T S6490C/1, copy of *Lia Fáil* newspaper, Nov. 1958.

16 Ó Tuathaigh, 'Land question', pp 180–1.

17 NAI, D/T S17032 A/61, Lemass to Ryan, 6 Mar. 1961. The Lemass initiative on small farms drew frequently on Pope John XXIII's papal encyclical *Mater et Magistra* (1961). The encyclical included a long commentary on social justice and rural life. Lemass quoted it frequently in his speeches.

18 NAI, D/T S17032 A/61, Smith to Lemass, 17 Feb. 1961. Smith mentioned the possibility of establishing an interdepartmental committee in the context of proposals to expand milk production in small farm areas, and to provide grants to fence and fertilise lands used for hill grazing.

Countrywomen's Assocation (ICA) in April 1961, Lemass acknowledged the
onerous task facing the new committee:

> There is a need for fresh thinking, and a re-examination of production
> possibilities, so that a way can be found, and a policy formulated, to
> make living on a small farm – as that term is understood in Ireland –
> more satisfying, and to offer a fair prospect of achieving through hard
> work and intelligent effort, living standards which conform to the
> national average ... It has always been our policy – it is indeed a
> directive principle of social policy prescribed in the Constitution – to
> seek to establish as many families as possible in economic security on
> the land. But the meaning of the term 'economic security' changes
> with the general conditions prevailing in the nation. It cannot mean a
> bare subsistence level. That is no longer acceptable. It must mean
> economic security comparable with that which can be gained in other
> activities, and, as general living standards rise, the standard on the
> small farms must be capable of rising with them, or this small farm
> problem will be always with us. The question is if this is possible, and,
> if so, how?

For Lemass, the initiative on which the government was embarking bore all
the hallmarks of a last-ditch attempt to avert the decimation of the small farming
community:

> If the small farm cannot be made an economic unit by bringing about
> changes in its production pattern and methods, then, notwithstanding
> the tenacity with which Irish people hold on to the ownership of land,
> we may expect a trend towards amalgamation into larger holdings, and
> fewer families living on the land. We see that something like this is
> happening in other countries. The small farms have, however, been
> such a typical feature of the Irish scene, and such strongholds of the
> Irish traditions which we value most highly, that I do not think that we
> should accept this change as inevitable until we have examined all
> other possibilities very thoroughly ... It is not very difficult to visualise
> the developments which we would like to see. It is a different matter to
> devise really effective plans and methods to bring these developments
> about, and still another matter to make all these plans and schemes
> fully operative in every locality.[19]

The consequent *Report by the inter-departmental committee on the problems of small
western farms*, published in April 1962, considered that the decline of small farms
and the general failure to make economic progress in the west of Ireland was due
to the disinclination of youth to remain on small holdings, the decline of
'farmyard income' through the loss of poultry and pig profits to customised mass

---

[19] NAI, D/T S17032 A/62, address by Lemass to the annual general meeting of the ICA at Mansion
House, Dublin, 11 Apr. 1961.

production units, the lack of industrialisation in the region, and the structural situation which determined that the general run of farmers were not in a position to benefit from fixed price crops such as wheat, barley, beet and milk. Despite these problems, the committee considered that the position of small farmers could not be improved in the long term either by subsidies or by special price supports as these would only act as palliatives rather than healing the economic ills of the area. The committee further considered that the economic pressures on small holdings were likely to persist, even intensify, in such a manner that "the weight of future efforts by the state in these districts should be directed to the possibilities of non-farm employment through industrialisation, forestry, tourist development, etc." Nonetheless, the report did stipulate a number of policy initiatives which might be taken to ameliorate the existing status of small farmers. In large measure, it marked a reiteration of long-standing aspirations. Expansion of educational and advisory services, improved grading and marketing systems, and a redesigned co-operative movement, were all deemed indispensable. There were also proposals to reorient the work of the Land Commission. It was proposed that the commission be given powers to buy holdings from elderly owners, control the undesirable agglomeration of holdings, and amend the old age pension criteria to allow for the transfer of land from older to younger farmers. Further, the policy on the size of holdings needed to be revised, low interest loans should be provided to western farmers to buy land in other regions and consideration should be given to empowering the acquisition of holdings let, but not properly worked, or left vacant, for five years. Attempts should be made to develop markets in such non-mainstream products as bull beef or mountain lamb, while the market for pig and eggs may improve so "the question of whether a calculated risk should be taken in developing pig and egg production and marketing on a co-operative basis should be considered."[20]

Reaction to the report, whose content had been toned down before publication on directive from the government, was generally positive, although the *Irish Times* did note:

> If the West of Ireland were to get everything recommended by the inter-departmental committee on small farms, the chances of its survival in prosperity would be much enhanced; though even then success would be far from certain. The sad and cynical history of Gaeltacht administration holds out no such prospect. Indeed, there is probably no sector of public policy in which promise has so replaced performance, and the people's confidence has been so abused.[21]

The paper called for the formulation of a coherent, realistic framework of development: "Erratic subvention is the mistake whose withered fruits can be seen in the deserted homes, untilled fields and empty schools of the Atlantic seaboard."[22]

---

20 *Report by the inter-departmental committee on the problems of small western farms* (1962), pp 7, 9, 34–5.
21 *Irish Times*, 25 Apr. 1962. See also NAI, D/T S17032 B/62, D/T note, 15 Apr. 1962, which recorded that even though the authors had been given anonymity, "it was found necessary to tone down some of the most critical references in the Report before it was published."

Within the government there was a clear acceptance that any initiative would have to come from official quarters as "the record of the agricultural organisations in this matter does not reflect any keenness to get involved even though the subject is of vital interest to the farming community."[23] Lemass canvassed opinions on the way forward from his cabinet. The Minister for Industry and Commerce, Jack Lynch, effectively abdicated responsibility when he claimed that he had tried to encourage industrial development in the west but was "not in a position to direct any industrial project to a particular area and the final decision regarding location in each case must be left to the promoters and to those proposing to invest their capital in the project."[24] In a typically off-beat contribution, the Minister for Transport and Power, Erskine Childers, noted that for all the income schemes attempted for small farmers, there was an inevitable move to agglomerate holdings and drift from the land:

> It will be fatal to our cause to try to deny these essential truths by announcing a policy that in fact will have only a marginal effect on the general prosperity of the farmer and to play up the policy and exaggerate the value of government aid ... Unless the will to improve can be stimulated – a spirit going far beyond mere profit incentive – the rest of the proposals are just props in a stage play that signify nothing.[25]

The Minister for Agriculture, Paddy Smith, offered a detailed appraisal of the recommendations made in the small farms report. With the exception of the proposal to empower the Land Commission to control the undesirable agglomeration of holdings, Smith agreed that all other recommendations were worthy of further investigation. He supported the suggestion that land division policy be redefined to facilitate not merely the upward revision of the size of holdings but also the extension of powers to ensure that land was not allowed to fall derelict. Smith was also particularly enthusiastic about the extension of educational and advisory services. He considered that this aspect was especially crucial in the light of attempts to extend the dairy industry through the west as "basic educational work is likely to be necessary before farmers in many of the areas concerned will be able to manage cows profitably."[26] For his part, the Minister for Finance reiterated these concerns on the extension of the dairy industry to the west but argued that the need for caution was rooted not just in technical aspects but "also by the world surplus in many dairy products, the difficulty of diversifying milk processing, and the heavy subsidisation which milk production requires." Indeed, the minister considered that "the fundamental requirement of any form of assistance for the West – as in any other part of the country – is that, whether or not initial grants or subsidies are given, the activity

---

22 *Ibid.*

23 NAI, D/T S17032 B/62, D/T note, 15 Apr. 1962.

24 NAI, D/T S17032 B/62, M/IC memo to govt., May 1962.

25 NAI, D/T S17032 B/62, Minister for Transport and Power memo to govt., 25 May 1962.

26 NAI, D/T S17032 B/62, M/A memo to govt., May 1962.

being started must be likely to operate economically."[27]

Lemass continued to drive his initiative forward at a pace unfamiliar to other agricultural initiatives. In June 1962 he called a conference of ministers to consider the report and the subsequent departmental contributions it had inspired. The decisions reached at that conference set the agenda for subsequent government action on small farms. In a somewhat ominous commentary on the future welfare of the small farm community, it was stressed at the outset that

> the weight of future efforts by the state in the west should be directed to the possibilities of non-farm employment through industrialisation, forestry, tourist development and any other possibilities offering a fair prospect of success. It was decided that all government departments, other public authorities and state-sponsored bodies should be asked to have regard to that objective in the formulation of plans and in the performance of their work.[28]

To this end, it was agreed that forestry work "should be pursued with the utmost vigour." Facilitating this would require new legislation further empowering the Minister for Lands to acquire blocks of suitable land between existing forest properties and would also require government authorisation of the migration from the west of the occupiers of land required for forestry purposes.[29]

In respect of land policy, it was decided that 40 to 45 acres of good land should be the desired size of any family farm, that the Land Commission should use its statutory powers to acquire holdings let or not properly worked, or left vacant, for five years and that the commission should also be given powers to purchase suitable holdings from elderly or incapacitated owners. This renewal of agricultural structural policy ultimately found expression in the Land Act, 1965. The Department of Social Welfare was asked to amend the old age pensions code to allow for the purchase price or life annuity received from any sale of land to be disregarded in the calculation of an old age pension. That department was also to examine the possibility of providing income supplements for smallholders in the congested districts. The Minister for Agriculture was instructed to conduct investigations and formulate comprehensive proposals on the best way to develop the advisory and educational services in the west, and "it was agreed that where a contribution from the exchequer was shown to be necessary to bring about the desired improvements, such a contribution should be given." Similarly, it was agreed that research be conducted into the development of specialised

---

[27] NAI, D/T S17032 C/62, M/F memo to govt., 16 Jun. 1962.

[28] NAI, D/T S17032 C/62, D/T memo on conclusions reached at conference of ministers on 19 Jun. 1962, 13 Jul. 1962

[29] It was accepted by the ministers that such migration would be particularly costly so "no publicity whatever would be desirable in relation to such an authorisation: publicity would involve grave danger of interrupting the normal flow of land purchase for forestry purposes by creating the false impression that migration would readily be offered where no agreement for cash purchase by the Minister was reached." *Ibid.*

commodities, but it was accepted that the future lay in the refinement of traditional product lines. In this respect, it was agreed that "concrete proposals" be formulated for the reorganisation and strengthening of the IAOS, and that there be examination of the "possibilities of securing, by co-operative action or otherwise, (a) a reduction in the costs of production and (b) better marketing arrangements, for pigs and eggs in the west."[30]

In August 1962, Lemass informed the Muintir na Tíre Rural Week in Thurles, Co. Tipperary of the developments in his initiative. Acknowledging the abject failure of previous attempts to devise a coherent policy, Lemass declared that development "cannot be achieved by wishing for it, but only by the consistent and vigorous application of well-conceived plans, related to the economic and social standards of the present age."[31] He determined that his present initiative was being carefully planned:

> the urgency of the problems of the small farming areas is not to be denied, and in settling policies to deal with them we must be sure that all the necessary information is available and all possible views assessed, so that our decisions may secure the widest possible measure of approval and be applied consistently over the years.

Lemass outlined the initiatives being assessed by various departments but also outlined the difficulties which were being encountered:

> one of the problems which arise in considering the application of a general plan of action to a particular area or areas is that the existing mechanism of government is not very well designed to that end. Government activities are organised vertically: the Departments of Agriculture, Education, Local Government and Lands and so on, have responsibilities related to economic and social matters within their defined spheres on a nation-wide basis. An organisation to apply a comprehensive economic and social programme within a particular area should, ideally, take a different form. The best substitute for it yet devised is some form of committee, inter-departmental or local, which can prepare a general programme but which, however, has then to be broken down into specific measures coming within the spheres of responsibility of particular departments, to be administered by those departments as part of their normal operations.[32]

Attempting to overcome the traditional obstacles to the formulation of coherent policy and to avoid stalling his initiative in the fault-lines running between the various government departments, Lemass co-ordinated the entire

---

[30] *Ibid.*

[31] NAI, D/T S17032 C/62, Lemass speech, 14 Aug. 1962.

[32] *Ibid.* Lemass stated clearly he did not believe that the transfer of the functions and powers of government to subordinate authorities would represent a viable alternative as this would "make more difficulties than it would solve."

operation from the Taoiseach's office. Through the remainder of 1962, monthly meetings were held at which ministers were asked to give progress reports on the efforts being made by their respective departments to implement the decisions outlined at the July conference. In some respects, decisions reached found almost immediate expression in policy, and, in others, legislation was enacted which brought a more long-term pursuit of stated aims. Small-scale directives involving minimal diversion of policy and funding such as the raising of the desired farm unit size to 40 to 45 acres of good land financed by a budget allocation rise from £750,000 to £1,000,000, enjoyed swift introduction.[33] Similarly, the deployment of greater numbers of agricultural advisers came as a direct consequence of the Lemass initiative.

Some departments moved with greater alacrity than others and certain ministers attempted to design innovative measures to solve the problems of smallholders. Fundamental reorientation of policy, though, proved beyond the capacity of ministers faced with the sheer enormity of the undertaking. Given the acknowledged potential of a vibrant, comprehensive co-operative movement to significantly aid the operations of smallholders, Lemass viewed a recasting of the IAOS as central to his entire project. He wrote to the Minister for Agriculture asking for a comprehensive account of the activities of the IAOS and pronounced his concern "at the apparent failure of the organisation to fulfil the primary objective for which it exists. He wishes that the memorandum should indicate the power or influence of the government in the activities of the organisation, with particular reference to its leadership."[34] The request sparked an internal debate within the Department of Agriculture on the reasons why the co-operative movement had failed to take root. Paddy Smith, did not agree with his departmental secretary, J.C. Nagle, that the lack of advisory officers had hindered the progress of the co-operative movement as he argued that "the co-operative movement took root when we had few advisory officers, and now that we have many it rarely takes a step forward at all."[35] For his part, Nagle argued that the co-operative movement had floundered in the absence of the provision of basic education for young people and that it was "really only in the last ten years or less that the number of agricultural advisers increased to any important extent, but by that time the co-operative movement had become more or less 'fossilised' and other kinds of rural organisations were taking over."[36] The Department of Agriculture submitted a proposal, subsequently accepted by the government, that "the best thing would be to arrange an independent survey carried out of the working of the co-operative movement (including the IAOS) by a recognised expert from outside the country."[37] This proposal was accompanied by a letter from Nagle which noted that the Minister for Agriculture had asked him to point out that

---

[33] NAI, D/T S6490 D/63, cabinet minutes, 7 Nov. 1963.

[34] NAI, D/T S1206/63, Lemass to Smith, 2 Aug. 1962.

[35] NAI, D/T S1206/63, Smith to Nagle, 19 Sept. 1962.

[36] NAI, D/T S1206/63, Nagle to Smith, 19 Sept. 1962

it would not, in his opinion, be justifiable to condemn the society [IAOS] which, in fact, has never possessed real powers of control over the co-operative movement. The society itself is a voluntary co-operative society, membership in which is open to all other co-operative societies which have elected to affiliate with it. The President and the committee of the IAOS are elected by representatives of the affiliated co-operative societies. The fact that the IAOS did not develop into a strong force in Irish agriculture would, therefore, appear to be primarily due to lack of real interest on the part of the co-operative movement generally in the further development of co-operatives in this country.[38]

This reluctance of the co-operative movement to co-operate even with itself was addressed in a report from an American expert, Joseph Knapp.[39] Knapp stressed he did not believe the problems faced by the co-operative movement could be solved easily but required long and continuous educational programmes. For Knapp, though, essential organisational change was fundamental in order to hasten progress and direct it towards the desired goals. To this end, his primary recommendation was that the IAOS be reinvigorated with a substantial grant of at least £100,000. This money should be used to provide the leadership and the technical services necessary to help farmers build strong co-operative organisations. Secondly, Knapp argued that the IAOS should be given full responsibility for the general reorganisation of the dairy industry through consolidation and mergers backed by research services. Thirdly, the dispute with the Dairy Disposal Company should be ended with the co-operativisation of that company under the aegis of the IAOS as "this decision would make clear the Government's confidence in the co-operative form of organisation, and would close the door on a controversy of over thirty years standing."[40]

Although the IAOS welcomed the report, other elements were less well disposed.[41] The Department of Agriculture forwarded to the government a letter received from the Dairy Disposal Company which pointed out that it was the single largest organisation in the dairying industry and claimed that the sources used by Knapp in the formulation of his report were inadequate. It firmly rejected any suggestion that the company should be liquidated.[42] Faced with two alternative courses of actions, the Minister for Agriculture chose neither. Smith invited the IAOS to put its businesses on a solid footing through merger and consolidation, but did not provide for any substantial redeployment of resources to facilitate this

---

[37] NAI, D/T S1206/63, D/A memo to govt., Sept. 1963.

[38] NAI, D/T S1206/63, Nagle to D/T, 26 Sept. 1962.

[39] NAI, D/T S1206/63, Lemass note, n.d., in which he mentioned that Henry Kennedy of the IAOS had agreed to the Department of Agriculture's suggestion on the utilisation of an outside expert to analyse the co-operative movement, although Kennedy did argue that what they really required were more resources.

[40] *An appraisal of agricultural co-operation in Ireland by Joseph G. Knapp* (1964), pp 107–8.

[41] *Irish Times,* 6 May 1964.

or other recommendations made by Knapp.[43] Indeed, such was the rearguard action by the Dairy Disposal Company and its proponents within the Department of Agriculture that a further report was commissioned from two other Americans, Cooke and Sprague. This report urged that the Dairy Disposal Company be expanded and given greater responsibilities as there was "little disposition among the co-operatives to unite and do the job."[44] In the years between the two reports, the reformation drive faltered and the co-operative movement rested in the paralysis which had gripped it for most of the century.

It was this paralysis which had prompted the Minister for Social Welfare, Kevin Boland, to write in May 1963 in support of his own proposal for a scheme of income supplements for smallholders that urgent action was needed "and this cannot be done without expense. Most of the other suggestions in the inter-departmental report are at best long-term and partial solutions and in some cases, I think, no more than pious hopes that are unlikely to be realised." Boland described his scheme, which would have allowed small farmers retain the profits of increased production while guaranteeing a basic income, as "complex" and "imaginative," noted that larger farmers living in more comfortable circumstances would receive more through fertiliser subsidies and rate relief than any smallholder would receive from his proposal, and claimed the net cost would be merely £2.9m for the congested districts or £6.1m for the entire country. Boland further believed his scheme would increase productivity as it would no longer be more valuable to a range of smallholders to keep their incomes low in order to qualify for existing social benefits, rather than passing above the limit on the means test and losing unemployment assistance with no guarantee of profiting from increased production. Equally, he stated that the money he believed necessary to fund his scheme was no more than the amount required to provide an urban worker with employment.[45]

Lemass had previously dismissed such an income support scheme in 1961 in the belief that "if in any area it proves impossible by means of agricultural policy to raise the income from these farms to a tolerable level, a system of paying the occupants to stay on them regardless of how badly they worked them would be a confession of defeat which would have a most demoralising effect."[46] In the context of his desire to aid smallholders he now defended Boland's proposals against attack from other ministers saying he believed "the Government will be prepared to support the principle of such a scheme provided it can be shown to be practicable within reasonable cost ... For my part I believe that such a scheme is justified in principle and will so contend when the matter comes to the government."[47] The departments of Finance and Agriculture were fundamentally opposed. Finance regarded all schemes offering income supplements as against

---

[42] NAI, D/T S1206 C/95, D/A memo to govt., 17 Jun. 1964.

[43] Hoctor, *The department's story*, p. 261.

[44] Smith and Healy, *Farm organisations*, p. 207.

[45] NAI, D/T S17474 A/63, Boland memo to govt., 9 May 1963.

[46] NAI, D/T S17032 A/61, Lemass to Boland, 25 Nov. 1961.

the principles of the *Programme for economic expansion* and opposed Boland's proposals at every juncture.[48] The Department of Agriculture, through Nagle, argued that the scheme

> raises the fundamental question whether it is to be the government policy (a) to perpetuate very small and uneconomic holdings, or (b) to go ahead gradually with a reasonable consolidation policy and the promotion of employment opportunities in industry and other non-agricultural occupations. In the opinion of the Minister, the policy at (a), which is implied by your department's proposals, is economically and socially unjustifiable. A gradual consolidation of very small holdings is the appropriate policy, and the minister would favour very generous financial terms to the owners of such holdings in order to induce them to sell the holdings to the Land Commission.

Overall, the income supplement scheme was viewed as one which could "offer little in the way of economic improvement – it may, in fact, impede it – and is likely to lead to more claims by farmers for help."[49]

Opposition to the scheme forced Boland to devise ever more complex methods of defining who would benefit from the assistance and its proposed administration soon spanned four departments – Agriculture, Social Welfare, Lands and Finance. Later, the scheme was side-tracked into devising notional systems of means assessment as Boland sought to deflect criticism that his supplement would prove a disincentive to work.[50] When Lemass informed Boland his proposal could not pass through government due to the objections of other ministers, the Taoiseach expressed his disappointment and urged Boland to seek new avenues, saying "it may not be possible to secure an adequate long-term solution at this stage, and we may have to do the best we can."[51] Ultimately, the proposals were lost and, in Boland's own words, joined the legions of "pious hopes that are unlikely to be realised."[52] And perhaps the most instructive moment of Boland's entire project came when, in preparing his proposals, he sought information on how many farmers might fall within his scheme of supplements, what their needs were and how best to address them.[53] None was available as the basic research into the problem simply had not been done.[54]

By the winter of 1963, the initiative had run out of steam – its momentum evaporating as the scale of the problem and the lack of deployed resources sapped the will. The emergence of a Co. Donegal-based priest, Fr James McDyer, as leader of the Charlestown Committee, a body proposing a series of initiatives purporting

[47] NAI, D/T S17474 A/63, Lemass to Boland, 24 May 1963.
[48] See, for example, NAI, D/T S17474 C/95, D/F memo to govt., 7 Aug. 1964.
[49] NAI, D/T S17474 B/63, Nagle to D/SW, 13 Dec. 1963.
[50] NAI, D/T S17474 D/95, D/SW memo to govt., 21 Dec. 1964.
[51] NAI, D/T S17474 C/95, Lemass to Boland, 6 Aug. 1964.
[52] NAI, D/T S17474 A/63, Boland memo to govt., 9 May 1963.
[53] NAI, D/T S17474 A/63, *passim.*

to benefit smallholders, somewhat altered the agenda. At a series of mass meetings across the west, McDyer proclaimed: "This is a revolution." He proposed the establishment of 12 pilot scheme areas of vegetable growing and processing involving Comhlucht Siúcre Éireann.[55] Such was the support the movement enjoyed that the government was forced to establish a committee to report on the proposals and, in March 1964, sanctioned a limited project.[56] McDyer believed it was merely an "anaemic version" of his scheme but, after further consultation, a pilot area programme was agreed for some western counties.[57] According to the report, the pilot areas would be used to "demonstrate what could be accomplished by community effort in making full and proper use of all available resources and facilities so that similar areas elsewhere may be encouraged to apply the same techniques and practices."[58] Only 5 per cent of the 106,000 farmers under 50 acres in the 12 counties involved fell within the remit of the pilot area programme.[59] This was neither the revolution sought by McDyer nor the social cohesion sought by Lemass – but it marked the apotheosis of the latter's initiative to address the position of smallholders in the west.

The relative position of that group continued to worsen and, by the end of the 1960s, "by far the most poverty stricken occupational group in Ireland was the small farmer class."[60] The failure of the state to develop a coherent policy or to provide meaningful support to a community eulogised in official rhetoric remained largely unchecked. Indeed, official policy – not least, subsidy policy – actually worsened the relative position of small farmers. Unable to benefit in any worthwhile manner from guaranteed grain prices, but forced to pay more for feeding stuffs because of these guarantees, the small farmer lost out to the larger farmer. Equally, small farmers in the west fared little better in dairying with, for example, Connacht farmers receiving only £1 million out of a total milk subsidy of £14 million in 1966.[61] Without effective state support, small farmers were exposed even more sharply to the "relentless workings of the market, and the consequences of an agricultural policy based primarily on official perceptions of

---

54 A contemporary request by Michael Kitt, who was in the process of preparing a lecture to a debating society in University College, Galway, for information on what was being done to help residents of the congested districts, led the Taoiseach's department to send a circular letter to each relevant department of government asking for precise information on the schemes implemented under their respective control. The subsequent replies were light on detail and entirely unconvincing, further underlining the incoherent formulation of policy. See NAI, D/T S15848 B/62, *passim.*

55 *The Kerryman*, 15 Jun. 1963

56 NAI, D/T S17032 G/95, Lemass to McDyer, 25 Mar. 1964.

57 *Western People*, 16 May 1964. In 1968, the pilot areas were extended to three times their original size. See *Dáil Debates*, vol. 232, no. 1, cols. 9–10, 31 Jan. 1968.

58 *Report on pilot area development by the inter-departmental committee on the problems of small western farms* (1964), p. 17. And given that it was intended that the pilot areas should inspire the rest of the farming populace with the image that they could aspire to the standards prevailing on the pilot farms, "it would be wrong to provide state help on too lavish a scale." *Ibid.*, p. 17.

59 Smith and Healy, *Farm organisations*, p. 195.

60 Damian F. Hannan, 'Peasant models and the understanding of social and cultural change in rural Ireland', in P.J. Drudy (ed.), *Ireland: Land, politics and people* (1982), p. 162.

61 R. O'Connor, 'Implications of Irish agricultural statistics', in I.F. Bailie and S.J. Sheehy (eds.), *Irish agriculture in a changing world* (1971), p. 36.

economic advantage."[62] Neither the short-term need to raise the standard of living of those presently on the land nor the long-term desirability of developing a viable agricultural farm structure found adequate expression in government policy. Increasingly, the struggle to hold onto small farms, however inadequate and poor, which had been handed through generations, was lost to the market dictate that agricultural prosperity necessitated a substantial degree of farm amalgamation. The stark reality was that Irish small farmers could not hew a profitable existence from their lands. Accordingly, small farms continued to disappear because "what is happening is too big, too widespread and too painfully logical to be reversed."[63]

II

Agriculture and the second programme for economic expansion

Although agricultural production rose through the years of the *Programme for economic expansion*, the failure to meet specified goals or to progress sufficiently in general terms, across the five years from 1958 fundamentally altered the role which the country's single largest industry was accorded in the *Second programme for economic expansion*. That *Second programme* was published in two parts, August 1963 and July 1964, and, in comparison with its predecessor, there was a singular shift in emphasis on the importance of agricultural development. From its primordial status as the engine of the economy, the determinant of national prosperity, the rising tide destined to lift all industrial boats, agriculture was now accepted as incapable of performing the tasks demanded of it. Political sensibilities required that the unveiling of this profundity could not be couched in language so vulgar as to offend the hundreds of thousands who continued to rely on farming for their livelihood – and who, equally, continued to vote. Increasingly, though, the weight of responsibility gravitated towards "industrial exports and services such as tourism rather than to agriculture. This was a profound change in thought."[64] The sounding of the death knell for agricultural pre-eminence in the Irish economy was unmistakable. Obviously, agriculture retained a huge presence, looming large over all economic discourse, but relative decline was officially accepted as now inevitable. Agriculture had not delivered, and could no longer be expected to deliver, national prosperity – what remained was to redefine its role as something

---

[61] R. O'Connor, 'Implications of Irish agricultural statistics', in I.F. Bailie and S.J. Sheehy (eds.), *Irish agriculture in a changing world* (1971), p. 36.

[62] Ó Tuathaigh, 'Land question', p. 181.

[63] *Irish Times*, 21 Nov. 1961.

[64] Meenan, 'Agricultural policies', p. 53.

other than the catalyst in the realisation of inherited social, cultural and economic aspirations.

The *Second programme* considered, albeit superficially, the dilemma of equating the "economic ideal" of producing an expanding supply of marketable foodstuffs through efficient use of manpower, land and other resources, with the "social ideal" of obtaining this increased production while retaining the maximum number of family farms. If that dilemma remained markedly unresolved in government policy, the task facing agriculture now was not to lead the other sectors of the economy to prosperity but to limit the disparity in income between farmers and other sectors of the workforce. Noting that the "maintenance of a reasonable balance between agricultural and non-agricultural incomes is by no means an easily achieved objective," it was, nonetheless, the "aim that the economic family farm should enjoy an acceptable living standard, bearing a reasonable relationship to the living standards afforded by other occupations."[65] Agricultural aspirations were now officially defined in negative terms and damage limitation would henceforth be the order of the day. Moreover, the income levels of farmers would depend on a continued drift from the land. The *Second programme* estimated that between 1960 and 1970 the numbers employed in agriculture would fall by 66,000 from 392,000 to 326,000 – an annual average decrease of 1.8 per cent.[66] The first part of the *Second Programme* proposed an annual average rate of growth for the agricultural sector of 2.7 per cent, thus ensuring that gross agricultural product would be 31 per cent greater in 1970 than it had been in 1960.[67] Significantly, this growth was not predicated on any overhaul of policy, rather "on the assumption that, in the second half of the 1960s, international market arrangements for our agricultural products ... will be considerably improved, as a result, *inter alia*, of our being admitted to membership of the EEC."[68] Notwithstanding the danger of retrospective clarity, this assumption seems to have been based on the shifting sands of wishful thinking rather than being rooted in realistic appraisal. The unequivocal failure of the British application for membership and the subsequent withdrawal of the Irish attempt in 1963 did not lend grounds for even moderate optimism of an early breakthrough on Europe. What likelihood there may have been of early entry was insufficient to serve as the guiding principle of any policy framework.

The publication of *Agriculture in the second programme for economic expansion*, produced by the Department of Agriculture, confirmed the broad thrust of aspiration, but offered little in the way of substantial policy initiatives. Known as the 'brown book', it was an extensive document which re-echoed the necessity to improve research, advisory and education facilities, to refine marketing processes,

---

[65] *Second programme for economic expansion*, part i (1963), pp 21, 22.

[66] *Ibid.*, p. 21. J.C. Nagle told a joint meeting of the Anglo-Irish economic committee that "a fall in the agricultural population was not undesirable." See PRO, MAF 276/37, minutes of meeting, 23 Nov. 1962.

[67] *Second programme for economic expansion*, part i (1963), pp 20–2. By contrast, industrial growth was expected to reach 7 per cent per annum.

[68] *Ibid.*, p. 22.

to expand credit and co-operative facilities, and to develop the main lines of the agricultural economy. The publication restated the growth targets for the rest of the decade as 2.9 per cent a year or a decade-long increase of 33 per cent in the gross product of agriculture. This increase would necessitate an increase of 3.9 per cent a year or 30.3 per cent in total of gross agricultural output by 1970. Fundamentally increased output would be reliant upon the major aim of increasing annual cattle output from 1,126,000 in 1963 to 1,500,000 in 1970.[69] Most pointedly, neither the *Second programme* nor its supplements, offered any firm indication of the level of government investment likely to fund the achievement of these objectives. Typical of this was the vague assurance in the *Second programme* that the government would "do all in their power to assist in the achievement of the agricultural target and will maintain the policy of substantial investment in, and support for, agriculture within the limits of their resources."[70]

Targets remained high, investment remained low, but suffusing the entire process was the implicit assertion that agriculture would no longer dominate the thinking of those charged with leading the state to prosperity. Seán Lemass did not shirk from acknowledging the symbolic passing of the broad policy framework enshrining agricultural dependency which had survived relatively unchallenged for more than four decades of independent government. Speaking in Limerick in the wake of the publication of the *Second programme*, Lemass acknowledged the impossibility of defying the logic of the march of economics across time:

> Change is the law of life, and while we may not always regard the cause of change as beneficial or desirable, it is rarely practical to stop it. There are always people who, in defiance of all human experience, like to think they can stop or put back the clock. But this is not given to us to do, and no matter how much we might yearn to have it otherwise, we must learn to come to terms with the inevitability of change, even when it signifies the passing of a social era which we ourselves have come to know and accept and even feel attracted to, and the ushering in of another about the character of which we may have doubts and fears.

The implacable fall in the numbers employed in agriculture represented a case in point:

> Governments who are trying to plan comprehensively for the future cannot shut their eyes to unattractive possibilities hoping that they will disappear if they are ignored ... The movement of population out of agriculture into other occupations has been going on for very many years and whether we regard it as desirable or not, it seems certain to continue for some time at least.[71]

What the *Programme for economic expansion* had intimated, the *Second*

---

[69] *Agriculture in the second programme for economic expansion* (1964).
[70] *Second programme for economic expansion, part one* (1963), p. 22.

programme confirmed. In defiance of generations of agrarian campaigners, the land was, after all, to be reserved for the bullocks.[72] Where the 1958 initiative had focussed on encouraging a more extensive use of inputs, through fertiliser subsidies, to increase the size of the Irish herd, the *Second programme* was accompanied by a specific fiscal incentive. If cattle output was to increase by the 33 per cent aspired to, an expanded breeding stock was an imperative. In October 1963 the government approved a Department of Agriculture proposal of a scheme of grants to encourage farmers to keep more cows and sought to increase the national herd from 1,300,000 to 1,700,000. Farmers were awarded £15 for each net additional calved heifer, in order to induce them to retain more breeding heifers on their farms rather than selling them as stores or fats.[73] The impact was immediate and, by June 1965, cow numbers had increased by 224,000 – the first truly significant increase in herd numbers in more than a century.[74] After June 1965, the rate of increase effectively stalled yet in June 1967 the cow herd numbered 1,547,800.[75] At that juncture the government agreed with Department of Finance complaints that the country just could not afford

> to pay a farmer £15 for buying or retaining a calved heifer, £30 annually in milk subsidies for milk produced by the heifer and sold to a creamery, a further £50 for an as yet unspecified increase in production whether in terms of milk or cattle or otherwise, and finally a beef subsidy of £15 to £20 at recent rates for each animal slaughtered and exported.[76]

An initial agreement to abandon the scheme was subsequently waived in favour of a Department of Agriculture proposal that the first two cows in the herd would be ineligible for the grant which would now be £8 a cow not selling milk. It was clearly stated that the aim of the scheme was to "discourage the trend towards dairying" and to provide an incentive towards beef production.[77] In its first four years, the scheme cost £8.5m and although its initial impact waned considerably, it was still the most successful domain of agricultural policy in this period.[78]

Overall, though, the mid-term review of the *Second programme* suggested that the general lack of faith in the potential for expeditious agricultural development was well-placed. In November 1966 the Department of Finance claimed that the

---

71 NAI, D/T S17673/95, Lemass speech in Limerick at the launch of the final report of the Limerick Rural Survey, 26 Nov. 1964.

72 Raymond Crotty commented that in setting the proposed 43 per cent increase in cattle output and 17 per cent decrease in employment in farming "the truly awesome thought does not seem to have occurred to the economic planners of the republic that in only one previous recorded decade did change of this order and nature take place in the cattle and human populations of Ireland. The decade was 1841–51." See Crotty, *Agricultural Production*, p. 204.

73 NAI, D/T S17535/63, D/A memo to govt., 19 Oct. 1963 and cabinet minutes, 22 Oct. 1963.

74 NAI, D/T 99/1/405, D/A memo to govt., 27 Nov. 1967, D/F memo to govt., 21 Dec. 1967 and cabinet minutes, 2 Jan. 1968.

75 *Ibid.*

76 *Ibid.*

77 NAI, D/T 99/1/405, D/A memo to govt., 16 Sept. 1968 and cabinet minutes, 1 Nov. 1968.

rate of growth in the agricultural sector between 1964 and 1966 was merely 1.5 per cent, only marginally above the annual average growth over the previous 20 years of 1.25 per cent.[79] The Minister of Finance, James Ryan, had predicted this failure to meet targets when he described the predictions of the Department of Agriculture, in 1963, as excessively optimistic. Ryan doubted the capacity to increase outputs and to find a market for any resultant surplus.[80] The Department of Finance believed that output over the following few years was "likely to reflect a continuation of past trends," and in order to reach projected 1970 targets, an "improbable," average growth rate of 5.75 per cent per annum would be required. It was further noted that all other government departments had agreed to a fundamental reappraisal of their aims and policies except the Department of Agriculture which was refusing to any adjustment to its targets which it claimed remained attainable. The Department of Agriculture made it clear that its refusal to entertain any prospect of a revision of its target growth rates was due, in part, to the clamour which would undoubtedly emerge from farming organisations who would use the downward revision of expectations to press for measures to reduce the disparities in income between its members and workers in other sectors.[81] In the ensuing stand-off with Finance, the Department of Agriculture position was summed up by J.C. Nagle as: "We think they are realistic and you think not. The judgement of which department is to be relied on?"[82]

Realising the aims of the *Second programme* was not facilitated by the poverty of the relationship between farming organisations and the Department of Agriculture. The growth of the ICMSA out of the milk strikes of the early 1950s and the foundation of the NFA in 1955 saw Irish farmers belatedly replicate the organisational moulds of their brethren in other European countries.[83] Previously, meaningful consultation with farmers was denied as a plethora of commodity-specific interest groups proved unable to present a united front.[84] The advent of

[78] *Ibid.*

[79] NAI, D/T 97/6/74, D/F memo to D/A, 4 Nov. 1966.

[80] NAI, D/T S17437 A/63, M/F to Lemass, 10 Jul. 1963.

[81] NAI, D/T 97/6/74, D/F memo to D/A, 4 Nov. 1966.

[82] NAI, D/T 97/6/74, Nagle to D/F, 11 Nov. 1966.

[83] A member of Kilkenny County Committee of Agriculture, M. Medlar, opined: "There is a dire need for a broad-minded farmers' organisation in this country, as Clann na Talmhan are not interested in the farmers any more than the man in the moon … Clann na Talmhan were not real farmers, but were uneconomic holders from the West of Ireland." J.E. Carrigan, the head of ECA in Ireland, was less colourful but no less emphatic, when he stated to Irish farmers: "By giving the Department so much authority you are sacrificing your independence. When you rely too much on the government you will find that you may lose control." See *IFJ*, 26 Feb. 1955 and 29 Jul. 1950. For the role of farming organisations in other European countries see, for example, Smith and Healy, *Farm organisations*, p. 48; Schmidt, 'German agriculture, 1945–53'; and Michele Micheletti, *The Swedish farmers' movement and government agricultural policy* (1990).

[84] Successive agriculture ministers posited the inability of Irish farmers to organise as a central reason why the Department of Agriculture had had to assume so much authority. Paddy Smith commented that he could never get from farmers "a unanimous suggestion as to the course that he and his Department should follow." James Dillon noted that he had to consult with sixty-three organisations to get the farmer's view. The NFA reckoned the number of farmers' groupings stood at ninety-seven. Thomas Walsh stated that, from his experience, a Minister for Agriculture "too often has the experience of receiving a deputation representing one agricultural interest or another and finding that the deputation itself is divided in its views." Smith and Healy commented that "a lesson was learned when Canon Hayes of Muintir na Tíre led Tipperary farmers to the Minister for Agriculture asking for higher grain prices and met a deputation of Cavan pig producers [who had] come to ask for a reduction in feed prices." See *Irish Press*, 14 Jan. 1948; Smith and Healy, *Farm organisations*, p. 22; and *IFJ*, 30 Apr. 1955.

the ICMSA and the NFA saw farmers organise more efficiently but there remained fundamental flaws in this mobilisation.[85] Not least, the deterioration of relations between the two bodies was a sordid affair. Initial failure to merge was succeeded by increasingly poisonous relations rooted in "pride, prejudice, personalities and party politics."[86] Increasingly, the two organisations grew more alike, to such an extent that practical differences in policy were seldom evident. And as similarities grew more pronounced, so also did the fractious nature of the affair. Duplicated delegations and progressively analogous methods neither eased the tension nor revealed the material relevance of its existence. Systematic and very public abuse, as well as the passing of rival pickets, undermined the capacity of either organisation to further the interests of farmers.

Relations between both organisations and the government were scarcely better. Dillon's initial response to ICMSA was to condemn them as "a tendentious political racket," with whom he did not intend to discuss "any matters relating to the creamery industry or anything else."[87] Paddy Smith was equally adamant in his opposition to representatives of both the ICMSA and the NFA. Smith believed that "this thing of deputations from all these conflicting interests in well overdone ... I find it hard to get myself to believe that these people are really serious."[88] By 1959, Smith was particularly exercised by the NFA's "vituperative press campaigns" and "misrepresentation and abusive attacks," while claiming that he himself had remained stoic despite "the medicine I have been swallowing all along." He claimed the NFA approach had been "90 per cent destructive" making it "impossible to establish the kind of policy partnership which you [the NFA] desire."[89] Attitudes hardened as the NFA became increasingly vocal under the leadership of Rickard Deasy after 1962.[90] Smith was distinctly precious in the face of criticism and when Seán Lemass encouraged him to mend fences, he replied:

> I can agree with your view that closer co-operation with the NFA is very desirable, and, apart from anything else, it would make life more pleasant for me and my officials. The real difficulty is to find a basis for fruitful co-operation while the NFA reserve the right to be destructively critical of every move made by me to help farmers, and to

---

[85] Many farmers did not see the need to join the nascent organisations. The NFA's first president, Juan Greene, wrote to Lemass that "the vast bulk of our farmers either do not appreciate the important work the Association is obliged to undertake on their behalf, more especially in the international field, or our mentality is such that we are willing to applaud provided the other fellow pays." See NAI, D/T S16719, Greene to Lemass, 23 Sept. 1959. Greene's views were embodied in a pamphlet issued by North Mayo NFA asserting that not joining its ranks was like drinking in a pub without buying a round: "Too many farmers are not pulling their weight in Ireland." Quoted in *IFJ*, 16 Dec. 1961.

[86] Smith and Healy, *Farm organisations*, pp 233–4. The words of leading NFA member, Joe Bruton, offer an insight: "We were just too far apart. I was there as an IFA man and also as a beef man and on either ground I could find too little in common with the dairy men who had their headquarters in the Golden Vale and, a lot of the time, their hind quarters in the civil war." Quoted in Larry Sheedy, *Milestones and memories: the life and times of Joseph Bruton* (1998), p. 48.

[87] Quoted in, Smith and Healy, *Farm organisations*, pp 221–2.

[88] NAI, D/T S2392 D/94, Smith to Lemass, 30 Dec. 1959.

[89] NAI, D/T S17543 A/63, Smith to Juan Greene, 25 Sept. 1959.

[90] Deasy replaced Juan Greene as President of the NFA in January 1962.

use meetings with me and my officials as the basis for biased attacks on us and on government policy.[91]

In January 1964, Lemass prepared a speech to be delivered at the opening of NFA offices in Limerick which would have elevated the NFA above the ICMSA as the premier representative body of farmers and would have accorded a genuine consultative role for the NFA on policy.[92] Smith replied that the speech could be taken

> to imply that the government's attitude to the NFA in the past has been faulty. In fact it has not been so any time while I've been here. I think that we should hear them out and quietly but firmly say our say ... I wouldn't suddenly forget their antics ... The NFA is ... composed of and controlled by people who never had a friendly attitude towards us as a party ... On the other hand, the ICMSA came into existence years before the NFA ... I know there is plenty of rascality and tangling in this organisation too but it doesn't deserve to be deserted merely in order to put the NFA on the map ... I strongly recommend again that you should not take any course of with them which would imply that they are being picked out by the government as the leading farmers' organisation ... I also think that the idea of your going to Limerick of all places to open the new NFA offices is preposterous.[93]

Again against the wishes of Smith, Lemass, in 1964, sought to present the NFA with a document outlining a blueprint for better relations and a framework for co-operation.[94] For a time such co-operation seemed possible. The replacement in 1964 of Smith as Minister for Agriculture by Charles Haughey suggested potential for an improved atmosphere between farmers and government. Both Haughey and Lemass spoke at a 1965 dinner to mark the tenth anniversary of the founding of the NFA but within a year the promise of progress had evaporated. Government could not respond to the demands of a farming community in decline. A fall in cattle prices, diminished yields and an Agricultural Institute report detailing the impoverished position of farmers fed growing resentment over perceived bias towards the services and industrial sectors. In the descent into acrimony neither side monopolised virtue or vice – but both suffered

---

[91] NAI, D/T S17543 A/63, Smith to Lemass, 20 Nov. 1963.

[92] NAI, D/T S17543 B/95, Lemass to Smith, 2 Jan. 1964.

[93] NAI, D/T S17543 B/95, Smith to Lemass, 8 Jan. 1964. For its part, in a memo the following day, the Department of Agriculture claimed that the "NFA is, unfortunately, still at an immature stage. Its claims and assertions are quite out of proportion to its real performance. The government's policy should be to intimate to the main farm organisations that none of them can at present be regarded as fully representative and that the only organisation the government can recognise as nationally representative will be one formed by the main organisations themselves." *Ibid.*

[94] NAI, D/T S17543 A/95, Lemass to Smith, 17 Jan. 1964 and Smith to Lemass, 14 Jan. 1964. The presentation that same month of the NFA's 'Green book' – a plan for agricultural expansion – was not welcomed by Lemass, though, who remarked: "I am sure that members of the NFA committees had a most enjoyable time putting down on paper all the different ways in which more public money could be spent for the benefit of farmers, but some of them must have had an inkling that, unless the Bog of Allen turns into gold, they were more often than not day-dreaming instead of preparing practical plans." See NAI, D/T S17543 B/95, Lemass speech, 8 Mar. 1964.

from faulty leadership at crucial junctures.[95] By the spring of 1966, the ICMSA was picketing the Dáil in search of higher milk prices and by the summer more than 450 of its members had been arrested. That autumn, the NFA adopted ICMSA methods "to the verge of demagoguery."[96] A farmers' rights march, huge rallies, boycotts, picketing, even a one-man hunger strike, saw events spiral ever-downwards. When farmers blockaded the roads and embarked on commodity strikes, Seán MacEntee later condemned it

> as a piece of egregious and short-sighted folly. Those engaged in it did not seem to be aware that they were embarking on a campaign which might have led to nothing short of civil war … The inevitable consequence of their evil counsels would be to raise the towns against the country; perhaps even bring about a condition verging upon agrarian war.[97]

A state of war – agrarian or civil – was never reached, but the catalogue of strikes, imprisonment and property seizures conspired to derail progress in the agricultural sector for much of the second part of the 1960s. As has been noted: "Most serious was the five-year disruption, even cessation of the work of preparation for the wider common market, for marketing boards, for re-organisation of creameries and marts." For the farmers, it was "a step backwards. It diverted the efforts of committees, NFA staff and organisation to agitation at the expense of planning and construction."[98] Members of the government, for their part, allowed the dispute so affect their judgement that progressive agricultural policies were effectively abandoned in response to immediate necessity. To this end, Neil Blaney, who was installed as Minister for Agriculture in 1966, sought to end NFA membership of the governing body of the Agricultural Institute. More pointedly, proposals on livestock marts were motivated by a desire to undermine the NFA who, Blaney considered, had tried to use the marts "in furtherance of their campaign."[99] The Livestock Marts Act, 1967 was passed after heated Dáil debates and accorded the Minister for Agriculture a wide range of arbitrary powers. It was found, subsequently, to be unconstitutional.

The entire set-to fundamentally impaired the capacity of the agricultural industry to progress. It compounded the debilitating sense that the *Second programme*, imitating its forerunner, "tended to focus on targets and projections as

---

95 According to John Healy in the *Western People* on 10 Sept. 1966, Deasy was too fond of "doing the God bit." In that same paper on 7 Jan. 1967, Healy also remarked on the replacement as Minister for Agriculture of Charles Haughey by Neil Blaney that: "Blaney is of a mould and a temper that he could see them frozen to the footpath and it will not worry him one whit." In respect of Haughey's performance as Minister for Agriculture, it was noted: "Lilies that fester smell far worse than weeds." See Smith and Healy, *Farm organisations*, p. 161.

96 Smith and Healy, *Farm organisations*, pp 236–7.

97 UCDA, Seán MacEntee papers, P67/736(2), MacEntee speech, n.d. The *Irish Press* also quoted MacEntee on 9 Dec. 1966, as saying that the farmers on the streets of Dublin were "landed gentry playing the part of layabouts."

98 Smith and Healy, *Farm organisations*, pp 210, 229.

99 See NAI D/T 98/6/453, D/A memo to govt., 22 May 1967 and NAI, D/T 98/6/920, D/A memo to govt., 23 May 1967.

the ultimate unknowns, as though in many cases the policy instruments could be taken for granted."[100] With the notable exception of the calved heifer scheme, the increase in Irish agricultural output seemed more related to the traditional forces of slow structural change and prevailing market forces than to any policy initiatives emerging from expansionist programmes, however extensive their influence on industry. With myriad factors restraining the capacity to proceed with structural change at a rate much in excess of that allowed by the demographic and societal shifts in Irish life, the dependence on foreign trade policy in the pursuit of agricultural expansion was heightened. Given the continued limited impact of various initiatives in the drive to increase output, the negotiation of profitable markets in Britain and Europe assumed an even greater importance. It proved a task no less arduous than any other undertaken by those involved in the formulation of agricultural policy.

III

In search of foreign markets

Irish economic isolation in the post-independence era seemed as much a matter of policy as of performance. Ireland abjectly failed to develop an industrial structure capable of competing in foreign markets – or, indeed, in home markets without the support of subsidy and tariff – and its limitations in the agricultural sphere were scarcely less damaging. The simple truth remained that, with the exception of store cattle, the Irish performance in efficiently producing marketable goods was so thoroughly inept it dislocated the economy into enforced isolation. The more clearly observable it became that the sale of store cattle to Britain was the sole guaranteed export market of note, the more government policy gravitated towards that practice. And the more it gravitated, the more difficult it became to conceive of a viable alternative. Even as the Irish economy threatened to wither and die in the 1950s, primarily due to the failure to develop a diversified economic culture, the sale of cattle remained the dominant feature in defining export policy. In the ultimate of ironies, so great was the dependency that Ireland could not survive without the trade whose nature threatened the country's very survival. It is in this context that the Irish response to the nascent moves to form trading blocs across Europe must be viewed.

Through the 1950s the post-war initiatives to redevelop European society, primarily through economic co-operation, gathered momentum. Although several of these initiatives, such as the proposed Green Pool, never came to fruition, the response of the Irish government to moves to redefine economic relations in Europe offered a vivid insight into the affairs of the nation. The Green

---

[100] Desmond Norton, *Problems in economic planning and policy formation in Ireland, 1958–74* (1975), p. 30.

Pool, discussions for which were held in Paris from March 1952 to June 1954, was essentially an attempt to establish a common agricultural authority operating on similar lines to the European Coal and Steel Community (ECSC). Eventually the difficulties encountered in attempting to harmonise the agricultural policies of the disparate European countries proved insurmountable and the enterprise ended in failure. The Irish quietly welcomed this failure as they had opposed the development from the outset. Considering the address which the Irish representative should give to a Green Pool meeting in Paris, the Department of Agriculture had commented:

> Careful consideration has been given to this matter and it has been concluded that the French plan is ... essentially inimical to the interests of this country. If the plan includes Britain, Ireland will lose her preferential position on that market both in regard to quantitative outlets and prices. If the plan excludes Britain but comprises the principal Western European countries, it may bring about strong political and economic pressure on the British to abandon or abate their preferential treatment of us ... The British have already indicated to the Irish Ambassador in London that they do not welcome the plan and that they are prepared to extend to it only the minimum international courtesies. It is not considered that this country should put itself in the position of making it more difficult for the British to resist these proposals which in the long run might be more to Ireland's disadvantage than to Britain's ... Ireland is in principle opposed to any line of policy liable to create upheavals in the social structure. This would be a logical effect of the implementation of the Plan ... It is important ... that we should fully realise where our real interests lie and do nothing which would encourage the development of the idea of an integrated market for agricultural products or make it more difficult for other countries to resist it.[101]

This ethos of apprehension defined the Irish approach to greater European integration over the following decade. Ireland operated on the premise that no benefits accruing from closer integration with the continent could make good the probable loss of agricultural preferences on the British market.[102] This perception remained unaltered through the negotiations on European free trade areas originating from OEEC proposals in 1956. In the wake of the move of ECSC to establish a customs union, these proposals involved the consideration of the creation of a free trade area between the six ECSC countries, and the remaining member states of the OEEC. The Irish reaction was unswervingly negative. The Department of Industry and Commerce commented that trade liberalisation was "something in which we had to acquiesce for the sake of international appearance

---

101 NAI, D/T S15011 A, D/A memo to govt., 21 Mar. 1952

102 See Brian Girvin, 'Irish agricultural policy, economic nationalism and the possibility of market integration in Europe,' in Richard T. Griffiths and Brian Girvin (eds.), *The Green Pool and the origins of the common agricultural policy* (1995), pp 239–71.

but which this country would be better off without."[103] There was no sense of either opportunity or of necessity: "Farmers generally, and this is any case true of our farmers, are rather conservative and are much more interested in the stability of markets than in ambitious schemes for international integration."[104] Accordingly, the departments of Agriculture, and Industry and Commerce did not feel the need to send representatives to the Paris negotiations although the government was represented by its ambassador to France and a governmental committee of secretaries was empowered to analyse the consequences of free trade on the Irish economy.[105]

In November 1957 the Department of Agriculture outlined its philosophy that the British market continued to offer the best prospects for Irish agriculture and that, in the event of a European free trade area, including Britain, being established, it would be best for Ireland if agriculture were excluded. This interpretation rested on the assertions that the opening of the Irish home market to foreign competitors in such products as butter would leave Irish producers at the mercy of the Dutch and the Danes, amongst others, and that Ireland would equally struggle to compete on an equal basis with OEEC countries in the British market. The department viewed with great concern the prospect that the link between Irish store cattle and the 1948 agreement would be endangered and, consequently, found itself in full support of the broad British negotiating position that agriculture be excluded from any free trade area.[106] A special delegation from the OEEC visited Dublin in June 1957 and was critical of the Irish approach, particularly its acceptance that agriculture should be excluded from any free trade arrangements. Highlighting the extreme dependence on the British market, the delegation considered that Ireland should attempt to expand its exports to the continent where access would improve through free trade and where markets could expand, notably through a projected rise in meat consumption.[107] This view was not adopted by the government who considered that its policy should continue to be based on the preservation of the existing preferences enjoyed by Irish agricultural produce in Britain. To this fundamental aim was added the secondary wish that OEEC countries would ease the restrictions placed on agricultural imports from states whose economies were dependent on the export of such products. It was a policy neatly outlined by the Minister for Agriculture, Seán Moylan: "We want non-discrimination on the continent and at the same time the preservation and strengthening of our present agricultural provisions in the British market."[108]

In an attempt to both clarify and further these policy aims, a series of meetings were held with British officials. These did nothing to ease the

---

[103] NAI, D/T S15281/A, D/IC memo to govt., 13 Oct. 1956.

[104] NAI, D/T S14638 N, Cremin to D/EA, 10 May 1954.[105] The members of the committee were the secretaries to the departments of Agriculture, Finance, Industry and Commerce, and External Affairs, respectively.

[106] NAI, D/T S15281 B, D/A memo to govt., 7 Nov. 1956.

[107] NAI, D/T S15281 I, report by W.P. Fay to Irish govt., 28 May 1957.

[108] NAI, D/T S15281 L, D/A memo to govt., 31 Oct. 1957.

apprehension of the Irish whose officials noted after one such meeting that the entire discussion was devoid of substance as the British clearly wished to avoid detailed analysis of the possible implications of a free trade area.[109] By November 1957 the Irish governmental delegation, in advance of a meeting with British counterparts, stressed its need to ascertain the British view of the "special relationship" between the two countries, as it "would not be realistic to go into this question until we had some idea of the British intentions in our regard."[110] Irish desires that they should obtain some commitment that their rights in the British market would be safeguarded regardless of free trade area developments were rejected by British officials determined not to make any commitments in advance of the Paris talks.[111] The Irish delegation, led by Lemass, took the opportunity, however, to press for the removal of the 3s 6d per cwt. differential in the application of the British price support scheme for store cattle. This was roundly rejected by the British side, one of whose officials complained that this request and "the other issues which Nagle raised of free entry in the UK market and joint consultation on agricultural policies are no more than an impertinence at this stage."[112] The position of the Irish was of little concern to the British and as a Treasury official noted, even the Irish advantage in store cattle would come under threat in the event of free trade area agreement:

> To the extent that continental countries cannot easily meet the requirements of our animal health regulations (e.g. as regards foot and mouth disease), the Irish Republic's market in the United Kingdom is fortuitously protected. This advantage could disappear if another Free Trade Area country, say France, succeeded in developing a regular disease-free exportable surplus of cattle.[113]

Lacking reassurance from the British, the Irish policy throughout 1958 was to hold the line in the hope that events would fall in their favour. The collapse of the negotiations to create a free trade area between the six members of the EEC, as the ECSC was restyled, and the other members of the OEEC brought temporary assurance that Ireland's position in the British market was not immediately threatened. The *Irish Farmers' Journal* did not feel moved to celebrate:

> For this melancholy ending to an expansionary dream we ourselves have a lot to explain. We neither determined nor fought for our objectives, we left it to others to make the running and we unfortunately prayed for this indecisive outcome so that we could relax in our customary uncomplicated dependence on the British market and our tariff structure.[114]

---

[109] NAI, D/T S14042 J, note on meeting with British officials, 6 Mar. 1957.
[110] NAI, D/T S14042 I, minutes of meeting of Irish delegation to discuss meetings with Britain on proposed free trade area, 7 Nov. 1957.
[111] NAI, D/T S14042 J, D/A memo to govt., 12 Dec. 1957.
[112] PRO, MAF 40/271, MAF note, 6 Dec. 1957.
[113] PRO, MAF 40/471, report by 'Closer economic association with Europe: working group on the Irish Republic', 1 Jan. 1958.
[114] *IFJ*, 23 Aug. 1958. Later, writing in the same newspaper, the columnist 'Farm Economist' considered that the failure to develop a wider free trade area would prove only a temporary drawback in what he considered a process which "long before it has tapered off, its explosive effects will have transformed Europe as profoundly as the Renaissance and the era of discoveries." *IFJ*, 15 Nov. 1958.

There was no opportunity to relax, however, as Britain led six other countries in the creation of a European Free Trade Association (EFTA) effectively dividing Europe into two trading blocs: the EEC and EFTA. Ireland did not seek involvement in EFTA which focused on industrial rather than agricultural trade, but chose instead to work for closer economic relations with Britain with a view to strengthening Ireland's position within the British market. The Irish approach was determined by the belief that none of the EFTA countries, with the exception of Britain, carried reasonable prospects of proving an export outlet for Irish livestock or livestock products, particularly given Denmark's more favourable geographical location.[115] This was in marked contrast to the Danish approach of participating in EFTA with a view to negotiating concessions in agricultural trade from its new partners.[116] By the middle of 1959, Denmark had negotiated a bilateral agreement with Britain which provided for the reduction of customs duties on imported Danish bacon and cheese. Further, the agreement effectively guaranteed Danish farmers an increased share in the British market and brought the commitment to provide reasonable safeguards in the event of the introduction of quantitative import restrictions.[117] A series of editorials in the *Irish Farmers' Journal* expressed increasing disillusion at the apparent failure to look beyond the British market, or even to safeguard its position in that market. Ireland was now "an island more isolated," and "the only major agricultural exporting European country without the framework for price improvement or expansion in volume of export." At the very minimum, the "revision of our existing agreements with Britain is now definitely demanded."[118]

In the second half of 1959, the Irish government pursued such a revision and sought, once more, the abolition of the 3s 6d per cwt. differential on store cattle, removal of the possibility of the imposition of quantitative restrictions on imports of Irish agricultural produce by Britain, the maintenance of existing preferential margins, and consultation on future agricultural and marketing policies.[119] The broad aim of the Irish was to secure, not free trade, but what effectively amounted to a common market on agriculture. It is a moot point whether the Irish seriously expected to obtain any of these goals (so reminiscent of ones sought in 1948) but, regardless, the initiative held no prospects for success.[120] Although the Irish sought "a form of economic association," a meeting

---

[115] D.J. Maher, *The tortuous path, 1948–1973* (1986), pp 91–3.

[116] Denmark made bilateral agreements with Britain (1960 and 1963), and with Sweden (1960 and 1963), Norway (1963) and Portugal (1965). See Historical Archives of the European Communities, OECD/1006.

[117] The NFA responded to the news of the Danish agreement with an article on trade policy entitled 'Now we're f**cked'. See Smith and Healy, *Farm organisations*, p. 140.

[118] *IFJ*, 27 Jun. 1959, 18 Jul. 1959 and 25 Jul. 1959.

[119] Maher, *Tortuous path*, p. 95.

[120] Brian Cowler has argued that contemporary statements by Lemass demonstrated that the Irish government never anticipated that the proposals made would be accepted. He quotes Lemass as implying that he merely presented the ideas to the British in an attempt to give the lie to the notion that a free trade area was an option. Lemass argued that unless he flushed out the proposal "the idea of such an arrangement would continue to be regarded by some of our people as feasible and would continue to be advocated, thereby distracting attention from the realistic aspects of our national economic development programme." See Brian Cowler, 'Irish agriculture and European integration 1956–72', (Ph.D., UCD, 1998), p. 89.

of British officials preparing for the talks noted "that nothing the Irish could say, would or could move Her Majesty's Government to 'improve' the terms of their agreement with us which in the [Board of Trade] President's view was too favourable to them already."[121] At the first of many meetings between the two sides between July 1959 and March 1960, Lemass attempted to pursue his government's international trading policy and was reported as stating that "the Republic was not a member of the General Agreement on Tariffs and Trade (GATT). They were thus able to think very much in terms of a bilateral solution to their problems ... He had in mind a movement towards the integration of the Irish and United Kingdom economies."[122] Later, a British Ministry of Agriculture official commented that Lemass "realises that there is no future for Ireland save in close connection with this country. Irish hopes of a market on the continent have completely evaporated ... He wants to turn the clock back – to say goodbye to the Battle of the Boyne."[123]

A series of meetings with British officials in the remaining months of 1959 did not hold out improved prospects of positive development. Indeed, the signing of the bilateral trade agreement between Britain and Denmark marked a further downturn in the Irish position. It signalled a definite change in British policy on agricultural imports and, as such fundamentally undermined Irish trade policy "one of whose principal objectives was to secure improved trading relations with Britain before that country entered into binding commitments with its partners among the Seven [EFTA]."[124] A meeting of British officials from a range of ministries remarked that the accord with the Danes should be kept in mind through the talks with the Irish.[125] The diminishing opportunities for Irish exports to Britain were noted in the acknowledgement that the agreement with the Danes would damage Irish bacon imports, that the increasing efficiency of Irish agriculture would allow "the prospect of no more than maintaining their place in an increasingly competitive market," and that it was "impossible to be optimistic about the Republic's economic future." Nonetheless, the officials did stress the value of offering some concession to the Irish in the interests of friendly relations and of seizing "this opportunity to recast the pattern of our trade with the Republic to our own advantage."[126] Emphasising the Irish incomprehension of the changing nature of trading relations, as well as the failure to draw significant concessions led Nagle to lament that "the English seemed to look upon this much more as a horse-trader's bargain than as a genuine attempt to get rid of Strongbow and Cromwell and to start a new spirit in Anglo-Irish relations."[127]

---

121 PRO, MAF 40/472, Irish govt. memo to British govt., 30 Jul. 1959 and MAF note, 9 Jul. 1959.

122 PRO, MAF 40/472, Minutes of meeting of Lemass and President of Board of Trade, 13 Jul. 1959.

123 PRO, MAF 40/472, R.E. Stedman note, 14 Jul. 1959. Stedman later noted that the Irish initiative was partly because "the creation of new groupings in Europe makes them feel very lonely." See PRO, MAF 40/473, Stedman note, 15 Dec. 1959.

124 Maher, *Tortuous path*, p. 99.

125 PRO, MAF 40/472, minutes of meeting between CRO, B/T, and Treasury officials, 11 Aug. 1959.

126 PRO, MAF 40/473, report of the working group on economic relations with the Irish Republic, 7 Dec. 1959.

127 PRO, MAF 225/978, A.J.D. Winnifrith note on private dinner with Nagle, 15 Feb. 1960.

The talks at Ministerial level were conducted amidst a heightened level of public expectation fostered by the Irish government as "with so much happening in Europe on the trade front and in particular the EFTA convention being signed shortly, Ministers in Dublin were under pressure to demonstrate that they were watching their own corner."[128] The British refrained from offering any meaningful concessions to Irish demands, arguing that the extra cost to their exchequer would prove unacceptable, and that British farmers would not tolerate the further extension of deficiency payments to Irish agricultural products. The developing trade relationships across Europe further limited room for manoeuvre, particularly the desire not to enter long-term commitments inimical to potential free trade interests. Ultimately, the arrangements reached in April 1960 allowed the removal of the 3s 6d per cwt. differential in the case of attested cattle, gave a formal contractual arrangement linking the prices of Irish sheep and lambs to British prices at a differential of ¾d per pound, and the agreement not to reduce or eliminate preferential margins without consultations with the Irish government. For the Irish, the agreement was a thorough disappointment offering only "minor concessions."[129] Even those concessions were hollow ones. The quantity of Irish store cattle then attested and available for export was so negligible as to render that clause of no immediate value, even if, potentially, it could prove worthwhile.[130] The right to consultation was dismissed privately by the British who noted "presentationally, this is a concession to the Irish but it does little more than give formal sanction to existing administrative arrangements." And even the contractual arrangement agreed on sheep was no call for celebration: "At no time have the Republic asked us to remove the differential on sheep and lambs. Although this concession was approved by the Cabinet, we have held it up our sleeve and there has been no necessity to offer it."[131] The context of broader European development compounded the disappointment of an agreement which left a bitter taste. Disillusioned, the *Irish Farmers' Journal* quoted a British journalist as remarking that "typically, the UK government has offered a carrot for the Irish donkey to strain after – little nibbles which do not cost much, but which will be the spur until a convulsive effort enables one big bite to be taken."[132]

---

[128] PRO, MAF 40/473, CRO note of discussions with Irish ambassador, McCann, 17 Nov. 1959.

[129] *IFJ*, 5 Mar. 1960.

[130] PRO, MAF 225/978, MAF note, Jan. 1960. It was estimated that this concession would cost the British £150,000 in 1960–61, rising eventually to a total cost of £750,000 per annum.

[131] PRO, MAF 225/978, CRO memo, 11 Mar. 1960.

[132] *IFJ*, 30 Apr. 1960. The comment was taken from the British *Farmers' Weekly* newspaper.

IV

Irish agriculture and Europe

Standing beyond the pale of two developing trading blocs was scarcely the most strategic position for a country with a recently avowed intent to expand its export markets as the cornerstone of an expansionary economic policy.[133] Nor did 'straining after carrots' conjure images of an alluring long-term vista – there was a resultant sense that Ireland remained trapped in an economic twilight zone. If official policy seemed to have reached something of an impasse, however, farmers increasingly called for a more integrated relationship with European markets. Originally, the NFA had fully supported government attempts to secure elevated status in the British market. Disenchanted by the 1960 Anglo-Irish trade arrangements, it despaired of the British market which had degenerated into "a food-dumping melee."[134] Although it had not managed to absorb all farmers' organisations into its structures following its foundation in 1954, the NFA was developing a potent voice and potential Irish membership of the EEC was the issue which saw it truly move to centre stage. As it became clear that the proposals for agriculture being formulated by the EEC seemed certain to benefit Irish farmers, the NFA intensified its demands that Ireland investigate the possibility of joining in the community "as a consequence of our failure to obtain a fairer deal for our agriculture in the recent review of the Anglo-Irish Trade Agreement, we should now make a serious and thorough examination of policy in consideration of becoming a partner in the EEC."[135]

Unburdened by the obligation to cater for the needs of the entire community rather than a sectional interest, the NFA saw Europe as a sanctuary offering immediate respite. It argued that an Irish application for membership could proceed regardless of British intentions on the matter. The NFA viewed with considerable relish the prospect that Irish farmers might have access to an expanding market uninhibited by a cheap food policy but committed to ensuring a comparable (and high) income for all sectors of the economy. It was attracted even more by the provision of guaranteed prices for many agricultural products at a relatively high level. By contrast, the Department of Agriculture was much more cautious in its approach. Although it welcomed the prospect of higher prices and expanding markets, it could not contemplate entry should Britain not accede at the same moment. It was perceived that association to British guaranteed prices on cattle might be threatened and, in the event of any restrictions on the entry of store cattle to Britain, the Irish economy would be in genuine difficulty.[136] The Department of Finance echoed these sentiments and reaffirmed the traditional

---

[133] *Programme for economic expansion* (1957), *passim.*

[134] *IFJ*, 8 Jul. 1961.

[135] NAI, D/T S16877 A, NFA D/A memo to govt., 20 Jul. 1960.

[136] NAI, D/T S16877 D, D/A memo to govt., 20 Jul. 1960.

wisdom which governed Irish export policy: "It does not appear that association in any form with the EEC, even if it included the full integration of our agriculture in the Common Market with long-term price stability at a fairly high level, would afford as good a basis for the expansion of Irish agricultural production as would similar arrangements with the UK."[137] From both departments, the inference was clear that Ireland should only consider applying for membership of the EEC if Britain was doing likewise. This effectively defined government policy and, although it was accepted that the best scenario would involve both countries entering the common market simultaneously, the prospects of British membership seemed so slight before 1961 that no worthwhile planning on process, prospects or policy was undertaken by the Irish who resumed their waiting game.

When, in the wake of intensive contacts between EEC members and the British government in the early months of 1961, the indications reached the Irish government that Britain was considering applying for membership, Ireland moved to shadow its neighbour. Lemass wrote to British Prime Minister, Harold Macmillan, asking to be kept informed of any prospective British move to membership and stating "should your government decide to take that step, my government would consider applying for membership also, endeavouring to secure such terms as would satisfactorily take account of our economic circumstances."[138] Forced to act by British moves to apply, the Irish government published a white paper on Ireland's relationship with the EEC.[139] The white paper offered little more than an historical record of the moves towards the creation of the EEC and the nature of that trading area, and it essentially restricted its policy analysis to reaffirming that the status of its trade with Britain would be the defining factor in any decision on whether or not Ireland should join the EEC.[140] The NFA considered that, in terms of offering an insight into government thought on the EEC, the white paper was "practically useless," and that it had expected a "more dynamic approach."[141] Neither was dynamism the characteristic most widely associated with the Department of Agriculture's activities in the light of the announcement on 31 July 1961 that Ireland was applying for membership of the EEC. As well as criticism from farming organisations, the department was condemned for the lethargy of its response by a host of newspapers and journals.[142] The department was inclined to blame the NFA for spreading black propaganda against it and this did little to facilitate a harmonious process of policy assessment. Pointedly, there was much unfavourable comparison with the energetic response of the Department of Industry and Commerce.

---

[137] Quoted in Cowler, 'Irish agriculture and European integration', p. 113. See NAI, D/T S16887 I, D/F memo to govt., n.d.

[138] PRO, PREM 11/4320, Lemass to Macmillan, 10 Jun. 1961.

[139] *European economic communities* (1961).

[140] *Ibid.*, p. 7.

[141] Quoted in, Cowler, 'Irish agriculture and European integration', p. 120.

[142] See, for example, criticism in *Irish Independent*, 30 Apr. 1962, *Irish Times*, 25 Apr. 1962 and *The Economist*, 28 Apr. 1962. See also Cowler, 'Irish agriculture and European integration', pp 125–7.

The department did commission reports from survey teams and from a team of European marketing consultants.[143] These reports were at one in stressing the need to improve virtually every aspect of the agricultural economy and laid great emphasis on the need to improve quality of product, as well as promotion and marketing. It was a timely reminder of Garret Fitzgerald's warning that "if we enter the common market suffering from the delusion that it will mean more money all round for Irish agriculture *as it is today,* the subsequent disillusionment could be disastrous."[144] Fitzgerald's words were supported by NFA president, Juan Greene, in June 1962 when he argued that "at all costs we must avoid the Common Market being used as an excuse for inaction and becoming a solution for all our ills; there is no utopia for agriculture ... The Common Market will provide us with a greater opportunity. It is for us to grasp and exploit to the best of our ability the opportunity it offers."[145] This did nothing to dampen the rampant enthusiasm of the majority of farmers and farm commentators who saw in Europe the panacea to Irish agricultural ills. Their views were condensed in the comment of ICMSA officials to Seán Lemass that "the Common Market is the answer to our problems and we should keep the traditional milk producer in production pending our entry."[146]

That Irish entry remained consequent on British negotiations with the EEC was never in real question. The Irish may have insisted in the light of their own application that they would pursue accession irrespective of the success of Britain's application, but this was not considered realistic by either the British or by the EEC members.[147] Throughout the talks there was close contact between the Irish and British governments, although the Irish were inevitably in the weaker position.[148] In preparation for meetings between Irish and British ministers to discuss their respective applications, the best assurance that the British could offer was the hope that, in the transition to Common Agricultural Policy (CAP) and Common Market *modus operandi* "the trade in agricultural products between our two countries was not subject to any sudden changes."[149] Nagle later commented that, at least for some sections of the Irish agricultural economy, the adjustment process "could be very painful."[150] Assessing the Irish application, British officials noted that "the Republic's main incentive for joining the Common Market would

---

143 *Report of the survey team on the dairy produce industry (1962); Report of the survey team on the bacon and pigmeat industry (1963); Report of the survey team on the beef, mutton and lamb industry* (1963); and, NAI, D/T S17426 R, report of market consultants on the marketing of Irish agricultural products in Europe, Jul. 1962.

144 *IFJ,* 15 Jul. 1961.

145 Quoted in, Smith and Healy, *Farm organisations,* p. 139.

146 NAI, D/T S11762 L/62, D/T note of ICMSA delegation meeting with Lemass, 14 Mar. 1962.

147 PRO, MAF 379/34, MAF note, 5 Oct. 1962.

148 In this respect, the Irish provided the British with a copy of their written replies to the EEC questionnaire which they were obliged to answer and copies of the records of their meetings with EEC officials. The British were not quite so forthcoming. In response to a reply to a request for information on British views on the CAP and its possible impact on British agricultural policy, the preparation of a memorandum which gave only the most vague of analyses drew approval from A.J.D. Winnifrith: "This is good anodyne stuff which won't add much to the sum of human knowledge." See PRO, MAF 379/33, Winnifrith note, 14 Jul. 1961.

be the protection of its trade with the United Kingdom. An additional incentive is the prospect of access to continental markets," and concluded that British interests would be "best served by the entry of the Irish Republic into the Common Market. Were she to stay out we should lose our privileged position in her market."[151]

Although the Irish policy was one of following Britain in respect of application, this did not extend to supporting the British negotiating position in agriculture. The finalisation of the CAP in January 1962 was swiftly followed by British attempts to renegotiate its terms in an attempt to safeguard their own farmers, the position of farmers from Australia and New Zealand, and its cheap food policy. Ireland opposed the British proposals which would effectively have amounted "to excluding a large part of agriculture from the Common Market altogether."[152] As these negotiations between the British and the EEC continued, Ireland was in large part a spectator – and when the British entry collapsed in January 1963, the Irish lapsed into limbo. Almost two years of drifting towards Europe ended in all too familiar isolation. Significantly, though, there was a sea change in public and political opinion – Europe had not brought salvation but the emerging consensus was that it retained that potential. Lemass told the Dáil that Ireland would "continue to prepare and plan for our entry to an enlarged Community, taking every step which will further this objective and avoiding any that might make it more difficult to attain."[153] In the meantime, the search for a more remunerative export market for agricultural produce returned to familiar territory.

---

[149] PRO, MAF 379/33, MAF note, 18 Jul. 1961. In preparation for the first of these meetings in July 1959 personality reports on the Irish representatives were circulated. These reports noted that Lemass "seems to have little of the typical Irishman in his make-up. He is said to be of Jewish origin and his appearance does not belie this theory ... [He is] pleasant and courteous to meet but is not endowed with much charm or personal magnetism." James Ryan, Minister for Finance was "an amiable but not very impressive man." Finally, in respect of the secretary of the Department of Agriculture, J.C. Nagle, it was noted: "though at first sight a lugubrious-looking individual (responsibility for maintaining Irish agricultural exports in the face of European economic groupings from which the Republic is excluded is a daunting one), his gloomy appearance conceals a sharp intellect and a considerable flair for patient and astute negotiation." See PRO, MAF 379/33, personality reports, Jul. 1961.

[150] PRO, MAF 276/37, minutes of meeting between MAF and D/A, 5 Oct. 1962.

[151] PRO, MAF 379/33, CRO note, 5 Jul. 1961.

[152] NAI, D/T S17426 M, D/A memo to govt., Jul. 1962.

[153] Quoted in, Maher, *Tortuous path*, p. 163.

V

Agriculture and the 1965 Anglo-Irish Free Trade Agreement

In another classic paradox of Irish trade policy, it was the belief that it was imperative to ultimately lessen dependence on the British market which led Ireland once again to seek still closer ties with that country. Within two months of the January 1963 debacle over Europe, Seán Lemass wrote to Harold Macmillan and espoused a general commitment "to maintain a pace of reorganisation and development which will bring us, as soon as possible, to a sufficiently high degree of economic strength and competitiveness to keep our place in a world of freer trade, and to assume, when the time comes the obligations of membership of the community." To this end, he stressed the importance of

> improved access to the United Kingdom market for our agricultural exports at prices giving a fair return to our farmers. We have no expectation of placing vastly increased supplies of agricultural products on your market; apart from cattle, our agricultural exports represent only a very modest proportion of your food imports. But it is very important, as I have already said, that we should have the support of an efficient and healthy agricultural industry for the economic development we wish to achieve in this decade.[154]

The twin pillars of export policy over the remainder of the decade came sharply into focus. Lemass was clearly intent on not merely improving the efficiency of the Irish economy in the expectation of alignment with a wider trading bloc, he was also motivated by a desire to defend the Irish position in the British market against its competitors and against British reforms of its agricultural policy. That policy reform saw Britain confirm its commitment to maintain a system of guaranteed prices and deficiency payments. A definite boundary of Exchequer outlay would be set, however. This boundary would be defined by placing a limit on the volume of home production which would qualify for guaranteed prices and by seeking agreements with overseas suppliers to regulate imports either by quantity or by minimum prices. In signalling the demise of open-ended commitment to agricultural supports in favour of a managed agricultural market, the British were jeopardising the entire Irish programme of agricultural expansion by restricting the prospects of sale on the sole export market of note. Lemass was moved to expand on his March letter with a further epistle in May 1963:

---

[154] PRO, MAF 276/38, Lemass to Macmillan, 27 Mar. 1963

We have in mind an arrangement which could be expressed in free-trade-area or common-market terms and thus satisfy international rules ... Basically what we would like to see is a gradual harmonisation of agricultural production and prices in the two countries ... Cattle are our staple export and ... the indications are that our dependence on them will be no less great in the future ... For butter, bacon and other products we need arrangements based on recognition of the fact that – due to various causes, including the distortion of competitive conditions – our agriculture has not had the opportunity contemplated in the 1938 and subsequent Trade Agreements of realising its potential and securing a reasonable share of your market. You will understand, therefore, that the freezing of the existing pattern of markets and trade would be unacceptable to us.

Lemass called again for detailed negotiations and for "Irish interests and objections" to be taken fully into account in formulating decisions on future food and agricultural policy.[155] There was certain sympathy on the British side to the renewed Irish approach, but this was political more than economic. The British ambassador in Dublin, Sir Ian McClennan, suggested that it would be a pity to "rebuff the Irish," especially as "it is not in our interest that this country should become impoverished. There is small place in a prosperous Republic for a militant IRA, but we have suffered in the past from an Ireland overpopulated and underemployed and we shall suffer again if these conditions return to the Republic."[156] These views were supported by the Commonwealth Relations Office which noted the "political advantage for us in drawing the Republic's economy even closer towards our own; this helps to soften Irish grievances about partition."[157] A Ministry for Agriculture official did not see any scope for compromise: "What more can we do for the Irish Republic on agriculture short of either in effect subsidising it or discriminating in some way against other suppliers. Neither of these highly unattractive prospects is at all compatible with the new agricultural policy, from which we could not exempt the Irish Republic."[158] A further official commented that "however much the more responsible Irish circles may be regretting the course of events since 1920," it seemed impossible that many concessions could be made, although, for political reasons, flat rejection was not considered appropriate either: "At the worst, discussions of this sort will simply run the whole issue into the sands; at the best, they could help to recommend our own proposals which will have to be put to the Irish as well as to our other suppliers for bacon, beef, mutton and lamb."[159] Throughout the early stages of this emerging

155 PRO, MAF 276/38, Lemass to Secretary of State, Duncan Sandys, 31 May 1963.

156 MAF 276/38, McClennan to MAF, 3 Apr. 1963.

157 PRO, MAF 276/38, CRO memo on Lemass proposals, 8 May 1963 and 18 Feb. 1964. The Home Office was not convinced of the validity of these arguments: "We are inclined to doubt whether prosperity in the Irish Republic does in fact reduce the risk of a recurrence of terrorist activities. The sort of men who make up the gangs are unlikely to be influenced by any rational considerations. On the other hand, it may well be that greater prosperity in the Republic diminishes the support for terrorist activities." See PRO, MAF 276/39, Home Office memo, 20 Feb. 1964.

158 PRO, MAF 276/38, MAF note, Jun. 1963.

159 PRO, MAF 276/38, MAF note, Jul. 1963.

process, the British were sceptical of the actual ends sought by the Irish. Mindful of the 1960 talks which had begun in a similar free trade vein but eventually focused on isolated commodity concessions, the British view was that "the Irish are hoping for something on bacon and meat ... all the other talk is just wrappings ... In short, we will have to go the long way round, via an inevitably fruitless discussion on the custom unions and free trade areas to get to the point about meat and bacon arrangements."[160]

The British ultimately decided on a reply to Lemass which was

guarded, but not altogether negative. It should offer to explore the Taoiseach's proposals in detail, so as at once to avoid giving offence, to keep open the possibilities of political advantage, to bring out the difficulties of significantly closer economic association, and perhaps to disclose whether a few minor concessions might not satisfy Eire.[161]

Eventually, in September 1963, Macmillan wrote to Lemass offering exploratory bilateral discussions at official level, the first of which could occur in November as part of the annual meeting so that "the press and the public would not suspect that anything was afoot."[162] As Whitaker noted to British officials, however, discussions between Britain and its other suppliers would be settled in pattern at that point and would "limit the freedom of manoeuvre in virtually every field in which the Irish could hope to improve their prospects in the United Kingdom ... He judged that from a realistic point of view the United Kingdom was pretty well determined on the course of its agricultural policy and that this would leave very little scope for an increase in the exports of Irish produce." Sir William Armstrong replied to Whitaker that he was, indeed, correct to assume there was little scope available.[163]

Armstrong's point was reinforced in November 1963 when a market-sharing accord on pigmeat was concluded. This agreement allocated all countries, including Britain, itself a quota, as well as a proportional share of any subsequent market expansion. The Irish quota of 27,000 tons of bacon per annum offered little possibility for significant expansion, even though this was an adequate figure in immediate terms and the Department of Agriculture considered that "the bacon position can be described as reasonably satisfactory in the circumstances."[164] This agreement also allocated to Ireland a confidential pork quota of 24,000 tons over five years to facilitate Irish expansion plans under the *Programme for economic expansion*. If the pork and bacon accords were accepted as reasonable, the market sharing arrangements on butter were regarded as entirely

---

[160] PRO, MAF 276/38, MAF note, 26 Sept. 1963.

[161] PRO, MAF 246/321, W.A. Nield report, 1 Aug. 1963.

[162] PRO, MAF 276/38, Macmillan to Lemass, 13 Sept. 1963.

[163] PRO, MAF 276/38, minutes of meeting between Irish and British officials at the Treasury, 18 Sept. 1963.

[164] NAI, D/T S12846 D/2/63, D/A memo to govt., 5 Nov. 1963.

unsuitable. Under a complex formula, related to existing and traditional performance on the British market, Irish exporters were originally granted a quota of 4,000 tons for 1961–2, but this was later increased to 12,000 tons for 1962–3. That increase was allowed only after the British government had imposed a prohibitive anti-dumping duty on Irish butter, pricing it completely out of the British market, after the Irish had refused initially to restrict exports.[165] Even the improved quota was a constant source of dispute between the two countries and was particularly opposed by the Irish in the light of the expansion in milk production in the early years of the 1960s. At the very moment that Ireland eventually secured a sustained increase in its dairy products, the British market progressively tightened, affording little prospect of increased Irish exports. The situation was beyond Irish control because, as one British official noted, the butter quotas "are mainly for the benefit of New Zealand and Australia."[166]

Following the talks on bacon imports, the Lemass initiative continued to be dominated by commodity issues as discussions on meat-market sharing loomed large. Within these talks on beef and cattle, the Irish "reiterated the need to regard Irish imports as, in fact, a facet of home production." The confirmation that there would be no limitation on stores was some consolation, but the inconclusive end to these multilateral talks in January 1964 was probably the optimum interim outcome for the Irish.[167] The general trend of agricultural policy was very worrying for the Irish, though, and the Department of Agriculture noted that market sharing "could operate to limit the rate of expansion in our agricultural exports and therefore reduce our rate of economic growth."[168] Commodity discussions did nothing to speed consideration of the proposed broader moves to free trade and, as one British official noted: "It really is absurd to be trying to take even a provisional view when the multilateral meat talks are within hours of their crisis."[169] The result was that the Lemass initiative "started as it were in the stratosphere and looks like ending up stalled twenty feet from the ground."[170] Detailed discussions were further delayed by the British general election in the spring of 1964 and talks at official level stuttered into the winter of that year without any meaningful progress. In the interim, the Irish government renewed its interest in applying to GATT. Although in November 1960, a GATT working party unanimously recommended that Ireland be invited to participate in the 1961 tariff negotiations with a view towards accession, the Irish decided to let their application lie until the application to join the EEC was assessed.[171] The Irish

---

[165] PRO, MAF 276/37, MAF memo., Nov. 1962.

[166] PRO, MAF 40/294, A.H. Reed note, 26 Oct. 1964.

[167] PRO, MAF 246/321, minutes of Irish and British officials' meeting on market sharing, 14 Jan. 1964 and 23 Jan. 1964.

[168] Quoted in Cowler, 'Irish agriculture and European integration', p. 157.

[169] PRO, MAF 276/39, N.J.P. Hutchinson note, 4 Feb. 1964.

[170] PRO, MAF 276/39, W.A. Nield memo on Lemass proposals, 17 Feb. 1964.

[171] PRO, MAF 40/294, Copy of GATT minutes, 14 Nov. 1961. The Irish stated that their limited resources did not permit them to undertake two sets of negotiations, simultaneously, although it was largely to protect their preferential relationship with the British economy that the application was withdrawn at the time.

revived their GATT application in April 1964 and the implications for the proposed free trade area with Britain were unmistakable. GATT rules defined a free trade area as a grouping of two or more territories in which duties and other restrictive regulations are eliminated with respect to substantially all the trade therein. There was no precise definition of 'substantially all the trade', but it was taken to amount to 90 per cent. By December 1964, duty free trade from Ireland to Britain stood at 93 per cent, although it totalled only 66 per cent in the opposite direction.[172] Parallel to the slow-moving talks on the proposed agreement with Britain, the Irish sought to enter GATT by participating in the proposed Kennedy round where it was hoped to reach some agreement on the principal agricultural commodities. The Irish sought consultations with the British over their respective offers to that process. Eventually, the British did provide the Irish with a copy of their provisional list of tariff reductions and the British embassy in Dublin reported the Irish to be "most perturbed," as the reduction in preferences in Britain would outweigh negligible gains from tariff reductions.[173]

In November 1964 the election as Prime Minister of Harold Wilson gave a certain impetus to the Anglo-Irish trade talks and an analysis was made of the prospects of developing an agreement conducive to GATT regulations where Ireland permitted a minimum of 85 per cent of imports duty free from Britain.[174] In March 1965 the British recorded that private soundings with GATT by the Irish had informed them that a minor freeing of trade would be insufficient to bring acceptance of a free trade area. The resultant determination of the Irish to press forward somewhat surprised the British who noted that "since the Irish are apparently prepared to go much further on the industrial side than we expected, they will expect from us a significant agricultural offer. Fundamentally, they are concerned with maintaining and expanding access to the British market for their main agricultural products at favourable prices."[175] Nonetheless, through the spring of 1965 there seemed only remote prospects of a wide-ranging agreement, despite the on-going discussions by the bilateral Anglo-Irish economic committee which continued to make some progress.

The major breakthrough came with the visit to London of Lemass who headed a delegation comprising his ministers of Finance, Agriculture, and Industry and Commerce in July 1965. Reviewing the discussions of the previous months, Lemass and Wilson reached the decision that both governments would consider the creation of a free trade area. It was acknowledged that much work remained to secure agreement on the exact nature of the area but this agreement in principle proved the key development in the negotiations. While negotiations continued at official level on the minutiae of detail, a further visit to London in

---

172 PRO, MAF 276/41, H.A.F. Rumbold, CRO, note, 18 Dec. 1964.

173 PRO, MAF 276/253, British embassy in Dublin to CRO, 6 Nov. 1964. Later the British determined to guard future offers more zealously with the Ministry of Agriculture citing the importance of not "giving any inkling to the Irish what our actual proposals are." See PRO, MAF 276/253, MAF note, 15 Feb. 1965.

174 See, for example, NAI, D/T S16674 Q, D/F memo to govt., Dec. 1964.

175 PRO, MAF 276/41, MAF note, 8 Mar. 1965.

December 1965 by Lemass for a summit with Wilson secured eventual accord. In its final form, the Anglo-Irish Free Trade Agreement was signed on 15 December 1965. Its preamble firmly rooted it within the context of the principles and objectives of GATT, the harmonious expansion of world trade through the removal of barriers, and as part of the continuing progress towards European economic co-operation. For industry, it was agreed that Britain would abolish all import duties on Irish goods on 1 July 1966. On that same date Ireland would cut import duties on all British goods by 10 per cent – and by that same proportion every year until their disappearance in 1975. For agriculture, the agreement allowed unrestricted, duty-free access to the British market for Irish store cattle, store sheep and store lambs. The Irish undertook to export at least 638,000 head of cattle per annum. The waiting period allowing those beasts to qualify for fatstock guarantee payments was reduced from three to two months, the ¾d per pound differential on guaranteed payments for sheep and lambs was abolished, and the British fatstock guarantee was extended to 25,000 tons of Irish carcass beef and 5,500 tons of Irish carcass lamb per year. In respect of other agricultural products, it was agreed that access to the British market would be related to international commodity agreements involving all substantial producers.[176]

In some respects, the eventual agreement bore out the fears expressed by the Minister for Foreign Affairs, Patrick Hillery, six weeks before negotiations were concluded. Hillery approved of the concept of free trade but noted that "all, as everyone accepts, depends on what advantages we have to gain from it in the agricultural field. It is here that I am now beset by anxiety because it seems to me that … what we had sought on the agricultural side has been whittled down." Indeed, Hillery believed that there were "reasons why even our original requests on agriculture, had they been granted in full, might not have been adequate compensation for the risks we are running in industry." In this respect, Hillery pointed out that "any concessions extended to us by way of price guarantees on meat are only possibilities for the future if conditions worsen to an extent that no-one now expects." Hillery wrote that his worries

> could all be summed up in the thought that free trade could work out reasonably well between equal partners or roughly equal partners; but there is no equality between the British and ourselves and there is no doubt that we will be taking a very big chance in opening our doors to them. I am worried about this anyhow but I am even more worried about the danger that we would open the door without having got other doors open to us and opened wide enough to enable us to be sure of making up what we lose.[177]

Lemass replied: "We have not got quite all that we have been looking for on

---

[176] See NAI, D/T 97/6/471; PRO, MAF 276/279 II; Maurice Fitzgerald, 'Ireland and the EEC, 1957 to 1966', (Ph.D., European University Institute, 1999), *passim.*; Cowler, 'Irish agriculture and European integration', pp 166–73; Maher, *Tortuous path*, pp 180–4.

[177] NAI, D/FA 2000/14/476, D/FA to D/T, 28 Oct. 1965.

agriculture, but there is a possibility that something more can be secured in further negotiations." The underlying rationale was clear: "of the various courses open to us, a free trade area arrangement with Britain was, in the circumstances in which we find ourselves, the one best calculated to enable us to achieve the aims of national economic policy."[178]

Reaction to the agreement was generally positive, though far from unanimously so. The *Carlow Nationalist* reported that the agreement had "pleased the farmers in this progressive agricultural region," and the *Nenagh Guardian* wrote of the "radical agreement, which may change the face of Irish life and bring a spirit of realism into our economic endeavours which is badly needed." By contrast, the *Donegal People's Press* said that for the predominantly small farmers of that region it was "simply just not enough ... Is it possible that so much stress will be laid on the benefits which the new agreement can bring to farmers in those areas better endowed for increased productivity than on the difficulties of those trying to eke out a bare existence in the North-West ?...".[179]

Despite the fears of small farmers, farm organisations generally welcomed the agreement, though there was no suggestion of euphoria. Indeed, beyond the provisions of the agreement, it was the statement by the Minister for Agriculture, Charles Haughey, that the agreement was the first step towards accession to the EEC – and the CAP – which drew greatest approval.[180] The *Irish Farmers' Journal* offered a warmer reception in its assessment that the prime contribution of the agreement was in "guaranteeing markets and outlets and at our present rate of expansion these are very important ... The agreement gives a good foot in the door of the UK market."[181] Between the predictable polarities of newspaper analyses and sectional interest groups, a more reasonable interpretation was offered by James Meenan who noted that, although the agreement was "very far from being a triumphant achievement," the fairest assessment was that it "at least stopped the gradual erosion of the Irish position in the British market and that, with all its imperfections, it was better to have it than to continue to rely on past agreements which were being rapidly emptied of their content."[182]

Although the agreement represented a radical step for industry through the steady dismantling of protective duties and tariffs, for agriculture, however, it was essentially the extension of existing policy. In December 1964 a British official had noted "on the agricultural front, they have asked for the moon and cannot possibly hope to get more than part of it."[183] In the event, what the Irish achieved ensured their feet remained firmly on the ground. The potential lines of expansion were unchanged and there remained only minimal prospects of restoring Irish advantage in such commodities as bacon, butter and eggs. In

---

[178] NAI, D/FA 2000/14/476, D/T to D/FA, 3 Nov. 1965.

[179] Quoted in NAI, D/T 97/6/471, n.d.

[180] Cited in, Cowler, 'Irish agriculture and European integration', p. 168.

[181] *IFJ*, 18 Dec. 1965.

[182] Meenan, 'Agricultural policies', p. 53.

[183] PRO, MAF 276/41, H.A.F. Rumbold, CRO note, 18 Dec. 1964.

keeping with historical trends, the agreement was fundamentally shaped to favour the export of store cattle. Indeed, notwithstanding the extension of guarantees to a limited tonnage of carcass meat export, the advantage given to stores secured, and even strengthened, the primacy of the live cattle trade. The increased butter quota – raised from 12,905 to 23,000 tons for the quota year 1966–7 – was acquired through the most strenuous of negotiations, and was valuable in the short term. The refusal to provide Irish exports of butter, cheese and bacon with unrestricted entry was crucial to expansionist hopes, however. In the circumstances of British domestic agricultural policy and its commitments to EFTA and the Commonwealth, it is difficult to see how the Irish could have negotiated a more favourable deal. That anything emerged, at all, was a tribute to Irish persistence in the face of British scepticism. Ultimately, though, the agreement blanched in comparison with the unrestricted markets and guaranteed prices apparently on offer to European farmers under the CAP.

VI

Conclusion

By 1965, Irish agriculture stood with "one foot in the subsistence type farming of the past and one in the business-farming world of the future."[184] The old traditions were dying away, but not without a struggle. The writer, Seán Ó Faoláin, remarked in 1949 that Irish small farmers

> held on with a tenacity that is the most moving and astonishing spectacle in the whole Irish story. For ... centuries, through generation after generation, starving not by thousands but by millions, falling into the earth like the dung of cattle, weeping and cursing as they slaved, patient alike under the indifference of God and of their masters, they clung to their wretched bits of land with a savage fierceness, clung as it were by their bleeding fingernails ... That epic of a peasant Israel is in the blood and bones of every Irishman, as inflammable as petrol; so that even when we are most bored, or utterly sick of the extravagances and crudities of Irish nationalism, we have to sympathise, and we try again to understand.[185]

---

[184] Thomas Walsh, 'Research and future agricultural developments', in I.F. Bailie and S.J. Sheehy (eds.) *Irish agriculture in a changing world*, pp 144–56, esp. p. 144.

[185] Seán Ó Faoláin, *The Irish: a character study* (1949), pp 95–6.

For Ó Faoláin, the "Irish peasant is the child of time. He is its guardian and its slave."[186]

The struggle in the post-war era to reconcile the demands of modern agriculture with the emotions and traditions of the past was not uniquely Irish. In many cultures, small farming communities were seen as the repository of racial purity and homage was paid to their intrinsic moral value. Cultural values were emphatically not immune from economic realities, however. Across the world, farmers, for so long a dominant force, were being pushed towards the margins. "The most dramatic and far-reaching social change of the second half of this [twentieth] century and the one which cuts us off for ever from the world of the past, is the death of the peasantry," wrote Eric Hobsbawm.[187] The drift from the land was a phenomenon well underway by the early years of the twentieth century and it steadily gathered pace as the decades rolled over. The consequences for the global economy were immense. The policy of successive Irish governments before the 1960s was to resist this process. Where other countries freed workers from agriculture to provide labour for industrial development, the Irish commitment to retain on the land as many family farms as was possible found expression in the state's constitution and in legislation. Policies giving expression to the social and cultural vision associated with the first generation of politicians to hold power in independent Ireland could not compete with the relentless economic forces sweeping the western world in the second half of the twentieth century. The ideal of Gaelic, industrious, prosperous (though not materialistic) farmsteads filling the countryside with an ancient and dignified way of life was fundamentally at odds with the forces governing the realities of rural life. The ideal was not, of itself, invalid, rather global economics rendered it hopelessly quixotic. Yet, political demands, as well as genuine fidelity to an inherited dream, severely restricted moves to restructure the Irish agricultural economy. Electoral imperatives ensured the continuance of, for example, a policy of land division long after it became apparent that such a policy was economically unsound. While farm sizes were increasing around the world, the Irish policy was to break up large-holdings and to continue to create holdings of less than fifty acres. This was in spite of the clear acknowledgement that expansion in output had proved persistently negligible on farms of that size. By the 1960s, Irish agricultural policy involved the existence of an ever greater number of schemes to support the occupants of small farms which had been created or sanctioned by the state. Survival, not prosperous expansion, remained the primary goal of the majority of small Irish farmers.

---

[186] *Ibid.*, pp 94–5. He continued: "He will preserve for centuries dull and foolish habits that those who neither love nor fear time or change will quickly cast aside, but he will also preserve dear, ancient habits that like wine and ivory grow more beautiful and precious with age, all jumbled with the useless lumber in that dusty cockloft which is his ancestral mind."

[187] In Spain, the percentage of farmers in the workforce fell from 47.6 per cent in 1949/51 to 27.6 per cent in 1964/66. In terms of numbers the decline of the those employed on the land was from 5.3 million in 1950 to 3 million in 1970. See Simpson, *Long siesta*, p. 29. See also Hobsbawm, *Age of extremes*, pp 289–91. In two post-war decades, the percentage of peasants halved in Columbia, Mexico and (almost) Brazil. It fell by almost two-thirds in the Dominican Republic, Venezuela and Jamaica. In Japan, farmers declined from 52.4 per cent of the labour force in 1947 to 9 per cent in 1985. In America, farmers constituted 30 per cent of the population in the 1920s but this had fallen to 3 per cent in the 1980s. See Gilbert Fite, *American farmers: the new minority* (1981), p. 11.

Restrictive international trade in agricultural products also undermined the ability of the Irish to expand their agriculture. Repeated insistence that agriculture would provide the engine of economic expansion bringing prosperity to the people of the island sought to ignore the realities of global trading patterns. Far from moving to free up trade in farm produce, most countries to whom Ireland could realistically expect to export were, instead, moving to subsidise their farmers through price supports or to protect them with tariffs. As other countries expanded their output, the Irish discovered that the potential for profitable export was severely curtailed. The desire to move towards national self-sufficiency in food and to reduce balance of payments difficulties contributed to progressively more difficult trade conditions. With few exceptions, the British market was the sole outlet of note for Irish agricultural exports. Even here, the nature of the trade agreements with Britain ensured that only in the export of cattle did Ireland command a substantial and viable trade. In terms of price and accessibility, no other commodity offered a profit margin worthy of the name. The production of cattle for export necessitated an extensive farming pattern inimical to the prospects of constructing a vibrant small farming community. Policy makers operated in the shadow of this conflict between economic and social needs. In tandem with export constraints, immense changes in international agriculture placed further demands on the Irish farmer. Across the world, a substantial rise in capital investment facilitated increased mechanisation which brought a rapid increase in productivity. There was also a trend towards greater specialisation of product. Comparative advantage was threatened, and increasingly negated, by a more scientific approach to agriculture. The application of advances such as artificial insemination, higher-yielding crop strains, chemical fertilisers and pest controls brought a revolution in agriculture. Farm sizes increased and labour productivity soared as workers left the land. For those who remained, the erosion of the relative importance of the agricultural sector was beyond question.

The Irish sought to deny this erosion. The project to root economy and society in a small-farming structure was condemned to failure as the forces of time and trade proved insurmountable. The 1962 *Report by the poultry production council on the broiler industry* epitomised the changed technical nature of the agricultural economy. Buoyed by decent prices and a favourable trade agreement, poultry exports were worth £7.5 million in 1952. It provided 'farmyard income' to thousands of small farmers. Within a decade, these farmers had been driven out of the market and the trade had disappeared. The development in the US and Britain through the 1950s of the broiler industry using the techniques of industrial mass production and distribution decimated the Irish export trade. Indeed, it was only regulations safeguarding against the introduction of disease into Ireland which prevented the inundation of cheap broilers from Britain. The report noted that production in Britain had risen from 75 million birds in 1959 to 135 million in 1961 and was projected to reach 250 million by 1965. It was a scenario "quite outside normal farming experience." Ireland's only possible response should it choose to enter the fray – and the report as much as suggested that this would not be advisable – would be a concentrated broiler project with a processing capacity of 4,000 birds per hour. The report concluded: "It is clear in an undertaking of this kind there is no room for the small producer."[188]

If technical change annihilated the prospects of the small farmer engaged in the poultry industry, the inability to find a profitable market gravely impaired expansion of the dairy industry. After the travails of the early 1950s when Ireland had been forced to import butter, increased output saw the emergence in the late 1950s of an exportable surplus. This was not necessarily a welcome eventuality. The 1957 surplus of 6,500 tons was exported by the butter marketing company at a loss of £821,442 to the state. Irish butter was uncompetitive in foreign markets without the assistance of subsidies.[189] As output improved, the disposal of dairy products presented a grave difficulty. For 1962/3 Ireland was accorded a fixed import quota of 12,000 tons of butter for the British market. Even though this quota was doubled under the 1965 Anglo-Irish free trade agreement, it did not present the opportunity for significant expansion.[190] Exports of cheese offered little prospects of salvation. The Irish quota for the years 1968 to 1970 was fixed at 35,000 tons over the two years, despite the fact that the Irish estimated they required a quota well in excess of that figure for those years. Unsuccessfully campaigning for an increase in import quotas, Irish Taoiseach, Jack Lynch, told the British "that the hopes we had in relation to the free trade area agreement were not being realised."[191]

Bacon exports matched dairy products in their inability to compete on foreign markets. Having long lost pre-eminence to the Danes, only ever-expanding subsidies allowed the Irish to retain even a foothold in the British market. In 1965, the government agreed to increase the exchequer provision of £1.8 million to meet bacon export supports by a further £950,000.[192] With bacon curers expected to make their profit in the protected home market, even the subsidies could not prevent a trade where "the export in bacon in fact takes place as a loss."[193] The growing use of industrial practices in the bacon industry drove the Irish small farmer out of the market. Even in 1960, pigs were kept on 38 per cent of all holdings, 75 per cent of them having less than ten animals at an average distribution of 8.1 pigs per holding.[194] By the end of the 1960s, though, it was clear that Irish farmers "who traditionally fattened a few pigs at a time, usually in the summer months, no longer regard the profit on this type of production as worthwhile and that the tendency is now more towards larger specialised pig units."[195] Better marketing and improved breeding contributed to a rise in the quality and quantity of exports – but it was the larger quasi-industrial units which profited, not the farmer who was unable to compete.

---

[188] *Report by the poultry production council on the broiler industry* (1962), p. 1.

[189] NAI, D/T S11762 G, D/A memo to govt., 14 Jan. 1958.

[190] See Hoctor, *The department's story*, pp 260–1.

[191] NAI, D/T 99/1/459, minutes of meeting between British and Irish delegations, 29 Nov. 1968.

[192] NAI, D/T 98/6/354, D/A memo to govt., 9 Dec. 1965 and cabinet minutes, 17 Dec. 1965.

[193] NAI, D/T 98/6/354, D/A memo to govt., 8 Feb. 1968.

[194] Gillmor, *Agriculture*, pp 134–5.

[195] NAI, D/T 98/6/354, D/A memo to govt., 8 Feb. 1968.

Although time and trade patterns operated ineluctably against the establishment of a profitable multi-commodity export trade, even within itself the Irish project was fundamentally flawed. Bucking international trends bore all the hallmarks of a Sisyphean task, but long before it entered the export market, Irish agriculture was impaled on its own sword. Various aspects of government policy corroded each other's worth to such an extent it appeared as if no policy was in existence. In essence, the expectation that agriculture could both drive the economy through export earnings and simultaneously preserve a way of life which was progressively more uneconomic was ill-conceived. Like other countries, Ireland wrestled with the dilemma of viewing agriculture as either a business or a way of life, and the Irish unequivocally regarded it as both. The resultant agricultural policy restricted the adoption of measures necessary to improve the competitiveness of Irish produce on the international market and also fostered a system of farming compatible with avowed social aims. As Raymond Crotty contended: "Assistance to the economic and to the uneconomic farmer is not of the same kind."[196] Irish agricultural policy largely failed to make the distinction, however, and far from pursuing a two-tiered approach, Irish policy makers invariably sought to build from the weakest.

The dairy industry offered the classic example of the conflict of attempting to improve the income of small farmers while promoting the efficiency which would allow Irish dairy products compete in the export market. A 1967 report noted how, since 1960, the cow population had risen significantly and how yields had improved but this progression was characterised by inefficiency which made products from surplus milk uncompetitive in international trade.[197] Significantly, it was in Connacht, the least profitable dairying area where the average number of cows per supplier was 4.2 and the yield was merely 341.7 gallons per cow, that the cow population had grown most in this era.[198] It was estimated that the threshold of viability for suppliers was 7,000 gallons per annum but only 14.4 per cent of Irish farmers reached that total, while 46 per cent of suppliers sold less than 2,000 gallons per annum.[199] The report did not envisage the elevation of economic priorities ahead of social ones as "in rationalising the industry, the people are more important than the milk."[200] The guaranteed price paid to farmers for the milk was a huge burden on the state, however, and moved the Department of Finance to decry it as "an utter waste of resources by comparison with using the land for any other purpose."[201] On this line, the Minister for Transport and Power,

---

[196] Crotty, *Agricultural Production*, p. 223.

[197] *Report by study group on two-tier milk system* (1967).

[198] *Ibid.*, p. 17. In Munster, the most profitable area for dairying, the number of dairying farmers had actually fallen, although amongst those who remained, the average number of cows per supplier was 10.8 and the yield was 488.7 gallons per cow.

[199] *Ibid.*, p. 18.

[200] *Report on Irish dairy industry organisation* (1968), p. 125. See also *Report by study group on two-tier milk system*, p. 25, which noted: "The family farm has a number of advantages which are not always appreciated … It fosters in farm children an understanding of the importance of work and a respect for authority from an early age. This contributes to stability of character and maturity in outlook which enables them to become staunch members of society later on."

[201] NAI, D/T 99/1/195, D/F memo to govt., 28 Oct. 1968.

Erskine Childers, wrote to the Taoiseach, Jack Lynch, in 1967 saying that the "supreme fact is that we cannot afford social payments until we earn them by production."[202]

The *ad hoc* nature of the attempts to prioritise economics in the formulation of agricultural policy was emphasised when, in 1950 the Department of Agriculture attempted to send an officer to the US on a six-month training programme in agricultural economics. Few of its officers held such training and

> consequently, the department is not at present adequately equipped to carry out the many detailed economic studies necessary in connection with the implementation of agricultural policy. There is, for example, no organisation for determining the economic results of farming or for investigating production costs in the various branches of the agricultural industry. This is a serious disadvantage.[203]

The officer was sent, but to little avail. By the mid-1960s, there was scant evidence of "the emergence of the agricultural economics profession as a potent influence on Irish agricultural policy."[204] Even, in 1959, the Department of Finance was writing that

> if Irish agriculture is to become more efficient and competitive, the aim should be to secure greater production from the personnel engaged rather than maximum employment for the production obtained ... The contrary policy means lower net output, weakens the competitive power of the industry and in the long run must lead to more unemployment.[205]

Compounding all else was the endeavour to ensure that policy was all things to all people. Isolated projects were venerated as shrines capable of curing a multitude of ills. Consequently, the Land Project was introduced with outrageous fanfare amid suggestions it would, single-handedly, drag Irish agriculture into a golden era. Expectation quickly soured to disillusion. The impossibility of anointing one scheme as the saviour of an industry became all too evident. Individual initiatives were rarely geared towards the solution of one problem or as a stimulant towards a particular aim, rather they were continually reshaped to appeal to as many disparate interests as possible. In part, this resulted from a political system where the larger parties cleaved over history more than over policy. The capacity to appeal to all sections of the farming community was crucial to political success. In the aftermath of World War II, differences between Fianna Fáil and inter-party government approaches to agriculture were dwarfed by the

---

[202] NAI, D/T 99/1/442, Childers to Lynch, 23 Jan. 1967.

[203] NAI, F 123/39/50, D/A to D/F, 10 Oct. 1950.

[204] A. Desmond O'Rourke, 'Towards an aggregate production function for Irish agriculture', *Economic and Social Review*, vol. 9, no. 3 (1977), pp 191–205.

[205] NAI, D/T S11042 E/95, D/F memo to D/LG, 7 Jan. 1959.

similarities. It was not a conformity rooted in conviction – nor always in economics – but unfailingly in electoral appeal. In 1962 J.C. Nagle told British officials: "The government would like to see the wheat acreage reduced but political factors imposed caution."[206] Populist political acts were determined by the permanent cries of crisis which filled the air. Endemic problems were most often treated with running repairs amid an inability to embark on large-scale structural overhaul. In reality, the Department of Agriculture existed primarily as an agency of aid administering succour rather than one concerned with matters of policy. Between 1928/9 and 1964/5, the expenditure of the department increased eighteenfold, as its administrative staff more than trebled. The multitude of schemes operated independently of any coherent framework of development and the notion was sustained of a department singularly unable to move beyond a groove of emergency containment.

The absence of a long-term view was partly because agriculture was forced to perform its many tasks without significant investment.[207] The proximate cause of Europe's unprecedented post-war economic growth was massive investment. Net investment rates stood nearly twice as high in Europe in the 1950s and the 1960s as in previous decades.[208] Irish farmers, though, were deeply reluctant to invest in a business which seemed to offer little chance of substantial returns. In this reluctance, they offered a mirror-image of the attitudes of a state which could never be accused of Byronic excess. Even under the proposed public capital programme announced in the *Programme for economic expansion*, agriculture was to receive only £37,660,000 from a total of £220,440,000 over five years.[209] In contrast to this paucity of deployed resources, the *Irish Farmers' Journal* commented how it was no surprise that "the farmers' reaction is all the more bitter ... because we read in the papers every day of some grandiose and expensive scheme for bolstering our ailing industrial arm."[210]

Government policy towards agriculture was deeply affected by conditions in other sectors of the economy. The failure of agriculture to meet the ambitions imposed on it was, in part, determined by the failure of industry. The foreign currency earned by agricultural exports was used to subsidise industrial development. Farmers also supported the inefficient fertiliser and chemical industries by paying prices above the world market. Further, Ireland's industrial economy was unable to pull under-employed labour from rural areas.

---

[206] PRO, MAF 276/37, minutes of Anglo-Irish economic committee meeting, 23 Nov. 1962.

[207] Plato's belief that the poet could get closer to the truth than the historian brings to mind the comment of the Monaghan poet, Patrick Kavanagh: "We loved our land with a wild jealous love, but the way a bad mother loves her children – doing nothing for them." See *IFJ*, 2 Aug. 1958. Through the late 1950s and early 1960s, Kavanagh wrote a weekly column, health permitting, for the paper.

[208] Barry Eichengreen, 'Institutions and economic growth: Europe after World War II', in Nicholas Crafts and Gianni Toniolo (eds.), *Economic growth in Europe since 1945* (1996), pp 38–72.

[209] *Programme for economic expansion*, appendix 2.

[210] *IFJ*, 1 Mar. 1958. It noted the establishment of a new transatlantic service with cheaper fares and commented that "no doubt these are intended for the farmers who will have no place in this great new industrial country."

Consequently, Irish farms absorbed far more labour than they could justifiably employ. There was little point in shifting labour out of agriculture when the alternatives were equally poorly paid industrial employment – or, more likely, no employment at all. There was only limited prospects of rationalising the agrarian structure given the dismal prospects of Irish industry for most of the period before 1965. Within that agrarian structure, policy was overwhelmed by economics as small farmers, unconvinced that virtue was a reward in itself, abandoned farming. As this previously hidden under-employed labour fled the land through the 1950s the full scale of the failure of the Irish project became evident. But, if Irish industry was unable to offer an outlet for excess labour, neither could it offer the possibility of diverting finance, as in other countries, to develop the farm sector. In America, the main tool of farm policy was price supports, funded substantially from industrial earnings. For a country such as Ireland, reliant upon its agricultural exports for foreign exchange earnings, greater difficulties existed in the construction of such a policy. In Ireland, price supports were also less useful, and certainly less feasible, as the agricultural population accounted for almost half of consumers, it accordingly paid a large proportion of its own price supports. The benefits of the price supports went mostly to large farmers who held the greatest sales and, further, once a large export surplus of bacon and butter became available the government could no longer afford to pay for price supports.

Price support policy contributed to the fractious relationship between government and agriculture in Ireland, but across the world, that relationship, regardless of political and economic systems, was less than harmonious. One critic noted that, in the US, agricultural policies

> have been ineffective or worse than that, that there has been and is a hodge-podge of badly-organized alphabetical agencies, each doing something for or to the farmers, and that a systemization of these agencies and an agreement on objectives are needed but will call for more wisdom, courage, and statesmanship than are likely to be found in Congress.[211]

In Canada, government land policy had been the cause of great suffering as prairie settlement on the basis of 160 acre farms was a serious handicap and fundamentally uneconomic.[212] The record of government assisted schemes in West Africa was "replete with cases of unsound planning, poorly-managed programmes, and projects frustrated by intractable environmental difficulties which deserve more than passing attention."[213] The Achilles heel of the Soviet economy in the aftermath of the revolution was agriculture. Although there was massive expansion of output, there were also three major famines, increasing inefficiency and mass corruption.[214] It was not merely Irish agriculture which passed through troubled times.

---

[211] John Ise, 'Review of Murray R. Benedict's, *Farm policies of the United States, 1790–1950* (1953)', in *AH*, vol. 28, no. 2 (1954), pp 95–6.

[212] V.C. Fowke, *The national policy and the wheat economy* (1957), *passim.*

[213] Raymond E. Dummett, 'Obstacles to government-assisted agricultural development in West Africa', in *AHR*, vol. 23, ii (1975), pp 156–72.

[214] Z.A. Medvedev, *Soviet agriculture* (1987), *passim.*

In the new economic order, the passage of time offered only limited hope that sustainable development was likely for agricultural communities. As Hoctor commented wistfully, for Irish agriculture, "Alps over Alps arise."[215] New obstacles continually emerged to compound the old ones restricting Irish agricultural development. Steady progress was made but so great were the impediments that that progress could never proceed sufficiently quickly to sate the evolving materialist needs of Irish society. By 1965, industry had displaced agriculture as the primary focus of moves to expand the Irish economy. Inevitably, the sheer scale of agriculture ensured it retained a formidable position in Irish society – and would continue to do so for many decades – yet its position as the fulcrum of the economy was lost. This was reflected in the political rhetoric of the years after the *Programme for economic expansion*. Industrial progress was now presented as central to Irish independence, to fidelity to the martyrs of the past, to the unification of Ireland, and to the restoration of the national language.[216] The unmistakable reality was that Ireland was shedding its agricultural past as it pursued an industrial future. Visions of a rural Elysium faded steadily into the background – defying global trends and reversing the sands of time proved impossible. Agrarian Ireland was in the throes of a long fade.

---

[215] Hoctor, *The department's story*, p. 275.

[216] In a series of speeches in 1959 and 1960, the Taoiseach, Seán Lemass, was quoted as saying that industrial development was crucial "to build up an Irish state which would be capable of maintaining permanent independence," that "if we fail now at this essential task we will have been false to our historic past and to the man and women who made it what it was," that "we have to confound those northern defenders of partition who contend that joining us in freedom would be an economic disadvantage to the north-eastern counties," and that "to assert that there is no unifying link between our language policy and our economic policy is a fundamental fallacy." See Susan Baker, 'Dependency, ideology and the industrial policy of Fianna Fáil in Ireland, 1958–72', (Ph.D., European University Institute, 1987), pp 223, 229, 231, 232–3.

List of Appendices[1]

1. Numbers of selected livestock, 1850-1930
2. Areas under selected crops, 1850-1930
3. Agricultural exports, 1929-42
4. Areas under selected crops, 1930-39
5. Number of holdings, 1855-1965
6. Numbers of selected livestock, 1940-65
7. Areas under selected crops, 1940-65
8. Population of Ireland, 1926-66
9. Males engaged in farm work, 1945-70
10. Value of Irish exports, 1945-65
11. State expenditure relating to agriculture, 1960-70
12. Irish agricultural output, 1926-66

---

[1] Appendices one, two, four, five, six, seven and eight are taken from the Central Statistics Office publication: *Farming since the famine: Irish farm statistics 1847-1996* (1997). Appendix three is from the *CIPEAP Majority Report*. Appendices nine and eleven are from the OECD publication, *Agricultural policy in Ireland* (1974). Appendix ten is from the *Statistical Abstract*. Appendix twelve is from James Meenan, *The Irish economy since 1922* (1970).

Appendix One

NUMBERS OF SELECTED LIVESTOCK (000s) 1850-1930

Year	Cattle	Cows	Sheep	Pigs	Poultry	Horses
1850	2252		1725	751	5388	405
1860	2898	1272	3350	1049	8161	480
1870	3081	1207	4065	1221	18948	411
1880	3212	1105	3341	728	10712	426
1890	3501	1107	3955	1286	11894	452
1900	3804	1157	3980	1045	13956	435
1910	3934	1190	3600	990	18200	483
1920	4261	1224	3016	887	17305	488
1930	4038	1225	3515	1052	22900	448

Appendix Two

AREAS UNDER SELECTED CROPS (000 HECTARES) 1850-1930

Year	Corn Crops	Wheat	Oats	Barley	Total Tillage	Hay & Pasture
1850	974	213	619	118	1403	3438*
1860	794	157	560	71	1319	3828
1870	645	80	461	97	1143	4063
1880	516	45	378	87	919	4202
1890	436	28	329	73	818	4228
1900	382	15	293	69	721	4355
1910	375	15	289	67	693	4222
1920	468	18	366	82	797	4015
1930	320	11	261	47	590	4199
					*TOTAL FOR 1851	

Appendix Three

AGRICULTURAL EXPORTS (£ MILLIONS) 1929-42

Year (1)	Agricultural Exports(2)	Livestock & Livestock Product Exports	(3) Aa A Percentage Of (2)
1929	35.9	35.0	97%
1935	13.5	13.1	97%
1936	15.6	15.2	97%
1937	16.8	15.5	92%
1938	19.9	19.0	95%
1939	22.7	22.1	97%
1940	27.8	26.7	96%
1941	24.0	23.1	96%
1942	26.4	25.7	97.5%

Appendix Four

AREAS UNDER SELECTED CROPS (000 HECTARES) 1930-1939

Year	Corn Crops	Wheat	Oats	Barley	Total Tillage	Hay + Pasture
1930	320	11	261	47 5	90	4199
1931	309	8	252	47	577	4169
1932	308	9 2	56	42	576	4143
1933	326	20	257	48	589	4147
1934	333	38	236	58	606	4127
1935	372	66	249	56	644	4050
1936	383	103	226	53	656	4041
1937	375	89	232	53	644	4062
1938	373	93	231	48	635	4078
1939	351	103	217	30	604	4093

Appendix Five

NUMBER OF HOLDINGS 1855-1965

Year	Acres 1-5	Acres 5-15	Acres 15-30	Acres 30-50	Acers 50-100	Acres 100-200	Over 200	Total Holdings
1855	61800	127200	101500	55600	44900	19300	9200	419500
1900	47700	115800	100200	57100	47700	20700	9000	398300
1930	31000	74400	91200	62500	50000	21100	7900	338000
1940	27400	67500	90800	62600	50100	21100	7300	326700
1945	26900	64200	88800	62600	50700	21400	7200	321800
1950	26200	62000	86600	62600	51500	21800	7200	317900
1955	25900	59100	83900	63100	52300	21900	7200	313000
1960	23300	47500	73300	62100	54200	22900	7100	290300
1965	23100	44900	68800	61200	55200	23300	7000	283500

Appendix Six

NUMBERS OF SELECTED LIVESTOCK (000s) 1940-65

Year	Cattle	Cows	Sheep	Pigs	Poultry	Horses
1940	4023	1230	3071	1049	19975	459
1941	4150	1214	2909	764	17393	459
1942	4084	1206	2693	519 1	7365	452
1943	4136 1	202	2560	434	17097	454
1944	4246	1218	2663	381	18330	459
1945	4211	1222	2581	426	18314	465
1946	4146	1201	2423	479	18276	452
1947	3950	1156	2094	457	17304	438
1948	3921	1134	2058	457	20790	421
1949	4127	1176	2192 6	75	22077	402
1950	4322	1209	2385	645	21132	391
1951	4376	1189	2616	558	18839	367
1952	4309	1159	2857	719	19379	342
1953	4397	1174	2930	882 1	9114	329
1954	4504	1204	3113	958	16062	313
1955	4483	1198	3269	799	16076	296
1956	4537	1187	3439	747	16362	276
1957	4417	1236	3720	900	14502	258
1958	4466	1260	4174	948	14078	244
1959	4684	1272	4412	852	13904	234
1960	4741	1284	4314	951	13047	224
1961	4713	1291	4528	1056	12843	207
1962	4742	1309	4671	1111	11870	196
1963	4860	1322	4691	1102	11888	190
1964	4962	1400	4950	1108	11627	180
1965	5359	1547	5014	1266	11405	172

Appendix Seven

AREAS UNDER SELECTED CROPS (000s HECTARES) 1940-65

Year	Corn Crops	Wheat	Oats	Barley	Total Tillage	Hay & Pasture
1940	454	124	276	54	747	3942
1941	572	187	317	66	905	3780
1942	666	233	355	75	981	3698
1943	673	206	379	85	995	3683
1944	715	260	383	68	1039	3638
1945	680	268	338	69	1001	3675
1946	659	260	336	58	977	3704
1947	632	235	334	59	937	3744
1948	618	210	356	48	925	3759
1949	491	147	278	64	770	3917
1950	449	148	249	50	716	3972
1951	434	114	251	68	695	3995
1952	444	103	247	91	696	3994
1953	452	143	231	76	709	3985
1954	480	197	216	66	732	3969
1955	454	145	221	86	699	4005
1956	448	137	212	96	691	4036
1957	476	164	186	124	711	4030
1958	482	170	185	125	720	3997
1959	439	114	187	135	669	4046
1960	456	148	172	133	678	3868
1961	437	140	149	146	647	3913
1962	435	127	140	164	642	3973
1963	405	94	134	174	612	4006
1964	391	87	117	184	582	4079
1965	380	74	115	188	564	4145

Appendix Eight

POPULATION OF IRELAND 1926-66

1926	2972000
1936	2968000
1946	2955000
1951	2961000
1956	2898000
1961	2818000
1966	2884000

Appendix Nine

MALES ENGAGED IN FARM WORK (000s) 1945-70

| | 1945 | 1955 | 1965 | 1970 | Annual % Rate of Decline | | |
					1945-55	1955-65	1965-70
18 AND OVER							
Members Of Family	356	298	250	223	1.8	1.7	2.3
Permanent Employee	84	57	35	24	3.8	4.8	7.3
Temporary Employee	51	40	26	18	2.5	4.2	7.1
14 And Under 18							
Members Of Family	24	18	14	7	2.8	2.	5 13
Permanent Employee	4.1	3.4	3	1.2	1.9	1.2	16.7
Temporary Employee	2.4	2.4	2.5	1.5	0	0	9.7
Total	522	418	330	274	2.2	2.3	3.7

Appendix Ten

VALUE OF IRISH EXPORTS (£ 000s) 1945-65

Year	Live Animals	Food, Drink & Tobacco	Total Exports
1945	17154	5317	35236
1946	19867	6077	38612
1947	22111	10719	38568
1948	22265	16306	47851
1949	27108	22023	58974
1950	29274	29396	70452
1951	29807	34515	79827
1952	32355	50750	99103
1953	32647	59869	111517
1954	41585	47039	111778
1955	44614	34676	107152
1956	45386	32172	104276
1957	54345	39973	126968
1958	47294	45719	126623
1959	39157	43593	126616
1960	44749	51206	147831
1961	55420	62658	175212
1962	47554	62565	168537
1963	52757	72093	191450
1964	66658	70816	217043
1965	56332	73540	214875

Appendix Eleven

STATE EXPENDITURE IN RELATION TO AGRICULTURE (£000s) 1960-70

	1960-61	1965-66	1970-71
1. PRICE SUPPORTS AND MARKETING AIDS			
DAIRY PRODUCE	2350	10704	28949
BEEF, MUTTON & LAMB		89	2893
BACON AND PORK	850	3100	3090
CEREALS	834	283	
TOTAL	4034	13893	35215
2. PRODUCTION INCENTIVES PAID DIRECT TO PRODUCERS			
BEEF CATTLE	4916	SHEEP	1326
OTHER	2852	393	
TOTAL	2852	6635	
3.PAYMENTS TO REDUCE PRODUCTION AND OVERHEAD COSTS			
LIME AND FERTILISER SUBSIDIES	2562	4421	6870
REDUCTION OF LAND ANNUITIES	863	1026	1260
RELIEF OF AGRICULTURAL RATES	5664	12487	20696
OTHER	44		
TOTAL	9133	17934	28826
4. LONG-TERM DEVELOPMENT AIDS OF A CAPITAL NATURE			
TOTAL	6320	12261	12381
5. DISEASE ERADICATION			
TOTAL	5050	2213	3820
6. EDUCATION, RESEARCH AND ADVISORY SERVICES			
EDUCATION	449	773	1621
RESEARCH	500	1633	2726
ADVISORY	339	693	1102
OTHER	270	689	972
TOTAL	1558	3788	6421
7. ADMINISTRATION OF ACTS, REGULATIONS AND SCHEMES			
TOTAL	194	587	890
TOTAL EXPENDITURE	26289	53528	94188

Appendix Twelve

ESTIMATED VALUE OF OUTPUT OF SOME AGRICULTURAL PRODUCTS
(£ 000s) 1926-68

	1926-7	1929-30	1934-5	1938-9	1947	1953	1966
Horses	1235	1382	604	794	2647	2799	3850
Cattle, Calves	12791	14960	5519	11920	24709	39502	69064
Sheep, Lambs	2634	2911	1683	1980	4186	6536	12111
Pigs	8271	8717	5120	6549	8875	21894	29572
Turkeys	560	630	500	590	1544	2595	1115
Other Fowl	1740	1715	1150	1412	2913	3843	5107
Milk							
(a) Consumed By Persons	3196	3258	2756	3538	7602	12967	17646
(b) Used in Industry	4228	5305	3734	4596	9370	19599	42754
Wool	685	822	377	494	1005	2525	3040
Eggs	6690	7113	4273	4666	10158	14782	9187
Wheat	142	111	703	1972	4686	11851	5747
Oats	1066	809	962	853	2433	2024	835
Barley	902	514	827	577	591	4252	10354
Sugar Beet	259	360	820	918	2058	5187	5863
Potatoes	3334	2530	2656	3268	8045	5997	8925
Hay	316	347	230	258	671	311	331
Turf	3377	3377	2813	3687	8990	7398	4998
Total (All Agricultural Output)	57837	61387	38813	52180	112271	171924	242528

BIBLIOGRAPHY
Primary Sources
Unpublished documents

Historical Archives of the European Communities, Florence
Directorates
Fay's Archive
OECD collection

Irish Folklore Archives, University College, Dublin
Ms. 32–54
Ms. 1162–1839

National Archives, Dublin
Cabinet Minutes
Department of Agriculture files
Department of Education files
Department of Finance files
Department of Foreign Affairs files
Department of Industry and Commerce files
Department of Taoiseach files

Public Record Office, London
Cabinet papers
Commonwealth Relations Office papers
Dominions Office papers
Foreign Office papers
Ministry of Agriculture papers

University College, Dublin Archives
Ernest Blythe papers
Michael Hayes papers
Seán MacEntee papers
Patrick McGilligan papers
Richard Mulcahy papers
Donnchadh Ó Briain papers

Official publications

Annual report of the Department of Agriculture
Dáil Debates
Seanad debates

Hansard
OECD reports, Ireland (various)
OEEC reports, Ireland (various)
Report on stock breeding farms for pure bred dairy cattle (1921)
Report of the commission on agriculture (1924)
Bunreacht na hÉireann (1937)
Report of the commission of inquiry into banking, currency and credit (1938)
Report of the tribunal of inquiry on fruit and vegetables (1943)
Report of the commission of inquiry on post-emergency agricultural policy (1945)
*Memorandum by the minister for agriculture: policy in regard to crops, pastures, fertilizers
    and feeding stuffs* (1946)
Guaranteed market and prices for dairy produce (1946)
Report on reorganisation of pig and bacon industries (1946)
Long-term recovery programme (1948)
Report by G.A. Holmes on the present state and methods for improvement of Irish land
    (1949)
Report of the commission on emigration and other population problems (1956)
Milling and baking quality of Irish wheat: interim report covering the 1956 harvest
    (1958)
Economic development (1958)
Programme for economic expansion (1958)
*Export marketing of Irish agricultural produce: statement of the government's policy on the
    recommendations of the advisory committee* (1959)
General aspects of Irish export trade in agricultural produce (1959)
Export of bacon and other pigmeat (1959)
Export of livestock and meat (1959)
Shell eggs and liquid eggs (1959)
Export of turkeys (1959)
Export of dairy produce (1959)
Survey of agricultural credit in Ireland (1959)
Export of poultry other than turkeys (1959)
Report of committee on the 1959 turkey export trade (1960)
Marketing of Irish butter in Britain (1961)
Report by the poultry production council on the broiler industry (1962)
Report of the survey team on the dairy product industry (1962)
National farm survey 1955/6–1957/8 (1962)
Report by the inter-departmental committee on the problems of small western farms (1962)
Report of the survey team on the oatmeal milling industry (1963)
Report of the survey team on the beef, mutton and lamb industry (1963)
Report of the survey team on the bacon and pigmeat industry (1963)
Report by poultry production council on the turkey industry (1963)
Second programme for economic expansion, part I 1963)
Study of wheat standards and marketing of wheat in Ireland (1964)
Agriculture in the second programme for economic expansion (1964)
An appraisal of agricultural co-operation in Ireland by Joseph G. Knapp (1964)
Poultry inquiry, 1960–61 (1964)

Report on pilot area development by the inter-departmental committee on the problems of
    small western farms (1964)
Review of the Irish agricultural advisory service (1967)
Report by study group on two-tier milk system (1967)
Report on Irish dairy industry organisation (1968)
Report of the study group on store cattle (1968)
Report by the survey team on the mushroom industry (1969)
 Report of the committee on the review of state expenditure in relation to agriculture (1970)
Agriculture in the west of Ireland: a study of low farm income (1971)

Newspapers

Carlow Nationalist
Cork Examiner
Donegal People's Press
Evening Mail
Farmers' Weekly
Grocers' Weekly
Irish Farmers' Journal
Irish Independent
Irish Press
Irish Times
Kilkenny People
Manchester Guardian
Nenagh Guardian
News Chronicle
Sunday Independent
Sunday Press
The Times
Western People

Secondary Sources

Periodicals and journals

Administration
Agricultural History (AH)
Agricultural History Review (AHR)
Agricultural Record

Capuchin Annual
Christus Rex
Economic and Social Review
Éire–Ireland
Farm Research News
History Ireland
Irish Economic and Social History   (IESH)
Irish Historical Studies
Journal of the Statistical and Social Inquiry Society of Ireland   (JSSISI)
Landmark
Political Studies
Rural Ireland
Studia Hibernica
Studies

Books, articles, pamphlets and theses

Allen, Kieran, *Is southern Ireland a neo-colony?* (1990).
Anderson, Desmond, 'Education and rural society in Ireland', in *Éire–Ireland*, vol. ii, no. 2 (1966), pp 89–94.
Arnold, Bruce, *Haughey: his life and unlucky deeds* (1993).
Attwood, E.A., 'Agriculture and economic growth in western Ireland', in *JSSISI*, vol. xx, v (1962), pp 172–95.
    'Trends in agricultural development in Europe and Ireland', in *JSSISI*, vol. xxi, i (1963), pp 31–49.
    Ireland and the European agricultural market (1963).
    'Some economic aspects of land use policy in Ireland', in *JSSISI*, vol. xxi, iii (1965).
Attwood, E.A., and Geary, R.C., *Irish county incomes in 1960* (1963).
Bailey, Richard, *Problems of the world economy* (1967).
Bailie, I.F., and Sheehy, S.J. (eds.), *Irish agriculture in a changing world* (1971).
Baker, Susan, 'Dependency, ideology and the industrial policy of Fianna Fáil in Ireland, 1958–72', (Ph.D., European University Institute, 1987).
Bannon, M.J.B., 'Urban growth and urban land policy', in P.J. Drudy (ed.), *Ireland: land, politics and people* (1982), pp 296–323.
Barton, R., 'Agricultural credit', in King, Frederick C. (ed.), *Public administration in Ireland* (3 vols, 1944–54), ii, 28–43.
Bax, Mart, 'The small community in the Irish political process', in P.J. Drudy (ed.), *Ireland: land, politics and people* (1982), pp 119–40.
Benn, Tony, *The Benn diaries* (1996).
Bew, Paul, 'The Land League ideal: achievements and contradictions', in P.J. Drudy (ed.), *Ireland: land, politics and people* (1982), pp 77–92.
Bew, Paul, and Patterson, Henry, *Sean Lemass and the making of modern Ireland*

(1982).

Birnie, J.E., 'Irish farming labour productivity: comparisons with the UK, 1930s-1990s', in *IESH*, vol. xxiv (1997), pp 22–41.

Bourke, Joanna, 'Dairywomen and affectionate wives: women in the Irish dairy industry, 1890-1914', in *AHR*, vol. 38, ii (1990), pp 149–164.

Bourke, Seamus, *Éire tomorrow: a sociological survey* (1943).

Bowers, J.K., 'British agricultural policy since the second world war', in *AHR*, vol. 33, i (1985), pp 66–76.

Bradley, Dan, *Farm labourers: Irish struggle, 1900-76* (1988).

Brassley, Paul, 'Silage in Britain, 1880-1990: the delayed adoption of an innovation', in *AHR*, vol. 44, i (1996), pp 63–87.

Bruton, Richard and Convery, Frank J., *Land drainage policy in Ireland* (1982).

Budd, Alan, *The politics of economic planning* (1978).

Cain, Leonard F., 'Land tenure in Ireland in the modern period', in *AH*, vol. 27, no. 1 (1953), pp 62–8.

Calvert, William L., 'The technological revolution in agriculture, 1910-55', in *AH*, vol. 30, no. 1 (1956), pp 18–27.

Carrigan, J.E., 'The Economic Co-operation Administration in Ireland', in King, Frederick C. (ed.), *Public administration in Ireland* (3 vols, 1944–54), ii, 11–7.

Clark, Samuel, 'The importance of the agrarian classes: agrarian class structure and collective action in nineteenth century Ireland', in P.J. Drudy (ed.), *Ireland: land, politics and people* (1982), pp 11–36.

Clarke, Marie, 'Vocational education in a local context, 1930-1997', (Ph.D., UCD, 1999).

Clarkson, L.A., 'Agriculture and the development of the Australian economy during the nineteenth century', in *AHR*, vol. 19, i (1971), pp 88–96.

Clawson, Marion, 'Israeli agriculture in recent years', in *AH*, vol. 29, no. 2 (1955), pp 49–65.

Commins, P., 'Land policies and agricultural development', in P.J. Drudy (ed.), *Ireland: land, politics and people* (1982), pp 217–40.

Conniffe, Denis (ed.), *Roy Geary 1896-1983: Irish statistician* (1997).

Cowler, Brian, 'Irish agriculture and the European Economic Community, 1956-72', (Ph.D., UCD, 1998).

Cox, Graham, Lowe, Phillip, and Winter, Michael, 'The origins and development of the National Farmers' Union', in *AHR*, vol. 39, i (1991), pp 30–47.

Cox, Lawanda F., 'The agricultural wage earner, 1865-1900: the emergence of a modern labour problem', in *AH*, vol. 22, no. 1 (1948), pp 95–114.

Coyne, E.J., 'The Agricultural Co-operative movement in Ireland', in King, Frederick C. (ed.), *Public administration in Ireland* (3 vols, 1944–54), ii, 18–27.

Crafts, N.F.R., 'The golden age of economic growth in post-war Europe: why did Northern Ireland miss out?', in *IESH*, vol. xxii (1995), pp 5–25.

Crotty, Raymond, *Irish agricultural production: its volume and structure* (1966). *Farming collapse: national opportunity?* (1973)

Daly, Mary E., 'Government finance for industry in the Irish Free State: the trade loans (guarantee) acts', in *IESH*, vol. xi (1984), pp 73–93.

Industrial development and Irish national identity, 1922–1939 (1992).

Daniel, T.K.D., 'Griffith on his noble head: the determinants of Cumann na nGaedheal economic policy, 1922–32', in *IESH*, vol. iii (1976), pp 55–65.

De Lillo, Don, *Underworld* (1998).

De Paor, Liam (ed.), *Milestones in Irish history* (1986).

Dooney, Sean, *Irish agriculture: an organisational profile* (1988).

Drudy, P.J., *Irish Studies 2: Ireland: land, politics and people* (1982).

'Land, people and the regional problem', in P.J. Drudy (ed.), *Ireland: land, politics and people* (1982), pp 191–216.

Dummett, Raymond E., 'Obstacles to government-assisted agricultural development in West Africa', *AHR*, vol. 23, ii (1975), pp 156–72.

Dusenberry, William, 'Foot and mouth disease in Mexico, 1946–51', in *AH*, vol. 29, no. 2 (1955), pp 82–90.

Fanning, Ronan, *The Irish Department of Finance* (1978).

Fennell, Rosemary, 'The domestic market for Irish agricultural produce', in I.F. Bailie and S.J. Sheehy (eds.), *Irish agriculture in a changing world* (1971), pp 98–117.

Ferriter, Diarmaid, '"A peculiar people in their own land". Catholic social theory and the plight of rural Ireland 1930–55' , (Ph.D., UCD, 1996).

Finnegan, Richard B. and Wiles, James L., 'The invisible hand or hands across the water?: American consultants and Irish economic policy', in *Éire–Ireland*, vol. xxx, no. 2 (1995), pp 42–55.

Fite, Gilbert C, 'Recent progress in the mechanization of cotton production in the United States', in *AH*, vol. 24, no. 1 (1950), pp 19–28.

Fitzgerald, Garrett, *Planning in Ireland* (1968).

Fitzgerald, Maurice, 'Ireland and the EEC, 1957 to 1966', (Ph.D., European University Institute, 1999).

Fitzpatrick, David, 'The disappearance of the Irish agricultural labourer, 1841–1912', in *IESH*, vol. vii (1980), pp 66–92.

'Class, family and rural unrest in nineteenth century Ireland', in P.J. Drudy (ed.), *Ireland: land, politics and people* (1982), pp 37–76.

Foster, H.G., 'Ireland's trade with Britain', in I.F. Bailie and S.J. Sheehy (eds.), *Irish agriculture in a changing world* (1971), pp 74–97.

Foster, Roy, *Modern Ireland, 1600–1972* (1988).

Fox, R.M., *James Connolly: the forerunner* (1946).

Foy, Michael, *The sugar industry in Ireland* (1976).

Ghatak, Subrata, and Ingersent, Ken, *Agriculture and economic development* (1984).

Gillmor, Desmond A., *Agriculture in the Republic of Ireland* (1977).

'The political factor in agricultural history: trends in Irish agriculture, 1922–85', in *AHR*, vol. 37, ii (1989), pp 166–179.

Girvin, Brian, *Between two worlds* (1989).

'Irish Agricultural policy, economic policy and the possibility of market integration in Europe', in Richard T. Griffiths and Brian Girvin (eds.), *The green pool and the origins of the common agricultural policy* (1995), pp 239–59.

Griffiths, Richard T. (ed.), *Explorations in OEEC history* (1997).

Grigg, David, *The dynamics of agricultural change* (1982).

The transformation of agriculture in the west (1994).

Halcrow, Harold G., Spitze, G.F., Allen-Smith, Joyce E., *Food and agricultural policy: economics and politics* (1994).

Hannon, Damian F., *Displacement and development: class, kinship and social change in Irish rural communities* (1979).

'Peasant models and the understanding of social and cultural change in rural Ireland', in P.J. Drudy (ed.), *Ireland: land, politics and people* (1982), pp 141–66.

Hannon, Damian F., and Katsiaoimi, Louise A., *Traditional families? From culturally prescribed to negotiated roles in farm families* (1977).

Haughey, Charles, 'Rural sociology and Ireland', in *Éire–Ireland*, vol. i, no. 4 (1966), pp 63–9.

Heavy, J.F., 'On farm efficiency', in I.F. Bailie and S.J. Sheehy (eds.) *Irish agriculture in a changing world* (1971), pp 118–129.

Hein, John, *Institutional aspects of commercial and central banking in Ireland* (1967).

Hobsbawm, Eric, *Age of extremes: the short twentieth century, 1914–91* (1994).

On history (1997).

Hoctor, D., *The Department's story: a history of the Department of Agriculture* (1971).

Holderness, B.A., *British agriculture since 1945* (1995).

Holmes, Colin J., 'Science and the farmer', in *AHR*, vol. 36, ii (1988), pp 77–86.

Horgan, S., *Seán Lemass: an enigmatic patriot* (1998).

Hughes, J.G., *The functional distribution of income in Ireland, 1938–70* (1972).

Ingersent, Ken A., and Rayner, A.J., *Agricultural policy in Western Europe and the United States* (1999).

Jacobsen, John Kurt, *Chasing progress in the Republic of Ireland: ideology, democracy and dependent development* (1994).

Jäger, Helmut, 'Land use in medieval Ireland', in *IESH*, vol. x (1983), pp 51–66.

Jenkins, J. Geraint, 'Technological improvement and social change in Cardiganshire', in *AHR*, vol. xiii (1965), pp 94–105.

Johansen, Hans Christian, *The Danish economy in the twentieth century* (1987).

Johnson, D. Gale, *World agriculture in disarray* (1973).

Johnson, D.S., 'Cattle smuggling on the Irish border, 1932–38', in *IESH*, vol. vi (1979), pp 41–63.

Jones, E.I., and Woolf, S.J., *Agrarian change and economic development* (1969).

Kennedy, Henry, 'Our agricultural problem', in King, Frederick C. (ed.), *Public administration in Ireland* (3 vols, 1944–54), ii, 44–58.

Kennedy, Kieran A., Giblin, Thomas, and McHugh, Deirdre, *The economic development of Ireland in the twentieth century* (1988).

Kennedy, Liam, *The modern industrialisation of Ireland 1940–1988* (1989)
Colonialism, religion and nationalism in Ireland (1996).

Kennedy, Michael, 'Towards co-operation: Seán Lemass and north–south economic relations, 1956–65', in *IESH*, vol. xxiv (1997), pp 42–61.

Keogh, Dermot, *Ireland and Europe, 1919–1989: a diplomatic and political history* (1990).

Twentieth century Ireland: nation and state (1994).

King, Frederick C., *Public administration in Ireland* (3 vols, 1944–54).

Knutson, Ronald D., Penn, J.B., Boehm, William T., *Agricultural and food policy* (1983).

Kuehn, Alfred, *Short-term economic forecasting and its application in Ireland* (1961).
Prospects of the Irish economy in 1962 (1962).

Lee, J.J., 'Irish agriculture', in *AHR*, vol. 17, i (1969), pp 64–76.
'The land war', in Liam de Paor (ed.), *Milestones in Irish history* (1986), pp 106–16.
Ireland, 1912–85: politics and society (1989).

Leneman, Leah, 'Land settlement in Scotland after world war one', in *AHR*, vol. 37, i (1989), pp 52–64.

Leser, C.E.V., *Imports and economic growth in Ireland, 1947–61* (1963).
The Irish economy in 1962 and 1963 (1963).
The Irish economy in 1963 and 1964 (1964).
The Irish economy in 1964 and 1965 (1965).
The Irish economy in 1965 and 1966 (1966).
The Irish economy in 1967 (1967).
A study of imports (1967).

Lewis, Colin A., 'Irish horse breeding and the Irish draught horse, 1917–78', in *AHR*, vol. 31, i (1983), pp 37–49.

Long, W. Harwood, 'The development of mechanization in English farming', in *AHR*, vol. 11, i (1963), pp 15–26.

Lynn, Richard, *The Irish brain drain* (1968).

Lyons, F.S.L., *Ireland since the famine* (1971).

MacAleese, Dermot, 'Political independence, economic growth and the role of economic policy', in P.J. Drudy (ed.), *Ireland: land, politics and people* (1982), pp 270–95.

McCarthy, John F. (ed.), *Planning Ireland's future: the legacy of T.K. Whitaker* (1990).

McCarthy, Vincent, *The formative years of seed testing in Ireland* (unpublished, 1996).

Mac Gréil, Mícheál (ed.), *Monsignor James Horan: memoirs, 1911–86* (1992).

Maher, D.J. *The tortuous path: the course of Ireland's entry into the EEC, 1948–73* (1986).

Maltby, Arthur, *Irish official publications: a guide to Republic of Ireland papers* (1980).

Manning, Maurice, *James Dillon* (1999).

Matthews, Alan, 'The state and Irish agriculture, 1950–80', in P.J. Drudy (ed.), *Ireland: land, politics and people* (1982), pp 241–69.

Meenan, James, *The Irish economy since 1922* (1970).
'Irish agricultural policies in the last twenty years', in I.F. Bailie and S.J. Sheehy (eds.), *Irish agriculture in a changing world* (1971), pp 44–55.

Mellor, John W., and Ahmed, Piasuddin (eds.), *Agricultural price policy for developing countries* (1988).

Micheletti, Michele, *The Swedish farmers' movement and government agricultural policy* (1990).

Milward, Alan S., 'The second world war and long-term change in world
   agriculture', in Alan S. Milward and Bernd Martin (eds.), *Agriculture and
   food supply in the second world war* (1985), pp 5–15.
   The European rescue of the nation-state (1992).
Moody, V. Alton, 'Europe's recurrent land problem, in *AH*, vol. 22, no. 4 (1948),
   pp 220–32.
Molohan, Cathy, *Germany and Ireland 1945–1955: two nations' friendship* (1999).
Murphy, John A., 'The European Economic Community', in Liam de Paor (ed.),
   Milestones in Irish history (1986), pp 138–51.
Murphy, Brian S., '"The land for the people, the road for the bullock": Lia Fáil,
   the smallholders crisis and public policy in Ireland, 1957–60', in Timothy
   P. O'Neill and William Nolan (eds.), *Offaly: history and society* (1998), pp
   855–87.
Murphy, William, 'In pursuit of popularity and legitimacy: the rhetoric of Fianna
   Fáil's social and economic policy 1926–34', (M.A., UCD, 1998).
Murray, A.C., 'Agrarian violence and nationalism in nineteenth century Ireland:
   the myth of ribbonism', in *IESH*, vol. xiii (1986), pp 56–73.
Nagle, J.C., *Agricultural trade policies* (1976).
   'Introduction', in I.F. Bailie and S.J. Sheehy (eds.), *Irish agriculture in a
   changing world* (1971), pp ix–xv.
Neenan, Michael, *A popular history of Irish agriculture* (unfinished manuscript,
   1996).
Nevin, Edward, *Public debt and economic development* (1962).
   Wages in Ireland, 1946–62 (1963).
Norton, Desmond, *Problems in economic planning and policy formation in Ireland,
   1958–74* (1975).
O'Brien, Flann, *The poor mouth* (Translation, 1973).
O'Brien, George, 'Patrick Hogan: Minister for Agriculture',
   Studies, 25 (1936), p. 37.
Ó Broin, Sean, 'The Department of Agriculture', in King, Frederick C. (ed.),
   Public administration in Ireland (3 vols, 1944–54), iii, 61–86.
O'Connor, R., 'The economic utilisation of grassland', in *JSSISI*, vol. xx, iii
   (1960), pp 71–96.
   The implication for cattle producers of seasonal price fluctuations (1969).
   'Implications of Irish agricultural statistics', in I.F. Bailie and S.J. Sheehy
   (eds.), *Irish agriculture in a changing world* (1971), pp 16–43.
   A study of the bovine tuberculosis eradication scheme (1986).
O'Connor, R., and Keogh, P., *Crisis in the cattle industry* (1975).
O'Connor, R., and Guiomard, C., 'Agricultural output in the Irish Free State
   area before and after independence', in *IESH*, vol. xii (1985), pp 89–97.
O'Connor, R., Baker, Terence J., and Dunne, Rory,
   A study of the Irish cattle and beef industries (1973).
O'Connor, R., Miceal Ross and Behan, Michael, *A linear programming model for
   Irish agriculture* (1977).
O'Donnell, Sean, 'Vetting the herd', *Éire–Ireland*, vol. xx, no. 2 (1985), pp 130–2.
   OECD, *Agricultural policy in Ireland* (1974).

The European reconstruction 1948–61 – bibliography on the Marshall plan and the OECD (1996).

Ó Faolain, Sean, *The Irish: a character study* (1949).

Ó Gráda, Cormac, *Ireland: a new economic history, 1780–1939* (1994).
  'Irish agricultural history: recent research', in *AHR*, vol. 38, ii (1989), pp 165–73.
  'Irish agriculture north and south since 1900', in Mark Overton and Bruce Campbell (eds.), *Land, labour and livestock* (1991), pp 439–56.
  A rocky road: the Irish economy since the 1920s (1997).

Ó Gráda, Cormac, and O'Rourke, Kevin, 'Irish economic growth, 1945–88', in Crafts and Toniolo (eds.), *Economic growth in Europe since 1945* (1996), pp 388–426.

O'Hagan, J.W., *The economy of Ireland: policy and performance of a small European country* (1995).

O'Higgins, Michael, and Gibbons, John P., 'Shopkeeper-graziers and land agitation in Ireland, 1895–1900', in P.J. Drudy (ed.), *Ireland: land, politics and people* (1982), pp 93–118.

O'Malley, Eoin, *Industry and economic development* (1989).

O'Rourke, A. Desmond, 'Towards an aggregate production function for Irish agriculture', in *Economic and Social Review*, vol. 9, no. 3 (1977), pp 191–205.

O'Shiel, Kevin, 'The work of the Land Commission', in King, Frederick C. (ed.), *Public administration in Ireland* (3 vols, 1944–54), ii, 59–74.

O'Toole, Fintan, *Meanwhile back at the ranch: the politics of Irish beef* (1995).

Ó Tuathaigh, M.A.G., 'The land question, politics and Irish society, 1922–60', in P.J. Drudy (ed.), *Ireland: land, politics and people* (1982), pp 167–90.

Overton, Mark and Campbell, Bruce (eds.), *Land, labour and livestock: historical studies in European agricultural production* (1992).

Parker, A.J., *Localism and bailiwicks: the Galway West constituency in the 1977 general election* (1983).

Parker, Garland G., 'British policy and native agriculture in Kenya and Uganda', in *AH*, vol. 26, no. 1 (1952), pp 125–31.

Pentony, P., *Psychological barriers to economic achievement* (1965).

Plunkett, Horace, *Ireland in the new century* (1904).

Press, J.P., 'Protectionism and the Irish footwear industry, 1932–39', in *IESH*, vol. xiii (1986), pp 74–89.

Pryor, Frederic L., *The red and the green: the rise and fall of collectivized agriculture in Marxist regimes* (1992).

Rafter, Kevin, *Neil Blaney: a soldier of destiny* (1993).
  The Clann: the story of Clann na Poblachta (1996).

Raymond, Raymond J., 'Thesis abstract: The economics of neutrality: the United States, Great Britain and Ireland's war economy, 1937–45', in *IESH*, vol. x (1983), pp 98–99.

Reynolds, D.J., *Inland transport in Ireland: a factual survey* (1962).
  Road transport: the problems and prospects in Ireland (1963).

Reynolds, Julian, 'The Shannon river', in Mary Tubridy (ed.), *The heritage of Clonmacnois* (1987).

Rippy, Merrill, 'Land tenure and land reform in modern Mexico', in *AH*, vol. 27, no. 1 (1953), pp 55–61.

Robinson, 'The extent of farm underdrainage in England and Wales prior to 1939', in *AHR*, vol. 34, i (1986), pp 79–85.

Rooth, T., 'Trade agreements and the evolution of British agricultural policy in the 1930s', in *AHR*, vol. 33, ii (1985), pp 173–90.

Ross, M., *Personal incomes by county 1965* (1969).

Further data on county incomes in the sixties (1972).

Ruane, J.B., 'The farmer in a changing industry', in I.F. Bailie and S.J. Sheehy (eds.), *Irish agriculture in a changing world* (1971), pp 130–43.

Salaman, R. N., *The influence of the potato on the course of Irish history* (1944).

Sammon, Patrick J., *In the Land Commission: a memoir, 1933–78* (1997).

Schmidt, Hubert G., 'Post-war developments in West German agriculture, 1945–53', in *AH*, vol. 29, no. 4 (1955), pp 147–60.

Scully, J.J., 'Agricultural adjustment in Ireland', in I.F. Bailie and S.J. Sheehy (eds.), *Irish agriculture in a changing world* (1971), pp 197–215.

Sheedy, Larry, *Milestones and memories: the life and times of Joseph Bruton* (1998).

Sheehy, S.J., 'EEC policy – the implication for Irish agriculture', in I.F. Bailie and S.J. Sheehy (eds.), *Irish agriculture in a changing world* (1971), pp 176–96.

Shiel, Michael J., *The quiet revolution: the electrification of rural Ireland 1946–76* (1984).

Short, Brian, 'The art and craft of chicken cramming: poultry in the weald of Sussex, 1850–1950', *AHR*, vol. 30, i (1982), pp 17–30.

Simpson, James, *Spanish agriculture: the long siesta, 1765–1965* (1995).

Skinner, Liam, *Politicians by accident* (1946).

Smith, Louis and Healy, Sean, *Farm organisations in Ireland: a century of progress* (1996).

Smith, Martin J., *The politics of agricultural support in Britain* (1990).

Solar, Peter M., 'The agricultural trade statistics in the Irish Railway Commissioners' Report', in *IESH*, vol. vi (1979), pp 24–40.

Spain, Henry, 'Agricultural education and extension', in I.F. Bailie and S.J. Sheehy (eds.), *Agricultural change in Ireland* (1971), pp 157–75.

Stokes, William S., 'The land laws of Honduras', in *AH*, vol. 21, no. 3 (1947), pp 148–54.

Symons, L., 'The pastoral economy of New Zealand', in *JSSISI*, vol. xx, iv (1961), pp 94–131.

Toniolo, Gianni, and Crafts, Nicholas (eds.), *Economic growth in Europe since 1945* (1996).

Tracy, M., 'Agricultural policies and the adjustment problem', in I.F. Bailie and S.J. Sheehy (eds.), *Irish agriculture in a changing world* (1971), pp 56–73.

Agriculture in western Europe (1982).

Turner, M., 'Output and productivity in Irish agriculture from the famine to the great war', in *IESH*, vol. xvii (1990), pp 62–78.

Tussing, A. Dale, *Irish educational expenditures – past, present and future* (1978).

Violin, Lazar, 'Land tenure and land reform in modern Russia', in *AH*, vol. 27, no. 1 (1953), pp 48–55.

Walker, David, *The allocation of public funds for social development* (1962). 'Agriculture and economic development', in I.F. Bailie and S.J. Sheehy (eds.), *Irish agriculture in a changing world* (1971), 1–15.

Walsh, Thomas, 'Research and future agricultural developments', in I.F. Bailie and S.J. Sheehy (eds.), *Irish agriculture in a changing world* (1971), pp 144–56.

Watson, James Scott, 'Some traditional farming beliefs in the light of modern science', in *AHR*, vol. I (1953), pp 4–8.

Weinryb, Bernard D., 'Middle-eastern agriculture in the inter-war years', in *AH*, vol. 26, no. 2 (1952), pp 52–8.

Whelan, Bernadette, 'Ireland and the Marshall Plan', in *IESH*, vol. xix (1992), pp 49–70.
        Ireland and the Marshall plan, 1947–57 (2000).

Whitaker, T.K., 'Ireland – land of change', in *Éire–Ireland*, vol. xxii, no. 2 (1987), pp 4–18.

Wintle, Michael, 'Agrarian history in The Netherlands in the modern period: a review and bibliography', in *AHR*, vol. 39, i (1991), pp 65–73.

Whyte, J.H., *Church and state in modern Ireland, 1923–79* (Second edition, 1984).

Index